THE BRONTËS: THE CRITICAL HERITAGE

THE CRITICAL HERITAGE SERIES

GENERAL EDITOR: B. C. SOUTHAM, M.A., B. LITT. (OXON.)
Formerly Department of English, Westfield College, University of London

For a list of books in the series see the back end paper

THE BRONTËS

THE CRITICAL HERITAGE

Edited by
MIRIAM ALLOTT
Reader in English Literature,
University of Liverpool

ROUTLEDGE & KEGAN PAUL: LONDON AND BOSTON

First published in 1974
by Routledge & Kegan Paul Ltd
Broadway House, 68–74 Carter Lane,
London EC4V 5EL and
9 Park Street,
Boston, Mass. 02108, U.S.A.
© Miriam Allott 1974
No part of this book may be reproduced in
any form without permission from the
publisher, except for the quotation of brief
passages in criticism

ISBN 0 7100 7701 7

Library of Congress Catalog Card No. 73-85426

Printed in Great Britain by
C. Tinling & Co. Ltd, London and Prescot

FOR
ADA HORROCKS
With love and gratitude

General Editor's Preface

The reception given to a writer by his contemporaries and near-contemporaries is evidence of considerable value to the student of literature. On one side we learn a great deal about the state of criticism at large and in particular about the development of critical attitudes towards a single writer; at the same time, through private comments in letters, journals or marginalia, we gain an insight upon the tastes and literary thought of individual readers of the period. Evidence of this kind helps us to understand the writer's historical situation, the nature of his immediate reading-public, and his response to these pressures.

The separate volumes in the *Critical Heritage Series* present a record of this early criticism. Clearly, for many of the highly productive and lengthily reviewed nineteenth- and twentieth-century writers, there exists an enormous body of material; and in these cases the volume editors have made a selection of the most important views, significant for their intrinsic critical worth or for their representative quality – perhaps even registering incomprehension!

For earlier writers, notably pre-eighteenth century, the materials are much scarcer and the historical period has been extended, sometimes far beyond the writer's lifetime, in order to show the inception and growth of critical views which were initially slow to appear.

In each volume the documents are headed by an Introduction, discussing the material assembled and relating the early stages of the author's reception to what we have come to identify as the critical tradition. The volumes will make available much material which would otherwise be difficult of access and it is hoped that the modern reader will be thereby helped towards an informed understanding of the ways in which literature has been read and judged.

B.C.S.

Contents

The novels of 'Ellis and Acton Bell', 1847–8

Wuthering Heights (1847) and *Agnes Grey* (1847)

CONTENTS

CONTENTS

Preface

The obtuseness and crudity of the early reviewers of the Brontës is a persistent part of the Brontë legend, but it is a part that will not stand up to examination. The legend was encouraged in the first place by Charlotte's sorrowful remarks about her sisters' critics in her 'Biographical Notice of Ellis and Acton Bell' of 1850, and in 1857 received further support from Mrs Gaskell, whose careful research for her *Life of Charlotte Brontë* stopped short at gathering and sifting the vast numbers of reviews and articles which had accumulated over the past ten years. For a long time in the twentieth century, ignorance of what Victorian reviewers actually wrote did nothing to correct received ideas concerning Victorian critical shortcomings. This situation has of course altered radically in recent years. Within the wide range of current Victorian studies, many anthologies of nineteenth-century criticism have played their own part in helping to set the record straight. It is hoped that the present collection will set the record straight for the Brontës' early reviewers and also represent the movement of opinion among their successors in the later years of the nineteenth century.

Acknowledgments

The editor and publisher would like to thank the following for permission to quote from copyright material: Manchester University Press for *The Letters of Mrs Gaskell* edited by J. A. V. Chapple and Arthur Pollard; Basil Blackwell & Mott Ltd for selections from *The Brontës: Their Lives, Friendships and Correspondence* edited by T. J. Wise and J. A. Symington.

For help received I should like to thank Professor Walter Houghton of the Wellesley Index; Professor James Bertram of the Victoria University of Wellington together with the authorities of the Alexander Turnbull Library, Wellington, and Mr T. J. Winnifrith of the University of Warwick. I should also like to acknowledge assistance from Mr R. H. Parker of the Department of Printed Books, the British Museum; Mr P. Allen of the Newspaper Library, the British Museum; Mrs M. M. Mackee of the University of London Library; Mr T. Walsh of the Manchester Central Library; Miss H. Lofthouse of Chetham's Library, Manchester; and the staff of the Harold Cohen Library at my own University. Thanks are also due to Mrs Barbara Wilson for her aid in translating the French reviews and to Mrs Joan Welford for her patient secretarial assistance. My greatest debt, as always, is to my late husband, Kenneth Allott, who throughout our working life together let me draw generously on his encyclopaedic knowledge of the Victorian period, and without whose advice and support neither this nor any other work of mine could have been completed.

Abbreviations

LL [i.e. *Life and Letters*]	*The Brontës: Their Lives, Friendships and Correspondence* vols 1–4, *The Shakespeare Head Brontë*, edited by T. J. Wise and J. A. Symington (1932).
BST	*Transactions of the Brontë Society.*
Letters of Mrs Gaskell (1966)	*The Letters of Mrs Gaskell*, edited by J. A. V. Chapple and Arthur Pollard (1966).
The George Eliot Letters (1954)	*The George Eliot Letters*, edited by Gordon S. Haight, seven volumes (1954).

Chronological Table

1812   The Reverend Patrick Brontë marries Maria Branwell (29 December).

1814   Maria Brontë born.

1815   Elizabeth Brontë born.

1816   Charlotte Brontë born (21 April).

1817   Patrick Branwell Brontë born.

1818   Emily Jane Brontë born (30 July).

1820   Anne Brontë born (17 January).
      The family moves to Haworth.

1821   Mrs Brontë dies (September). Her sister, Miss Elizabeth Branwell, takes charge of the house and family.

1824   Maria and Elizabeth go to the Clergy Daughters' School at Cowan Bridge (July); Charlotte joins them in August, Emily in November.

1825   Maria leaves the school because of illness (14 February) and dies (6 May). Elizabeth leaves for the same reason (31 May) and dies (15 June). Charlotte and Emily are taken away from the school (1 June).

1826   Beginning of the Brontës' childhood fantasy games centred on the toy soldiers given to Branwell by his father (June).

1831   Charlotte goes to Miss Wooler's school at Roe Head (January). Meets Ellen Nussey and Mary Taylor.

1832   Charlotte leaves Roe Head to take charge of her sisters' education at home. By now the family's fantasy games have grown into the Angrian saga shared by Charlotte and Branwell and the Gondal saga shared by Emily and Anne.

1835   Charlotte returns as governess to Roe Head (July), Emily accompanies her as a pupil but becomes homesick and leaves (October). Anne replaces her (January 1836–December 1837). Charlotte leaves 1838 (May).

1837   Emily a governess at Miss Patchett's school at Law Hill near Halifax. Leaves after some months (exact period not known).

1839   Anne a governess with the Ingram family, Blake Hall, Mirfield, (April–December).

Charlotte a governess with the Sidgwick family, Stonegappe Hall, near Skipton (May–July).

1840 Charlotte, Emily and Anne together at Haworth.

1841 Anne a governess with the Robinson family, Thorp Green Hall, near York (March 1841–June 1845; Branwell joins her as tutor January 1843). Charlotte a governess with the White family, Upperwood House, Rawdon (leaves December 1841).

1842 Charlotte and Emily go to Brussels to study in the Pensionnat Heger (February); they are called home on their aunt's death (November). Charlotte returns alone to Brussels and stays for a further year (January 1843–January 1844).

1844 Failure of the plan to set up a school at Haworth (first mooted summer 1841).

1845 The family together at Haworth (Anne leaves Thorp Green in June; Branwell dismissed in July). Charlotte finds Emily's poems and projects the publication of a selection of poems by the three sisters (autumn).

1846 *Poems, by Currer, Ellis and Acton Bell* published by Aylott and Jones (May). *Jane Eyre* begun (August).
The Professor, *Wuthering Heights* and *Agnes Grey* finished and begin their tour of the publishers (summer).

1847 *Wuthering Heights* and *Agnes Grey* accepted by Thomas Newby (summer) and published after a long delay (December). *The Professor* (after at least three rejections during its solitary tour) rejected by Smith, Elder (August). *Jane Eyre* accepted by Smith, Elder (August) and published six weeks later (October).

1848 *The Tenant of Wildfell Hall* published by T. C. Newby (summer). Charlotte and Anne visit Smith, Elder in London to set the record straight after Newby's misrepresentations concerning the authorship of novels by 'the Bells' (July).
Branwell dies (24 September).
Emily dies (29 December).

1849 Anne dies (28 May).
Shirley published by Smith, Elder (October).
Charlotte visits London; meets Thackeray and Harriet Martineau (November–December).

1850 Charlotte visits London; meets G. H. Lewes and dines at Thackeray's house (June).
Meets Mrs Gaskell and Matthew Arnold during her visit to the Kay Shuttleworths at Windermere (August).

Prepares and publishes the memorial edition of *Wuthering Heights* and *Agnes Grey*, containing her 'Biographical Notice of Ellis and Acton Bell' and preface to *Wuthering Heights*, and a further selection of Emily's and Anne's poems from their MSS; the edition appears under the imprint of Smith, Elder who secure the rights from Newby (September–December). Visits Harriet Martineau at Ambleside (December).

1851   Charlotte visits London; sees the Great Exhibition and attends Thackeray's lectures (May–June).

Visits Mrs Gaskell in Manchester (June; second and third visits, April 1853, May 1854. Mrs Gaskell visits Haworth September 1853).

1852   The Reverend Arthur Nicholls (curate at Haworth since 1845) proposes to Charlotte and is refused because of Mr Brontë's disapproval (December). He leaves Haworth May 1853.

1853   *Villette* published by Smith, Elder (January).

1854   Charlotte becomes engaged to Arthur Nicholls, who returns to Haworth as curate (April); they marry two months later (June).

1855   Charlotte dies (31 March).

1857   Mrs Gaskell's *Life of Charlotte Brontë* published by Smith, Elder (March).

The Professor published by Smith, Elder, with a preface by Arthur Nicholls dated 22 September 1856.

1860   'Emma', fragment of Charlotte's unfinished story, published in *Cornhill Magazine* with an introduction by Thackeray (April).

Introduction

The body of writing published during their lifetimes by the Brontës is not large. It comprises *Poems by Currer, Ellis and Acton Bell* (1846); *Jane Eyre* (1847), *Shirley* (1849) and *Villette* (1853) by Charlotte Brontë ('Currer Bell'); *Wuthering Heights* (1847) by Emily Brontë ('Ellis Bell'); and *Agnes Grey* (1847) and *The Tenant of Wildfell Hall* (1848) by Anne Brontë ('Acton Bell'). Charlotte Brontë's earliest novel, *The Professor*, which she wrote during 1845-6, was published posthumously in 1857, with the author's name still appearing as 'Currer Bell'. Other material gradually came to light after Charlotte's death in 1855 (Emily died in 1848, Anne in 1849). It included letters and poems; the fragment of a new novel by Charlotte; the juvenilia written by Charlotte and her brother Branwell as chronicles of their fantasy realm, Angria (Emily's and Anne's corresponding chronicles of their own fantasy realm, Gondal, have not been found); exercises written by Charlotte and Emily for their Brussels teacher, M. Heger; and the poignant birthday 'diary-papers' in which Emily and Anne tried to look into their future. But even with these additions, the total amount of material is still modest, and anyone wishing to study the Brontës can readily familiarize himself with all of it.

The case is very different with criticism of the Brontës. During the past thirty years or so it has grown enormously, but interest in the Brontës on the part of the general reading public was already thriving by the turn of the century, when Mrs Humphry Ward, who is still one of their most discerning critics, was preparing her introductory essays for the Haworth edition of their works.[1] She speaks with some feeling of the nature and scale of this interest in her preface to *Jane Eyre*:

Judging by the books that have been written and read in recent years, by the common verdict as to the Brontë sisters, their story and their work, which prevails, almost without exception, in the literary criticism of the present day; by the tone of personal tenderness, even of passionate homage, in which many writers speak of Charlotte and Emily; and by the increasing recognition which their books have obtained abroad, one may say with some confidence that the name and memory of the Brontës were never more alive than now, that

'Honour and Fame have got about their graves' for good and all, and that
Charlotte and Emily Brontë are no less secure, at any rate, than Jane Austen
or George Eliot or Mrs Browning of literary recollection in the time to
come . . .

This lively interest in the Brontës had its beginnings long before
1899 in the immediate and dramatic success of *Jane Eyre* in October
1847, and was kept alive during the next two years by the mystery of
'the Bells'' identity and sex, which was a favourite topic of contemporary literary gossip. Then in 1850 came Charlotte's arresting information about her dead sisters in the memorial edition of *Wuthering
Heights* and *Agnes Grey*, which revealed that the three 'brothers' who
had been taken to task often enough for being 'coarse' and 'violent'
were, startlingly, three young unmarried sisters from a remote country
parsonage near the Yorkshire moors, two of whom were now tragic-
ally dead, carried off within months of each other by the family disease
of tuberculosis. The death of Charlotte herself five years later encouraged readers to reflect once more – as so many readers have
reflected since – on the disparity between the restrictedness of her own
and her sisters' lives and the vitality of their creative imagination. It
was the pity, respect and admiration called forth by hearing their
story that drew Mrs Gaskell to Charlotte when they first came to
know each other in 1850, and after Charlotte's death in 1855 led her
to collect all the materials necessary for the writing of a biography of
her dead friend. The work took two years to complete. *The Life of
Charlotte Brontë* (1857) was widely read and reviewed, the reviewers
including several prominent literary figures of the day. Thereafter
there is continuous evidence throughout the century of the fascination
which the Brontë story held for the general reading public, a fascination which then and in our own century has often done its subjects a
disservice by drawing attention away from their work to concentrate
upon the details of their lives.

SCOPE AND ARRANGEMENT OF THE COLLECTION

Anyone wishing to study contemporary critical attitudes to the Brontë
sisters must sort through quantities of material, for Charlotte's novels
in particular were extensively reviewed in daily and weekly newspapers and in almost all the monthly and quarterly periodicals of any
standing. The generous space devoted at the time to the reviewing of
novels must be a matter of envy to the modern novelist; most notices,

even of novels by unknown writers, included a comprehensive account of the story along with extensive extracts illustrating the author's style, characterization and powers of description. By today's standards, many reviews of *Wuthering Heights* and *The Tenant of Wildfell Hall* – *Agnes Grey* was always more skimpily discussed – are remarkably substantial and well-documented. Yet these look meagre in number and scale when measured against the commentaries on *Jane Eyre*, *Shirley* and *Villette*. The abundance of material, then, presents some problems, but there is the additional difficulty of selecting and arranging the material so that justice will be done to the impression made by the Brontës as a family group as well as to the individual impression made by each sister. The task is complicated by the fact that so long as 'the firm of Bell and Co', as an American reviewer described them (No. 20), were, so to say, in business together, there was some blurring by the public of their individual creative identities, the confusion being worse confounded by the shady dealing of Emily's and Anne's publisher, Thomas Newby, who exploited the situation to promote his sales (see pp. 10–12). It is of some help that in the period between 1847 and 1850 the reviews devoted to Emily, whose novel usually impressed itself strongly if not necessarily agreeably on its readers, are phrased with sufficient emphasis to ensure that this 'Bell' would not be readily confused with either of the other two. Again, although many critics in this period incorporated into their reviews general reflections about the puzzling group, they still managed to concentrate attention on the particular novel under discussion. So it is still possible when reading these earliest reviews to make out the emerging pattern of each sister's developing reputation. Sensitivity to their individual tones of voice could develop more freely once Charlotte had brought out her 'Biographical Notice' in 1850. Finally, when all three sisters were dead, and the first full record of their lives and achievements had been put before the public by Mrs Gaskell, it became a critical habit to attempt some evaluation of their relative stature, a process from which Emily early emerges as the force most to be reckoned with for originality and power while Charlotte remains for some twenty years or so the figure who commands from Brontë enthusiasts the warmest feelings of allegiance and admiration. From the 1870s onwards her work tends increasingly to be measured not only against that of her sister but also against the major literary achievements of the age, a process from which for many readers – including her publisher George Smith – she emerges as a gifted but limited writer whose place must be situated some way below the first rank.

The material in this volume is arranged to shed light on these stages in the development of the Brontës' nineteenth-century critical reputation. The first of the three main sections covers the years from 1846 to the early 1850s, that is from *Poems by Currer, Ellis and Acton Bell* to the publication of *Villette*. The second section concentrates on the movement of opinion throughout the 1850s, the decade in which critical opinion was affected first by the memorial edition of 1850 and then by the further reassessments following Charlotte's death in 1855 and the publication of Mrs Gaskell's *Life* in 1857. The third section includes a selection of statements made about their work during the rest of the century up to (and including) Mrs Humphry Ward's outstanding essays, written as introductions for the Haworth edition of the Brontës' collected works published in 1899–1900. In the first section each sister's work is treated separately, even though this means that there is some chronological overlapping (and that in one case a particular critique, which discusses each of the Bells in some detail, has had to be represented more than once). Exceptions are the early joint reviews of *Wuthering Heights* and *Agnes Grey*, which were published together in 1847 to make up an edition of the popular 'three-decker' size. The fact that some of these early reviews decided notwithstanding to ignore *Agnes Grey* has its own importance here. The commentaries of 1857 by their nature require that what is said should not be broken up in order to preserve the separate treatment accorded to the sisters in the first section. The same principle holds for much of the material in the third section, an additional interest for the student of the Brontës being the incidence and timing of critiques, essays and full-length studies devoted exclusively to the work of any one sister.

In all three sections an attempt has been made to represent as wide a spectrum of opinion as possible. In other words, faced with the problem of what to leave out for the sake of economy (and readability), the decision has been made to extract the gist of many commentaries rather than to represent a few in more detail. Since, as I have said, the illustrative detail is usually copious, the danger of serious misrepresentation does not seem to me to be acute, and in any case it seems less serious than the injustices which may creep in with the elimination of one series of reviews in the interests of another. All the major controversial reviews are represented here, together with many others, including most of those which Charlotte Brontë herself commented upon in her letters. In some cases – for example Sydney Dobell, Swinburne (on Charlotte, not Emily), Peter Bayne and Eugène Forçade – hard pruning may be said to have done the authors some service. After all, closely sustained argument and analysis is not necessarily looked for in the occasional writing which provides the staple material for collections of this kind. Leslie Stephen's measured pieces for the *Cornhill Magazine* are exceptional and his contribution here is treated accordingly. Of all the contributions gathered in this volume, those by Mrs Humphry Ward are both the most substantial and the most considered, which is unsurprising in view of her assignment and the resources which she brought to it. Her work it is which has suffered most severely at my hands, but I take comfort from the fact that her essays are more accessible to the general reader than most of the other materials collected in this book.

THE BRONTË SISTERS BECOME 'THE BROTHERS BELL'

The circumstances surrounding the transformation of Charlotte, Emily and Anne Brontë into 'Currer, Ellis and Acton Bell' have been related many times since the first brief account given by Charlotte in her 'Biographical Notice of Ellis and Acton Bell' for the 1850 edition of *Wuthering Heights* and *Agnes Grey*. Anyone even slightly familiar with the story of the Brontës knows that as a family they had been making up stories since their early childhood days, and that from the 'Young Men' plays (inspired by the wooden soldiers which their father, Patrick Brontë, brought home for their brother Branwell one day in the June of 1826) grew the celebrated cycles of tales about two fantasy realms, the realm of Angria created by Charlotte and Branwell, and the realm of Gondal, created by Emily and Anne. 'Resident in a remote district,' wrote Charlotte in 1850,

where education had made little progress, and where, consequently, there was no inducement to seek social intercourse beyond our own domestic circle, we were wholly dependent on ourselves and each other, on books and study, for the enjoyments and occupations of life. The highest stimulus, as well as the liveliest pleasure we had known from childhood upwards, lay in attempts at literary composition.

Life in a quiet country parsonage, with a large family, narrow means and plenty of books has often proved to be a valuable forcing ground for the creative imagination. What is remarkable in the Brontë sisters is the intensity and persistence of their possession by their own imagination. Charlotte was still writing Angrian tales celebrating the flamboyant Duke of Zamorna when she was in her early twenties, and at the ages of twenty-eight and twenty-five respectively Emily and Anne were still producing fresh chronicles of Gondal and acting out the parts of their heroes and heroines. 'The Gondals still flourish bright as new', Emily wrote in her birthday diary-paper of 30 July 1845: 'I am at present writing a work on the First Wars. Anne has been writing some articles on this, and a book by Henry Sophona. We intend sticking firm by the rascals as long as they delight us.'[2] That the sisters could be troubled by the strength of their addiction seems clear from Emily's poems addressed to her own imagination – for example, 'Who weary with the long day's care . . .', and 'O thy bright eyes must answer now . . .', both written in the autumn of 1844[3] – and from Charlotte's determination to pitch her first novel, *The Professor*, in a subdued imaginative key.[4] The anxiety probably played a part in the sisters' attempts to channel their creative talents in a new direction during 1845. In spite of Emily's remarks in her diary-paper, the Gondals were facing competition. Anne's companion diary-paper, written on the following day, 31 July 1845, records that the Gondals were 'not in first-rate playing condition' and adds 'Emily is . . . writing some poetry . . . I wonder what it is about? I have begun the third volume of "Passages in the Life of an Individual". I wish I had finished it.'[5] As we now know, Emily had been writing verse for several years, much of it personal as well as 'Gondalian', while Anne's 'Passages in the Life of an Individual' became the novel known as *Agnes Grey*. It is generally accepted today that both *Wuthering Heights* and *The Professor* – which had been incubating at least since Charlotte's return from Brussels in 1844 – must have been fairly well under way by the end of 1845. (*Jane Eyre* was not begun until the following August.) During that year, as Charlotte was to explain in 1850, the sisters were reunited for the first time after a long separation. In spite of their happiness at being together, this seemed to be, on the face of it, a barren and disappointing period. Charlotte's existence had been darkened since her return by her hidden unanswered passion for her Brussels teacher, M. Heger. There was no compensating hope to be had from the family plan to set up a school in the parsonage, which fell through from want of support. Branwell, the only son of the house, had been dismissed in disgrace from his post of tutor at Thorp Green and was already set on his course of self-destruction. In spite of or perhaps because of these frustrations, the parsonage was alive with literary activity. Not long after Emily and Anne had written their diary-papers (Emily's is notably cheerful in tone), on 'a day in the autumn of 1845', Charlotte 'accidentally lighted on a MS. volume of verse . . . in Emily's handwriting'.[6] The history of 'the Bells' and their publications had begun.

Charlotte's immediate judgment that Emily's verse deserved to be published chimed in with 'the honourable ambition' which she shared with her sisters – 'we had very early cherished the dream of one day becoming authors' – and it was perhaps this ambition that eventually triumphed over Emily's fierce reticence. Few aspiring writers can have been as ignorant as they were of the ways of the publishing world, but once they had agreed to try to get a small selection of their poems into print, Charlotte's pertinacity carried the project through and rallied the others to renewed creative efforts when the fate of their initial venture looked bleak.

One of their first practical problems was to select suitable pen-names. 'Averse to personal publicity,' Charlotte tells us, 'we veiled our names under those of Currer, Ellis and Acton Bell.' Her explanation reveals the sisters' characteristic blend of unworldliness, shrewd observation and moral principle. The 'ambiguous choice' was dictated[7]

by a sort of conscientious scruple at assuming Christian names positively masculine, while we did not like to declare ourselves women, because – without at that time suspecting that our mode of writing and thinking was not what is called 'feminine' – we had a vague impression that authoresses are liable to be looked on with prejudice, we had noticed how critics sometimes use for their chastisement the weapon of personality, and for their reward, a flattery, which is not true praise.

Charlotte must have been recalling, as she wrote this, recent reviews of her second novel, *Shirley* (published not long before, in October 1849) which were affected by the now generally accepted opinion that 'Currer Bell' was indeed a woman. 'I was hurt', she wrote to G. H. Lewes concerning his review of January 1850 which discussed characteristics of female authorship, 'because after I had said earnestly that I wished critics would judge me as an *author*, not as a woman, you so roughly – I even thought so cruelly – handled the question of sex.'[8]

PUBLISHING HISTORY OF THE 'BROTHERS BELL' (1846–57)

That the brothers found the 'bringing out of our little book . . . hard work' is unsurprising in view of their inexperience and the current lack of enthusiasm for poetry on the part of most publishers, a state of affairs acknowledged by Charlotte in her letter of September 1848 to George Smith, '. . . "the Trade" are not very fond of hearing about Poetry . . . it is but too often a profitless encumbrance on the shelves of the bookseller's shop.'[9] As a last resort Charlotte applied for advice to the Scottish publishers, W. & R. Chambers of Edinburgh, who sent a short sensible reply, 'on which we acted and at last made way'.[10] The 'way' lay through Messrs Aylott and Jones of Paternoster Row, London, who were booksellers and stationers as well as publishers. As G. D. Hargreaves argues in his pioneering essay on the publishing of the *Poems*, Chambers probably recommended the firm to Charlotte 'in the role of stationers who would be prepared to undertake the publication . . . "on the authors' account", as Charlotte's first letter to them, on 28 January 1846, suggests'.[11] The procedure was common practice, and the agreement probably stipulated that the authors would retain their copyright, pay production costs, receive the money from sales, and pay the publishers a commission for their help in getting the book out. The records show that the cost of production in this case (including printing, paper and advertising) was at least £37.18.3. It appears that 1,000 copies were printed, a huge over-estimate (250 copies would have been nearer normal practice).[12]

Once the agreement was completed, things moved fast; Charlotte sent off the MS. (now lost) on 5 February, learning some two weeks later that the volume would be 'thinner' than she had thought;[13] proofs arrived throughout April; three advance copies in their green cloth binding had arrived at the parsonage by 7 May; and the volume was out by the end of May 1846. One year later, Charlotte posted copies to various well-known literary figures, notably Wordsworth, Tennyson, Lockhart[14] and De Quincey, accompanied in each case by the same wry little missive, dated 16 June 1847:

. . . our book is found to be a drug; no man heeds or needs it. In the space of a year our publisher has disposed of but two copies, and by what painful efforts he succeeded in getting rid of these two, himself only knows.

Before transferring the edition to the trunkmakers, we have decided on distributing as presents a few copies of what we cannot sell – we beg to offer you one in acknowledgment of the pleasure and profit we have often derived from your works (*LL*, ii, 136).

This sad anti-climax does not reflect the kindly opinions which the poems won from the handful of people who read them, and the book's subsequent history was brighter. Some eighteen months later, Charlotte's new publishers, Smith, Elder and Company, who were now enjoying *Jane Eyre*'s success, met Aylott and Jones's inquiry about the disposal of the remaining 961 copies by buying up the stock at 6d a copy.[15] They reissued the work almost at once, in the autumn of 1848, with a new binding and title-page, but retaining the original date. The new edition made no dramatic impact, but had sold 279 copies by July 1853. The publishers appear to have had good hopes that sales would benefit by the publication of Mrs Gaskell's *Life of Charlotte Brontë*, for in 1857 they had 450 copies bound up in readiness.[16] They were right to the extent that the principal reviews of the *Life* reconsidered the Brontës' poems, along with the rest of their writings, giving them closer and more discriminating attention than any they had yet received.

During the April of 1846, encouraged by the excitement of seeing their first work in proof, the sisters offered to Aylott and Jones[17]

... a work of fiction, consisting of three distinct and unconnected tales which may be published either together as a work of 3 vols of the ordinary novel size, or separately as single vols. as shall be deemed most advisable ...

This time, the authors had no intention of publishing the work 'on their own account'. The 'tales' were *The Professor*, *Wuthering Heights* and *Agnes Grey*, on which the sisters had been working closely for several months. As 'the brothers Bell', they may have had in mind, as a precedent for separate tales published together, the work of the 'brothers O'Hara', otherwise John and Michael Banim, who published their *Tales by the O'Hara Family* in 1825. *Wuthering Heights* fleetingly recalled to one early reviewer (No. 63), John Banim's addition to the O'Hara tales, *The Nowlans* (1826). Aylott and Jones refused the undertaking,[18] but offered useful advice and the tales were sent out with a brief covering letter, dated 4 July 1846, to Henry Colburn, the first of the publishers upon whom, during 1846-7, the MSS were, in Charlotte's words, 'perseveringly obtruded'. Her own and Mrs Gaskell's accounts differ over the exact length of time that elapsed and the number of publishers who were approached before *Wuthering Heights* and *Agnes Grey* were accepted by Thomas Newby some time in the summer of 1847. Nor is it clear at what stage in its pilgrimage *The Professor* was offered separately from the other two. Charlotte's 'Biographical Notice' of 1850 has it that 'various' publishers were approached 'for the space of a year and a half' until Emily's and Anne's novels 'were accepted on terms somewhat impoverishing to the two authors. Currer Bell's book found acceptance nowhere . . . As a forlorn hope he tried one publishing house more – Messrs Smith and Elder.'

According to Mrs Gaskell, 'the three tales . . . tried their fate in vain together; at length they were sent forth separately, and for many months with still-continued ill success.'[19] We do know from Charlotte's letters that the MS. of *The Professor* was rejected six times before being sent to Smith's on 15 July 1847 (see p. 13), and that proof sheets of Emily's and Anne's novels were ready at Newby's by the beginning of August;[20] Mrs Gaskell adds that their MSS were 'lying in his hands . . . during all the months of early summer . . .'[21]

Seemingly, then, Emily and Anne had to wait rather less than a year, not 'a year and a half', before Thomas Cautley Newby, the publisher, bookseller and printer, whose list of authors included 'the O'Haras', the prolific G. P. R. James and, for a brief spell, Anthony Trollope, agreed to publish *Wuthering Heights* and *Agnes Grey*. He has won no golden opinions for this transaction for his terms were ungenerous and he was dilatory in honouring them. His dishonesty in exploiting other publishers' successes which so distressed 'the Bells' (their mysterious identities were a windfall for him), was also to distress George Eliot twelve years later at the time of *Adam Bede*. Charlotte's allusions to Newby are invariably uncomplimentary, and his chief claim to fame today is the procrastination which permitted 'Ellis's' and 'Acton's' work to languish on his shelves throughout most of the period – mid-July to October 1847 – during which the energetic George Smith first rejected 'Currer's' *The Professor*, and then accepted, published and successfully launched her *Jane Eyre*. 'Mr Newby does not do business like Messrs Smith and Elder,' Charlotte wrote on 10 November 1847 to W. S. Williams, the firm's sympathetic literary adviser, 'Mr Newby shuffles, gives his word and breaks it . . . I have to acknowledge the benefits of a management at once businesslike and gentlemanlike, energetic and considerate.'[22] By this time, Newby, stung into action by *Jane Eyre*'s success, had sent proof-sheets to Haworth for correction. The two novels were published in the following month, December 1847, in a three-volume edition, with *Wuthering Heights* occupying two volumes and *Agnes Grey* making up the third.

Charlotte's distrust of Newby was justified. According to her account of his agreement with her sisters, he arranged to print 350 copies of the edition, to receive £20 from the authors towards expenses, and to refund this on the sale of 250 copies, which would 'leave a surplus of £100 to be divided';[23] yet by September 1850, when the work was, as Charlotte says, seemingly entirely out of print, no part either of the £50 or the promised £100 had been received.[24] Moreover the first copies, as Charlotte complained in December 1847, were shoddily produced and abounded in printing errors.[25] More serious still, Newby had set about his task of confusing the identities of the Bells – and so affecting the course of contemporary criticism – by phrasing his advertisements so that his 'Ellis Bell' might be taken for Smith's best-selling 'Currer Bell'. *Wuthering Heights* was advertised as 'By the successful New Novelist' (*Douglas Jerrold's Magazine*, 5 February 1848), and as 'Mr Bell's new novel' (*Examiner*, 19 February 1848). The climax of his sharp practice came in the summer of 1848, though some of the blame for this must be shared by Emily and Anne, whose scruples forbade them to transfer their allegiance to Charlotte's publishers.[26] Emily's continued commitment seems to be indicated by Newby's letter expressing 'great pleasure in making arrangements for your next novel',[27] and Anne let him have her second novel, *The Tenant of Wildfell Hall*, which she had been working on since the winter of 1847 and which he published in 1848. His terms were better than before,[28] but his behaviour was not. His juggling advertisements now suggested that it was 'Acton' who had written all the 'Bell' novels. Impressive passages were lifted from reviews of *Wuthering Heights* – 'the work is strangely original. It reminds us of *Jane Eyre*. The author is a Salvator Rosa with his pen' (*Britannia*, No. 60), 'A Colossal Performance' (see the *Atlas*, No. 63) – to imply that 'Acton's' *Agnes Grey* had prompted this praise. Worst of all, he encouraged Harper Brothers of New York to bid for *The Tenant of Wildfell Hall*, this time by allowing them to believe that it was written – along with all the other 'Bell' novels – by 'Currer Bell'.[29] The news got back to Smith's, who had made their own arrangements with another American publisher for the sale of *Jane Eyre*. Newby's manoeuvres shocked even more the three sisters at Haworth. When Smith's inquiry reached them, on 7 July 1848, Charlotte and Anne at once made their celebrated journey to London to set the record straight by presenting to George Smith at least two of the 'brothers Bell' for the first time in person. (Emily, as usual, was not to be dislodged, and kept the fort at home.)

Newby's part in the publishing history of the Bells was now virtually over. In the excitement of the first encounter with Smith, vividly described by Charlotte in her letter to Mary Taylor, their interview with Newby seems to have paled into insignificance, for Charlotte barely mentions it; we do learn, though, that when 'explanations were rapidly gone into', Smith reacted robustly and Newby was 'anathematised, I fear, with undue vehemence . . .'[30] He seems to have tried his old tricks again at the close of 1848, for Charlotte wrote to W. S. Williams on 7 December,

. . . I am indeed surprised that Mr Newby should say that he is to publish another work by Ellis and Acton Bell. Acton has had quite enough of him . . . by . . . petty and contemptible manoeuvring he throws an air of charlatanry over the works of which he has the management. This does not suit 'the Bells'; they have their own rude north-country ideas of what is delicate, honourable and gentlemanlike . . .

She also informs him that[31]

'Ellis Bell' is at present in no condition to trouble himself with thoughts either of writing or publishing. Should it please Heaven to restore his health and strength, he reserves to himself the right of deciding whether or not Mr Newby has forfeited every claim to his second work . . .

Twelve days later Emily was dead. Anne died in the following May. In the winter of 1850, Smith obtained from Newby his rights to their novels and published a second edition, adding a selection of their poems along with Charlotte's 'Biographical Notice' and her critical preface to *Wuthering Heights*, all of which helped to settle most of the lingering doubts about the separate identities of 'Currer, Ellis and Acton Bell'.

'Currer Bell's' publishing history is altogether more straightforward, thanks to 'the management at once businesslike and gentlemanlike, energetic and considerate' – though less financially rewarding than it should have been – which she encountered at Smith, Elder, to whom she had sent the MS. of *The Professor* in July 1847, 'as a forlorn hope'. George Smith recalled in 1900 the arrival of the MS.[32]

. . . addressed to the firm, but bearing the scored out addresses of three or four publishing houses, showing that the parcel had been previously submitted to the publishers. This was not calculated to prepossess us in favour of the MS . . .

The story was lacking in colour and narrative interest, and was too short to sell widely at a time when the 'three-decker' was in vogue. But the reasons for refusing it were courteously given, literary promise was detected, and it was added 'that a work in three volumes would meet with careful attention . . .'[33] Charlotte replied on 6 August that she had a narrative of this length in progress, 'to which I have endeavoured to import a more vivid interest . . . In about a month I hope to finish it.'[34] In fact she posted the MS. of *Jane Eyre* to Smith's on 24 August 1847, just a year after she had begun work on it,[35] and less than three weeks after writing this letter. It was published only six weeks later on 16 October in a three-volume edition entitled *Jane Eyre. An Autobiography. Edited by Currer Bell*. A second edition was called for by the end of the year and a third by the spring of 1848. For the second edition, the title was changed to *Jane Eyre. An Autobiography. By Currer Bell* (the fiction about the 'editor' was inadvertently preserved on the spine), and a preface added, in which 'Currer Bell' thanked the public, the press and the publishers for their generosity to an unknown author. She also included a dedication, cast in elevated terms, to her admired fellow-novelist, Thackeray. The third edition, published in April 1848, carried an author's 'Note' disclaiming all titles to any novels other than 'this one work alone', an obvious attempt to dispel the confusion about the identity of 'the Bells' which had recently been increased by Newby's chicanery.

Charlotte's second novel, *Shirley*, meditated as early as mid-December 1847,[36] took her nearly twice as long to complete. The first two volumes went well until the bleak months from September 1848 to May 1849 when she saw first her brother and then her two sisters die one after another. She toiled slowly through the third volume during the lonely summer of 1849, dispatched the MS. in early September, and saw the novel published on 26 October 1849. It was reissued in a one-volume edition three years later, on 19 August 1852. Her third novel, *Villette*, published 24 January 1853, again took her virtually two years to write. She began it early in 1851, worked on it laboriously with intermissions of ill-health and depression, and finally managed to finish it by November 1852.

Earlier, she had made two unsuccessful attempts to interest the firm in publishing a revised version of *The Professor*, once in the winter of 1847–8,[37] and again early in 1851. By 5 February 1851, she had 'yielded with ignoble facility in the matter of *The Professor*', as she put it in her letter to Smith, adding wryly, '[it] has now had the honour of being rejected nine times by the "Trade" (three rejections go to your own share).'[38] Eventually, in 1856, the year after her death, the MS. was carried off in triumph by Mrs Gaskell, who, with the aid of Sir James

Kay Shuttleworth, rescued it with other Brontë papers from the guarded possession of Charlotte's husband, the Reverend Arthur Nicholls.[39] After various misgivings, including Nicholls's fear that the story might seem merely to go over the same ground as *Villette*, and Mrs Gaskell's worries about the possible need for revision, it was published, unrevised, in 1857, with Charlotte's preface and a brief note by Arthur Nicholls, dated 22 September 1856. The note states that Charlotte had written her preface 'shortly after the publication of *Shirley*', which suggests that she had given *The Professor* further serious thought late in 1849.[40]

One must assume that Smith, Elder concluded their agreement to publish *The Professor* on the same terms that had been agreed with Charlotte for her other three novels. Details concerning the editions and sales of all the Brontë novels are lodged – for the moment inaccessibly – with the publishing house of John Murray,[41] but we do know from Charlotte that she earned in all £1,500 from her novels (£500 each). Considering that she was a best-selling author, and certainly enhanced her publishers' reputation, this was not a great deal. She herself expected more generous treatment for *Villette*: 'Papa . . . expected me to earn £700 – nor did I – myself – anticipate that a lower sum would be offered; however £500 is not to be despised.'[42] Mrs Gaskell was much tougher with Smith. Reminding him that she had received £600 from Chapman for *North and South*, she stood out successfully for £800 in payment for *The Life of Charlotte Brontë*.[43]

CHARLOTTE BRONTË AND W. S. WILLIAMS

It would be unjust and inaccurate to discuss Charlotte's early literary reputation without recording the part played in its initial stages by George Smith's literary adviser, William Smith Williams (1800–75), the mild-mannered older man whom Smith had rescued from his detested post of book-keeper with the firm of lithographers undertaking Smith, Elder's artistic work.[44] The prompt action was characteristic of the energetic practical intelligence which ensured the firm's success. George Smith (1824–1901) was only twenty-three when Charlotte first sent her work to him and had recently assumed responsibility for the business,[45] whose standing so far had rested chiefly on the Annual, *Friendship's Offering* (1823–43), and a series on scientific voyages, including Darwin's *Voyage of the Beagle* (1839). It was after their initial dealings with Charlotte that the firm added to their lists the names of Matthew Arnold, Ruskin, Browning, Thackeray and Mrs Gaskell (the inclusion of the last two was largely owed to the firm's success with Charlotte). In these undertakings Smith's enterprise was complemented by the sensitive judgment of his reader. Williams, who was perhaps a writer *manqué*, had been involved in literary affairs since his days as an apprentice with Keats's publishers, Taylor and Hessey; in 1820 he saw Keats off to Italy on his last journey, and it is thought that he may have been the author of an early pseudonymous sonnet in praise of Keats's poetic achievement.[46] He had met various other writers of the Romantic period, and when Smith discovered him in 1845 he was trying to keep up his literary interests by writing dramatic reviews for the *Spectator*, though he found the editor, R. S. Rintoul, excessively chilly – 'The *Spectator* is *not* enthusiastic', Rintoul is reported to have said, 'and must not be.'[47] Williams may well have related this tale to Charlotte when the *Spectator*'s reviews of her own and her sisters' work continued to abide by this principle (see p. 22). His special liking for Turner won him the respect of Ruskin, a selection of whose writings he published in 1861. He displayed his habitual discernment when he saw that if *The Professor* must be rejected, its author must nevertheless be encouraged to try again. He did everything to promote *Jane Eyre* once it was out, skilfully selecting recipients of presentation copies from among contemporary literary personalities – his most striking choice, as it turned out, was G. H. Lewes, who was one of the keenest and certainly the most persistent of the Brontës' Victorian reviewers (see p. 24). Williams then urged Charlotte to persevere with her 'second attempt', wrote encouragingly to her during the long periods of depression in 1849, and again during the months of loneliness and ill-health in 1851–2 when she was writing *Villette*. Throughout the entire period, he helped her by his friendly sober letters, filled with good advice, discussions of her reviews and general literary talk – all of which can be glimpsed through her replies. He stimulated, then, most of her exclusively 'literary' letters. These provide, among other things, a lively running commentary on her own critics and reviewers, which itself throws light on our 'critical heritage' and is in consequence liberally drawn upon in the headnotes below. Her letters to Williams also include her revealing reactions to the regular, thoughtfully selected, gifts of books sent by himself and Smith, possibly the most influential gifts ever made by a publishing firm to one of their writers. The books were eagerly awaited, read and talked over by the inmates of the parsonage during 1848, and later were opened in solitude by the lonely survivor, whose major link with the outside world they remained until December 1853, when the pattern of her life began to change and she requested her correspondent, a little brusquely, 'not to select or send any more books. These courtesies must cease some day, and I would rather give them up than wear them out . . .'[48] Her respect for Williams was saluted after her death by Mrs Gaskell. 'My own feeling as to any revision [of The Professor]', she told George Smith in 1856, 'would be that Mr Williams should undertake it. I believe . . . that he would have been the person she would have chosen . . .'[49] His liking for that novel had survived Charlotte's two unsuccessful attempts to persuade the firm to publish a revised version; '. . . its merits, I plainly perceive,' she had said in 1851, 'will never be owned by anybody but Mr Williams and me . . .'[50]

THE BRONTËS' EARLY CRITICAL REPUTATION (1846–56)

The first decade of the Brontës' critical reputation opens with the publication in 1846 of the Poems and closes with the earliest attempts to set before the public substantial biographical and critical accounts of 'the Bells'. Even though recognition would be dramatically extended the following year with the publication of Mrs Gaskell's Life, it is still true to say that by 1856 Charlotte's literary reputation was secure, Emily's originality was acknowledged – it is in the 1850s that a growing number of contemporary literary figures begin to express their admiration for her peculiar gifts – and Anne, after the flurry about her 'disagreeable' subject-matter in The Tenant of Wildfell Hall had died down, was already settled in her familiar shaded place beside her more famous sisters. In December 1852, that is even before the publication of Villette, the Nonconformist enthusiastically welcomed the cheap edition of 'the series of noble novels by the Bells', spoke sympathetically of 'the author of Wuthering Heights' and found her novel to be 'nearly as wonderful in its way as Jane Eyre'.[51]

The twentieth century, then, cannot claim any monopoly of insight in distinguishing the Brontës' giftedness, since there was early recognition for their grasp of particular detail, their lively feeling for character, and their possession of a creative intensity which did not stop to calculate the ins and outs of current tastes and expectations. Nor was it long before there was acceptance as well as recognition of the fact that their genius was entangled with elements of the crude and naïve, though perhaps it has needed the longer perspective of the present age to see that these ingredients were an inevitable part of their genius, at once ensuring and restricting its imaginative vitality. If we set aside the more sophisticated methods of modern academic criticism, early-Victorian reviews differ noticeably from our own chiefly because of the long-winded style then favoured (the habit of moral expatiation is closely associated with it) and the absence of detailed attention to particular narrative procedures, though interest in the novel as a literary form is lively and grows with the growing import-ance of the novel throughout the nineteenth century.[52] A nearer approach to the cooler manner and the more searching assessments found acceptable today is discovered in some later criticism, for example Leslie Stephen's dryly intelligent piece of 1877 on Charlotte Brontë, included in his *Hours in a Library* (1879), which replies to Swinburne's verbose eulogy in his monograph of the same year, *A Note on Charlotte Brontë* (Nos 108, 109). Swinburne's perceptive later piece on Emily Brontë, written in 1883 as a notice of Mary Robinson's recently published *Emily Brontë* (Nos 111, 112), is a very different matter, anticipating among other things twentieth-century interest in the nature and effects of the 'poetic' novel.[53]

Poems by Currer, Ellis and Acton Bell (1846)
Although the *Poems* received only three reviews of any substance, all of which are represented below, the tone of each was friendly, and two out of the three made a point of distinguishing 'Ellis' from her sisters. The *Critic* (No. 1), which alone devoted its attention exclusively to 'the Bells', quoted three of 'Ellis's' poems to 'Currer's' two and 'Acton's' one, and the *Athenaeum*, in its survey of current verse entitled 'Poetry of the Million' (No. 2), judged that 'Acton's' qualities 'require the indulgence of affection', 'Currer's' muse 'walks half way' between 'Acton's' and 'Ellis's', and 'Ellis's' gifts 'rise into an inspiration which may yet find an audience in the outer world'. The third review, in the *Dublin University Magazine* (No. 3), praised the three 'Bells' with less discernment as 'uniform in a sort of Cowperian amiability and sweet-ness'. This article, unsigned like the others but now known to have been written by William Butler, Professor of Moral Philosophy at Trinity College, Dublin, is an excessively long-winded and rambling commentary, designed to be the first in a series entitled 'Evenings with our Younger Poets'. Apparently it greatly impressed Charlotte and her sisters (see p. 63).

It was not for want of trying that the book was sparsely reviewed. On 7 May 1846, in the first flush of that hopeful 'effort to succeed', Charlotte had directed Aylott and Jones to send copies of the *Poems* and advertisements 'as soon as possible' to eight periodicals (*Colburn's New Monthly Magazine, Bentley's Miscellany, Hood's Magazine, Jerrold's Shilling Magazine, Blackwood's Magazine*, the *Edinburgh Review, Tait's Edinburgh Magazine* and the *Dublin University Magazine*) and two newspapers (the *Daily News* and the *Britannia*).[54] The publishers, it seems, added to the list the *Athenaeum*, the *Literary Gazette*, the *Critic* and *The Times*.[55] The sisters were thus in a sense indebted to their publishers for their two most perceptive reviews. During the next few years most of these (and many other) newspapers and periodicals would be reviewing work by one or other of the Brontës as a matter of course. The *Britannia*, which did not review the *Poems*, nevertheless remembered the *Poems* in its review of *Shirley* (No. 31), and devoted space to linking Charlotte's narrative poems with her novelistic skills; it was also to carry one of the more discriminating of the first reviews of *Wuthering Heights* (No. 60). Of the periodicals which did notice the *Poems*, the *Critic* always remained kindly disposed to all the Brontës, thus ensuring Charlotte's gratitude, for she was quick to respond whenever her sisters' qualities were recognized (headnote, No. 32). The *Athenaeum*, in spite of what Charlotte considered to be its somewhat lofty tone (headnote, No. 7), sustained its interest over a period of nearly forty years; it joined in controversies over details in Mrs Gaskell's *Life* and in 1883 it published Swinburne's influential essay on Emily Brontë, thus finally setting the seal on its early prophecy about her future fame.

The Brontës' companions in these reviews of their *Poems*, and the reviewers' uncomplimentary references to the many small volumes of new verse which they had ignored, help to explain why 'the Bells' were not widely noticed and why 'the Trade' was so little interested in publishing poetry (see p. 8). 'Amid the heaps of trash and trumpery in the shape of verses which lumber the table of the literary journalist,' remarked the *Critic*, 'this small book . . . has come like a ray of sunshine . . .' William Butler's 'trembling candidates for fame' include – 'the Bells' apart – no figures more dazzling than Claire Toumlin and the not-so-young R. H. Horne.[56] In this context the Brontës' restricted range mattered less than their 'true voice of feeling', the quality by which in the end all their work, unequal as it is, must either stand or fall. The quality may have recalled to these reviewers the memory of more distinguished poetic figures. The *Critic* discovered 'traces of Wordsworth, perhaps of Tennyson'. Butler, who shared his age's veneration for Wordsworth (he had just visited him in the Lakes), muses at length upon Wordsworth's achievement and upon the characteristics, as he sees them, of modern poetry, especially its plangent melancholy, its 'refined Pantheism' and the not-too-rarefied idealism informing its treatment of love. He does not situate 'the Bells' in this context beyond offering them benevolent encouragement to persevere. So long as there is the smallest indication of talent in a newcomer, he says, he is prepared to set aside for a time Shakespeare, Milton and 'the glittering *eau de vie* of Moore . . . the sterling "parliament" of George Crabbe . . . the "half and half" of Southey and Shelley and Keats . . .',[57] a catalogue which has its own interest as an index of current literary taste. Butler's encouragement and his general reflections prompted Charlotte to write a letter of thanks to the editor of the *Dublin University Magazine* (see headnote, No. 3). She also proposed to Aylott and Jones that a short extract from the review in the *Critic* should be used in any further advertisements of their book (see headnote, No. 1).

It is likely that 'Currer' and 'Acton', without 'Ellis' to support them, would have won no more enthusiastic response than the *Athenaeum*'s forbearing remarks about the two Hersee sisters, members of whose family, it was felt, would be gratified by their appearance in print. Charlotte, as she explains, brought her own poems out of hiding chiefly in order to overcome Emily's distaste for publicity, and Anne had followed suit. She had no illusions about their quality (though their narrative interest is more engaging than Anne's melancholy piety), and in 1850 described them as 'juvenile productions written . . . before taste was chastened or judgment matured . . . they now appear to me very crude.'[58] The handful of rather colourless but not disrespectful reviews of the reprint of the *Poems* in 1848 gave her little pleasure. The *Standard of Freedom* and the *Morning Herald* ought to have 'more fully recognised Ellis Bell's merits', and the *Spectator* (No. 4) especially incensed her because, 'blind as any bat', it had failed to recognize Emily's supremacy.[59] She would have warmed to such readers as Peter Bayne and the unidentified 'W.P.P.', who ten years later, took Emily's poems seriously (No. 93 and see p. 21), and even more to those reviewers of Mrs Gaskell's *Life* in 1857 who made a point of celebrating Emily's 'wild and plaintive music', which was so hauntingly associated with the purity and austerity of her literary style.

Some readers who were at first unenthusiastic – for example, Charles Kingsley (No. 96) – were drawn to look again at her poetry and found that they had earlier missed the signs of a genuine imaginative talent But it was not until much later that any real attempt was made to link Emily's poetry with her novel, and even so more than another half century had to pass before the thought and feeling in the one was related to the impassioned themes and disciplined structure of the other.[60] By this time criticism was able to benefit from C. W. Hatfield's authoritative text of all Emily's poems, based on careful research into the original manuscripts.[61] Such research also helped to establish which of the poems had originated in Emily's Gondal stage and which were 'personal', though the critical consensus understandably remaining today is that in most important respects this is a distinction without a difference.

Jane Eyre (1847); Shirley (1849); Villette (1853)

Throughout her lifetime, Charlotte's reputation as a novelist rested upon the above three books. Its progress is not hard to outline, though the movements of critical opinion shaping it are sufficiently complex. With Jane Eyre, Charlotte found herself overnight the author of an immediate popular success. Jane Eyre became at once a fashionable topic of conversation in literary circles and also the target for a few self-appointed guardians of public morality who warned against its 'improprieties'; but its author's claim to serious literary standing was left open until the publication of Villette. Since the successor to a best-selling first novel invites a reaction of disappointment, Charlotte's second book needed to be very strong indeed in order to win a genuine succès d'estime. As it turned out, Shirley received wide attention, most of it respectful; a minority even applauded because it was less melodramatically colourful than its predecessor. But its virtues, notably its sharp observation of Yorkshire scenes and characters, were ultimately found insufficient to make up for its diminished narrative verve, the improbabilities in its main story, and its loose construction. Judgment concerning 'Currer Bell's' literary position was accordingly suspended until the appearance of Villette, when most doubts were removed. Lucy Snowe's sombre autobiographical narrative made painful reading for many admirers, but the book won acclaim for its truth, intensity and elevated moral feeling. Reproach for the melancholy which broods over the work in spite of its lively feeling for persons and places was usually offered in sorrow rather than anger, for by this time most reviewers knew who 'Currer Bell' was and what her life had been. On Charlotte Brontë's death in 1855 these feelings of admiration and pity were widely shared. 'W.P.P.', who himself 'felt no ordinary sorrow', quotes representative passages from the torrent of obituaries in the press:

softly, quietly, she went her way . . . such memorials of her as are ours have become pregnant with new meanings,

and again:

Her name is one which belongs to no dilettante associations, no trivial anecdote, no trapping of literary pomp and vanity . . . Henceforth it is a thought for the wakeful midwatches of the night, is a household word for the melancholy dusk. Behold! how we loved her.[62]

The *Daily News* carried Harriet Martineau's well-known (and luckily more trenchantly expressed) tribute to the 'gifted creature' whose loss would be felt throughout the country (No. 88). *Fraser's Magazine* printed 'Haworth churchyard', Matthew Arnold's elegiac tribute to all three sisters (No. 89).

The early controversies about the 'immorality' of the Brontës were recalled after Charlotte's death by admirers whose views suggest that it is not easy to draw a clear line, as has been attempted, between the relatively open-minded 1840s and the increasingly prudish 1850s.[63] The *Oxford and Cambridge Magazine* of 1856 (No. 91) placed Charlotte beside Thackeray – the comparison would have gratified her deeply – as a ruthless adversary of pretence, and scorned those who saw *Jane Eyre* as 'an immoral production and Currer Bell as the treacherous advocate of contempt of established maxims and disregard of the regulations of society'. Such an attitude exemplified the fault 'which the Pharisees found with the teachings of the Saviour'. 'W.P.P.' saw the sisters as highly educated women who 'evinced their true modesty most forcibly by writing freely and truthfully on all subjects whether they were what Mrs Grundy – detestable old bugbear! – would call delicate or not'.

It is impossible to separate the reasons for early misgivings about 'Currer Bell's' moral values from those which made her work so attractive to the majority of her readers. She was, in effect, an original writer and the mixed reactions are in keeping. The spectrum of contemporary opinion about her is reflected in the periodicals whose particular religious or political bias usually flavours their literary reviews. The radical *Examiner*, though it could be shrewdly critical, always approved of 'Currer Bell' (as she approved of it); the high-and-dry 'organs of the High Church', the *Guardian* and the *Christian Remembrancer*, though wishing to be liberal, took exception to her unsettling individualism; and R. S. Rintoul's *Spectator*, watchful for the 'respectable families' for whom it catered,[64] failed to unbend until seemingly convinced by *Villette* that 'Currer Bell' was unlikely to bring a blush to the domestic cheek. On the other hand, the *Quarterly Review*'s celebrated attack on *Jane Eyre* in no way reflected editorial opinion, since Lockhart was enthusiastic about the Brontës and seems not to have foreseen that his reviewer, Elizabeth Rigby, would find the book offensive (Nos 13, 22).

Whatever the political or religious leanings of individual reviewers, there was general agreement about the new writer's 'extraordinary freshness and originality'. The phrase is taken from the review of *Jane Eyre* in the *Church of England Quarterly* for April 1848, which broke its rule never to review novels, because this one was so enthralling and had created such a powerful impression in the six months since its appearance. Its praise was tempered with the warning that 'Currer Bell's' heroine was 'a merely moral person', and, for any real sign of Christianity discoverable in her nature, 'might have been a Moham-medan or a Hindoo'.[65] 'Power', 'originality', 'freshness', 'vigour', 'truth' are the key words in the reviews of 1847 to 1848. This novel was 'different'. According to an early notice in the *Weekly Chronicle* it was 'the most extraordinary production that has issued from the press for years'.[66] For the *Tablet*, in another early notice, 'it was not at all a conventional novel.'[67] Some attempts were made to show how it was 'different'. For example, the *Era* of November 1847 (No. 11) refused to describe it as a 'mere novel' because

there is nothing but truth and nature about it . . . nothing morbid, nothing vague, nothing improbable . . . no high life glorified, caricatured, or libelled; nor low life elevated to an enviable state of bliss; neither have we vice made charming. The story is . . . unlike all that we have read . . . Bulwer, [G.P.R.] James, D'Israeli, and all the serious novel writers of the day lose in comparison.

The qualities associated by the *Era* with 'mere' novels and its unimpressive roll-call of authors are a reminder that 'Currer Bell's' success with *Jane Eyre* owed much to its timing. Her first novel made its appearance in the somewhat dismal interval between, on the one hand, the days of Jane Austen and Scott, and, on the other, the most eventful period in the novel's history. Looking back in 1883, Swinburne compared the rise of the Victorian novel to the flowering of Elizabethan drama, a comparison also made by several other critics writing after the 1850s. The range and variety which prompted the comparison began to manifest themselves in the three years immediately following the publication of *Jane Eyre*, when there appeared Thackeray's masterpiece, *Vanity Fair* (1847–8); Trollope's first two novels, *The Macdermots of Ballycloran* (1847) and *The Kelly's and the O'Kelly's* (1848); Mrs Gaskell's first novel, *Mary Barton* (1848); Dickens's *David Copperfield* (1849–50); and Charles Kingsley's social novels, *Yeast* (1848) and *Alton Locke* (1850). All the Brontë novels, with the exception of *Villette*, belong to the same short period. Within a decade, these writers, who were by then established household names, were to be joined by George Eliot, whose major achievement spans the mid-Victorian years.

But the reviewers of the late 1840s and early 1850s could not know that they stood on the threshold of so rich an age for fiction. Charlotte's companions in early reviews include numbers of minor writers whose names are now hardly remembered outside specialist studies – Mrs Marsh, Lady Georgina Fullerton, Marmion Savage, Harriet Smythies. Signs of the changing times emerge in comparisons which begin to be made quite soon between 'Currer Bell's' Lowood and Dickens's Dotheboys Hall; in the reviewing from late 1848 of *Jane Eyre* alongside *Vanity Fair*; and in the various parallels drawn in 1849 between *Shirley* and *Mary Barton* and in 1853 between *Villette* and *Ruth*. Even so, it was still possible for a reviewer of *Villette* in the *Morning Advertiser* of 4 February 1853 to write in much the same terms as the *Era*'s review of *Jane Eyre* in 1847. 'Currer Bell's' books could not be classed, he felt, under the 'generic term "novel"', because they replaced 'frivolity of style', 'morbid excitement' and 'defiance of probability' with 'the strength of true feeling . . . and robust common sense'.[68]

In spite of failures by reviewers to discern larger movements at work in the fiction of the time, there was no mistaking that 'Currer Bell's' personal innovations lay, as the *Morning Advertiser* emphasized, in her truthful observation of everyday reality heightened by intense feeling, a combination which betrays her affinity with one strain of Romanticism. Mrs Humphry Ward, in 1899, was the first to attempt a close definition of the Brontës' relationship with the whole movement of European Romanticism, but early reviewers glance at Byronic elements in her work (see, for example, the *Examiner*, No. 27) and link her with George Sand, towards whom Charlotte, like many of her contemporaries, was strongly drawn. The *Dublin University Magazine*, for example, detected a resemblance between Jane Eyre and Consuelo.[69] Swinburne was to return to this comparison in the 1870s (No. 108), but among early reviewers it was George Lewes who was most impressed by the kinship. He lent Charlotte some of George Sand's novels in the autumn of 1850 and received an enthusiastic letter in response.[70] One of the latest of his many reviews of the Brontës opens with the declaration, 'In Passion and Power – those noble twins of Genius – Currer Bell has no living rival except George Sand' (No. 45).

Lewes, who also responded ardently to Emily's *Wuthering Heights* (Nos 83, 94), was the most energetic spokesman for those who felt that the union of truthful observation and personal feeling in 'Currer Bell' made up for the weaknesses and improbabilities which in any less passionate writer would be fatally disabling. His enthusiasm derived from his delight in the writer's individual voice, the truth in the depiction of her central figures, her lively descriptive gifts and fresh sense of place, the robust English style which served these gifts, and – informing all – her 'passion and power'. His unfavourable review of *Shirley* (No. 39) made her 'sick' with distaste because of its clumsy insistence on the role of women writers and, though she only hints at this, its painful home truths about the inexperience of life which impaired the portrayal of Caroline's mother, Mrs Prior.[71] But his central criticism sprang in fact from his disappointment at the disappearance of the personal urgency which drives on the narrative in *Jane Eyre*. Its return in *Villette* he warmly welcomed (No. 45). He understood that the extravagances which had marred *Jane Eyre* and which also disfigured *Shirley* – for example, in the improbable behaviour of the Moore brothers – originated in that same powerful feeling, but in these instances undisciplined by truthful observation of human behaviour. This attitude explains his prescribing for Charlotte a course of reading in Jane Austen, thus eliciting from his correspondent some of the liveliest condemnations of that novelist to appear.[72] The vigour of Charlotte's general reaction to Lewes indicates the degree to which she took what he said to heart. The entire relationship between Lewes and Charlotte is of peculiar interest. Whatever he was to become once his life was bound up with George Eliot's, and whatever may be said concerning the Goethean 'neo-classicism' of other of his reviews, his response to the Brontës – and especially to Emily, his '*bête fauve*' – was the impassioned response of a strongly romantic temperament.[73]

G. H. Lewes was certainly not the only admirer who tried to strike a balance between the weaknesses and strengths of Charlotte Brontë's novels. Albany Fonblanque of the *Examiner* – whom with the Frenchman, Eugène Forçade, she counted among the most discerning of her critics (see headnote, No. 21) – attempted in his review of *Shirley* (No. 27) to explain what was meant by the 'coarseness' which for many had spoilt *Jane Eyre*:

We have it in a less degree in *Shirley*, but here it is. With a most delicate and intense perception of the beautiful, the writer combines a craving for stronger and rougher stimulants. She . . . lingers with evident liking amid society as rough and stern as the forms of nature which surround them . . . dwelling even on the purely repulsive in human character.

She has 'vividness', 'reality', 'vigour', and her 'power of graphic delineation . . . is intense . . .', but she lacks any quality, particularly humour, with which 'to soften and relieve the habit of harsh delineation . . .' 'Coarseness' was an indefinite term. For Fonblanque, it seems to be chiefly associated in this case with the provincial setting, speech and behaviour of Charlotte's Yorkshire characters. For others it was associated with Charlotte's 'indecorous' presentation of her characters' love affairs. In *Jane Eyre*, the new author had disconcertingly chosen to make her heroine plain and poor but passionate, and to permit her to live under the same roof as Mr Rochester in a situation which invited charges of impropriety. There were fewer risks to social decorum in her later novels, but the lovers were still uncommonly bold in expressing their feelings, the passionate nature of the heroines was still insisted upon, and the principal male characters, eccentric in manner and inelegant in speech, were still as far as possible from being what Keats called 'Mr Lovels'. For others again, 'coarseness' had principally to do with the manner in which the author dealt with church matters and with religion, whether she was castigating curates or shuddering away from the excesses of 'Romanism'.

The underlying cause of the general uneasiness, whatever the particular 'coarseness' singled out, is perhaps best summed up by the *Christian Remembrancer*'s declaration in the spring of 1848 that 'moral Jacobinism burned in every page of *Jane Eyre*' and that ' "unjust, unjust" is the burden of every reflection upon the things and powers that be' (No. 16). Matthew Arnold, it will be remembered, detected 'hunger, rebellion and rage' yeasting everywhere in *Villette* (No. 53).[74] This impassioned individualism – akin in feeling if not belief to the 'proud, rugged, intellectual republicanism . . . bidding cant and lies be still', for which Froude in 1849 felt that the 'clergy gentleman, and the Church turned respectable' could be no match[75] – was precisely the quality most admired by Eugène Forçade (Nos 21, 33).

The fact that Charlotte was what the *Christian Remembrancer* called 'a good hater' of the 'things and powers that be' may well have stimulated the special animosity colouring the few really hostile attacks on her work, notably Elizabeth Rigby's attack on *Jane Eyre* in the *Quarterly* (No. 22). The severity of this review is remarkable since the reviewer, then on the eve of her happy marriage to the painter and art historian, Sir Charles Lock Eastlake (they married in 1849 and he was knighted in 1850), was, on all the evidence, not only lively and attractive but herself somewhat unconventional.[76] She condemned the heroine's 'vulgarity', Mr Rochester's coarseness and brutality, the author's ignorance of fashionable dress and behaviour, and the 'anti-Christian' nature of the book as a whole. If the novelist was female, then she must have 'for some sufficient reason long forfeited the society of her own sex', and if male, as the ignorance about women's clothes suggested, then the writer was no artist (this illogicality was immediately pounced on by the deeply offended Charlotte). Lockhart had passed on with the assignment the rumour that 'the Bells', a copy of whose *Poems* he had received in 1847, were Lancashire weavers,[77] one of the bizarre tales current at the time, and this may have produced its effect.

Elizabeth Rigby's piece appeared towards the close of 1848, more than a year after *Jane Eyre*'s publication, and provided talking-points for commentaries on the same book which, remarkably, were still coming out in 1849, and for the new crop of notices greeting *Shirley* at the end of that year. Her points about 'vulgarity' and 'lack of principle' were generally taken up only to be dismissed out of hand or placed in a reasonable critical perspective. There was still some surprised comment in the notices of *Shirley* about Charlotte's treatment of the relationship between men and women, though the growing consensus that 'Currer Bell' was a woman produced a mawkish tone in certain reviews which irritated her (headnote, No. 24). But her book generally gave little offence. The *Church of England Quarterly Review* in its brief notice (No. 37) now pronounced 'the moral tendency not open to serious objection', and appeared rather less pleased about this than disappointed that *Shirley* had less 'originality and freshness' than *Jane Eyre* and was 'inferior in point of interest'. The *Spectator* (No. 28), though chilly, found 'less coarseness', welcomed the greater variety of characters and, not unreasonably, preferred the vivid realization of the social and historical background to the love relationships, which, as Lewes recognized, had more 'feeling' than 'truth'. Fonblanque, besides attempting to explain what he meant by 'coarseness', picked up from the *Examiner*'s earlier review of *Jane Eyre* (No. 10) its comparison of 'Currer Bell's' novels with those of Godwin (both shared a greater interest in 'mental analysis as opposed to . . . events'), now adding that it 'might have taken Lord Byron within the range of comparison'. But 'Currer Bell' was found better than either writer, because she did not, like Godwin, 'subordinate human interests to moral theories, nor, like Byron, waste her strength in impetuous passion. Keen intellectual analysis is her forte . . .' (No. 27).

Setting aside the dismissive piece in *The Times* (No. 35), which stung her to tears by finding *Shirley* 'puerile', 'commonplace', and simultaneously 'high flown and dull', Charlotte had little to complain of in the treatment of *Shirley*. Nor could she complain about the response to *Villette* some three years later, in spite of two reviews, both written by women, which were in their various ways as upsetting as the *Quarterly*'s review of *Jane Eyre* and the remarks from Lewes and *The Times* concerning *Shirley*. Apart from these there was little serious condemnation. 'Coarseness' was not mentioned with any strong emphasis, pleasure was taken in 'Currer Bell's' return to her absorbing autobiographical method, and everyone was intrigued – and many captivated – by her eccentric hero, Paul Emanuel. Even the two reviews by women admired the new book's skill and power.

The controversial reviews in question were Harriet Martineau's in the *Daily News* and Anne Mozley's in – once again – the *Christian Remembrancer* (Nos 41, 54). Both were unsigned, but Charlotte immediately recognized Harriet's authorship:[78]

Extremes meet, says the proverb . . . Miss Martineau finds with *Villette* nearly the same fault as the Puseyites – She accuses me with attacking Popery with virulence – of going out of my way to assault it 'passionately' . . . In other respects she has shown . . . a spirit . . . strangely and unexpectedly acrimonious.

Harriet was a staunch rationalist. Her 'Puseyite' opposite number in this case was Anne Mozley, sister of James Mozley, editor of the *Christian Remembrancer*. In her lengthy (and frequently admiring) article, Anne Mozley recalled the periodical's earlier attack on the 'outrages on decorum' in *Jane Eyre*, found some improvement in this respect in *Villette*, but deplored the narrowness displayed in the author's views on

'Romanism'. She ended by attacking the author's support for feminine independence, since a 'restless and vagrant imagination, though owned by woman, can have no sympathy or insight into the really feminine nature . . .' It is in the 'daily round of simple duties and pure pleasures' that its 'true happiness and satisfaction lie'. From her diametrically opposite point of view, Harriet also attacked Charlotte's view of women. She disliked the novel's overwhelming 'subjective misery' and the excessive concern of the female characters with the need for love – women, she argues, do have other interests, and the failure to take this into account is a limiting weakness in an otherwise splendid, even Balzacian, tale.

Charlotte found it difficult to forgive either reviewer. She wrote a pained letter to the editor of the *Christian Remembrancer* (headnote, No. 54 and p. 370 n.), and felt betrayed by Harriet, with whom – radically different as they were in outlook and temperament – she had been friendly since December 1849, and to whom she had gone for advice when bewildered by repeated references to the indelicate behaviour of her heroes and heroines. 'She could not make it out at all,' Harriet records, 'and wished that I could explain it.' Harriet tried to do so: 'I had not seen that sort of criticism then . . . but I had heard *Jane Eyre* called "coarse". I told her that love was treated with unusual breadth, and that the kind of intercourse was uncommon, and uncommonly described, but that I did *not* consider the book a coarse one.' Charlotte begged her to read the book again, and to tell the truth as she saw it.[79] Later again she begged Harriet, in even more pressing terms, to tell her the truth about *Villette*. Harriet did this, both in a private letter and in her review. The 'truth' was too much for Charlotte, who broke off the correspondence and put an end to the friendship.[80]

Wuthering Heights (1847); *Agnes Grey* (1847); *The Tenant of Wildfell Hall* (1848)

It is hard to say how Emily's and Anne's novels would have fared in these early years without either the lively discussions aroused by their sister's work or her memorial to them in 1850. An early reviewer of *Wuthering Heights* and *Agnes Grey*, in the *Atlas* of January 1848 (No. 63), felt that *Jane Eyre* had done much 'to ensure a favourable reception for the volumes now before us'; and throughout the next two years comparisons with the first of the 'Bell' novels feature constantly in reviews of 'Ellis's' and 'Acton's' work. 'The first is still the best' was a common judgment, even when there was renewed admiration for the family's characteristic gifts of 'vigour' and 'genuineness'. *The Tenant of Wildfell Hall* caused some stir on its own account in the summer of 1848, but confusion about 'the Bells' was then at its height. The American periodical, the *Literary World*, reviewing Anne's new novel in August (No. 74), forecast 'an infinite series of novels of a new class, which would be strung on, like the knotted tail of a kite, to the popular work *Jane Eyre*'; and in referring to 'the author's mingled strains of harshness and genius' – this perception was by now a critical commonplace in reviews of the Brontës – it implied that 'Acton Bell' had produced *Jane Eyre* and *Wuthering Heights* as well as *The Tenant of Wildfell Hall*. Confusion still reigned two years later when Sydney Dobell wrote his tribute to *Wuthering Heights* (No. 80) as the most impressive, if still immature, achievement so far produced by 'Currer Bell', whom he took to be the author of all the 'Bell' novels; he had refused to be shaken even by Charlotte's disclaimer in the third edition of *Jane Eyre* (see pp. 277–8).

In spite of such confusion, it is obvious that Emily's individual gifts strongly impressed her earliest readers. Even if these turned to *Agnes Grey* with relief because it was 'sunnier' or more 'measured', they found it untouched by the imaginative qualities which lifted *Wuthering Heights* out of the ordinary. Most reviews merely confined themselves to a few remarks about Anne's more placid story; some devoted their attention exclusively to its companion, among them Charlotte's favourite periodical, the *Examiner* (No. 59). There were many bewildered allusions to 'Ellis's' gloom and violence, and to the particular brand of the family 'coarseness' found in her book, the term being used this time to indicate the effect of her characters' unrestrained behaviour and habits of speech, both of which gave offence. But in the same breath that they expressed their misgivings, critics also expressed their admiration. *Wuthering Heights* was much more than a 'mere' novel for the reviewers in, among others, the *Britannia, Douglas Jerrold's Weekly Newspaper* and the *Atlas* (Nos 60, 61, 63), from all of which Newby was able to cull glowing passages for use in promoting *The Tenant of Wildfell Hall* (see p. 11).

The mistaken belief that early critics failed to do justice to Emily and Anne originated in 1850 with Charlotte's 'Biographical Notice' and was consolidated by Mrs Gaskell, whose statements about the early critical reception of the Brontës are highly misleading.[81] The mistake is understandable, since in 1850 and throughout her friendship with Mrs Gaskell, which dates from the same year, Charlotte saw her sisters through a haze of grief which magnified every adverse criticism into a wrong added in the general cruelty of destiny. She probably remembered with especial bitterness some of the last reviews of their own work seen by the sisters, including Edwin Whipple's abrasive pieces in the *North American Review* (Nos 69, 75). Others, even at the time, placed the situation in clearer perspective. Extracts from reviews printed in the 1850 edition in order to encourage sales, including tributes from the *Britannia* and the *Atlas*, led George Lewes to comment in his notice of the new edition for the *Leader* (No. 83) that, contrary to Charlotte's opinion, the critics had been 'excessively indulgent'; some of them, including the reviewer in the *Examiner*, even expressed their annoyance at being so sadly misrepresented (see No. 82). Passages extracted from reviews for the purpose of puffing look different in their proper context, but in this case the tributes had genuine force and discernment. The *Britannia* saw that the novel was produced by 'a mind of limited experience but of original energy and of a singular and distinctive cast', while Douglas Jerrold's reviewer (see headnote, No. 61) thought 'the writer . . . wants but practised skill to make a great artist; perhaps a great dramatic artist', thus foreshadowing Dobell's (and, later, Swinburne's) feeling for the affinity of *Wuthering Heights* with poetic drama. Such judgments make nonsense of Charlotte's belief that 'the immature but very real powers revealed in *Wuthering Heights* were scarcely recognised'. Emily's combination of strength and naïvety is precisely what these early readers were quick to see.

But we cannot blame Charlotte for saying that 'the import and nature of the book were misunderstood', since these are still debated, the main difference then being that the book's violent and unorthodox elements were not only puzzling but also disturbing. Charlotte's 'moral Jacobinism' and sturdy dismissal of many reassuring stock ingredients of fiction paled into insignificance beside her sister's more startling departures from custom. As she always recognized, Emily's mind and imagination were more daringly speculative than her own (No. 68), and the nature and reach of the exploratory statements in *Wuthering Heights* were subversive in a manner that was never fully understood – there is no hint in Charlotte of, for example, the cosmic outlawry which troubles Catherine Earnshaw in recounting her dream to Nelly Dean in the book's ninth chapter. Charlotte's fine preface of 1850 itself suggests her own trouble over Emily's creation of Heathcliff (No. 81). 'Strange' is one of the commonest of the more neutral epithets applied to the book in the reviews. It was 'strange' partly because of its emphatic insistence on contrasts of violence and harmony. Douglas Jerrold's reviewer was struck by the proximity of passages 'of powerful testimony to the supreme power of love' and others where 'The reader is shocked, disgusted, almost sickened by details of cruelty, inhumanity and the most diabolical hate and vengeance.' It was 'strange' even more because, although the violence and destruction seemed to cry out for condemnation, they were dramatized with an intensity that implied the author's sympathy with them. Strangest of all, perhaps, was the absence of any single authoritative viewpoint from which the reader could take his moral bearings in this world of extremes. He might be disturbed by Jane Eyre, but no moral ambiguity clouded her farewell to Rochester: 'The more solitary, the more friendless, the more unsustained I am, the more I will respect myself. I will keep the law given by God; sanctioned by man. I will hold to the principles received by me when I was sane, and not mad as I am now.' There is no such central authority in *Wuthering Heights*. Modern readers, having read their James and Conrad, are more at home with the multiple perspectives of Emily's indirect narrative method. But for them, as for their predecessors, it is the 'dark' elements, chiefly concentrated in the figure of Heathcliff, which overshadow the sunnier and more 'normal' aspects of life also depicted in the novel. They still find it easy not to notice that half the total number of chapters is given to the story of Heathcliff's and Catherine's successors in the next generation, and to the unfolding of events leading Cathy and Hareton out of the turbulent 'Heights' to the ordered life of the valley. The effect indicates the bias of Emily's creative imagination rather than the carelessness of her readers. All the same, at least one early reader (No. 67) perceived the importance of the two locations – the moorland and the valley – as central in the book's effort to establish a balance of forces, and thus as something more than an excuse to display that robust gift for natural description which characterized each of 'the Bells'. This reviewer was the author of the discerning, and still unidentified, notice, a cutting of which was found preserved in Emily's desk after her death.

But there was no recognition of the book's reliance on a firmly symmetrical structure or its employment of an intricate chronological scheme.[82] Everyone, even the most kindly disposed, found the composition confusing. No wonder, then, that there were so many helpless gestures towards the absence of any ostensible 'moral purpose'. The *Spectator*, naturally, disapproved (No. 57), while the *Examiner*, hastening to declare its breadth of outlook – 'We detest the affection and frippery . . . frequent in the modern novel and willingly trust an author who goes . . . fearlessly into the moors and desolate places for his heroes . . .' (No. 59) – still exhorted this author not to lay so much weight on whatever of the 'coarse and loathsome' he discovered in his wanderings. Chorley's plea in the *Athenaeum* – 'Never was there a period in our history . . . when we English could so ill afford to disperse with sunshine . . .' (No. 58) – reminds us again of the 'hungry Forties' and the uneasiness produced by Charlotte's intransigent individualism. Yet it was from across the Atlantic that the sternest moral condemnations arrived, many of these couched in colourful language.[83] The reviewer in *Graham's Magazine* (No. 66), recalling an old saying about eating toasted cheese and dreaming of the devil, had his own views about 'Ellis's' diet. Edwin Whipple (No. 69) found that 'the whole firm of Bell & Co seem to have a sense of the depravity of human nature peculiarly their own. It is the yahoo, not the demon, that they select for representation.'

It was Whipple who regarded *Wuthering Heights* 'as the last desperate attempt to corrupt the virtues of the sturdy descendants of the Puritans', a pronouncement which unwittingly leads straight into the heart of the matter, that is to the particular kind of romanticism informing Emily's work. The well-known complexity in the response of the American 'puritan ethic' towards romantic movements of feeling is apparent in most of the American reviews of the Brontës. In England, as we have seen, there was a considerable degree of sympathetic insight into Charlotte's romantic affinities, with special recognition for her French affiliations. In English reviews of *Wuthering Heights*, as in reviews of Charlotte's work, there were allusions to Byron (*The Examiner*, for example, compared Heathcliff with Byron's Corsair). There was also recognition here and there of a resemblance between *Wuthering Heights* and some German 'Gothic' tales; the parallel with Hoffman was first drawn by the *Britannia* in 1848, and taken up again in 1857 by Émile Montégut in the *Revue des deux mondes* (No. 102) and in 1895 by 'Vernon Lee' in the *Contemporary Review*. The 'French' and 'German' aspects of Charlotte's and Emily's work were to receive more informed attention at the end of the century from Mrs Ward, who made a genuine attempt at a scholarly investigation of their possible 'sources' (No. 116). When the new edition of *Wuthering Heights* appeared in 1850, most reviewers were too surprised and interested by the new information which it contained to do more than rehearse the biographical facts and exclaim about them. But some readers thought anew about *Wuthering Heights* itself, and in such cases it is the larger-than-life romantic scale of the emotions found in it that they find attractive. The passionate feeling and poetic power which excited the poet Sydney Dobell in his wordy but keenly responsive article, written just before the new edition appeared (No. 80), also aroused George Lewes's admiration. He had already reviewed by now both *Jane Eyre* and *Shirley* (Nos 14, 15, 39), and while it was again the Brontëan 'truth' of feeling which he noticed, it was the strong pulse of this particular Brontë's feeling that captivated him. The book was 'sombre, rude, brutal, yet true'. In the next years, between 1850 and 1857, we find others among Emily's fellow-writers, including D. G. Rossetti and Matthew Arnold (Nos 87, 89), responding as ardently to her poetic power.

There could be no such ardent response to Anne, whose lesser imaginative gifts were recognized then as now. In the first months of her career, from December 1847 until the following summer, 'Acton' was regarded as the least controversial – in other words, the least interesting – of the 'three Bells'. *Agnes Grey* was briefly but not un-favourably noticed. It suffered as an individual achievement because it was usually drawn into the current of the reviewer's general views concerning the family's literary characteristics. The *Britannia*'s greater interest in *Wuthering Heights* in 1848 (No. 60) left it room only for a fleeting acknowledgment of 'Acton's' 'nicely sketched characters and scenes'. The *Atlas* (No. 63) saw it as 'a coarse imitation' of one of Jane Austen's 'charming stories' and felt that it might be effaced by the next new novel, 'but *Jane Eyre* and *Wuthering Heights* are not things to be forgotten.' Chorley in the *Athenaeum* (No. 58) drew both *Agnes Grey* and *Wuthering Heights* into his closing remarks, for there was 'much feeling for character and nice marking of scenery in both', so that it was worth warning these two 'Bells' to avoid spoiling their next work by once again emphasizing the uglier and more painful aspects of existence.

Chorley was to be disappointed, since Anne's acute sense of duty made her see her moral responsibility as a writer in a different light. Branwell's dissolution and its effect on his sisters' imaginative life would not become a matter of extensive critical discussion until the 1870s. The extent of this influence on Charlotte's and Emily's work must remain a matter of conjecture but for Anne's second novel it was crucial. She took it on herself to display to others as an awful warning the destructive effects of the type of self-indulgence which for some four years had provided so gruelling a spectacle in her daily life at Haworth. To her dismay, she found that she had made herself vulnerable to the charge so often levelled against her sisters, of a gratuitous liking for sensationalism. The novel's strong flavour, however, paid off; the book quickly went into a second edition and she was able to add a – discreetly – explanatory preface, explaining the moral purpose behind the story of Henry Huntington's alcoholism and its disastrous consequences (No. 72).

In spite of distaste for the theme, many reviews are again, as in the case of all 'the Bells', remarkable more for discernment and tolerance than for any cripplingly narrow moralistic judgment. Setting aside *Sharpe's Magazine* and the *Rambler* (Nos 76, 77), in which such judgments predominate (they embrace all the Brontës' novels, including *Jane Eyre* which, for the *Rambler*, is a very '*bad*' book), there is a general sense that, to borrow the *Athenaeum*'s metaphor, 'the metal from the Bell foundry' was far from base, even if it was not always put to good use. Indeed the *Athenaeum*, in spite of Anne's disregard for Chorley's warning, recommended her book to its readers as 'the most interesting novel which we have read for a month past'. Even the *Spectator* recognized its author's ability (though, of course, finding this misused). The two reviews of most interest for the general moral debate about the family's work were the unsigned notice by Charles Kingsley in *Fraser's* (No. 78) and the long commentary in the American periodical the *Literary World* (No. 74). Of these, Kingsley's defends the propriety of using such subject-matter in terms similar to those employed by some commentators in 1856 (see p. 21). The writer in the *Literary World*, believing that all 'the Bell' novels were written by 'Acton' (see p. 11), took a different line from his American colleagues: 'We do not believe one word in the charge of immorality ... brought against these books. An aberration of taste, an ignorance of society must by no means be confounded with a departure from principle.' He pointed to the common fallacy of confounding an author with his characters, and emphasized the 'vividness and fervour' of the writer's imagination. He had no doubt about 'Acton Bell's' sex. What is 'good or attractive in the male characters is womanish', what is bad is imported from 'the flash English novel' or 'the melodramas of Kotzebue's day'. He was shrewder than he realized, for Branwell's utterances – as we know them from his letters and surviving tales – have much of this flavour about them.

Charles Kingsley agreed about the writer's sex, and for similar reasons, but differed over the 'truth' of the book, which in the light of his own Christian socialist principles is its strongest moral defence. The 'very coarseness and vulgarity is just such as a woman, trying to write like a man, would invent'. But she cannot be despised for attempting to expose some of the

> ... foul and accursed undercurrents ... in this same smug, respectable, white-washed English society ... we must not lay Juvenal's coarseness at Juvenal's door, but at that of the Roman world which he stereotyped in his fearful verses ...

When Charlotte's explanations of 1850 arrived to support Anne's preface of 1848, the whole matter fell into a different perspective, and so, too, did the 'vigour' of her book. For even in 1848, those among her reviewers who disliked the subversive elements in 'the Bells', for example Edwin Whipple (No. 75) and the reviewer in *Sharpe's London Magazine* (No. 76), had found mitigating qualities in her work which separated it from that of her sisters. By the 1850s, when Emily's gifts were being thrown more and more into relief, her own achievement in *The Tenant of Wildfell Hall* came to seem much less extraordinary. This growing interest in Emily and its inevitable effect upon Anne's reputation was disregarded by George Moore, Anne's major champion in the twentieth century. He claimed in his *Conversations in Ebury Street* (1930) that critics were encouraged in 'their depreciation of Anne' by Charlotte's remarks in the 'Biographical Notice' concerning her sister's misdirected zeal. *Agnes Grey* was for him 'the most perfect prose narrative in English literature ... the one story in English literature in which style, characters and subject are in perfect keeping'. Moreover, in the first part of *The Tenant of Wildfell Hall* the 'weaving of the narrative reveals a born story-teller, just as the knotted and tangled threads in *Wuthering Heights* revealed the desperate efforts of a lyrical poet to construct a prose narrative.' It was 'not lack of genius' but inexperience that made Anne lose her way in the middle of her story. 'The diary broke the story in halves', and all would have been saved had Helen related her story herself.[84]

THE REVIEWERS AND MRS GASKELL'S *The Life of Charlotte Brontë* (1857)

The virtues of Mrs Gaskell's biographical study have little to do with its critical insight into Charlotte's novels, and everything to do with those gifts of quick observation and human sympathy which ensured its author's own success as a novelist. It was a success as different as possible from that of any of the Brontës; indeed it was partly the keenness of her feeling for the differences separating herself and Charlotte that intensified her interest and concern when they first met in 1850. But there were qualities of mind and imagination in each member of the family which necessarily eluded the reach of her generous but relatively conventional kind of insight. The woman who later heroically struggled with her own moral distaste for George Eliot's irregular partnership with Lewes, because the 'noble' sentiments in *Adam Bede* could not have been expressed by anyone 'bad', displays the same half-admirable, half-obtuse play of mind in her defence of Charlotte's 'coarseness' (see No. 98, p. 356). Emily, naturally, was yet more remote from her. They had never met, so Mrs Gaskell knew her only through Charlotte's recollections, which were coloured by grief and her peculiarly intense feelings of love and awe. Mrs Gaskell's personal comments on Emily in the *Life* are confined to the sentence quoted from her letter late in 1853: 'Emily must have been a remnant of the Titans, great-granddaughter of the giants who used to inhabit the earth.'[85] This remark, together with the space given to stories about Emily's ruthlessness in life – the punishment of her dog, the cauterizing of her own arm with the hot iron – and her stoicism in the face of death, must bear much of the responsibility for the persistent image of a gaunt, preternatural creature, totally separated from humour, gaiety and almost all ordinary human sympathies. Various attempts (notably by Ellen Nussey, a family friend) to set the record straight had little effect until Mary Robinson attempted to do for Emily what Mrs Gaskell had done for Charlotte and produced in 1883 the first full-length biographical study. Mrs Gaskell found Anne easier to describe, but since the details that she collected chiefly emphasized Anne's quiet sedentary ways and her increasing melancholy in the last years of her short life, the portrait did little for her literary reputation apart from fixing her in the role of gentle sister to two talented writers.

The most important consequences of Mrs Gaskell's *Life* for the course of the Brontës' subsequent critical history stem from the stimulus which it gave to speculations about the connection between a writer's actual experience and the products of his creative imagination. The relationship has a special importance in Victorian times, for the pulse of urgent personal feeling beats in the work of most of the celebrated story-tellers – certainly in the Brontës, Dickens and George Eliot – as well as in that of various 'non-novelists', for example J. H. Newman and Froude, who turn to fiction to explore in disguise pressing personal dilemmas. In the event, inquiry into this question of the interplay between 'life' and 'art' was to produce studies of widely varied quality, the crudest of them promoting a belief in a simple correspondence between a writer's subject-matter and his day-to-day experience. The tendency to identify life and art was encouraged in the case of the Brontës by the exceptional fascination of their personal history, which, perhaps more than in the case of any other literary figures, drew many of their admirers to employ their work primarily as a quarry for future information about their lives. Emily was in the end the worst sufferer since she was the most perplexing and the least known of the three. This kind of interest culminated in the founding of the Brontë Society in the 1890s.

Mrs Gaskell's personal reputation in 1857, as the author of *Mary Barton* (1848), *Ruth* (1853), *Cranford* (1853) and *North and South* (1855), ensured a wide and also an informed welcome for her work. Several of her reviewers were themselves known in the world of letters; she also received private tributes in letters from fellow-writers which help us to follow more intimately some movements of feeling about the Brontës in the late 1850s. But it must be remembered that Charlotte and her sisters were by this time themselves very well known indeed and that this fact was one strong reason for Mrs Gaskell's undertaking the *Life* in the first place. The most striking biographical revelations had been made by Charlotte in 1850, and after her death in 1855 numbers of articles and monographs appeared containing further information, for example 'W. P. P.'s' *Jottings* (1856), and, in June 1855, the piece in *Sharpe's London Magazine*, 'A Few Words about Jane Eyre',[86] which set in train the process leading to the *Life*. Besides recalling feverish early gossip about 'the Bells' in the late 1840s, the revelations of 1850, and the sorrow over Charlotte's recent death, the article relates from unspecified sources two anecdotes, one concerning Patrick Brontë's first intimation that his daughter was a novelist, the other recounting the first meeting between the author of *Jane Eyre* and 'a lady, who afterwards became intimate with Miss Brontë'.[87] It was Ellen Nussey's desire for a more accurate record that encouraged Patrick Brontë to approach Mrs Gaskell as 'the best qualified' person 'to publish a long or short account of her life and works ... as you may deem expedient and proper'.[88] Mrs Gaskell's personal prestige, then, counts for much in her book's subsequent fortunes, but the fame of the Brontës counts for still more.

With all this information, the reviewers of 1857 were better placed than those of 1850. They had no need to exclaim over the unravelling of a three-year-old mystery, they could look at the Brontës' work as a whole instead of piecemeal – even *The Professor* came out in time to be included in their surveys – and they gained from the perspective afforded both by the natural distancing processes of time and by the artful ordering of Mrs Gaskell's narrative. It is a tribute to her self-effacing manner that they were free to devote their attention to the Brontës rather than to her. Notices in the dailies and weeklies – the *Critic* and the *Athenaeum*, for instance[89] – chiefly went over the main events of the story and commended Mrs Gaskell's treatment. The important monthlies and quarterlies, with more space at their command, displayed a stronger sense of occasion. John Skelton in *Fraser's*, W. C. Roscoe in the *National Review*, and E. S. Dallas in *Blackwood's* produced substantial review-articles in which they analysed what seemed to them to be the essential imaginative qualities displayed by each of the three sisters (Nos 95, 98, 99). There was a similar concentration of interest in some influential foreign periodicals. *La Revue des deux mondes* followed its earlier notices by Eugéne Forçade with Émile Montégut's now well-known essay (No. 102), and in America Mrs Sweat (No. 103) helped the *North American Review* to make amends for Edwin Whipple's harshness in 1848.

Thanks to Mrs Gaskell's skill in picturing the Yorkshire setting of the Brontës, these particular reviewers had in common a quickened sense of the 'wilder' world in which the sisters grew up. This better understanding disposed of the narrower moral issues in the old controversy about the Brontës' 'coarseness' and 'immorality'. None of these reviewers had much patience with criticism conducted simply at this level. They did concern themselves, rightly, with the risks incurred by the narrow range of tone and subject-matter found on one side of the Brontëan 'medal of so strange an alloy', of which the other side is passion and power.

At the same time, their interest in the influence of the Brontës' environment and experience upon their work did not prevent them from recognizing, in Skelton's words, that 'the experience can never entirely explain the work'. Skelton observed, as others did (for Montégut the matter was of prime importance), the reflection in her novels of Charlotte's personal life, but between the experience and the work lies 'the mystery of Genius'. Roscoe – perhaps not fully comprehending the issues – even disagreed with Lewes over his advice to her to look more directly at life; she was at her best when she freed her gifts from the portraying of 'real' people – such as the curates and the Yorkes in *Shirley* – and permitted them to transmute experience into something new. He singled out the figure of Paulina, also in *Shirley*, though he might possibly not have done so had Mrs Gaskell presented straight-forward evidence of a model.

To some extent this desire to separate 'life' from 'art' is associated with contemporary distaste for publicizing personal details of any private life. Roscoe opened on this note, praising Mrs Gaskell's skill while thinking it misdirected. The distaste for personal revelation was shared by Mrs Gaskell herself[90] and persisted late into the century, as Henry James reminds us in several of his 'little tales'. It is ironical that the same age should have produced so many outstanding biographies, including, besides Mrs Gaskell's, Lockhart's *Life of Scott* (1837–8), A. P. Stanley's *Life of Arnold* (1844) and Cross's *Life of George Eliot* (1885), all of which were greeted with more interest than repugnance. These complex feelings concerning the sanctity of private experience invite speculation about the connection between these feelings and the strong 'personal impress' in so many Victorian novels. The reviewers of 1857 share an enthusiasm for the strong individuality in the Brontë novels. 'A personal impress is strongly marked on them', says Roscoe: 'It is curious that, though the writers all had strong imaginations, not one of them had the power to get rid for a moment of her own individuality. It permeates with its subtle presence every page they write.' E. S. Dallas, looking back to the *Poems*, saw the individual 'handwriting' there too, 'so that in taking up any one of the poems, it is not difficult to discover the writer.' Skelton, also re-reading their verse, was again sensitive to their individual voices, 'And because of this ... they never imitate ... The writers speak out plainly and calmly what they have felt themselves.' He saw, moreover, something else in the poems: 'There are deeps of passion underneath the passion-less face. The estimation of life is studiously grave and sombre, but at times an intoxicating sense of liberty thrills their blood, and the wild gladness of a Bacchante sparkles in their eyes.'

This response to the strong feelings associated with a passionate individualism, that *amour de soi* which later critics were to identify as the most characteristic expression of the Brontës' individual romantic temper, was most marked in the singling out of Emily as the member of the family endowed with the strongest imaginative gifts. Charlotte, naturally, was given the most space and was preferred for her relatively wider range and her less 'abnormal' qualities, as she was also praised for her vigour and independence, and her racy, accurate English. Anne was the one least attended to, though Roscoe went out of his way to praise her for one quality in which she surpassed her sisters, namely that she was more of an 'artist' in that her work was more consistently ordered and therefore more 'homogeneous'.[91] It was Emily, though, who called out the most resonant passages of appreciation. Her 'power, splendour, and wildness' fascinated George Lewes (No. 94). She was 'the most powerful' of the sisters for Skelton, and again for Roscoe, who found in her poems how far she excelled in 'force of genius, in the power of conceiving and uttering intensity of passion'. Dallas followed Skelton in stressing her gift in the early poems, which were singled out 'even at the time . . . and that verdict is not likely to be disputed'. Like Roscoe, he saw that Mrs Gaskell's limitations were a hindrance to her appreciation of the Brontës' less conventional qualities, though his own explanation of the differences separating Mrs Gaskell from Emily required him to paint a dramatic portrait of Emily as a despairing figure burdened by her tragic sense of life.

But if Dallas's portrait of Emily as an individual was exaggerated, his feeling for the genre to which her novel belongs was not. With Skelton and Roscoe, he saw that its mixture of naturalistic and non-naturalistic elements calls for comparisons with poetic drama. His reading over-emphasized the 'pitiless fatality' in *Wuthering Heights*, but his parallel with Greek tragedy was at least suggestive. Roscoe, too, was arrested by her 'wealth of tragic utterance' and by 'some strange sympathy' in her nature with the 'harsh natures she revels in delineating'. It was to Shakespearian rather than Greek tragedy that Skelton looked when he noticed the resemblance between Ophelia's madness and Catherine's deathbed recollections of the birds which she and Heathcliff watched in their childhood days on the moors.[92] It was he, again, who invoked the memory of Kyd and Ford when repudiating the old charges of immorality levelled against Charlotte; their themes, like the Brontës' themes, involved pain, violence, grief and separation.

These commentators had travelled far from the more simplistic readings of the earliest critics. The allusions to Shakespeare in discussing Emily, which increase with time (see, for instance, No. 115), imply some feeling for the movement in her novel through violence and destruction to balance and reconciliation. Skelton understood the mingling of peace and conflict in her work, even pointing to the attractive wildness of the youthful Heathcliff, which is associated with the 'charm of the bleak hillsides and savage mountains', and which is later lost; and he understood a quality of tenderness in the handling of both the Catherines. Émile Montégut, who, like the rest, gave most of his space to Charlotte and least of it to Anne, was as impressed as everyone else by Emily. He reprinted his essay in 1885 and in a footnote expressed at once his delight at the comparatively recent recognition of her merit by Swinburne and his pleasure at what he took to be his own unique percipience in 1857. In fact several of his English fellow-critics had anticipated to a remarkable degree what Swinburne had to say in 1883 concerning the 'fresh dark air of tragic passion' in *Wuthering Heights*.

JUDGMENTS AND OPINIONS (1857–89)

Thirty years after the publication of Mrs Gaskell's *Life*, *Blackwood's Magazine* carried in its issue for January 1887 a Jubilee article entitled 'The Literature of the last Fifty Years',[93] written by the tireless Mrs Oliphant. In her view Charlotte's 'impassioned revelation' of 'feminine distresses' had won her a temporary fame, while Anne and Emily – the latter as the author of an 'extraordinary and feverish romance' – probably had owed their 'former' reputations chiefly to Mrs Gaskell, 'herself . . . also well worthy of note as a novelist'. They all belong, she claims, to the beginning and end of the Victorian period, a period 'when society was purer and manners better' and now clearly regarded by the writer as over and past beyond recall.[94]

Mrs Gaskell has fallen into that respectful oblivion which is the fate of a writer who reaches a sort of secondary classical rank . . . for *Jane Eyre*, though it has a much stronger power of survival than *Mary Barton*, it is necessary now to look in private libraries or in the old-fashioned circulating libraries of our youth . . . Circulating libraries in watering places where Mudie is not supreme . . . are the places to make sure of Mrs Gaskell, and even to bring oneself once more under the powerful spell of Lucy Snowe and Jane Eyre . . .

This is potboiling journalism, but it was surely a strange oversight which led Mrs Oliphant to ignore the fact that over the past fifteen years interest in the Brontës, so far from fading, had been rapidly gathering new momentum. Publications about the Brontës were certainly infrequent in the decade immediately following the *Life*, since attention was naturally drawn to major new literary events –

Mrs Oliphant in retrospect saw, for example, that another woman had been the first to 'attain the highest place in literature. The position of George Eliot is unique.' Even so, there was a trickle of published material throughout the 1860s. W. C. Roscoe reprinted his 1857 review in his *Poems and Essays* (1860); the study by 'Camille Selden', *L'esprit des femmes de notre temps* (1865), containing 'Charlotte Brontë et la vie morale en Angleterre', was reviewed in 1866 at some length in the *Catholic Herald*; *Harper's New Monthly Magazine* carried in 1865 a tribute to 'Charlotte Brontë's Lucy Snowe'; Harriet Martineau reprinted her obituary of Charlotte in her *Biographical Studies* of 1869. Throughout the same period, too, allusions to the Brontës appear in many of the numerous review-articles now dedicated to the task of keeping up with the novels coming weekly from the presses. V. H. Hobart singled out the primitive power and truth in *Wuthering Heights* in his 'Thoughts on Modern English Literature' for *Fraser's Magazine* of July 1859.[95] Alexander Smith, in 'Novels and Novelists of the Day' for the *North British Review* of February 1863, calculated that 'two novels, or six volumes, every week are produced in England', most of them 'worthless', but, 'as a set-off we have more eminent names in this special literary walk than any other'. He was representative in using the Brontës as a measure of comparison when discussing George Eliot, who had 'less than Charlotte Brontë of lyrical impulse and impetuosity, – fewer of those unexpected, passionate intense sentences . . . which readers of *Jane Eyre* and *Villette* know so well, – she has quite as much passion, only . . . in equally diffused heat rather than sparkles of flame . . .' Smith was also one of many to deplore the appalling feebleness of so many current novels, a theme taken up again by Mrs Oliphant herself in *Blackwood's* for September 1867 (No. 105), where she plays her own part in keeping Charlotte in the public memory by presenting her as the only begetter of the new palpitating heroines who excitedly await the heroes' 'flesh and muscles . . . strong arms . . . and warm breath' in the sensational pages of Annie Thomas, Miss Braddon, Rhoda Broughton and 'Ouida'.

References to the Brontës in the 1870s indicate more clearly how strongly interest in them had survived, the interest now being increasingly biographical. It was in these years that the Brontë legends began to grow.[96] At the same time, the new biographical studies prompted new critical assessment, as the *Life* had done in the late 1850s, and now, as then, the biographers applied for help to Ellen Nussey, whose presence at this time is increasingly felt in the background of Brontë studies. As the oldest accessible friend of the family and owner of a large number of obviously extremely valuable letters, she was in a difficult position. The strain told on her sensitive if somewhat conventional spirit and led her to make some unwise judgments, but much is owed to her, including her earlier support for Mrs Gaskell, and her 'Reminiscences of Charlotte Brontë' for *Scribner's Monthly Magazine* in May 1871, in which she undertook to refute the charge of 'irreligion' against Charlotte. This was a matter which, like many others affecting the Brontës' good name, assumed exaggerated proportions in her mind. In fact the article is of more value for its record of hitherto unknown details about the brighter and more mischievous side of Emily's character – she played the piano, we are told, with precision and brilliancy and was known for her gaiety and sense of fun when out on the moors with her family. Two years later, in July 1873, George Smith contributed 'The Brontës' to the *Cornhill Magazine*, a critical reappraisal which suffers from its unexpectedly heavy-going style – he reserved his personal reminiscences of the Brontës for his second much livelier *Cornhill* article of 1900. Here the three points of most interest are – once again – warm praise for Emily, whose novel 'stands as completely alone in the language as . . . *Paradise Lost* or the *Pilgrim's Progress*' and whose Heathcliff 'has no match outside Shakespeare'; the preference of *Jane Eyre* over *Villette*, whose reputation Smith considered to have been inflated and which, it appears, had never sold as well as its prestige had led him to expect; and the placing of Charlotte, who 'eclipses novelists of the highest reputation in isolated qualities' but whose 'genius is intense . . . not broad, and it is breadth alone which distinguishes the loftiest minds'. One can understand Mrs Oliphant in 1887 overlooking these two essays of 1871 and 1873 by Ellen Nussey and George Smith, but it is difficult to see how she could neglect Thomas Wemyss Reid's biography of Charlotte in 1877, which had first appeared in a shorter form as a series of articles for *Macmillan's Magazine* in the autumn of 1876 (No. 107). This work touched off a fresh debate about the Brontës, which was still going on when she was writing and continued into the 1890s when the Brontë Society was founded and work was begun on the Haworth Edition. Reid's work breaks little new ground so far as Charlotte is concerned, since he wished chiefly to recall attention to her by telling again the story of her life and work, with some additional material from her correspondence, but he corrects Mrs Gaskell by devoting special attention to Emily as a compellingly talented writer. Reid's book was accompanied in 1877 by two critical essays which are among the *loci classici* of Brontë studies, the first being Swinburne's monograph, *A Note on Charlotte Brontë* (1877), and the second Leslie Stephen's reply, 'Charlotte Brontë', published in the *Cornhill* for December 1877 (Nos 108, 109). The tone of Swinburne's essay was affected by what he regarded as the unspeakably inadequate praise for Charlotte offered by Reid's reviewer in the *Spectator*. In his own heatedly verbose eulogy he prophesied that Charlotte would survive all the 'female immortals' of the hour and would be read with delight and admiration 'when even *Daniel Deronda* has gone the way of all waxworks, when even Miss Broughton no longer cometh up as a flower, and even Mrs Oliphant is at length cut down like the grass'. It was his unusual exaltation of Charlotte at the expense of George Eliot, whose 'exceptional intellectual power' was exactly what made the cultivated reader set her above every other contemporary novelist, that seemed so extraordinary to Leslie Stephen. His cool, measured reply was based on the view that if 'criticism cannot boast of being a science, it ought to aim at something like a scientific basis . . .' His penetrating analysis separated Charlotte's strengths from her weaknesses. The latter include her want of general ideas, the lack of universality in her major figures, not excluding the widely admired Paul Emanuel, and, above all, the inherent flaw in her thinking which carried her to protest against conventionality while adhering to society's conventions. These weaknesses ensure that she cannot be placed in the highest rank. She is foremost among those who have suffered unresolved emotional conflicts, have felt passionately 'the necessity of consolation', and have drawn their readers to them through their powerful expression of human distress.

Were it not for one fact this essay might be taken as the coming-of-age of Brontë criticism. But the coolness of temper which makes Stephen's reply to Swinburne so telling also restricts the range of his sympathies. Although not hostile and plainly not unintelligent, his remarks about Emily indicate his lack of engagement by her 'naturally subjective mode of thought', her reflection of 'the mood of pure passion', and her 'lyric cry'. His attitude, moreover, was out of keeping with the prevailing feeling about Emily, who in the 1880s began to replace Charlotte as the centre of attention. In 1877 Reid saw her as 'a rare and splendid genius', and Swinburne in the same year linked her with Charlotte as exemplifying a genius which reaches 'a quite incomparable degree of excellence'. He records his lifelong admiration for her in his letter to Reid of September 1877 (No. 112) and his 'Note' on Charlotte includes a salute to Emily which anticipates his essay of 1883; the true voice of feeling is heard in Jane's response to Rochester, and it is heard as clearly in Catherine's celebrated cry, 'Nelly, I *am* Heathcliff.' Five years before this, an American reviewer, in the New York *Galaxy* (No. 106), inspired by Smith, Elder's uniform edition of the Brontës' novels and poems, devoted a long article exclusively to Emily's 'Life and Writings'. The article made amends for 'the wholesale condemnation and unqualified abuse' which had been heaped on Emily's work in America, and anticipated her special importance for English readers in the 1880s.

This decade opened with Peter Bayne's second, yet more copious, essay on the Brontës in *Two Great Englishwomen* (1881), in which he re-examined at length the work of the three sisters and expressed renewed, if even more troubled, admiration for Emily as a powerful writer, the clue to whose writings lies in her unsuccessful quest for some evidence of the existence of God (No. 110). The major landmark of the period, however, was the first full-length biography of Emily. This was published by Mary Robinson in 1883 and prompted Swinburne's second Brontë essay, which was written as a review-article for the *Athenaeum* in the same year (No. 112). Mary Robinson, who had gathered fresh materials from Ellen Nussey,[97] was particularly interested in the religious and autobiographical sources of *Wuthering Heights*. At the same time, like the reviewers of 1857, she tried hard to avoid making simple correspondences between 'life' and 'art' and took issue with Reid over his view that Heathcliff was drawn directly from Branwell.[98] Even so, Swinburne found that she made too much of Branwell's effect on Emily, whose naturally sombre vision, as he saw it, did not need this kind of stimulus. His review finally set the seal on the conception of *Wuthering Heights* as an outstanding work of the poetic imagination. The 'inner harmony', which is 'the first and last necessity . . . for a poem worthy of the name', and which characterizes *King Lear* and *The Duchess of Malfi* as it characterizes Scott's *The Bride of Lamermoor* and Victor Hugo's *Notre Dame de Paris*, is everywhere apparent in *Wuthering Heights*, and finally 'distinguishes the hand of Emily from the hand of Charlotte'. Moreover, it follows from Emily's 'passionate straightforwardness' that the 'prevailing atmosphere of the book', so far from being morbid and brutalizing, is high and healthy'.

There were still those, of course, who, like Frederic Harrison, could only think of *Wuthering Heights* as a 'grisly dream' and looked on Charlotte as the single Brontë meriting serious attention.[99] But the central movement of feeling is felt in passing references in a number of literary essays, for example 'Vernon Lee's' 'On Literary Construction' for the *Contemporary Review* in 1895, where Emily's principle of composition is a flaw in 'one of our greatest masterpieces of passion and romance'.[100] By 1896, Clement Shorter was able to write of Emily Brontë as 'the sphinx of our modern literature', whose 'cult . . . started with Mr Sydney Dobell . . . found poetic expression in Mr Matthew Arnold's fine lines on her . . . and culminated in an enthusiastic eulogy by Mr Swinburne, who placed her in the very forefront of English women of genius.'[101] This whole movement of feeling, in which the relative strengths of Charlotte and Emily tell more and more in favour of Emily, finds its ultimate expression in Mary Ward's intelligent well-informed commentaries for the Haworth edition of the Brontës' work (No. 116), published in seven volumes, in 1899–1900, as *The Life and Works of Charlotte Brontë and her Sisters*. The edition included as well as the novels, *Poems* (1846), the selection from Emily's poems printed by her sister in the 1850 edition of *Wuthering Heights* and *Agnes Grey*, Patrick Brontë's *Poems* (1811), and Mrs Gaskell's *Life*. The latter carried an introduction and notes by Clement Shorter, who had already made a major contribution to Brontë studies in 1896 with his *Charlotte Brontë and her Circle*.[102] Mary Ward's breadth and sense of proportion (which would have gratified her uncle, Matthew Arnold), her familiarity with English, French, German and even Russian literature, and her natural feeling for the novelist's processes of re-creating actual experience, enable her to come as close as anyone has done to understanding the quality of the Brontë sisters' artistic achievement and their particular brand of romanticism. She discussed the effects on Charlotte's work of her hereditary Celtic strain and her Yorkshire Pennine environment, and also noted her response to contemporary French literature. 'The dithyrambs of *Shirley* and *Villette*, the "Vision of Eve" of *Shirley* and the description of Rachel in *Villette*, would have been impossible to Emily; they come to a great extent from the reading of Victor Hugo and George Sand.' Perhaps she over-estimated the German 'Gothick' influences on Emily, who certainly learned German and was familiar with tales from the German published in *Blackwood's Magazine* in the 1830s and 1840s, but she was right to notice the difference between the sisters. Most modern readers will find themselves in sympathy with her final assessments. She spoke comparatively little, though not slightingly, of Anne. She recognized in Charlotte and Emily, in spite of the dithyrambs and amateurish 'lack of literary reticence' of the one and the occasional crudities of the other, a 'similar *fonds* of stern and simple realism' and a 'similar faculty of observation at once shrewd and passionate'; and she found in the end that the differences between them are 'almost wholly in Emily's favour'.

THE BRONTËS IN THE TWENTIETH CENTURY

One may say, then, that if Mrs Ward's work provides a fitting close to the story of the Brontës' literary reputation from 1846 to 1900, it also points to a certain continuity of critical opinion concerning their achievement which links the nineteenth century to the twentieth. But it must be added at once that there can be no expectation of providing within the space allotted here anything like an adequate account of the ways in which her views have since been expanded or modified. A glance at any responsible bibliographical survey of Brontë criticism will immediately indicate why. In the *Cambridge Bibliography of English Literature, Nineteenth Century* (1969 edition), the list of works about the Brontës occupies some six columns of small print, of which three columns cover most of the important studies which appeared up to 1940. The remaining three columns represent the vast proliferation of work which has taken place since. In Mildred Christian's comprehensive chapter, 'The Brontës', in *Victorian Fiction, a Guide to Research*, edited by Lionel Stevenson (1964), the fourth section – the first three deal with bibliographies, manuscripts, editions and biographies – offers a descriptive account of about a hundred books, articles and shorter notices published during the previous thirty years. Obviously, then, all one can do here, and in the Bibliography at the close of this collection, is to indicate briefly some of the principal movements of opinion, and mention – however invidiously – a handful of the commentators most closely identified with them.

One point that can be made with some confidence is that the movement of allegiance away from 'Charlotte's more simple certainties to Emily's wild and puzzling questions'[103] has continued throughout most of the twentieth century, while Charlotte has remained for most of the period in the secondary position – *vis à vis* both Emily and other Victorian novelists – to which from the 1870s many even of her warmest admirers felt obliged to consign her.[104] It seems right to add that the most influential of the Brontës' modern critics in encouraging these attitudes has been Lord David Cecil in the chapters 'Emily Brontë and *Wuthering Heights*' and 'Charlotte Brontë', which form part of his *Early Victorian Novelists: Essays in Revaluation* (1934). His views chime in with Mrs Ward's, since he too recognizes that Charlotte's novels are crippled by weaknesses, and yet are transfigured by their passionate intensity of feeling. Again like Mrs Ward, he has no doubt at all that Emily is the greater writer. He emphasizes her toughness of structure, her firm grip on the actual, and the vivid particularity of her descriptive details. Still more important for its effect on subsequent criticism is his attempt to arrive at a coherent reading of her book as a 'metaphysical' novel, a reading which takes account of its 'moral unorthodoxy' and its mixture of naturalism and non-naturalism, and which has something in common with Virginia Woolf's brief imaginative comments in her essay of 1916 on the two Brontë sisters (included in *The Common Reader* (1925)) concerning Emily's 'gigantic ambition' to unite in a book a world 'cleft into gigantic disorder'. Since 1934, whatever the measure of agreement or disagreement with Cecil's interpretation, whole legions of articles about theme and symbol in *Wuthering Heights* have sprung into being, so that the subject as a critical theme seems to me to have been by this time pretty well run into the ground.[105] Twenty years after the publication of Cecil's essay, Emily's modern French critic Jacques Blondel, in his monumental study, *Emily Brontë: Expérience Spirituelle et Création Poétique* (1955), was able to view his subject in the new perspective of modern criticism and research. He offers the fullest exploration yet to appear of every aspect of her work, her poetry included, and lays particular emphasis on her art as a highly individual blend of realism and romanticism, in which her *amour de soi* – compare Mrs Ward's phrasing[106] – prompts her to create a powerful myth at the same time as it prevents her achieving anything approaching a genuine Shakespearian detachment.

Throughout the same period, that is until the mid-1950s, critical studies of Charlotte are much fewer in number and generally less interesting, since, whatever her intensity of feeling, she has a less arrestingly original, and therefore less intellectually stimulating, quality of mind and vision. The issue most canvassed in the period concerns the relative merits of her two most successful novels, *Jane Eyre* and *Villette*. Certain later nineteenth-century readers had come to think less highly of *Villette* than their predecessors had done[107] but many modern readers have once again singled out this novel because it appears to them to demonstrate the successful culmination of its author's struggle to come to terms with 'reality' (as against, that is, the powerful counter-attractions of romantic fantasy). Such a view is implied in Kathleen Tillotson's chapter on *Jane Eyre* in her *Novels of the Eighteen-Forties* (1954), and it provides the central theme for Robert Colby's '*Villette* and the Life of the Mind' (*PMLA*, 1960). Towards the end of the 1950s, however, the first efforts begin to be made to restore Charlotte to a position of primacy among the three sisters. Even so, many of the new apologias are based on the claim that her novels to be properly appreciated must be read in the same way as *Wuthering Heights*, that is, as 'poetic' novels illustrating the imaginative organization which encouraged Emily's perceptive early readers to refer in the same breath to her novel and to the poetic dramas of Webster and Shakespeare. The singular inappropriateness of this approach was pointedly argued by D. W. Crompton in his brief note, 'The New Criticism: a Caveat' (*Essays in Criticism*, 1960).

This renewal of interest in Charlotte has coincided with a fresh determination to look at the work of all three Brontë sisters with as little reference as possible to biographical material;[108] the interference of the 'Brontë story' with dispassionate appreciation of their work was recognized as early as 1899 by Mrs Ward in the opening pages of her Introduction to *Jane Eyre* for the Haworth edition. Among those critics who have eschewed biography and at the same time found strongly for Charlotte – though without necessarily incurring the risks warned against by D. W. Crompton – are R. B. Martin in *Accents of Persuasion* (1966), the first substantial full-length study devoted exclusively to Charlotte's work, and Wendy Craik in *The Brontë Novels* (1968). Mrs Craik's book can be linked with Mrs Ewbank's *Their Proper Sphere* (1966) in that each represents a return to the habit of examining the work of the sisters as a family group, with due respect for the qualities of Anne, who has received some additional recognition in this century from W. T. Hale's *Anne Brontë: Her Life and Writings* (1929), Ada Harrison's and Derek Stanford's *Anne Brontë* (1959), and Winifred Gérin's *Anne Brontë* (1959). However, Anne's present-day status is perhaps still best indicated by the implication in Norman Sherry's title for his introductory primer, *The Brontës: Charlotte and Emily* (1969), a study which gets a lot of material into a short space. This critic, moreover, makes no bones about holding to his belief in Emily's greater originality and in paying tribute to the ultimately 'Shakespearian' nature of her vision, in which a good natural order is shown re-establishing itself after temporary disruption by the forces of evil. Allowing for variations of emphasis and for the diverse effects of personal bias, the critical attitudes to the Brontës indicated in Professor Sherry's brief account seem to me to represent sufficiently accurately the current consensus of informed critical opinion. As to popular opinion, this has barely changed much over the years. Everyone knows – or knows of – *Jane Eyre* and *Wuthering Heights*, both of which continue to be dramatized, filmed, televised and read over the air. A recent television adaptation of *Villette* demonstrated that Charlotte's feeling for persons and places can still have vitality for a modern audience. But it is the powerful feeling and larger-than-life romantic appeal of *Jane Eyre* and *Wuthering Heights* which keep them alive in the popular mind, and if the response of new readers is anything to go by, it is *Wuthering Heights*, of the two, which still arouses the stronger feelings and produces the more powerful imaginative impress.

NOTES

1 See pp. 46–7.

2 *LL*, ii, 49–50.

3 *The Complete Poems of Emily Jane Brontë*, ed. C. W. Hatfield (1941), 205–6, 208–9.

4 See her letter to G. H. Lewes, 6 November 1847 (*LL*, ii, 152–3) and her preface (*c.* 1849) to *The Professor* (1857).

5 *LL*, ii, 52.

6 'Biographical Notice'.

7 Ibid.

8 *LL*, iii, 68; and see No. 39.

9 *LL*, ii, 254.

10 Robert Chambers (1802–71), who founded the firm with his brother, had established in 1832 *Chambers's Journal*, which was designed to provide 'information for the people'. *Chambers's Encyclopaedia* was begun 1859 (completed 1868).

11 G. D. Hargreaves, 'The publishing of *Poems by Currer, Ellis and Acton Bell*', *B.S.T.* (1969), vol. 13, no. 4, 294.

12 For further discussion of these and other details, see ibid., 294–300.

13 That is, 163 pages of foolscap octavo instead of 'from 200 to 250 pages' of the octavo volume which she wished to be 'of the same quality paper and size of type as Moxon's last edition of Wordsworth' (*LL*, ii, 81, 82–3).

14 The gesture in this case was to have unlooked for repercussions (pp. 22, 26).

15 Aylott and Jones could thus repay the Bells £24.0s.6d. of their original outlay.

16 G. D. Hargreaves, *op. cit.*, 299 n.

17 *LL*, ii, 87.

18 Aylott's daughter records his preference for 'publishing classical and theological books' and his refusal to publish novels 'as he was rather old-fashioned and had very narrow views regarding light literature' (*LL*, ii, 80).

19 *Life*, chapter 15 (Haworth edn, 313).

20 *LL*, ii, 154.

21 *Life*, chapter 16 (Haworth edn, 324).

22 *LL*, ii, 154.

23 The usual price for a 'three-decker' at the time was 31s.3d.

24 Charlotte's letter to George Smith, 18 September 1850 (*LL*, iii, 160).

25 *LL*, ii, 162, 165.

26 See Charlotte's letter to George Smith, 17 February 1848 (*LL*, ii, 190).

27 For details concerning this letter, which was found in Emily's desk after her death, see *LL*, ii, 187–8.

28 Anne was to receive £25 on publication, a further £25 on the sale of 250 copies; and two further payments of £50, one on the sale of 400 copies, and the second on the sale of 500 copies. The book had a minor *succès de scandale* (see p. 34) and brought him more money than he deserved; yet by 13 September 1850, six months after Anne's death, only two instalments of £25 each had been paid (*LL*, iii, 156–7, 159).

29 See Charlotte's letter to Mary Taylor, 4 September 1848 (*LL*, ii, 250–1).

30 Ibid., 252.

31 *LL*, ii, 290–1.

32 George Smith, 'Charlotte Brontë', *Cornhill Magazine*, December 1900, 780.

33 'Biographical Notice'.

34 *Life*, chapter 16 (Haworth edn, 327–8).

35 While staying in Manchester, 19 August–28 September 1846, as companion to her father during his treatment for cataract.

36 Letter to W. S. Williams, 14 December 1847 (*LL*, ii, 161).

37 Letter to W. S. Williams, 14 December 1847 (*LL*, ii, 161–2).

38 *LL*, iii, 206–7.

39 Mrs Gaskell's letter to George Smith, 25 July 1856, *Letters of Mrs Gaskell* (1966), 398.

40 For Charlotte's revisions of her novel see M. M. Brammer, 'The MS. of *The Professor*', *R.E.S.*, n.s. 11 (1960).

41 Smith, Elder survived until 1917 and was then incorporated into the house of John Murray.

42 Letter to Margaret Wooler, 7 December 1852 (*LL*, iv, 23).

43 Letters to George Smith, 26 and 29 December 1856, *Letters* (1966), 430, 431–2.

44 George Smith, *loc. cit.*, 780–1.

45 His father, who had founded the firm with his fellow Scot, Alexander Elder, in 1816, had died in 1846; Elder had retired in 1845.

46 *Keats: The Critical Heritage*, ed. G. M. Matthews (1971), 29.

47 George Smith, *loc. cit.*, 781.

48 *LL*, iv, 100; Charlotte had been corresponding with Arthur Nicholls throughout the summer of 1853 and became engaged to him in April 1854.

49 Letter to George Smith, 1 August 1856, *The Letters of Mrs Gaskell* (1966), 401.

50 Letter to George Smith, 5 February 1851, *LL*, iii, 206. For other brief commentaries on W. S. Williams see *LL*, ii, 171–2 and Clement Shorter's *Charlotte Brontë and her Circle* (1896), 370–2.

51 Unsigned notice of the one-volume reprint of *Shirley*, *Nonconformist*, 15 December 1852.

52 See Richard Stang, *The Theory of the Novel in England 1850–1870* (1959), and Kenneth Graham, *English Criticism of the Novel 1865–1900* (1965).

53 For instance, G. D. Klingopulos, 'The novel as dramatic poem: *Wuthering Heights*', *Scrutiny* (1947), xiv, 269–86.

54 *LL*, ii, 93.

55 The titles are added to Charlotte's list in brackets and in a different hand.

56 Richard Hengist Horne (1803–84), joint author with Elizabeth Barrett Browning of *The New Spirit of the Age* (1844). His dense moral allegory in nine books, *Orion: an Epic Poem* (1843) had just reached its sixth edition; he sent Charlotte a copy in December 1847, when *Jane Eyre* had made 'Currer Bell's' name better known, and received a warm reply (*LL*, ii, 163).

57 *Dublin University Magazine*, October 1846, xxviii, 384.

58 Letter to Miss Alexander, 18 March 1850 (*LL*, iii, 86).

59 Letters to W. S. Williams, 2 and 6 November 1848 (*LL*, ii, 268, 269).

60 See Peter Bayne's and Mary Robinson's comments in 1881 and 1883 (Nos 110, 111) and compare Mary Visick's pioneering study, *The Genesis of Wuthering Heights* (1958; revised 1965).

61 See Bibliography, p. 462.

62 'W.P.P.', *Jottings on Currer, Ellis and Acton Bell* (1856), 19. 'W.P.P.'s' monograph consists of random observations concerning the Brontës' subject matter and style and is warm-hearted rather than critically shrewd. The author's identity is unknown; the essay has a faintly clerical flavour.

63 See, for example, Kathleen Tillotson, *Novels of the Eighteen-Forties* (1954), 54–73.

64 See G. M. Young, *Early Victorian England* (1934), ii, 47.

65 *Church of England Quarterly Review*, April 1848, xxiii, 491–2.

66 *Weekly Chronicle*, 23 October 1847, 3.

67 *Tablet*, 23 October 1847, 675.

68 *Morning Advertiser*, 4 February 1853, 6.

69 *Dublin University Magazine*, May 1848, xxxi, 614.

70 *LL*, iii, 171-3. For her earlier reading of George Sand see her letter to Lewes, 12 January 1848 (*LL*, ii, 180).

71 She praised Henry Bagshawe's review in the *Dublin Review* (March 1850, xxviii, 209-33) as 'very able' and affording 'a curious contrast to Lewes in the Edinburgh' (*LL*, iii, 93). Besides quoting liberally from *Jane Eyre* and *Shirley*, Bagshawe made a point of commending her treatment of Mrs Prior.

72 Letters to G. H. Lewes, 12 and 18 January 1848 (*LL*, ii, 179-81).

73 Useful commentaries on Lewes include F. Gary's 'Charlotte Brontë and George Henry Lewes', *PMLA*, 1936, li, 518-42 and various entries in Richard Stang, *op. cit.*, notably 79-86, 129-30, 171-6.

74 Thackeray also sensed an angry frustration in her work, but seems to have ascribed it exclusively to her thwarted longing for sexual love (see No. 51).

75 J. A. Froude, *The Nemesis of Faith* (1849), 153.

76 Her varied life and the gist of other of her reviews are recorded in Marion C. Lochhead's *Elizabeth Rigby, Lady Eastlake* (1961).

77 Clement Shorter, *Charlotte Brontë and her Circle* (1896), 348-9.

78 Letter to Margaret Wooler, 13 April 1853 (*LL*, iv, 58); George Smith had confirmed Harriet's authorship in the preceding February (*LL*, iv, 46).

79 *LL*, iv, 54; Mrs Gaskell's *Life*, chapter 26.

80 See her letter to George Smith, 26 March 1853 (*LL*, iv, 55).

81 See, for example, her views about the reception of *Jane Eyre*, *Life*, chapter 16 (Haworth edn, 332-3).

82 Such recognition had to wait for C. P. Sanger's seminal analysis in *The Structure of Wuthering Heights* (1926).

83 For an account of some of these early reviews see Helen Arnold, 'First American reviews of the Brontës', *BST*, 1964, xiv, 39-44.

84 George Moore, *Conversations in Ebury Street* (1930), 219-20, 218, 216.

85 *Letters of Mrs Gaskell* (1966), 249; *Life*, chapter 27 (Haworth edn, 619). She seems to have wanted to say more; see her letter to R. S. Oldham, 1 June 1857: 'Emily impresses me as something terrific. Much could not be told of small details which would have made them understood.' *Letters of Mrs Gaskell* (1966), 448.

86 *Sharpe's London Magazine*, June 1855, n.s. vol. 5, 339-42.

87 Ibid., 342. The 'lady' must be Mrs Gaskell; the account is similar to, but not identical with, the description in her letter to Catherine Winkworth, 25 August 1850, *Letters of Mrs Gaskell* (1966), 123.

88 Letter to Mrs Gaskell, 16 July 1855 (*LL*, iv, 190).

89 *Critic*, 15 April 1857, 168-71; *Athenaeum*, 4 April 1857, 427-9. Other reviews which concerned themselves rather less with criticism than biography (including in some cases the rights and wrongs of writing

biographies at all) include the *Christian Remembrancer* (No. 100), the
Christian Observer (which was strongly hostile to the book and its subject),
and the *New Monthly Magazine*. A brief account of these appears in A. B.
Hopkins's *Elizabeth Gaskell, Her Life and Work* (1952), chapter 10, 189–92.
The *Dublin University Magazine* (July 1857, 1, 88–100) used the occasion
chiefly to notice Charlotte's mixed achievement in *The Professor*.

90 See her letters of 10 May and 4 June 1865, *Letters of Mrs Gaskell* (1966),
761. Her personal distaste may well have been increased by the protracted
controversies over references in the *Life* to various living people (see, for
example, A. B. Hopkins, *op. cit.*, chapter 10).

91 Thus anticipating George Moore in 1930 (see p. 35 above).

92 The parallel has also been noticed by modern readers, for example,
Arnold P. Drew, 'Emily Brontë and *Hamlet*', *Notes and Queries*, no. 9,
n.s. 1 (1954), 81–2, and Lew Girdler, '*Wuthering Heights* and Shakespeare',
Huntington Library Quarterly, 19, no. 4 (August 1956), 389–90.

93 *Blackwood's Magazine*, January 1887, cxli, 757–8.

94 Ibid.

95 Reprinted in *Fragments* (1875). See also his references to *Wuthering Heights*
in *Essays and Miscellaneous Writings* (1885).

96 Studies appearing in the 1870s–1890s which fostered this kind of interest
include F. H. Grundy's 'Patrick Branwell Brontë', *Pictures of the Past*
(1879); J. H. Turner's *Haworth Past and Present* (1879) and *Brontëana*
(1898); W. Scruton's *The Birthplace of Charlotte Brontë* (1884) and *Thornton
and the Brontës* (1898); F. A. Leyland's *The Brontë Family with special
reference to Patrick Branwell Brontë* (1886); and N. Wright's apocryphal
The Brontës in Ireland (1893).

97 For the relevant correspondence see *LL*, iv, 267–83. Ellen Nussey was
dissatisfied with many elements in the biography, as she was dissatisfied
in some degree with almost everything written about the Brontës, not
excluding Mrs Gaskell's *Life*.

98 The view is tentatively expressed in his *Charlotte Brontë* (1877), but Mary
Robinson cites an unpublished lecture by him which deals more directly
with the subject. See her *Emily Brontë* (1883), p. 436 below.

99 Frederic Harrison, 'Charlotte Brontë's place in literature', *Forum*, March
1895, reprinted in *Studies in Early Victorian Literature* (1895). For George
Saintsbury's want of enthusiasm in the same period, see Mary Ward,
p. 454 below.

100 *Contemporary Review*, July–December 1895, lxviii, 409–10.

101 Clement Shorter, *Charlotte Brontë and her Circle* (1896), 144, 145–6.

102 This was revised in 1914 as *The Brontës and their Circle*. Shorter's other
studies include *Charlotte Brontë and her Sisters* (1905), and *The Brontës:
Life and Letters* (1908).

103 I am indebted for this phrasing to Judith O'Neil's useful short study,
Critics on Charlotte and Emily Brontë (1968), 7.

104 See above, pp. 42, 43, 44–7.

105 I have tried to trace some ins and outs of this area of Brontë criticism in *Wuthering Heights: Casebook*; see Bibliography, p. 461.

106 See p. 456 below.

107 Among them George Smith (see p. 43), and Leslie Stephen (No. 109).

108 For the outstanding biographical studies published in this century see the Bibliography, p. 462 below.

Note on the Text

The materials in this volume follow the original texts in all important respects. Passages quoted from the novels of the Brontës have usually been omitted for the sake of brevity. These omissions have been indicated in the text. Typographical errors have been silently corrected and in a few cases spelling has been modernized.

Part 1

The critical reputation of the 'brothers Bell', 1846-53

POEMS BY CURRER, ELLIS AND ACTON BELL

May 1846

1. From an unsigned review, *Critic*

4 July 1846, 6–8

See Introduction, pp. 18–19. Charlotte described the review to W. S. Williams on 9 October 1847 as 'unexpectedly and generously eulogistic', while that in the *Athenaeum* was 'more qualified, but still not discouraging' (*LL*, ii, 147–8). The passage which particularly pleased the authors is indicated below.

No preface introduces these poems to the reader. Who are Currer, Ellis, and Acton Bell, we are nowhere informed. Whether the triumvirate have published in concert, or if their association be the work of an editor, viewing them as kindred spirits, is not recorded. If the poets be of a past or of the present age, if living or dead, whether English or American, where born, or where dwelling, what their ages or station – nay, what their Christian names, the publishers have not thought fit to reveal to the curious reader. Perhaps they desired that the poems should be tried and judged upon their own merits alone, apart from all extraneous circumstances, and if such was their intent, they have certainly displayed excellent taste in the selection of compositions that will endure the difficult ordeal.

Indeed, it is long since we have enjoyed a volume of such genuine poetry as this. Amid the heaps of trash and trumpery in the shape of verses, which lumber the table of the literary journalist, this small book of some 170 pages only has come like a ray of sunshine, gladdening the eye with present glory, and the heart with promise of bright hours in store. Here we have good, wholesome, refreshing, vigorous poetry –

no sickly affectations, no namby-pamby, no tedious imitations of familiar strains, but original thoughts, expressed in the true language of poetry – not in its cant, as is the custom with mocking-bird poets. The triumvirate have not disdained sometimes to model after great masters, but then they are *in the manner* only, and not servile copies. We see, for instance, here and there traces of an admirer of Wordsworth, and perhaps of Tennyson; but for the most part the three poets are themselves alone; they have chosen subjects that have freshness in them, and their handling is after a fashion of their own. To those whose love of poetry is more a matter of education than of heart, it is probable that these poems may not prove attractive; they too much violate the conventionalities of poetry for such as look only to form, and not to substance; but they in whose hearts are chords strung by nature to sympathize with the beautiful and the true in the world without, and their embodiments by the gifted among their fellow men, will recognize in the compositions of Currer, Ellis and Acton Bell, the presence of more genius than it was supposed this utilitarian age had devoted to the loftier exercises of the intellect.[1]

Being such, we make no apology for extracting from these poems more largely than is our custom, or, rather, than the worthlessness of most of the books of verses submitted to us will permit . . .

The first poem in the book is one of the most original and powerful in the collection, but, unfortunately, its length forbids its being transplanted entire. . . .

[quotes Charlotte's 'Pilate's Wife's Dream' stanzas 1–6]

The next we take is Ellis. A trite topic, but how newly handled!

[quotes 'The winter wind is loud and wild . . .']

The following reminds us of some quaint but powerful productions of the close of the Elizabethan age.

[quotes Anne's 'Vanitas vanitatum, omnia vanitas']

How sweet and pure is this by Ellis!

[quotes 'The linnet in the rocky dells . . .']

Currer has contributed the following exquisitely beautiful sketch – a

---

[1] Charlotte suggested that the passage 'they in whose hearts . . . exercises of the intellect' should be used in advertising the *Poems* (*LL*, ii, 102; see headnote).

picture in words as full of colour as any that ever came from the easel of an R.A.

[quotes 'The Letter']

Lastly, we extract, because it is short, some stanzas by Ellis, on 'Sympathy'.

[gives both stanzas]

And we might copy twenty equally beautiful and original with the above, and they will, we are sure, recommend the volume that contains them to the regards of all lovers of true poetry.

2. From an unsigned notice, *Athenaeum*

4 July 1846, 682

From 'Poetry of the Million', which notices collections by S. and E. Hersee, E. J. Hughes, E. L. Harvey, C. E. Kennaway and Mrs Thomas. The reviewer turns to 'the Bells' after discussing S. and E. Hersee's *My Dream, and Other Poems*. See Introduction, pp. 17, 18 and No. 1.

The second book on our list furnishes another example of a family in whom appears to run the instinct of song. It is shared, however, by the three brothers – as we suppose them to be – in very unequal proportions; requiring in the case of Acton Bell, the indulgences of affection . . . and rising, in that of Ellis, into an inspiration, which may yet find an audience in the outer world. A fine quaint spirit has the latter, which may have things to speak that men will be glad to hear, – and an evident power of wing that may reach heights not here attempted.

[quotes 'The Philosopher', stanzas 3–5]

How musical he can be, and how lightly and easily the music falls from his heart and pen, a verse or two from a 'Song' may testify.

[quotes 'The linnet in the rocky dells . . .', stanzas 1-2, 5-7]

The little poem that follows, which we give complete, furnishes a hint as to the writer's moods; yet he is no copyist. There is not in this volume enough to judge him by – but, to our mind, an impression of originality is conveyed, beyond what his contributions to these pages embody.

[quotes 'Hope was but a timid friend . . .']

The Muse of Currer Bell walks half way betwixt the level of Acton's and the elevation attained by Ellis. It is rarely that the whole of one of his poems is up to the scale registered by parts. A bit here and there from the 'Monologue of the Teacher' in his lonely schoolroom, away from the friends and fields of happier and less toilsome days, may give the tone and manner of his singing.

[quotes 'The Teacher's Monologue', ll. 41-70, 79-82]

And a few lines from the dying words of the apostate lady to the pleading priest.

[quotes 'Apostasy', ll. 65-76]

3. W. A. Butler, from an unsigned notice, *Dublin University Magazine*

October 1846, xxviii, 383–91

William Archer Butler (1814–48), Professor of Moral Philosophy at Dublin (1837–48), besides contributing to this periodical, published his *Sermons* (1855–6) and *Lectures* (1856). He visited Wordsworth in 1844. Charlotte wrote to the editor on 6 October 1846:

I thank you in my own name and that of my brothers ... for the indulgent notice ... of our first humble efforts in literature; but I thank you far more for the essay on Modern poetry which preceded that notice – an essay in which seems ... to be condensed the very spirit of truth and beauty (*LL*, ii, 112).

See Introduction, p. 19.

Of the triad of versemen, who style themselves 'Currer, Ellis and Acton Bell', we know nothing beyond the little volume in which, without preface or comment, they assume the grave simplicity of title, void of *proenomen* or *agnomen* ... Whether ... there be indeed 'a man behind' each of these representative titles; or whether it be in truth but one master spirit – for the book is, after all, not beyond the utmost powers of a single human intelligence – that has been pleased to project itself into three imaginary poets, – we are wholly unable to conjecture ... The tone of all these little poems is certainly uniform; this, however, is no unpardonable offence, if they be, as in truth they are, uniform in a sort of Cowperian amiability and sweetness, no-wise unfragrant to our critical nostrils. The fairest course may, perhaps, be, to present a little specimen from each of the three.

The following pretty stanzas are from Currer's pen.

[quotes 'The Wife's Will']

Ellis contributes this touching 'Death-Scene'.

63

[quotes 'O Day! he cannot die . . .']

And now *loquitur* Acton Bell.

[quotes 'A Reminiscence']

There are pleasing thoughts, too, in Ellis's poem about the 'Stars' ['Ah! why, because the dazzling sun . . .']; and his 'Prisoner' ['In the dungeon-crypts idly did I stray . . .']; and Currer's 'Gilbert' is impressively told. Altogether, we are disposed to approve of the efforts of 'these three gentlemen aforesaid' . . . their verses are full of unobtrusive feeling; and their tone of thought seems unaffected and sincere.

4. From an unsigned notice, *Spectator*

11 November 1848, xxi, 1094–5

The second issue of the *Poems*, now under Smith, Elder's imprint, appeared early in November 1848 (see Introduction, p. 9).

To those who think the subject worth attention, this volume will furnish data for examining the resemblances that have been observed and the differences detected in the prose fictions published separately under the names of Currer, Ellis, and Acton Bell. We do not know that it will settle the question as to whether the writers are identical or merely akin. The mass of the poems in this volume are occasional, and often on such common subjects as are usually found in 'miscellanies': the more peculiar pieces (as far as subject is concerned) are chiefly by Currer Bell, but furnish little means of judging; since all the Bells selected incidents and persons of a singular character, produced by circumstances of a rare kind, or arising from isolated modes of life. In the prose works, the story, however strange and coarse, was consistent with itself and distinct in its purpose. In the larger narrative poems by Currer Bell, both these qualities are wanting: there is often neither head nor tail; or, when the story is distinctly told, it is not only unlikely, but inconsistent with itself. As far as execution is concerned, the poems under the signature of Currer are entitled to the preëminence. They exhibit more power and possess a greater interest: but this is not conclusive as to difference of authorship. Part of the comparative inferiority of the others may arise from the greater quietness of a small or the triteness of a common subject; it may be accident, or even art.

The essence of poetry – that quality so difficult to define yet so easy to recognize – is rare in the volume. Of the formal and secondary properties there is a good deal. The poems have frequently much strength of thought and vigour of diction, with a manner which, though degenerating into manner*ism*, is very far removed from commonplace; while in the poorest 'stanzas,' without a subject at all, there is still a style which separates them from the effusions of poetasters. The effect of the volume, however, is by no means proportioned to the abilities possessed by the authors. The novels of the Bells have stopped short of an excellence that seemed attainable, from ill-chosen subjects, alike singular and coarse. This defect is visible enough in the poems; but a greater cause of ill success is a disregard of the nature of poetical composition. Where the knack or gift exists, verse can possibly be written with as much certainty as prose, if with less readiness and in less abundance: but the result is the kind of poetry which is not endured by gods, men, or bookstalls. If the structure of the piece does not require more thought than in prose, it requires as much; and, most assuredly, an incident or a narrative that would never be ventured in plain prose, is not from its excess of incongruity adapted to verse. Yet 'Pilate's Wife's Dream,' 'Gilbert,' and perhaps nearly all the story pieces by Currer Bell, are really in this predicament. As regards the sentiments and 'composition' of poetry, there is no doubt but that a careful selection of the thoughts and the exercise of the *labor limæ* are more essential than in prose. Few persons who write down any sudden thoughts that strike them would dream of publishing them in prose; and wherefore in verse? A promising idea rises in the poet's mind, and he commits it to paper; but time is needed to test its value – careful labour to elicit its full proportion, and to clothe it in the most apt language; after all, it may be doomed to the flames, as falling short of necessary excellence. We suspect such kind of care has not been bestowed upon this volume: the indispensable arts of selection and of blotting are yet to be learned by the Bells. If, as seems not unlikely, they are infected with a rage for literary experiment and an itch of writing, they will by no means fulfil the expectation which some have formed of them, or even hold their ground; especially as their experience or their taste seems limited to one kind of life, and that both peculiar and extreme.

One merit belonging to the Bells, especially to Currer, is occasionally found in these pieces, – an easy naturalness, that imparts strength to common things without impairing their homely truth. Such are these lines; which, however, open a tale without intelligible drift.

[quotes 'Mementos', ll. 1–36]

The following verses, under the signature of 'Ellis,' are called a song, though without any lyric quality: they are nearer the short ballad. But we quote them as exhibiting a specimen of the taste which the works of these writers show for local manners, or singular feelings, thoughts, and actions.

[quotes 'The linnet in the rocky dells . . .']

JANE EYRE

October 1847

5. From an unsigned review, *Atlas*

23 October 1847, 719

The *Atlas* was attentive to the Brontës (see Nos 25, 63) and gave them substantial space in its review columns. The omitted passages here include further details of the story with quotations from chapter 9 to illustrate 'the character of the little governess as sketched by Rochester ... in the guise of a gipsy hag', and from chapter 27 to give 'a sample of the dialogue from a long scene of absorbing interest' after the wedding 'has been broken off at the very altar foot'.

This is not merely a work of great promise; it is one of absolute performance. It is one of the most powerful domestic romances which have been published for many years. It has little or nothing of the old conventional stamp upon it; none of the jaded, exhausted attributes of a worn-out vein of imagination, reproducing old incidents and old characters in new combinations; but is full of youthful vigour, of freshness and originality, of nervous diction and concentrated interest. The incidents are sometimes melo-dramatic, and, it might be added, improbable; but these incidents, though striking, are subordinate to the main purpose of the piece, which depends not upon incident, but on the development of character; it is a tale of passion, not of intensity which is almost sublime. It is a book to make the pulses gallop and the heart beat, and to fill the eyes with tears.

Jane Eyre tells her own story. She is an orphan child, outwardly adopted but inwardly repudiated by a hard, unfeeling woman, her aunt, who outrages the affections of the child, and would fain crush her spirit. The little girl turns at times against her oppressor; and resistance strengthens the hatred and stimulates the cruelty of the bad woman. Jane is sent to a charitable institution, where she spends eight years of her life, emerging thence, at the age of eighteen, in the character of a governess. Here the interest of the story commences. The history of Jane's life at the Lowood institution is, perhaps, unnecessarily lengthened out. There is an air of truth about it; and we do not doubt that the character of Helen Burns – a youthful inmate of the asylum, who is the very incarnation of Christian charity and forbearance – is an especial favourite with the writer. Helen Burns is just one of those idealities in which young writers are fain to revel – conjuring up with the enchanter's wand beings who belong to a higher sphere and a purer atmosphere than this – dream-children, with the unspotted hearts of babyhood and the wisdom of adolescence. Creations such as these are very beautiful, but very untrue.

Jane obtains a situation as a governess in an old country house, ostensibly tenanted only by a venerable housekeeper, a few servants, and a little girl, the ward of the absent master. Mr. Rochester – such is his name – returns from abroad, and before long conceives a grand passion for the little teacher. Jane Eyre is not pretty, but she is very piquante. Her manner attracts Mr. Rochester – a man of forty, with strongly-marked and somewhat harsh lineaments both of countenance and character. His curiosity is excited; his interest awakened; he is charmed – fascinated. A bungler would certainly, under such circumstances, have painted the heroine in radiant colours. She would have been, in a novel of approved manufacture, a beauty of the first water. The author of Jane Eyre has too deep an insight into human character – too profound a knowledge of the sources of human passion, to commit any such mistake. It was precisely because Jane Eyre was not a beauty of the recognised stamp that Rochester, who had mixed largely with the world, who had tasted of satiety, who had been in his day almost a libertine – the libertine of circumstances, not of a corrupt heart – was stimulated into an intensity of love and desire . . .

We know not whether this powerful story is from the pen of a youthful writer; there is all the freshness and some of the crudeness of youth about it, but there is a knowledge of the profoundest springs of human emotion, such as is rarely acquired without long years of bitter experience in the troubled sea of life. The action of the tale is sometimes unnatural – but the passion is always true. It would be easy to point out incidental defects; but the merits of the work are so striking that it is a pleasure to recognise them without stint and qualification. It is a book with a great heart in it; not a mere sham – a counterfeit.

6. Thackeray, from a letter

23 October 1847

Letter to W. S. Williams from *The Letters and Private Papers of W. M. Thackeray*, edited Gordon N. Ray (1947) ii, 318–19. Charlotte wrote to Williams on 28 October 1847:

I feel honoured in being approved by Mr. Thackeray . . . I have long recognised in his writings genuine talent, such as I admired, such as I wondered and delighted in . . . One good word from such a man is worth pages of praise from ordinary judges . . . The plot of *Jane Eyre* may be a hackneyed one. Mr. Thackeray remarks that it is familiar to him. But having read comparatively few novels I never chanced to meet with it, and I thought it original (*LL*, ii, 150).

The plot may have reminded Thackeray of his own marital tragedy, but see the *Athenaeum* (No. 7). For his later comments see No. 51.

I wish you had not sent me Jane Eyre. It interested me so much that I have lost (or won if you like) a whole day in reading it at the busiest period, with the printers I know waiting for copy. Who the author can be I can't guess – if a woman she knows her language better than most ladies do, or has had a 'classical' education. It is a fine book though – the man & woman capital – the style very generous and upright so to speak. I thought it was Kinglake for some time. The plot of the story is one with w^h., I am familiar. Some of the love passages made me cry – to the astonishment of John who came in with the coals. S^t. John the Missionary is a failure I think but a good failure there are parts excellent I dont know why I tell you this but that I have been exceedingly moved & pleased by Jane Eyre. It is a womans writing, but whose? Give my respects and thanks to the author – whose novel is the first English one (& the French are only romances now) that I've been able to read for many a day.

7. H. F. Chorley, unsigned review, *Athenaeum*

23 October 1847, 1100–1

Hugh Fothergill Chorley reviewed widely for the *Athenaeum* during 1833–68, including reviews of *Jane Eyre* and *Wuthering Heights* (see L. A. Marchand, *The Athenaeum: A Victorian Mirror of Culture* (1941), 192); he was the author of the book referred to below as 'a now-forgotten novel – *Sketches of a Seaport Town* [1834]'. Charlotte met him in December 1849 and found him 'a peculiar specimen' (*LL*, iii, 62). Of the *Athenaeum*, which regularly noticed the Brontës' work (see Introduction, p. 18), she wrote on 26 October 1847: '[it] has a style of its own, which I respect, but cannot exactly relish; still . . . journals of that standing have a dignity to maintain . . . I suppose there is every reason to be satisfied' (*LL*, ii, 149–50).

There is so much power in this novel as to make us overlook certain eccentricities in the invention, which trench in one or two places on what is improbable, if not unpleasant. Jane Eyre is an orphan thrown upon the protection – or, to speak correctly, the cruelty – of relations living in an out-of-the-way corner of England; who neglect, maltreat, chastize, and personally abuse her. She becomes dogged, revengeful, superstitious: and, at length, after a scene, – which we hope is out of nature now that 'the Iron Rule' is over-ruled and the reign of the tribe Squeers ended[1] – the child turns upon her persecutors with such precocious power to threaten and alarm, that they condemn her to an *oubliette* – sending her out of the house to a so-called charitable institution. There she has again to prove wretchedness, hard fare and misconstruction. The trial, however, is this time not unaccompanied by more gracious influences. Jane Eyre is taught, by example, that patience is nobler than passion; and so far as we can gather from her own confessions, grows up into a plain, self-sustained young woman,

[1] Dickens's *Nicholas Nickleby* was published in 1839. See Introduction, p. 23.

with a capital of principle sufficient to regulate those more dangerous gifts which the influences of her childhood had so exasperated. Weary of the monotonous life of a teacher, she advertises for the situation of a governess; and is engaged into an establishment – singular, but not without prototype – to take care of the education of the French ward of a country gentleman; which said girl proves, when called by her right name, to be the child of an opera *danseuse*. The pretty, frivolous little fairy Adèle, with her hereditary taste for dress, coquetry and pantomimic grace, is true to life. Perhaps too – we dare not speak more positively – there is truth in the abrupt, strange clever Mr. Rochester; and in the fearless original way in which the strong man and the young governess travel over each other's minds till, in a puzzled and uncomfortable manner enough, they come to a mutual understanding. Neither is the mystery of Thornfield an exaggeration of reality. We, ourselves, know of a large mansion-house in a distant country where, for many years, a miscreant was kept in close confinement, – and his existence, at best, only darkly hinted in the neighbourhood. Some such tale as this was told in a now-forgotten novel – *Sketches of a Seaport Town*.[1] We do not quarrel with the author of *Jane Eyre* for the manner in which he has made the secret explode at a critical juncture of the story. From that point forward, however, we think the heroine too outrageously tried, and too romantically assisted in her difficulties: – until arrives the last moment, at which obstacles fall down like the battlements of *Castle Melodrame*, in the closing scene, when 'avenging thunder strikes the towers of Crime, and far above in Heaven's etherial light young Hymen's flower-decked temple shines revealed.' No matter, however: – as exciting strong interest, of its old-fashioned kind *Jane Eyre* deserves high praise, and commendation to the novel-reader who prefers story to philosophy, pedantry, or Puseyite controversy.[2]

---

[1] See headnote, and also No. 6.

[2] As in, for example, Elizabeth Harris's *From Oxford to Rome, and how it fared with those that lately made the journey* (1847). 'Puseyite Novels' are discussed in the *Prospective Review* 1850, vi, 512–34. A lively account of Victorian religious novels, including those stemming directly from the Oxford Movement, appears in Margaret Maison's *Search Your Soul, Eustace* (1961).

8. From an unsigned review, *Critic*

30 October 1847, 277–8

See No. 1. The rest of the review consists of an outline of the story and extracts from descriptions of life at Lowood gathered under the heading 'A Charity School'.

Our readers will probably remember a volume of poems, the joint production of three brothers, Bell, which, albeit little noticed by our critical brethren, took our fancy so much, as seeming to be freighted with promise, that we dedicated several columns to a review . . . , and, as we are informed, thereby contributed mainly to establish for the authors a reputation which we hope was something more than nominal.

The performance before us, by one of the brothers, proves the justice of those anticipations. Currer Bell can write prose as well as poetry. He has fertile invention, great power of description, and a happy faculty for conceiving and sketching character. *Jane Eyre* is a remarkable novel, in all respects very far indeed above the average of those which the literary journalist is doomed every season to peruse, and of which he can say nothing either in praise or condemnation, such is their tame monotony of mediocrity. It is a story of surpassing interest, riveting the attention from the very first chapter, and sustaining it by a copiousness of incident rare indeed in our modern English school of novelists, who seem to make it their endeavour to diffuse the smallest possible number of incidents over the largest possible number of pages. Currer Bell has even gone rather into the opposite extreme, and the incidents of his story are, if any thing, too much crowded. But this is a fault which readers, at least, will readily pardon . . . We can cordially recommend *Jane Eyre* to our readers, as a novel to be placed at the top of the list to be borrowed, and to the circulating-library keeper, as one which he may safely order. It is sure to be in demand.

9. From an unsigned review, *Spectator*

6 November 1847, xx, 1074–5

The coolest of the early reviews (see Introduction, pp. 15, 19, 34). Charlotte wrote on 10 November 1847: 'The way to detraction has been pointed out, and will probably be pursued . . . I fear this turn of opinion will not improve the demand for the book – but time will show' (*LL*, ii, 155).

Essentially, *Jane Eyre, an Autobiography*, has some resemblance to those sculptures of the middle ages in which considerable ability both mechanical and mental was often displayed upon subjects that had no existence in nature, and as far as delicacy was concerned were not pleasing in themselves. There is, indeed, none of their literal impossibilities or grotesqueness – we do not meet the faces of foxes or asses under clerical hoods; neither is there anything of physical grossness. But, with clear conceptions distinctly presented, a metaphysical consistency in the characters and their conduct, and considerable power in the execution, the whole is unnatural, and only critically interesting. There is one fault, too, in *Jane Eyre*, from which the artists of the middle ages were free – too much of artifice. Their mastery of their art was too great to induce them to resort to trick to tell their story. In the fiction edited by Currer Bell there is rather too much of this. Dialogues are carried on to tell the reader something he must know, or to infuse into him some explanations of the writer; persons act not as they would probably act in life, but to enable the author to do a 'bit o' writing'; everything is made to change just in the nick of time; and even the 'Returned Letter Office' suspends its laws that Jane Eyre may carry on her tale with 'effect'.

The fiction belongs to that school where minute anatomy of the mind predominates over incidents; the last being made subordinate to description or the display of character. Jane Eyre, the heroine, is exhibited in three leading positions. At first we see her as an orphan, dependant upon a rich aunt by marriage, and subject to the bad treatment of a poor ill-favoured relation. Her temper is soured by the oppression of grown-up people and the tyranny of children; and the first act ends at a half-charity school for orphans, whither she is sent as a punishment. The second part exhibits Jane as governess to the protégé of a Mr. Rochester, – a hard, peculiar, and to the reader a rather disagreeable person of forty, in whom there is much talk and some little mystery. The mystery, however, is explained, when after a course of hardly 'proper' conduct between a single man and a maiden in her teens, the marriage between Jane and Mr. Rochester is stopped by the 'lawful cause and impediment' of another wife being in the way ... Mr. Rochester, in spite of his exposure, persists in wishing Jane to live with him; which leads to the third act. Dreading her own weakness, she elopes in the night; and after three days' fatigue, and all but death from starvation (not likely, but serving to write about), she is assisted by a clergyman and his sisters. Then she passes some time as the mistress of a private charity school; after which, the convenient but not very novel resource of an unknown uncle dying abroad makes her independent, and discovers relations in the friendly divine and his sisters. In the interim, Mr. Rochester's house is burned down, Mrs. Rochester is killed off, and Rochester is maimed and blinded through the heroic manner in which he exposes himself. The upshot of a wedding may be divined without particulars; but the close is the best-managed part of the book.

A story which contains nothing beyond itself is a very narrow representation of human life. Jane Eyre is this, if we admit it to be true; but its truth is not probable in the principal incidents, and still less in the manner in which the characters influence the incidents so as to produce conduct. There is a low tone of behaviour (rather than of morality) in the book; and, what is worse than all, neither the heroine nor hero attracts sympathy. The reader cannot see anything loveable in Mr. Rochester, nor why he should be so deeply in love with Jane Eyre; so that we have intense emotion without cause. The book, however, displays considerable skill in the plan, and great power, but rather shown in the writing than the matter; and this vigour sustains a species of interest to the last.

Although minute and somewhat sordid, the first act of the fiction is the most truthful; especially the scenes at the philanthropic school. There are many parts of greater energy in Jane Eyre, but none equal to the following.

[quotes from chapter 9 the death of Helen Burns]

10. A. W. Fonblanque, from an unsigned review, *Examiner*

27 November 1847, 756–7

Probably by the radical journalist, Albany William Fonblanque (1793–1872). The *Examiner* (launched by John and Leigh Hunt 1808) was edited by him (1830–47) and by John Forster (1847–55); he continued to contribute reviews after 1847 (see No. 27). Charlotte seems to have been assured of his authorship of this review. See her letters to Williams of 1 December 1847: 'The notice in the *Examiner* . . . appears to be from the pen of an able man . . . approbation from such a quarter is encouraging' (*LL*, ii, 158), and 11 December 1847: 'I can hardly credit that anything I have done should . . . give even transitory pleasure to such men as Mr Thackeray, Sir John Herschel, Mr Fonblanque, Leigh Hunt and Mr Lewes' (*LL*, ii, 160).

The rest of the review consists of an outline of the story up to the beginning of Jane's love affair with Rochester (who is regarded as one of the book's failures), together with lengthy extracts from Jane Eyre's experience at Thornfield Hall (close of chapter 22, opening of chapter 23); her lonely wanderings (chapter 28); and her relationship with St John Rivers (chapter 35).

This book has just been sent to us by the publishers. An accident caused the delay, and is responsible for what might else have seemed a tardy notice of the first effort of an original writer.

There can be no question but that *Jane Eyre* is a very clever book. Indeed it is a book of decided power. The thoughts are true, sound, and original; and the style, though rude and uncultivated here and there, is resolute, straightforward, and to the purpose. There are faults, which we may advert to presently; but there are also many beauties, and the object and moral of the work is excellent. Without being professedly didactic, the writer's intention (amongst other things) seems to be, to show how intellect and unswerving integrity

may win their way, although oppressed by that predominating influence in society which is a mere consequence of the accidents of
birth or fortune. There are, it is true, in this autobiography (which
though relating to a woman, we do not believe to have been written
by a woman), struggles, and throes, and misgivings, such as must
necessarily occur in a contest where the advantages are all on one side;
but in the end, the honesty, kindness of heart, and perseverance of the
heroine, are seen triumphant over every obstacle. We confess that we
like an author who throws himself into the front of the battle, as the
champion of the weaker party; and when this is followed up by bold
and skilful soldiership, we are compelled to yield him our respect.

Whatever faults may be urged against the book, no one can assert
that it is weak or vapid. It is anything but a fashionable novel. It has
not a Lord Fanny for its hero, nor a Duchess for its pattern of nobility.
The scene of action is never in Belgrave or Grosvenor Square. The
pages are scant of French and void of Latin. We hear nothing of
Madame Maradan; we scent nothing of the bouquet de la Reine. On
the contrary, the heroine is cast amongst the thorns and brambles of
life; – an orphan; without money, without beauty, without friends;
thrust into a starving charity school; and fighting her way as governess,
with few accomplishments. The hero, if so he may be called, is (or
becomes) middle-aged, mutilated, blind, stern, and wilful. The sentences are of simple English; and the only fragrance that we encounter
is that of the common garden flower, or the odour of Mr. Rochester's
cigar.

Taken as a novel or history of events, the book is obviously defective; but as an analysis of a single mind, as an elucidation of its progress
from childhood to full age, it may claim comparison with any work of
the same species. It is not a book to be examined, page by page, with
the fictions of Sir Walter Scott or Sir Edward Lytton or Mr. Dickens,
from which (except in passages of character where the instant impression reminds us often of the power of the latter writer) it differs
altogether. It should rather be placed by the side of the autobiographies
of Godwin and his successors, and its comparative value may be then
reckoned up, without fear or favour. There is less eloquence, or rather
there is less rhetoric, and perhaps less of that subtle analysis of the
inner human history, than the author of *Fleetwood* and *Mandeville* was
in the habit of exhibiting; but there is, at the same time, more graphic
power, more earnest human purpose, and a more varied and vivid
portraiture of men and things.

The danger, in a book of this kind, is that the author, from an extreme love of his subject, and interest in the investigation of human motives, may pursue his analysis beyond what is consistent with the truth and vitality of his characters. In every book of fiction, the reader expects to meet with animated beings, complete in their structure, and active and mingling with the world; and he will accordingly reject a tale as spurious if he finds that the author, in his love of scientific research, has been merely putting together a metaphysical puzzle, when he should have been breathing into the nostrils of a living man.

The writer of *Jane Eyre* has in a great measure steered clear of this error (by no means altogether avoiding it), and the book is the better for it. But it is time to introduce the reader a little into the secrets of the story.

11. From an unsigned review, *Era*

14 November 1847, 9

Charlotte wrote to Williams on 17 November 1847:

The perusal of the *Era* gave me much pleasure, as did that of the *People's Journal* [No. 12]. An author feels peculiarly gratified by the recognition of a right tendency in his works . . . if what he writes does no good to the reader, he feels he has . . . wasted . . . his labour. *The Spectator* [No. 9] seemed to have found more harm than good in *Jane Eyre* . . . I acknowledge that distressed me a little (*LL*, ii, 155).

This is an extraordinary book. Although a work of fiction, it is no mere novel, for there is nothing but nature and truth about it, and its interest is entirely domestic; neither is it like your familiar writings, that are too close to reality. There is nothing morbid, nothing vague, nothing improbable about the story of Jane Eyre; at the same time it lacks neither the odour of romance nor the hue of sentiment. On the other hand, we are not taken to vulgar scenes, and made acquainted with low mysteries. We have no high life glorified, caricatured, or libelled; nor low life elevated to an enviable state of bliss; neither have we vice made charming. The story is, therefore, unlike all that we have read, with very few exceptions; and for power of thought and expression, we do not know its rival among modern productions. Bulwer, [G. P. R.] James, D'Israeli, and all the serious novel writers of the day lose in comparison with Currer Bell, for we must presume the work to be his. It is no woman's writing. Although ladies have written histories, and travels, and warlike novels, to say nothing of books upon the different arts and sciences, no woman *could have* penned the 'Autobiography of Jane Eyre.' It is all that one of the other sex might invent, and much more, and reminds us of *Caleb Stukeley, Ten Thousand a Year*,[1] and one or two domestic novels that have come out in strong relief within these few years. The tale is one of the heart, and the working out of a moral through the natural affections; it is the victory of mind over matter; the mastery of reason over feeling, without unnatural sacrifices. The writer dives deep into human life, and possesses the gift of being able to write as he thinks and feels. There is a vigour in all he says, a power which fixes the reader's attention, and a charm about his 'style and diction' which fascinates while it edifies. His pictures are like the Cartoons of Raphael. The figures are not elaborately executed, but true, bold, well-defined, and full of life – struck off by an artist who embodies his imaginings in a touch.

[briefly outlines the 'unique' story]

The apt, eloquent, elegant, and yet easy mode by which the writer engages you, is something altogether out of the common way. He fixes you at the commencement, and there is no flagging on his part – no getting away on your's – till the end. You discover, in every chapter, that you are not simply amused, not only interested, not merely excited, but you are improved; you are receiving a delightful and comprehensible lesson, and you put down the volume with the consciousness of having benefited by its perusal. Such a work has no ordinary attractions, and it will be found that we have not overdrawn them. There is much to ponder over, rejoice over, and weep over, in its ably-written pages ... The obvious moral thought is, that laws, both human and divine, approved in our calmer moments, are not to be disobeyed when our time of trial comes, however singular the 'circumstances' under which we are tempted to disregard them; that

[1] Samuel Phillips, *Caleb Stukely* (1844); Samuel Warren, *Ten Thousand a Year* (1841).

there is an immaterial world about us, one wherein disobedience is sure to bring punishment; and that although to be truly wise is not, as a certain and immediate consequence, to be truly happy, the practice of simple propriety, founded on strict morality and religious principles, is the sure road to ultimate bliss, and a means of securing many beautiful and encouraging prospects along its borders, however rugged be the journey.

12. From an unsigned review, *People's Journal*

November 1847

Reprinted in *People's Journal* ed. John Saunders, 1848, iv, 269–72.

See No. 11. With the *Critic* and *Britannia* [Nos 8, 31] one of the few to refer to Charlotte's poems. The omitted passages include an outline of the story and extracts from descriptions of Lowood, including Jane Eyre's first impressions (chapter 5) and Helen Burns's character and death (chapters 6, 7).

This is one of the most notable domestic novels which have issued from the press in this country for many years past. We have had so much waste paper sent into the world recently, under the false pretence of being the literature of fiction, that it is quite a relief to find a really good and striking production. English 'fiction' is *not* entirely a 'fraud,' as we were really beginning to suspect. *Jane Eyre* is a very remarkable work. The style is bold, lucid, pungent; the incidents are varied, touching, romantic; the characterisation is ample, original, diversified; the moral sentiments are pure and healthy: and the whole work is, in its high and headlong course, calculated to rivet attention, to provoke sympathy, to make the heart bound, and the brain pause.

Mr. Currer Bell is already slightly, but rather favourably, known to the public, as one of the writers of a small volume of poems, which was published several months ago as the joint production of three brothers – Currer, Ellis, and Acton Bell. The contributions which bore the signature of Currer Bell in this collection, evidenced some power of thinking, and an uncommonplace turn of mind; but it is no disparagement of the author to say that they hardly afforded any sign of the vigorous intellect, shrewd observation, and great, if undisciplined, powers, unquestionably manifested in the story of *Jane Eyre*. Yet this novel is far more significant as a promise than it is as a performance. It implies still finer and stronger qualities than it produces – qualities as yet lying fallow in the author's mind; quickening into consciousness, but not yet developed into the fulness of life. *Jane Eyre* is a prophecy of greater things to come – the herald of loftier and more perfect creations which are to follow her: as such we accept and welcome it . . .

It is impossible to deny that the author possesses native power in an uncommon degree – showing itself now in rapid headlong recital – now in stern, fierce, daring dashes at portraiture – anon in subtle, startling mental anatomy – here in a grand allusion, there in an original metaphor – again in a wild gush of genuine poetry. Discipline and deeper study will enable him to turn these attributes to better account, will give him what he most needs, artistic skill, the capacity to construct and to co-ordinate.

The very selection of so homely a name for the heroine is an omen of good. It indicates a departure from the sickly models of the Minerva Press.[1]

---

[1] Well known in the late eighteenth and early nineteenth centuries for the flood of romantic novels appearing under its imprint.

13. J. G. Lockhart, from a letter

29 December 1847

Letter to Mr and Mrs Hope, from Andrew Lang's *The Life and Letters of J. G. Lockhart* (1897) ii, 307. The phrase 'fifty Trollopes' is an allusion to Frances Trollope (1780–63).

John Gibson Lockhart (1794–1854), author of the *Life of Scott* (1838), the *Life of Burns* (1828) and several novels, was editor of the *Quarterly Review* 1825–53. His chosen reviewer of *Jane Eyre* for the *Quarterly* was notoriously less enthusiastic (see Introduction, pp. 22, 26 and No. 22).

I have finished the adventures of Miss Jane Eyre, and think her far the cleverest that has written since Austen and Edgeworth were in their prime. Worth fifty Trollopes and Martineaus rolled into one counterpane, with fifty Dickenses and Bulwers to keep them company; but rather a brazen Miss. The two heroines exemplify the duty of taking the initiative, and illustrate it under the opposite cases as to worldly goods of all sorts, except wit. One is a vast heiress, and beautiful as angels are everywhere but in modern paintings. She asks a handsome curate, who will none of her, being resolved on a missionary life in the far East. The other is a thin, little, unpretty slip of a governess, who falls in love with a plain stoutish Mr Burnand, aged twenty years above herself, sits on his knee, lights his cigar for him, asks him flat one fine evening, and after a concealed mad wife is dead, at last fills that awful lady's place. Lady Fanny will easily extract the moral of this touching fable.

14. G. H. Lewes, from an unsigned review, *Fraser's Magazine*

December 1847, xxxvi, 686–95

The first of several notices of work by the Brontës from George Henry Lewes (1817–78); see Nos 15, 39, 45, 83, and Introduction (pp. 24, 30). Lewes records in his letter to Mrs Gaskell (reproduced in her *Life of Charlotte Brontë*) the delight which he felt on reading his presentation copy of *Jane Eyre* (see Introduction, p. 15) and his immediate offer to review it for *Fraser's*. The editor, J. W. Parker, 'would not consent to an unknown novel . . . receiving such importance, but thought it might make one on "Recent Novels: English and French"' (*LL*, ii, 152). The other English novel is Marmion Savage's *The Bachelor of the Albany*. The French novels include Frédéric Soulié's *L'Histoire d'Olivier Duhamel*, Balzac's *Cousin Pons* and George Sand's *Piccanino* (which was a disappointment; cp. Introduction, p. 24). The review opens with general reflections on three types of novel reader (those who 'adore' novels, those who 'despise' them as frivolous, and those who don't 'devour' but greatly enjoy them) and continues by applauding 'truth in the delineation of life and character', a quality found in Jane Austen and Fielding but less in Scott, who is an 'Ariosto to Shakespeare'. Scott lacks 'that singular faculty of penetrating into the most secret recesses of the heart . . . he has not, above all, those two Shakespearian qualities – tenderness and passion . . .' Charlotte Brontë wrote to Williams on 11 December 1847: 'Mr Lewes is very lenient . . . The notice differs from all other notices. He must be a man of no ordinary mind' (*LL*, ii, 159–60). Lewes's enthusiasm seems to have infected George Eliot after he met her in 1852 (see Nos 17, 48).

After laughing over the *Bachelor of the Albany*, we wept over *Jane Eyre*. This, indeed, is a book after our own heart; and, if its merits have not forced it into notice by the time this paper comes before our readers let us, in all earnestness, bid them lose not a day in sending for it. The writer is evidently a woman, and, unless we are deceived, new in the world of literature. But, man or woman, young or old, be that as it may, no such book has gladdened our eyes for a long while. Almost all that we require in a novelist she has: perception of character, and power of delineating it; picturesqueness; passion; and knowledge of life. The story is not only of singular interest, naturally evolved, un-flagging to the last, but it fastens itself upon your attention, and will not leave you. The book closed, the enchantment continues. With the disentanglement of the plot, and the final release of the heroine from her difficulties, your interest does not cease ... Reality – deep, significant reality – is the great characteristic of the book. It is an autobiography, – not, perhaps, in the naked facts and circumstances, but in the actual suffering and experience. The form may be changed, and here and there some incidents invented; but the spirit remains such as it was ... This gives the book its charm: it is soul speaking to soul; it is an utterance from the depths of a struggling, suffering, much-enduring spirit: *suspiria de profundis*!

When we see a young writer exhibiting such remarkable power as there is in *Jane Eyre*, it is natural that we should ask, Is this experience drawn from an abundant source, or is it only the artistic mastery over small materials? Because, according as this question is answered, there are two suggestions to be made. Has the author seen much more and felt much more than what is here communicated? Then let new works continue to draw from that rich storehouse. Has the author led a quiet secluded life, uninvolved in the great vortex of the world, undisturbed by varied passions, untried by strange calamities? Then let new works be planned and executed with excessive circumspection; for, unless a novel be built out of real experience, it can have no real success. To have vitality, it must spring from vitality. All the craft in the circulat-ing-library will not make that seem true which is not true ...

It is too often forgotten, that the most ignorant reader is a competent judge of truth in this sense ... *Hamlet, Don Quixote, Faust*, marvellous creations as they are, with roots diving deep into the profoundest regions, and with branches rising into the highest altitudes of thought, do, nevertheless, powerfully interest even the foolishest readers. There is a chord in the human breast which vibrates sympathetically whenever it be touched; and no artist need fear that, if he touch it with skill, his skill will be thrown away.

Quite true it is that the merest platitudes will also gain attention;

true that a novelist, scorning all experience, may give such a representation of life as, while outraging everything we know of life, while substituting the empty phantasmagoria of the library for breathing flesh and blood, shall, nevertheless, enchain the reader's attention, and create for the author a certain vogue ... We often hear professed novel-readers declare, that however stupid, trashy, and absurd the novel, they must finish it, 'to see what becomes of the hero and heroine!' They are compelled to finish; but they never go back to it, never think of it afterwards. Whereas, if to that curiosity about the story there are added scenes which, being transcripts from the book of life, affect the reader as all truth of human nature must affect him, then the novel rises from the poor level of street-conjuring into the exalted region of art.

Of this kind is *Jane Eyre*. There are some defects in it – defects which the excellence of the rest only brings into stronger relief. There is, indeed, too much melodrama and improbability, which smack of the circulating-library, – we allude particularly to the mad wife and all that relates to her, and to the wanderings of Jane when she quits Thornfield; yet even those parts are powerfully executed. But the earlier parts – all those relating to Jane's childhood and her residence at Lowood, with much of the strange love story – are written with remarkable beauty and truth. The characters are few, and drawn with unusual mastery: even those that are but sketched – such as Mr. Brocklehurst, Miss Temple, Mrs. Fairfax, Rosamond, and Blanche – are sketched with a vividness which betrays the cunning hand: a few strokes, and the figure rises before you. Jane herself is a creation. The delicate handling of this figure alone implies a dramatic genius of no common order. We never lose sight of her plainness; no effort is made to throw romance about her – no extraordinary goodness or cleverness appeals to your admiration; but you admire, you love her, – love her for the strong will, honest mind, loving heart, and peculiar but fascinating person. A creature of flesh and blood, with very fleshly infirmities, and very mortal excellencies; a woman, not a pattern: that is the Jane Eyre here represented. Mr. Rochester is also well drawn, and from the life; but it is the portrait of a man drawn by a woman, and is not comparable to the portrait of Jane. The way in which the authoress contrives to keep our interest in this imperfect character is a lesson to novelists. St. John Rivers, the missionary, has a touch of the circulating-library, but not enough to spoil the truth of the delineation; there is both art and artifice in the handling, and, although true in the main, and very powerful in parts, one feels a certain misgiving about him: it is another example of the woman's pencil. Helen Burns is lovely and lovable; true, we believe, even in her exalted spirituality and her religious fervour: a character at once eminently ideal and accurately real.

The story is so simple in its outlines yet so filled out – not spun out – with details, that we shall not do it the injustice of here setting down the mere plot . . . We have spoken of the reality stamped upon almost every part; and that reality is not confined to the characters and incidents, but is also striking in the descriptions of the various aspects of Nature, and of the houses, rooms, and furniture. The pictures stand out distinctly before you: they *are* pictures, and not mere bits of 'fine writing' . . .

It would be exceedingly easy to quote many examples, but we will content ourselves with this very brief passage, strongly characterised by the reality we speak of. It occurs in the third page: –

Folds of scarlet drapery shut in my view to the right hand; to the left were the clear panes of glass, protecting, but not separating, me from the drear November day. At intervals, while turning over the leaves of my book, I studied the aspect of that winter afternoon. Afar, it offered a pale blank of mist and cloud; near, a scene of wet lawn and storm-beat shrub, with ceaseless rain sweeping away wildly before a long and lamentable blast.

Is not that vivid, real, picturesque? It reads like a page out of one's own life . . .

This faculty for objective representation is also united to a strange power of subjective representation. We do not simply mean the power over the passions – the psychological intuition of the artist, but the power also of connecting external appearances with internal effects – of representing the psychological interpretation of material phenomena. This is shewn in many a fine description; but we select that of the punished child shut up in the old bed-room, because it exhibits at the same time the power we speak of, and the power before-mentioned of representing the material aspects of things. The passage about the looking-glass, towards the close, strikes us as singularly fine.

[quotes from chapter 2, 'The red room was a spare chamber . . . returned to my stool']

We have no space to go on quoting charming passages . . . We have already given enough to make both the authoress and the reader understand what we mean by our praise. To her we emphatically say, Persevere; keep reality distinctly before you, and paint it as accurately as you can, invention will never equal the effect of truth.

15. G. H. Lewes, unsigned notice, *Westminster Review*

January 1848, xlviii, 581–4

Coincides with the appearance of the second edition of *Jane Eyre*; Charlotte wrote to Williams on 4 January 1848: 'What makes you say that the notice in the *Westminster Review* is not by Lewes? It expresses precisely his opinion, and he said he would perhaps insert a few lines in that periodical' (*LL*, ii, 174).

Decidedly the best novel of the season; and one, moreover, from the natural tone pervading the narrative, and the originality and freshness of its style, possessing the merit so rarely met with now-a-days in works of this class, of amply repaying a second perusal. Whoever may be the author, we hope to see more such books from her pen; for that these volumes are from the pen of a lady, and a clever one too, we have not the shadow of a doubt: nor can there be any question as to the reality of many of the scenes and personages so artistically depicted; the characters are too life-like to be the mere creations of fancy, and sketchy as some of them are, they are wondrous telling: several of them we almost feel persuaded we have met with in real life. The Rev. Mr. Brocklehurst, with his 'straight, narrow, sable-clad shape, standing erect on the rug; the grim face at the top being like a carved mask, placed above the shaft by way of capital;' the lady-like Miss Temple; sweet Helen Burns, whose death-scene is so touchingly narrated; the neat and prim little Mrs. Fairfax, and the eccentric Mr. Rochester, whom with all his faults and eccentricities one can't help getting to like; are but a few of the characters in the drama, though essential ones, and cleverly struck off.

16. From an unsigned review, *Christian Remembrancer*

April 1848, xv, 396–409

One of the 'organs of the High Church Party' which recognized Charlotte's gifts but expressed concern about the moral implications in her novels; see especially its review of *Villette* (No. 54). The omitted passages include a confessedly 'rambling disquisition' on the growing importance of the novel as a literary form and the consequent need of novelists to face up to their responsibilities as potentially influential directors of moral behaviour. Charlotte wrote to Williams on 3 March 1848:

> . . . written with some ability – but to do justice was evidently not . . . the . . . main object . . . C. Bell is . . . rather encouraged than dispirited . . . hard-wrung praise extorted reluctantly from a foe is the most precious praise . . . the reviewer has too high an opinion of my abilities . . . he aims his shafts in the dark . . . the ill success of his hits makes me laugh rather than cry. I hope . . . that if the spirit moves me in future to say anything about priests etc. I shall say it with the same freedom as heretofore (*LL*, ii, 195).

Since the publication of *Grantley Manor*,[1] no novel has created so much sensation as *Jane Eyre*. Indeed, the public taste seems to have outstripped its guides in appreciating the remarkable power which this book displays. For no leading review has yet noticed it,[2] and here we have before us the second edition. The name and sex of the writer are

---

[1] *Grantley Manor, a Tale* (1847) by Lady Georgina Fullerton.
[2] An odd remark in the circumstances.

still a mystery. Currer Bell (which by a curious Hibernicism appears in the title-page as the name of a female autobiographer) is a mere *nom de guerre* – perhaps an anagram. However, we, for our part, cannot doubt that the book is written by a female, and, as certain provincialisms indicate, by one from the North of England. Who, indeed, but a woman could have ventured, with the smallest prospect of success, to fill three octavo volumes with the history of a woman's heart? The hand which drew Juliet and Miranda would have shrunk from such a task. That the book is readable, is to us almost proof enough of the truth of our hypothesis. But we could accumulate evidences to the same effect. Mr. Rochester, the hero of the story, is as clearly the vision of a woman's fancy, as the heroine is the image of a woman's heart. Besides, there are many minor indications of a familiarity with all the mysteries of female life which no man can possess, or would dare to counterfeit. Those who have read Miss Edgeworth's Montem,[1] and know how a lady paints the social nature of boys and the doings of boys' schools, may judge *e converso* what work a man would have made of the girls' school in the first volume of Jane Eyre. Yet we cannot wonder that the hypothesis of a male author should have been started, or that ladies especially should still be rather determined to uphold it. For a book more unfeminine, both in its excellences and defects, it would be hard to find in the annals of female authorship. Throughout there is masculine power, breadth and shrewdness, combined with masculine hardness, coarseness, and freedom of expression. Slang is not rare. The humour is frequently produced by a use of Scripture, at which one is rather sorry to have smiled. The love-scenes glow with a fire as fierce as that of Sappho, and somewhat more fuliginous. There is an intimate acquaintance with the worst parts of human nature, a practised sagacity in discovering the latent ulcer, and a ruthless rigour in exposing it, which must commend our admiration, but are almost startling in one of the softer sex. Jane Eyre professes to be an autobiography, and we think it likely that in some essential respects it is so. If the authoress has not been, like her heroine, an oppressed orphan, a starved and bullied charity-school girl, and a despised and slighted governess (and the intensity of feeling which she shows in speaking of the wrongs of this last class seems to prove that

---

[1] *Montem* was the triennial celebration of Eton, held on Whit-Tuesday, when the boys went in procession to the mound known as Salt Hill; it was first recorded in 1561 and last observed in 1844. Maria Edgeworth gives an inaccurate account in one of her children's playlets.

they have been her own), at all events we fear she is one to whom the world has not been kind. And, assuredly, never was unkindness more cordially repaid. Never was there a better hater. Every page burns with moral Jacobinism. 'Unjust, unjust,' is the burden of every reflection upon the things and powers that be. All virtue is but well masked vice, all religious profession and conduct is but the whitening of the sepulchre, all self-denial is but deeper selfishness. In the preface to the second edition, this temper rises to the transcendental pitch. There our authoress is Micaiah, and her generation Ahab; and the Ramoth Gilead, which is to be the reward of disregarding her denunciations, is looked forward to with at least as much of unction as of sorrow ...

We select the following extract as an illustration of our remarks.

[quotes from chapter 21, '"I am very ill I know ..."' to 'Neither of us had dropt a tear']

All the expressions of tenderness and forgiveness, on the part of the injured Jane, are skilfully thrown in so as to set off to the utmost the unconquerable hardness of the dying sinner's heart. They are the pleadings of the good angel, made audible, and rejected to the last. We are compelled to see and acknowledge beyond the possibility of doubt, that Mrs. Reed dies without remorse, without excuse, and without hope.

The plot is most extravagantly improbable, verging all along upon the supernatural, and at last running fairly into it. All the power is shown and all the interest lies in the characters ...

The character of Mr. Rochester, the hero, the lover, and eventually the husband, of Jane Eyre, we have already noticed as being, to our minds, the characteristic production of a female pen. Not an Adonis, but a Hercules in mind and body, with a frame of adamant, a brow of thunder and a lightning eye, a look and voice of command, all-knowing and all-discerning, fierce in love and hatred, rough in manner, rude in courtship, with a shade of Byronic gloom and appetizing mystery – add to this that when loved he is past middle age, and when wedded he is blind and fire-scarred, and you have such an Acis as no male writer would have given his Galatea, and yet what commends itself as a true embodiment of the visions of a female imagination. The subordinate characters almost all show proportionate power. Mr. Brocklehurst, the patron and bashaw of Lowood, a female orphan school, in which he practises self-denial, *alieno ventre*, and exercises a vicarious humility, is a sort of compound of Squeers[1] and Pecksniff, but more probable than either, and drawn with as strong a hand . . . Mrs. Reed is a good type of the 'strong-minded' and odious woman. Excellent too, in an artistic point of view, is the character of St. John Rivers, the Calvinist clergy-man and missionary, with all its complex attributes and iridescent hues – self-denial strangely shot with selfishness – earthly pride and restless ambition blending and alternating with heaven-directed zeal, and resignation to the duties of a heavenly mission. The feeblest character in the book is that of Helen Burns, who is meant to be a perfect Christian, and is a simple seraph, conscious moreover of her own perfection. She dies early in the first volume, and our authoress might say of her saint, as Shakespeare said of his Mercutio, 'If I had not killed her, she would have killed me.' In her, however, the Christianity of Jane Eyre is concentrated, and with her it expires, leaving the moral world in a kind of Scandinavian gloom, which is hardly broken by the faint glimmerings of a 'doctrine of the equality of souls,' and some questionable streaks of that world-redeeming greed of Christ, 'which being emancipated from narrow human doctrines, that only tend to elate and magnify a few,' is seldom invoked but for the purpose of showing that all Christian profession is bigotry and all Christian practice is hypocrisy.

In imaginative painting Jane Eyre is very good.

[quotes from chapter 9, 'I discovered . . . wild primrose plants')

The rather ambitious descriptions of manners and social life which the book contains are, we are bound to say, a most decided failure. Their satire falls back with accumulated force upon the head of the satirist. It is 'high life below stairs' with a vengeance; the fashionable world seen through the area railings, and drawn with the black end of the kitchen poker.

[quotes from chapter 17 Blanche Ingram's exchanges with her mother and Rochester]

To say that Jane Eyre is positively immoral or antichristian, would be to do its writer an injustice. Still it wears a questionable aspect . . .

The authoress of Jane Eyre will have power in her generation, whether she choose to exercise it for good or evil. She has depth and breadth of thought – she has something of that peculiar gift of genius, the faculty of discerning the wonderful in and through the commonplace – she

[1] See above, p. 71, n.

has a painter's eye and hand – she has great satiric power, and, in spite
of some exaggerated and morbid cynicism, a good fund of common
sense. To this common sense we would appeal. Let her take care that
while she detects and exposes humbug in other minds, she does not
suffer it to gain dominion in her own. Let her take warning, if she will,
from Mr. Thackeray, to whom she dedicates her second edition, whom
she thinks 'the first social regenerator of the day,' and whose 'Greek-
fire sarcasm' and 'levin-brand denunciation' she overwhelms with such
extravagant panegyric. Let her mark how, while looking every where
for 'Snobs' to denounce, he has himself fallen into one, and not the
least vicious, phase of that very character which he denounces ... Let
her cease, if she can, to think of herself as Micaiah, and of society as
Ahab. Let her be a little more trustful of the reality of human goodness, and a little less anxious to detect its alloy of evil. She will lose
nothing in piquancy, and gain something in healthiness and truth. We
shall look with some anxiety for that second effort which is proverbially
decisive of a writer's talent, and which, in this case, will probably be
decisive of the moral question also.

17. George Eliot, from a letter

11 June 1848

Letter to Charles Bray, *The George Eliot Letters* (1954) i, 268. For
her increased enthusiasm in 1853 see Nos 14, 48.

I have read *Jane Eyre*, mon ami, and shall be glad to know what you
admire in it. All self-sacrifice is good – but one would like it to be in a
somewhat nobler cause than that of a diabolical law which chains a
man body and soul to a putrefying carcase. However, the book *is*
interesting – only I wish the characters would talk a little less like the
heroes and heroines of police reports.

18. Mary Taylor, from a letter

24 July 1848

Letter to Charlotte Brontë from Wellington, New Zealand
(*LL*, ii, 235–9).

Mary Taylor, Charlotte's school friend and origin of Rose Yorke
in *Shirley*, emigrated in 1845 (she returned to England *c.* 1859).
She published *The First Duty of Woman* (1870) and *Miss Miles;
a Tale of Yorkshire Life Sixty Years Ago* (1890).

About a month since I received and read *Jane Eyre*. It seemed to me
incredible that you had actually written a book. Such events did not
happen while I was in England. I begin to believe in your existence
much as I do in Mr Rochester's . . . Your novel surprised me by
being so perfect as a work of art. I expected something more change-
able and unfinished. You have polished to some purpose. If I were
to do so I should get tired, and weary every one else in about two
pages. No sign of this weariness in your book – you must have had
abundance, having kept it all to yourself!

You are very different from me in having no doctrine to preach. It
is impossible to squeeze a moral out of your production. Has the world
gone so well with you that you have no protest to make against its
absurdities? Did you never sneer or declaim in your first sketches? I
will scold you well when I see you. I do not believe in Mr Rivers.
There are no *good* men of the Brocklehurst species. A missionary either
goes into his office for a piece of bread, or he goes from enthusiasm,
and that is both too good and too bad a quality for St John. It's a bit
of your absurd charity to believe in such a man. You have done wisely
in choosing to imagine a high class of readers. You never stop to
explain or defend anything, and never seem bothered with the idea – 'If
Mrs Fairfax or any other well-intentioned fool gets hold of this, what
will she think?' And yet, you know, the world is made up of such, and
worse. Once more, how have you written through three volumes
without declaring war to the knife against a few dozen absurd doc-

93

trines, each of which is supported by 'a large and respectable class of readers'? Emily seems to have such a class in her eye when she wrote that strange thing *Wuthering Heights*. Anne, too, stops repeatedly to preach commonplace truths. She has had a still lower class in her mind's eye. Emily seems to have followed the bookseller's advice. As to the price you got, it was certainly Jewish.[1] . . .

I mention the book to no one and hear no opinions. I lend it a good deal because it's a novel, and *it's as good as another*! They say 'it makes them cry.' They are not literary enough to give an opinion. If ever I hear one I'll embalm it for you.

---

[1] Charlotte received £500 for each of her three novels. See Introduction, p. 14.

19. John Eagles, from an unsigned notice, *Blackwood's Magazine*

October 1848, lxiv, 459–74

From 'A Few Words About Novels' by 'Aquilius', i.e. John Eagles (1783–1855), author and regular contributor to *Blackwood's* during 1831–55. Before turning to *Jane Eyre*, Eagles welcomes the increasing popularity of novels, argues that the age of 'sickly sentimentality' is over, and discusses (among other things) eighteenth-century literature, Dickens's 'false view of life' (*Dombey and Son* is 'his greatest failure'), the unjust charges of 'coarseness and vulgarity' levelled against Frances Trollope, and the pleasures of 'the mysterious' in *The Arabian Nights* and Shakespeare. He also notices H. W. Torrens's novel, *Madam de Malguet: A Tale of 1820* (1848). Charlotte wrote on 6 October 1848 (Branwell had died 24 September): '*Blackwood's* mention of *Jane Eyre* gratified me much – and will gratify me more I daresay, when the ferment of other feelings than that of literary ambition, shall have a little subsided' (*LL*, ii, 263).

AQUILIUS. – But now, Eusebius, we have read the novels brought to us. The first, *Jane Eyre*, has been out some time: not so the other, *Madame de Malguet*, which has only now made its first appearance. I do not think it fair, though it is a common practice with critics, to give out a summary of the tales they review – for this is sure to spoil the reading. I will resume, then, the dialogue, omitting such parts as may be too searching into the story.

LYDIA. – Well, I am glad we read *Jane Eyre* first, for I should have been sorry to have ended with tears, which she has drawn so plentifully; and not from my eyes alone, though both you men, as ashamed of your better natures, have endeavoured to conceal them in vain.

AQUILIUS. – It *is* a very pathetic tale – very singular; and so like truth that it is difficult to avoid believing that much of the characters and incidents are taken from life, though woman is called the weaker sex.

Here, in one example, is represented the strongest passion and the strongest principle, admirably supported.

CURATE. – It is an episode in this work-a-day world, most interesting, and touched at once with a daring, yet delicate hand. In spite of all novel rules, the love heroine of the tale has no personal beauty to recommend her to the deepest affection of a man of sense, of station, and who had seen much of the world, not uncontaminated by it. It seems to have been the purpose of the author to show that high and noble sentiments, and great affection, can be both made subservient, and even heightened, by the energy of practical wisdom. If the author has purposely formed a heroine without the heroine's usual accomplishments, with a knowledge of the world, and even with a purpose to heighten that woman in our admiration, he has made no small inroad into the virtues that are usually attributed to every lover, in the construction of a novel. He, the hero, has great faults – why should we mince the word? – vice. And yet so singular is the fatality of love, that it would be impossible to find two characters so necessary to exhibit true virtues, and make the happiness of each. The execution of the painting is as perfect as the conception.

LYDIA. – I think every part of the novel perfect, though I have no doubt many will object, in some instances, both to the attachment and the conduct of Jane Eyre.

AQUILIUS. – It is not a book for Prudes – it is not a book for effeminate and tasteless men; it is for the enjoyment of a feeling heart and vigorous understanding.

LYDIA. – I never can forget her passage across the heath, and her desolate night's lodging there.

CURATE. – But you will remember it without pain, for it was at once the suffering and the triumph of woman's virtue.

AQUILIUS. – To my mind, one of the most beautiful passages is the return of Jane Eyre, when she sees in the twilight her 'master' and her lover solitary, and feeling his way with his hands, baring his sightless sorrow to the chill and drizzly night.

20. 'Novels of the Season', *North American Review*

October 1848, cxli, 354–69

The article, by 'E.P.', i.e. Edwin Percy Whipple (1819–86), American critic and lecturer, reviews eight novels, of which the first three discussed are *Jane Eyre*, *Wuthering Heights* (No. 69) and *The Tenant of Wildfell Hall* (No. 75); the other novels noticed include Bulwer Lytton's *Harold, the Last of the Saxon Kings* (1848), Lady Georgina Fullerton's *Grantley Manor, a Tale* (1847) and Thackeray's *Vanity Fair* (1848). Whipple was among the first to review the works of 'Bell & Co' together, though not the first to emphasize family resemblances and confuse the identities of the authors. For Charlotte's well-known sardonic comments on the article see headnote, No. 69, and for the general flavour of current American attitudes to 'the Bells', Introduction, p. 32.

The first three novels on our list are those which have proceeded from the firm of Bell & Co. Not many months ago, the New England States were visited by a distressing mental epidemic, passing under the name of the 'Jane Eyre fever,' which defied all the usual nostrums of the established doctors of criticism. Its effects varied with different constitutions, in some producing a soft ethical sentimentality, which relaxed all the fibres of conscience, and in others exciting a general fever of moral and religious indignation. It was to no purpose that the public were solemnly assured, through the intelligent press, that the malady was not likely to have any permanent effect either on the intellectual or moral constitution. The book which caused the distemper would probably have been inoffensive, had not some sly manufacturer of mischief hinted that it was a book which no respectable man should bring into his family circle. Of course, every family soon had a copy of it, and one edition after another found eager purchasers. The hero, Mr. Rochester ... became a great favorite in the boarding-schools and in the worshipful society of governesses. That portion of Young America known as ladies' men began to swagger and swear in the presence of the gentler sex, and to allude darkly to events in their lives which excused impudence and profanity.

While fathers and mothers were much distressed at this strange conduct of their innocents, and with a pardonable despair were looking for the dissolution of all the bonds of society, the publishers of *Jane Eyre* announced *Wuthering Heights*, by the same author. When it came, it was purchased and read with universal eagerness; but, alas! it created disappointment almost as universal. It was a panacea for all the sufferers under the epidemic. Society returned to its old condition, parents were blessed in hearing once more their children talk common sense, and rakes and battered profligates of high and low degree fell instantly to their proper level. Thus ended the last desperate attempt to corrupt the virtue of the sturdy descendants of the Puritans.

The novel of *Jane Eyre*, which caused this great excitement, purports to have been edited by Currer Bell, and the said Currer divides the authorship, if we are not misinformed, with a brother and sister. The work bears the marks of more than one mind and one sex, and has more variety than either of the novels which claim to have been written by Acton Bell. The family mind is strikingly peculiar, giving a strong impression of unity, but it is still male and female. From the masculine tone of *Jane Eyre*, it might pass altogether as the composition of a man, were it not for some unconscious feminine peculiarities, which the strongest-minded woman that ever aspired after manhood cannot suppress. These peculiarities refer not only to elaborate descriptions of dress, and the minutiæ of the sick-chamber, but to various superficial refinements of feeling in regard to the external relations of the sex. It is true that the noblest and best representations of female character have been produced by men; but there are niceties of thought and emotion in a woman's mind which no man can delineate, but which often escape unawares from a female writer. There are numerous examples of these in *Jane Eyre*. The leading characteristic of the novel, however, and the secret of its charm, is the clear, distinct, decisive style of its representation of character, manners, and scenery; and this continually suggests a male mind. In the earlier chapters, there is little, perhaps, to break the impression that we are reading the autobiography of a powerful and peculiar female intellect; but when the admirable Mr. Rochester appears, and the profanity, brutality, and slang of the misanthropic profligate give their torpedo shocks to the nervous system, – and especially when we are favored with more than one scene given to the exhibition of mere animal appetite, and to courtship after the manner of kangaroos and the heroes of Dryden's plays, – we are gallant enough to detect the hand of a gentleman in the composition. There are also scenes of passion, so hot, emphatic, and condensed in expression, and so sternly masculine in feeling, that we are almost sure we observe the mind of the author of *Wuthering Heights* at work in the text.

The popularity of *Jane Eyre* was doubtless due in part to the freshness, raciness, and vigor of mind it evinced; but it was obtained not so much by these qualities as by frequent dealings in moral paradox, and by the hardihood of its assaults upon the prejudices of proper people. Nothing causes more delight, at least to one third of every community, than a successful attempt to wound the delicacy of their scrupulous neighbours, and a daring peep into regions which acknowledge the authority of no conventional rules. The authors of *Jane Eyre* have not accomplished this end without an occasional violation of probability and considerable confusion of plot and character, and they have made the capital mistake of supposing that an artistic representation of character and manners is a literal imitation of individual life. The consequence is, that in dealing with vicious personages they confound vulgarity with truth, and awaken too often a feeling of unmitigated disgust. The writer who colors too warmly the degrading scenes through which his immaculate hero passes is rightly held as an equivocal teacher of purity; it is not by the bold expression of blasphemy and ribaldry that a great novelist conveys the most truthful idea of the misanthropic and the dissolute. . . .[1]

[1]Continued on p. 247.

21. Eugène Forçade, from a review, *Revue des deux mondes*

31 October 1848, tome 4, 471–94

Eugène Forçade, regular contributor to this influential French journal, won Charlotte's warm praise for his reviews of her first two novels (see Nos 33, 52). His '*Jane Eyre*: Autobiographie' is very long (the passages omitted here include the most minutely analytical account of the story to appear) and reflects its author's concern with current political troubles in his own country, against which he measures 'Currer Bell's' truth and independence of mind (see Introduction, pp. 25–6). Charlotte wrote on 16 November 1848:

The notice . . . is one of the most able, the most acceptable to the author of any that has yet appeared. Eugène Forçade understood and enjoyed *Jane Eyre*. I cannot say that of all who professed to criticise. The censures are as well-founded as the commendations (*LL*, ii, 271).

The vicissitudes and sorrows of the present time lend a particular interest to romantic literature. The events which have interrupted numbers of careers, have consigned a host of distinguished people to that life of retirement, rest and contemplation which is, as it were, the environment in which this kind of literature most readily flourishes . . .

It seems to me that such conditions and such a mood should call forth their own novelist and inspire . . . something more than works of pure entertainment or mere literary craft . . . if art still wields any real power in society, if literature still retains any effective influence on manners and morals, then art and literature are solemnly called upon to fulfil a practical, social function. What is the sickness of our time? Utopia, the false ideal that makes an absurd and untrue image of man, that realizes the dictum of Montaigne and Pascal: in seeking to make man an angel, it intoxicates and degrades him to the level of a beast. Utopia dreams of a mechanical perfection for man, a perfection that is monotonous and stupid . . . and it should prove especially attractive to men who . . . pursue the illusory ideal of rest under the leveller of humanitarian tyranny in order to free themselves from the proud and harsh duties of freedom and personal responsibility ... Poetry, that flame of human liberty, ... has as deep an interest as society itself in refuting the impossible ideal of the socialists. The most powerful weapon of poetry is the philosophy of the passions, whose intimate depths it alone can plumb and which it alone can express with its irresistible eloquence. And this is where the novel has a part to play, for the novel is the form of poetry devoted to the individual history of human emotion and it is therefore for the novel above all to formulate the protest of society and art against socialism and to force the lay figure of humanitarianism to make way for the breathing reality of man himself.

These thoughts came to mind as I read the book, which has attracted a good deal of notice in England ... *Jane Eyre* is the first novel of a writer whose identity is concealed from the curious by a pseudonym. Who has written these swift and vehement pages? A young man, some say; others, a woman ... Internal evidence and certain details of the book do strongly suggest that *Jane Eyre* is in fact the work of a woman; but whoever the author of this novel may be ... one thing struck me about *Jane Eyre* and that is the eminently and vigorously personal character of the book. *Jane Eyre*, I must warn you, is not at all a story of universal interest, one of those tales independent of place which may be read with the same pleasure in Paris, Madrid or Moscow. Nor is *Jane Eyre* a literary work of deep significance, but it is a highly curious and engaging moral study for those who, like myself, cannot – even though they are French – bring themselves to turn socialist. It is a book that is completely English in the moral sense of the word. One feels all through it the spirit of that Anglo-Saxon race, crude if you will – you Frenchmen who still imagine yourselves Athenians in 1848 – but masculine, inured to suffering and hardship ... They firmly implant in the hearts of their children the feeling for freedom and responsibility; they have given the world not Saint-Simon and Fourier but William Penn, Daniel Defoe and Benjamin Franklin. This is the aspect that interests me in the story told us by the author of *Jane Eyre*, the story of a child, an orphan, cast alone on the world and fighting a solitary battle. The account vibrates with a feeling which seems sometimes to bear the accent of a personal confession and it has that passion and animation which always inspire the beginner in the zest of a first work. But what especially charmed me was that the author has relied solely on the eloquence of the emotions depicted and has not for a moment thought of calling down a fiery judgment

on society in a drama in which society nevertheless plays more or less
the cruel and tyrannical role assigned to fate in the tragedies of antiquity.

And the author of *Jane Eyre* is all the more to be admired for having
disdained the declamatory resources offered by the subject in that she
has systematically created other and singular difficulties for herself . . .
Jane Eyre is not one of those beautiful, smiling young ladies pursued
by elegant suitors, idealized in the golden light of girlish dreams . . .
The novelist has taken the bold step of making his hero and heroine
decidedly ugly, allowing them to catch here and there as best they may
under the influence of emotion, that chance beauty which we call the
beauty of the devil. There is another resource in common use among
English novelists which is likewise eschewed in *Jane Eyre*: I mean the
depiction of life in high society which of itself has guaranteed the
success of a number of fashionable novels. In its setting *Jane Eyre* is
quite simply a novel of country life. This book contains not a hint of
a description of a London season, a stay in a watering-place, or a point-
to-point race; no social lions appear, not even the briefest sketch of the
Beau Brummell or the Comte d'Orsay of the day: no stroll in the
park, no dinner at Richmond, not a trace of fashionable ranting . . .
It is a sober and serious tale concerned to bring to life the poor and
dependent situation of a highly interesting class of person and one that
is very numerous among women in England. And for us, as foreigners,
the romantic attraction of such a picture is perhaps nothing more than
an inquisitive interest in scenes of everyday life in another country . . .
In England the old order still exists . . . The political, colonial and
mercantile activities of the English people, that spirit of enterprise that
takes Anglo-Saxons to every corner of the world, do it is true redress,
for men, the effects of the law of primogeniture. It is not quite the
same for women; they have not the same means of winning a place in
the sun. Among the middle classes especially, how many girls belonging
to the junior branch of the family, must decline through poverty to
dependence and destitution! How often must one find, especially
among these Englishwomen, that inner conflict, that fatality arising
from their situation, so cruelly felt by our needy middle classes, and
which grows out of a disharmony between birth, education and
fortune. It is in this class that our author has chosen the heroine of her
novel . . . We first meet Jane Eyre . . . persecuted and trembling, in the
house of her aunt, Mrs. Reed, who is as hard and hateful as a step-
mother; she is brought up with Mrs. Reed's children, two daughters
who look down on her as an inferior, and a mischievous little rascal

for whom she is a plaything and a victim . . . Jane Eyre is intense and taciturn. Her aunt and the servants of the house accuse her of being underhand and use this as a pretext for treating her worse than ever. The author summarizes in a few scenes the martyrdom of Jane Eyre's childhood. This procedure of going back to the earliest years of life to seek the development of character and of tracing the man in the child is a familiar one among English novelists. Nothing could be more logical. In these lively and sensitive natures which form the subject of novels, childhood contains the seed and key to the whole life. Note the pleasure, the delighted and minute attention with which those poets who have left us their memoirs linger over their first memories; look at Goethe and Rousseau.

[quotes the final paragraph of chapter 1 and all chapter 2, continuing with a detailed account of the story incorporating further lengthy extracts]

A novel is made up of three things: situation, characters and plot. The author of *Jane Eyre* has chosen a really interesting and romantic situation. This young girl, orphaned, educated on charity, entering the world with a cultivation of mind second to none but in a subordinate and inferior station, brought into contact with everything that her intelligence and feeling equip her to understand, merit and desire but that fate denies her, receiving at last through love full entry into life – this story will always be touching . . . Nor have I any reproach to level at the characters in *Jane Eyre*: they are energetic and emphatic rather than delicate; but they are true, that of Jane especially, and every scene in the novel gives them in the smallest details a solidity which is full of life. But the plot, here is the weak side of the work. I cannot understand why the author of *Jane Eyre* could not have found a simpler action through which to develop her situation and characters; I cannot understand why she should have thought she needed to have such complicated and disjointed incidents, often improbably linked . . . the author of *Jane Eyre* had quite enough talent to create a complete and irreproachable work.

But what I shall never cease to praise is the vigorous, healthy, moral spirit that informs every page of *Jane Eyre*. Whatever our novelists may say, this book proves once more that there are infinite resources for fiction in the depiction of the upright morals and straightforward events of real life and the simple and open development of the passions. When will we French stop investigating in our novels with such obsessive relentlessness the metaphysics, the subtle and sometimes profound politics of depraved instincts, corrupt emotions, monstrous attachments, of everything bred of the fermentation of evil in human nature? ...

22. Elizabeth Rigby, from an unsigned review, *Quarterly Review*

December 1848, lxxxiv, 153–85

The controversial review by Elizabeth Rigby (1809–93), contributor to the *Quarterly* since 1842 and author of *A Residence on the Shores of the Baltic* (1841). She married in 1849 Sir Charles Lock Eastlake (President of the Royal Academy 1850–65). Her later works include a translation of Waagen's *Treasures of Art in Great Britain* (1854–7) and *Five Great Painters* (1883); her journals and correspondence appeared in 1895. Her article is often commendatory but its snobbish criticisms (which provoked sharp reactions from many of Charlotte's later reviewers) are at variance with the feelings of the *Quarterly's* editor, J. G. Lockhart (No. 13), and seemingly also with her own general temper and behaviour (see Introduction, p. 26). Her authorship of the article was revealed to Charlotte by W. S. Williams some time in February 1849 (see *LL*, ii, 307, 314; iii, 12), but was not generally known until the 1890s (Marion Lochhead, *Elizabeth Rigby, Lady Eastlake* (1961), 64). Charlotte's initial response was blunted by grief over Emily's recent death. She wrote on 2 January 1849: 'The lash of the *Quarterly* cannot sting . . . Currer Bell feels a sorrowful independence of reviews and reviewers' (*LL*, ii, 298), and on 4 February 1849: 'I read the *Quarterly* without a pang . . . the critic seems anxious to let it be understood that he is a person well acquainted with the habits of the upper classes . . . I am afraid he is no gentleman' (*LL*, ii, 307). The criticisms rankled, however, judging by her intention in August 1849 (promptly discouraged by her publishers) to include a 'Note' to the *Quarterly* in her preface to *Shirley* (*LL*, iii, 12, 15–16). The article opens by discussing Thackeray's *Vanity Fair* and closes with a notice of the Report for 1847 of the Governesses' Benevolent Institution. Omitted passages include an account of the narrative and a generous selection of extracts.

Jane Eyre, as a work, and one of equal popularity, is, in almost every respect, a total contrast to *Vanity Fair*. The characters and events, though some of them masterly in conception, are coined expressly for the purpose of bringing out great effects. The hero and heroine are beings both so singularly unattractive that the reader feels they can have no vocation in the novel but to be brought together; and they do things which, though not impossible, lie utterly beyond the bounds of probability. On this account a short sketch of the plan seems requisite; not but it is a plan familiar enough to all readers of novels – especially those of the old school and those of the lowest school of our own day. For Jane Eyre is merely another Pamela, who, by the force of her character and the strength of her principles, is carried victoriously through great trials and temptations from the man she loves. Nor is she even a Pamela adapted and refined to modern notions; for though the story is conducted without those derelictions of decorum which we are to believe had their excuse in the manners of Richardson's time, yet it is stamped with a coarseness of language and laxity of tone which have certainly no excuse in ours. It is a very remarkable book: we have no remembrance of another combining such genuine power with such horrid taste. Both together have equally assisted to gain the great popularity it has enjoyed; for in these days of extravagant adoration of all that bears the stamp of novelty and originality, sheer rudeness and vulgarity have come in for a most mistaken worship.

The story is written in the first person. Jane begins with her earliest recollections, and at once takes possession of the reader's intensest interest by the masterly picture of a strange and oppressed child she raises up in a few strokes before him. She is an orphan, and a dependant in the house of a selfish, hard-hearted aunt, against whom the disposition of the little Jane chafes itself in natural antipathy, till she contrives to make the unequal struggle as intolerable to her oppressor as it is to herself. She is therefore, at eight years of age, got rid of to a sort of Dothegirls Hall,[1] where she continues to enlist our sympathies for a time with her little pinched fingers, cropped hair, and empty stomach. But things improve: the abuses of the institution are looked into.

[outlines the rest of the story, noting the 'scenes of truly tragic power' following the interrupted wedding]

Such is the outline of a tale in which, combined with great materials

[1] Cp. pp. 71, n., 91.

for power and feeling, the reader may trace gross inconsistencies and improbabilities, and chief and foremost that highest moral offence a novel writer can commit, that of making an unworthy character interesting in the eyes of the reader. Mr Rochester is a man who deliberately and secretly seeks to violate the laws both of God and man, and yet we will be bound half our lady readers are enchanted with him for a model of generosity and honour. We would have thought that such a hero had had no chance, in the purer taste of the present day; but the popularity of *Jane Eyre* is a proof how deeply the love of the illegitimate romance is implanted in our nature. Not that the author is strictly responsible for this. Mr Rochester's character is tolerably consistent. He is made as coarse and as brutal as can in all conscience be required to keep our sympathies at a distance. In point of literary consistency the hero is at all events impugnable, though we cannot say as much for the heroine.

As to Jane's character – there is none of that harmonious unity about it which made little Becky so grateful a subject of analysis – nor are the discrepancies of that kind which have their excuse and their response in our nature. The inconsistencies of Jane's character lie mainly not in her own imperfections, though of course she has her share, but in the author's ... The error in Jane Eyre is, not that her character is this or that, but that she is made one thing in the eyes of her imaginary companions, and another in that of the actual reader ... We hear nothing but self-eulogiums on the perfect tact and wondrous penetration with which she is gifted, and yet almost every word she utters offends us, not only with the absence of these qualities, but with the positive contrasts of them, in either her pedantry, stupidity, or gross vulgarity ... Even in that *chef-d'oeuvre* of brilliant retrospective sketching, the description of her early life, it is the childhood and not the child that interests you. The little Jane, with her sharp eyes and dogmatic speeches, is a being you neither could fondle nor love. There is a hardness in her infantine earnestness, and a spiteful precocity in her reasoning, which repulses all our sympathy. One sees that she is of a nature to dwell upon and treasure up every slight and unkindness, real or fancied, and such natures we know are surer than any others to meet with plenty of this sort of thing. As the child, so also the woman – an uninteresting, sententious, pedantic thing; with no experience of the world, and yet with no simplicity or freshness in its stead.

[quotes from chapter 13 her 'governessy effusions' about '*cadeaux*']

Let us take a specimen of her again when Mr Rochester brings home his guests to Thornfield. The fine ladies of this world are a new study to Jane, and capitally she describes her first impression of them as they leave the dinner table and return to the drawing-room – nothing can be more gracefully graphic than this . . . But now for the reverse. The moment Jane Eyre sets these graceful creatures conversing, she falls into mistakes which display not so much a total ignorance of the habits of society, as a vulgarity of mind inherent in herself. They talked together by her account like parvenues trying to show off. They discuss the subject of governesses before her very face, in what Jane affects to consider the exact tone of fashionable contempt. They bully the servants in language no lady would dream of using to her own – far less to those of her host and entertainer – though certainly the 'Sam' of Jane Eyre's is not precisely the head servant one is accustomed to meet with in houses of the Thornfield class . . .

But the crowning scene is the offer [of marriage] – governesses are said to be sly on such occasions, but Jane outgovernesses them all – little Becky would have blushed for her . . . Although so clever in giving hints, how wonderfully slow she is in taking them! Even when, tired of his cat's play, Mr Rochester proceeds to rather indubitable demonstrations of affection – 'enclosing me in his arms, gathering me to his breast, pressing his lips on my lips' – Jane has no idea what he can mean. Some ladies would have thought it high time to leave the Squire alone with his chestnut tree; or, at all events, unnecessary to keep up that tone of high-souled feminine obtusity which they are quite justified in adopting if gentlemen will not speak out – but Jane again does neither. Not that we say she was wrong, but quite the reverse, considering the circumstances of the case – Mr Rochester was her master, and 'Duchess or nothing' was her first duty – only she was not quite so artless as the author would have us suppose . . . A little more, and we should have flung the book aside to lie for ever among the trumpery with which such scenes ally it; but it were a pity to have halted here, for wonderful things lie beyond – scenes of suppressed feeling, more fearful to witness than the most violent tornados of passion – struggles with such intense sorrow and suffering as it is sufficient misery to know that any one should have conceived, far less passed through; and yet with that stamp of truth which takes precedence in the human heart before actual experience. The flippant, fifth-rate, plebeian actress has vanished, and only a noble, high-souled woman, bound to us by the reality of her sorrow, and yet raised above us by the strength of the will, stands in actual life before us. If this be Jane Eyre, the author has done her injustice hitherto, not we. Let us look at her in the first recognition of her sorrow after the discomfiture of the marriage.

[quotes from chapter 26, 'Only the clergyman stayed . . . the floods overflowed me']

We have said that this was the picture of a natural heart. This, to our view, is the great and crying mischief of the book. Jane Eyre is throughout the personification of an unregenerate and undisciplined spirit, the more dangerous to exhibit from that prestige of principle and self-control which is liable to dazzle the eye too much for it to observe the inefficient and unsound foundation on which it rests. It is true Jane does right, and exerts great moral strength, but it is the strength of a mere heathen mind which is a law unto itself. No Christian grace is perceptible upon her. She has inherited in fullest measure the worst sin of our fallen nature – the sin of pride . . . she looks upon all that has been done for her not only as her undoubted right, but as falling far short of it. The doctrine of humility is not more foreign to her mind than it is repudiated by her heart. It is by her own talents, virtues, and courage that she is made to attain the summit of human happiness, and, as far as Jane Eyre's own statement is concerned, no one would think that she owed anything either to God above or to man below. She flees from Mr Rochester, and has not a being to turn to. Why was this? . . . Jane had lived for eight years with 110 girls and fifteen teachers. Why had she formed no friendships among them? Other orphans have left the same and similar institutions, furnished with friends for life, and puzzled with homes to choose from. How comes it that Jane had acquired neither? . . .

Altogether the autobiography of Jane Eyre is pre-eminently an anti-Christian composition. There is throughout it a murmuring against the comforts of the rich and against the privations of the poor, which, as far as each individual is concerned, is a murmuring against God's appointment – there is a proud and perpetual assertion of the rights of man, for which we find no authority either in God's word or in God's providence – there is that pervading tone of ungodly discontent which is at once the most prominent and the most subtle evil which the law and the pulpit, which all civilized society in fact has at the present day to contend with. We do not hesitate to say that the tone of the mind and thought which has overthrown authority and violated every code human and divine abroad, and fostered Chartism and rebellion at home, is the same which has also written Jane Eyre.[1]

Still we say again this is a very remarkable book. We are painfully alive to the moral, religious, and literary deficiencies of the picture, and such passages of beauty and power as we have quoted cannot redeem it, but it is impossible not to be spellbound with the freedom of the touch. It would be mere hackneyed courtesy to call it 'fine writing.' It bears no impress of being written at all, but is poured out rather in the heat and hurry of an instinct, which flows ungovernably on to its object, indifferent by what means it reaches it, and unconscious too. As regards the author's chief object, however, it is a failure – that, namely, of making a plain, odd woman, destitute of all the conventional features of feminine attraction, interesting in our sight. We deny that he has succeeded in this. Jane Eyre, in spite of some grand things about her, is a being totally uncongenial to our feelings from beginning to end. We acknowledge her firmness – we respect her determination – we feel for her struggles; but, for all that, and setting aside higher considerations, the impression she leaves on our mind is that of a decidedly vulgar-minded woman – one whom we should not care for as an acquaintance, whom we should not seek as a friend, whom we should not desire for a relation, and whom we should scrupulously avoid for a governess.

There seem to have arisen in the novel-reading world some doubts as to who really wrote this book; and various rumours, more or less romantic, have been current in Mayfair, the metropolis of gossip, as to the authorship. For example, Jane Eyre is sentimentally assumed to have proceeded from the pen of Mr Thackeray's governess, whom he had himself chosen as his model of Becky, and who, in mingled love and revenge, personified him in return as Mr Rochester. In this case, it is evident that the author of *Vanity Fair*, whose own pencil makes him grey-haired, has had the best of it ... To this ingenious rumour the coincidence of the second edition of Jane Eyre being dedicated to Mr Thackeray has probably given rise. For our parts, we see no great interest in the question at all. The first edition of *Jane Eyre* purports to be edited by Currer Bell, one of a trio of brothers, or sisters, or cousins, by names Currer, Acton and Ellis Bell, already known as the joint-authors of a volume of poems. The second edition the same – dedicated, however, 'by the author,' to Mr Thackeray; and the dedication (itself an indubitable chip of Jane Eyre) signed Currer Bell ...

[1] See Introduction, pp. 25–6.

Whoever it be, it is a person who, with great mental powers, combines a total ignorance of the habits of society, a great coarseness of taste, and a heathenish doctrine of religion. And as these characteristics appear more or less in the writings of all three, Currer, Acton, and Ellis alike, for their poems differ less in degree of power than in kind, we are ready to accept the fact of their identity or of their relationship with equal satisfaction. At all events there can be no interest attached to the writer of *Wuthering Heights* – a novel succeeding *Jane Eyre*, and purporting to be written by Ellis Bell – unless it were for the sake of more individual reprobation. For though there is a decided family likeness between the two, yet the aspect of the Jane and Rochester animals in their native state, as Catherine and Heathfield, is too odiously and abominably pagan to be palatable even to the most vitiated class of English readers. With all the unscrupulousness of the French school of novels it combines that repulsive vulgarity in the choice of its vice which supplies its own antidote. The question of authorship, therefore, can deserve a moment's curiosity only as far as *Jane Eyre* is concerned, and though we cannot pronounce that it appertains to a real Mr Currer Bell and to no other, yet that it appertains to a man, and not, as many assert, to a woman, we are strongly inclined to affirm . . . No woman – a lady friend, whom we are always happy to consult, assures us[1] makes mistakes in her own metier – no woman trusses game and garnishes dessert-dishes with the same hands, or talks of so doing in the same breath. Above all, no woman attires another in such fancy dresses as Jane's ladies assume – Miss Ingram coming down, irresistible, 'in a morning robe of sky-blue crape, a gauze azure scarf twisted in her hair! !' No lady, we understand, when suddenly roused in the night, would think of hurrying on 'a frock.' They have garments more convenient for such occasions, and more becoming too. This evidence seems incontrovertible. Even granting that these incongruities were purposely assumed, for the sake of disguising the female pen, there is nothing gained; for if we ascribe the book to a woman at all, we have no alternative but to ascribe it to one who has, for some sufficient reason, long forfeited the society of her own sex.

And if by no woman, it is certainly also by no artist. The Thackeray eye has had no part there. There is not more disparity between the art of drawing Jane assumes and her evident total ignorance of its first principles, than between the report she gives of her own character and the conclusions we form for ourselves. Not but what, in another sense,

[1] Cf. Anne Mozley's similar fiction about her sex in her review of *Villette* – see p. 207.

the author may be classed as an artist of very high grade. Let him describe the simplest things in nature – a rainy landscape, a cloudy sky, or a bare moorside, and he shows the hand of a master; but the moment he talks of the art itself, it is obvious that he is a complete ignoramus.

We cannot help feeling that this work must be far from beneficial to that class of ladies whose cause it affects to advocate. Jane Eyre is not precisely the mouthpiece one would select to plead the cause of governesses, and it is therefore the greater pity that she has chosen it: for there is none we are convinced which, at the present time, more deserves and demands an earnest and judicious befriending.

23. James Lorimer, from an unsigned review, *North British Review*

August 1849, xi, 455–93

By James Lorimer (1818–90), jurist and political philosopher, member of the Faculty of Advocates of Scotland 1845, appointed to the chair of 'The Law of Nature and of Nations', Edinburgh, 1865; his books include *Political Progress not necessarily Democratic* (1857). His piece has some interest, in spite of its critical limitations, as one of many rebuttals of the *Quarterly*'s strictures concerning the 'vulgarity' of *Jane Eyre*. Charlotte wrote on 16 August 1849:

> Much of the article is clever . . . yet . . . I do not respect an inconsistent critic. He says, if *Jane Eyre* be the production of a woman, 'she must be a woman unsexed'. In that case the book is an unredeemed error . . . Jane Eyre is a woman's autobiography . . . If it is written as no woman would write, condemn it with spirit and decision . . . do not apologise and then detract . . . There is a . . . comment . . . having no pretence to either justice or discernment on the works of Ellis and Acton . . . I have read no review since either of my sisters died which I could have wished *them* to read (*LL*, iii, 11–12).

The rest of the review discusses Mrs Stirling's *Fanny Hervey; or the Mother's Choice* (1849) and Anne Marsh's *Emilia Wyndham* (1846). Omitted passages include a lengthy analysis of the success with women won by masterful men like Rochester.

It is now full time we were looking after Miss Eyre . . . and the first favour we shall do her . . . will be to acquit her of the charge of conventional vulgarity, which has been brought against her by a contemporary.[1] There is an old proverb which prohibits the throwing of stones to those who dwell in palaces of glass; and we think there is enough that comes to light, in the pages of our contemporary, to show that a bandying of conventionalities was a sport in which he could not very safely indulge. There is a continual anxiety to display his acquaintance with the little social peculiarities of civilized life, which we never

[1] Elizabeth Rigby; see No. 22.

find in those to whom they are habitual; and there are observations on blue-crape dresses, and other pieces of female gear, which would lead us to suppose that the article (if written by a man at all) was the production of a man-milliner; and if Mr. Mantalini[2] had not long since become 'a body,' we should infallibly have suspected him. Notwithstanding, then, this authority, we venture to assert that, neither conventionally nor absolutely, is Jane vulgar; and we go so far as to say that, with her organization, mental and physical, (unless the book had been a blunder from beginning to end, which is not alleged) it was scarcely possible that she should be so. Where great intellectual power and activity, accompanied, as it usually is, by the gift of entering into the feelings of others, is united to a nervous temperament of the most sensitive texture, the result must be a person to whom conventional refinements, which others must painfully learn, (and of which they are sometimes painfully vain) will be intuitive . . . But we are by no means clear that graver faults might not have been assigned to Jane. Though there is nothing that is coarse as a human being, there is much about her that is hard, and angular, and indelicate as a woman. Notwithstanding her love for Rochester, we feel that she is a creature more of the intellect than of the affections; and the matter-of-course way in which she, a girl of nineteen, who had seen nothing of the world, receives his revelations of his former life, is both revolting and improbable . . . We cannot blame her for ultimately falling in love with Rochester, for in doing so she did nothing more than every woman who has read the book has done since. Proud, tyrannical, violent, and selfish though he was, he had the element of power, which, involuntarily and almost unconsciously, in a woman's eyes, supplies the deficiency of every other good quality . . . By an affectation of indifference he contrived, in the midst of his passion, to retain the air of superiority, which was one of the principal charms which belonged to him, and to bring matters at last to such a pass that her pride consisted, not in resisting, but in being vanquished . . . He had one of the most enviable attributes of genius, that of sympathizing and of calling forth sympathy . . . This power of entering into the nature of another, is indeed one of the most indispensable qualities of the poet – it is the feeler which he stretches out into the waters of life, and in the possession of it, as in many other respects, Mr. Rochester comes nearer to the man of genius than any hero of romance that we know . . .

The great defect in the otherwise most successful character of

[1] In Dickens's *Nicholas Nickleby* (1839); cp. p. 71, n.

Rochester, consists in representing his life as utterly objectless. This we look upon as a positive artistical blunder. No such man could have been contented, during his whole life, to sit tamely and silently by, and see the affairs of mankind, his own included, managed by others. Duty being altogether out of the question, a sort of internal necessity would have prompted him, sooner or later, to make his voice heard. Ambition, in some form, is seldom wanting to the powerful, and Rochester's love of enjoyment, which seems never to have gained the mastery over his reason, so far from indicating an inaptitude for affairs, went rather to prove the completeness of his nature . . .

Of the crime which Rochester committed in attempting to marry Jane whilst his wife was alive, we do not think it necessary to say much. A transgression of so heinous a nature, as to come within the reach even of human laws, is not likely to become attractive in the eyes of many. But there are more latent objections to the tendency of this powerful book . . . In Jane herself there is a recklessness about right and wrong which is very alarming, and although in the great action of her life, that of leaving Rochester, she valiantly resists a very powerful temptation, and her general conduct is not very reprehensible, the motive by which she is actuated is seldom a higher one than worldly prudence; and there is often a kind of regretful looking-back, which makes us fear that the fate of Lot's wife may overtake her. In the other novels, *Wuthering Heights* and *The Tenant of Wildfellhall*, these, like all the other faults of Jane Eyre, are magnified a thousand-fold, and the only consolation which we have in reflecting upon them, arises from the conviction that they will never be very generally read. With *Wuthering Heights* we found it totally impossible to get along. It commences by introducing the reader to a perfect pandemonium of low and brutal creatures, who wrangle with each other in language too disgusting for the eye or the ear to tolerate, and unredeemed, so far as we could see, by one single particle either of wit or humour, or even psychological truth, for the characters are as false as they are loathsome. How it terminates we know not, for the society which we encountered on our first introduction was so little to our taste, that we took the liberty of declining the honour of a farther acquaintance. *The Tenant of Wildfellhall* has a better beginning, and the conclusion is an unimpeachable instance of poetical justice; but in the body of the tale there are scenes in which the author seems to pride himself in bringing his reader into the closest possible proximity with naked vice, and there are conversations such as we had hoped never to see printed in English.

There is a coarseness and brutality in the manner of speaking of almost all the characters, never to be met with among gentlefolks, however depraved; and there is a continual use of 'slang' throughout the book, even where the author speaks in his own person, which might well have justified our contemporary, if he had pronounced over it, instead of Jane Eyre, the social anathema of vulgarity. There is even a frequent inaccuracy of style, and an apparently involuntary slipping into provincialisms, which would lead us to think that, if Currer Bell be the editor of Acton Bell's books, as would seem from their title-pages, he must have been napping on the occasion of this publication.

But with all their faults, there is no denying the family resemblance between these unpleasing productions, and their more happily constituted elder sister. They are vigorous dwarfs, in whose mis-shapen limbs the idea of the same powerful nature is still to be traced; of whom we can say, that if they had not been dwarfs, they would have been strong and beautiful beings. Their fault is deformity, not weakness. Nor is this resemblance perceptible in the characterization only. In the scenery it is even more striking. There is always a wild upland district, with the wind howling through a few gnarled and weather-beaten Scotch firs, or an old untenanted manor-house, buried in trees, and haunted by horrors – not supernatural. In the colouring, so to speak, there is an unity of tone throughout. It is *grey*, and there is an evident partiality for rough and boisterous weather. The artist has a contempt for 'the pretty,' which might have satisfied our poor friend David Scott himself;[1] but the sketches show an acquaintance with nature in her rougher moods not often to be met with. In two or three words we have the scene so vividly before us, that we seem to experience with our bodily senses the phenomena described. The following picture of a 'drear November day' makes us cold and comfortless. 'Afar it offered a pale blank of mist and cloud; near, a scene of wet lawn and storm-beat shrub, with ceaseless rain sweeping away wildly before a long and lamentable blast.' [chapter 1]

We shall not attempt to resolve the much agitated question of the sex of the author of these remarkable works. All that we shall say on the subject is, that if they are the productions of a woman, she must be a woman pretty nearly unsexed; and Jane Eyre strikes us as a personage much more likely to have sprung ready armed from the head of a man, and that head a pretty hard one, than to have experienced, in any shape, the softening influence of female creation.

[1] The melancholy Romantic painter who had recently died (born 1806).

SHIRLEY

October 1849

24. From an unsigned review, *Daily News*

31 October 1849, 2

One of the first reviews and of some interest as heralding the general recognition that 'Currer Bell' must be a woman. Charlotte wrote on 1 November 1849: '... my heart sickened over it ... [its] inexpressible ignorance first stuns and then stirs me' (*LL*, iii, 30), and on 6 November 1849:

I was sadly 'put out' by the *Daily News* ... good resolutions ... were tried this morning by another notice in the same style in the *Observer*. The praise of such critics mortifies me more than their blame.... To speak of the press being still ignorant of my being a woman! Why can they not be content to take Currer Bell for a man? I imagined, mistakenly, it now appears, that *Shirley* bore fewer traces of a female hand than *Jane Eyre*; that I have misjudged disappoints me a little, though I cannot exactly see where the error lies (*LL*, iii, 34).

The omitted passages include two extracts from chapter 7, the first introducing Caroline Helstone and the second describing Robert Moore's coldness towards her.

There are few things more forbidding than the commencement of a novel by the author of *Jane Eyre*. Like people who put dwarfs and monsters to keep their gates, or ugly dogs to deter idle folk from entering, so doth this writer manage to have an opening chapter or two of the most deterring kind. What so disgusting as the family in the midst of whom Jane Eyre is first discovered? The three curates and their junketting, with whom *Shirley* commences, is quite as vulgar, as unnecessary, and as disgusting.

If you do not mind these monstrosities at the entrance, you will be both welcomed and repaid by the graceful and the beautiful, when you enter the mansion. Palace it is not. The abodes haunted and peopled by Mr. Currer Bell's imagination are middle-class ones, with the peculiar kind of refinement, purity, and feeling which pervade them: gentility without its nonsense, industry without its coarseness.

The story is in keeping with the scenes and the class in which it is laid. The adventures are simple, brief, and few: scarcely culled indeed, but almost carelessly taken from every-day life; a love story of the simplest, chequered by the very smallest of obstacles, and solved by the most awkward of devices. If the adventures are not the most stirring, the characters are not of the most striking. But what is striking is the sentiment. *Shirley* is the anatomy of the female heart. By *Shirley* we mean the book, and not the personage; for the true heroine is the rector's niece, the history of whose heart is one of the most beautiful chronicles ever set down by a female pen. For that Currer Bell is petticoated will be as little doubted by the readers of her work as that Shirley Keeldar is breeched.

The merit of the work lies in the variety, beauty, and truth of its female character. Not one of its men are genuine. There are no such men. There are no *Mr. Helstones*, *Mr. Yorkes*, or *Mr. Moores*. They are all as unreal as Madame Tussaud's waxworks. And in truth the mind of the writer must have been darkened by the shade of some lay figure, some wooden man stuck up between the light and the easel used in painting. The sentiments of this man, or men on womankind, are all fictitious, and evidently thrust therein by a woman's imagination or resentment. Let Currer Bell get some one else to paint men, and himself do none but the female figures, or dissect at least none save female hearts.

Although the incidents of the book be few, they are powerfully imagined and well told. *Moore*, the hero, is a mill-owner, who persists in introducing machinery. He makes sore enemies of his hands, who plot against him, break his frames, and at last attack his mill. The Yorkshire rioters are sketched with a pencil of truth. But the author cares not to dwell upon them. Mr. Bell prefers establishing a microscopic opening into the breast of some young lady, and writing all the phenomena of that wonderful and delicate work of nature or of art ... *Shirley*, a book which, like its predecessor, indicates exquisite feeling, and very great power of mind in the writer, though he too much disdains art, has too much tolerance for common place, and dilates too much not merely on what is conventional, but what is real vulgarity, too trivial to expose and too trifling to condemn. The women, however, are all divine, and *Shirley* is indeed an intellectual harem.

25. From an unsigned review, *Atlas*

3 November 1849, 696–7

The omitted passages include extracts from Louis Moore's dialogue with Henry Sympson and his subsequent interview with Shirley (chapter 28); also shorter selections from conversations between Shirley and Caroline, including Caroline's painful recollection of her behaviour towards Robert Moore (chapter 12), which prompts the comment, 'We might be sure that a woman wrote this passage, though she should array her ladies in azure crepe for morning costume' (see Elizabeth Rigby's review, No. 22).

Not for many years has a second appearance been looked for so eagerly as the second appearance of the author of *Jane Eyre*. The public waited long and anxiously for it; but in spite of the tardy advent of the new claimant we never forgot the piquant Jane, with her plain black gown, her insignificant stature, her irregular features, her somewhat brusque style of address, and her wonderful fascinations. More than two years have passed since *Jane Eyre* was published; but it has never ceased to be a constant object of inquiry wherever the English language is read, and never has the third volume of that indescribable fiction been laid down without a longing after more fruit from the same tree and a singular interest in its development. But for the causes of delay, we should have rejoiced that the second appearance of Currer Bell has been so long retarded. It has left full time for *Jane Eyre* to be appreciated. The new has not come too soon to supersede the old, even if the new work were another *Jane Eyre*. But it is not another *Jane Eyre*. In some respects it is superior; but we do not like it half as well – or, we should say, we do not succumb to it half as much. *Shirley* we have quite in our power. In *Jane Eyre* there was an irresistible spell; one was not, for some time, the same as before after reading it. It would take a great many *Shirleys* to put *Jane Eyre* out of our heads.

Now *Jane Eyre* has taken a high, a very high, place among English novels; but whether Currer Bell could take a high place among English novelists remained to be proved – nay, it still remains to be proved. We will not admit that *Shirley* settles the question. If we thought it did, our decision would be against the claims of Currer Bell. We should be obliged to confess that the author of *Shirley* is singularly destitute of invention. The leading idea of this new story is the same as the leading idea of the old. The sexes are only reversed. Instead of a gentleman of property and a governess, we have a lady of property and a tutor. *Mutatis mutandis*, Shirley (such is the lady's somewhat masculine baptismal name) and Louis Moore are but a reproduction of Rochester and Jane Eyre. The points of resemblance are so many that we cannot venture to particularise them. The scenery and costume of the story are very much the same as we have in the preceding fictions of the Bell family. There is a wild north-country landscape – an old manorial house, of which the proprietor comes to take possession – and a somewhat rude state of society obtaining in all the neighbourhood. 'Remote from towns,' the people run a rather godless and very uncivilised race; and, to our southern visions, the entire environments of the piece seem somewhat strange and uncouth, but not without a possible reality, which, though one's experience cannot, one's imagination can readily embrace.

There is one thing which may be said, without any misgivings, after even a careless perusal of *Shirley*. It sets at rest now and for ever all question of the sex of the writer. For our own parts, we could never acknowledge that there was any question about it; but it was pertinaciously raised and volubly discussed, in the face of the strongest possible evidence of female workmanship. The reasons for the entertainment of an opposite faith, put forth by the *Quarterly Review* [No. 22] and other grave authorities, always appeared to us of the weakest . . . But now the most sceptical will cease to doubt. There is woman stamped on every page of the present fiction.[1]

In spite of even more deplorable evidences of bad taste than disfigure the former work of Currer Bell, *Shirley* is a more womanly book

[1] See headnote to No. 24.

than *Jane Eyre*, and on the whole more pleasing. The charm of the story lies in its exquisitely truthful delineation of female character. There is nothing to our taste so piquante – nothing to our mind so interesting – as dear Jane Eyre; but Caroline Helstone, the real heroine of *Shirley*, is a sweeter, gentler creature; more of a 'young lady' – fitter for everyday life and genteel society – and will, peradventure, have the suffrages of the many. The progress of an attachment, fluctuating between hopelessness and full assurance, through all the varying grades of pleasing and painful doubt, has seldom been traced with more delicacy and truth. The reader who wants strong stimulants will probably be disappointed. There is very little action in *Shirley*. The story is but a slender one. The *dramatis personae* do little; but they feel much. It is the deep under-current of womanly emotion, whose windings he must be content to follow. The narrative, indeed, is throughout rather psychological than dramatic; although in form it is more dramatic than *Jane Eyre*, and it is written almost wholly in dialogue. It is the inner rather than the outer world, that is set forth; and the effort to impart something more of social life to the story is singularly unsuccessful. And it is not a mere negative failure. The minor characters are, for the most part, extraordinarily unreal and repulsive. There is, for example, a batch of curates, who act as a sort of *chorus* to the piece; but there is no dramatic fitness in their introduction; they are in harmony with nothing; what they have been obtruded upon us for it is very difficult to say. They occupy the stage at the first drawing up of the curtain, like a bevy of goblins in a pantomime; and are almost as much out of place as if such an introduction were to usher in the romantic love-drama of *Romeo and Juliet*.

The first chapter of *Shirley* is enough to deter many a reader from advancing a step further than the threshold. It required all the remembered fascinations of *Jane Eyre* to keep down the feelings of dissatisfaction (we had nearly written another word with the same commencement) which the first chapter of *Shirley* raised up within us. All this is very coarse – very irreverential. And there is besides, discernible in other parts, an unseemly mode of allusion to solemn topics, a jesting with scriptural names, and a light usage of scriptural expressions, which will grate painfully upon the feelings of a considerable number of Currer Bell's many-minded readers . . . *Shirley* is better written than *Jane Eyre*; but there is less power in it. There is nothing like the originality of the little governess in these pages . . . Still it is a very noticeable book . . . It has the stamp of genius upon it.

26. From an unsigned review, *Athenaeum*

3 November 1849, 1107–9

For Charlotte's comment see No. 32. The omitted passages include quotations to 'exhibit the author in her more favourable light as an adjuster of separate scenes', including Mrs Pryor's nursing Caroline Helstone (chapter 24) and Louis Moore's proposal to Shirley Keeldar (chapter 36).

That *Jane Eyre* is a book of more than ordinary power and cleverness, we said among the foremost [No. 7] – that it is a world's wonder of power or passion we have never admitted . . . The novel pleased the many because it contained yet one more protest against social conventionalisms and inequalities – yet one more expression of aching discontents and vague ambitions, uttered through the medium of eccentric characters and startling incidents, and combined with descriptions of scenery and pictures of manners the strangeness of which gave them a welcome relish. Critics and coteries fell upon the book with an eagerness whimsically proving how young Old England is in spite of all John Bull's mishaps, – and how precious is a literary sensation even in this over-wrought London of ours. Parties ran high and waxed hot in discussing whether *Jane Eyre* owned a masculine or a feminine parentage . . . Subsequently, other tales appeared by other Bells, and the attempt to ascertain whether they were kindred or identical kept up the excitement: – so that the intrinsic qualities of the novel in question, and the power of its writer to maintain a high place, ran small chance of being calmly considered or fairly determined.

We have always felt that the question was adjourned till the appearance of Currer Bell's second venture . . . And to do the writer justice, – it is obvious . . . that she (for we will assume at once that these books are from a female hand) has taken every possible pains to justify her first success, by diligence and deliberation in her second appeal to the public. Whatever be thought of *Shirley*, it is neither a slight nor a slighted book, – but one demanding close perusal and careful consideration.

It is not easy to convey to the reader any idea of the story of *Shirley* – because story has been obviously not the motive uppermost with the writer. Her main purpose has been, to trace the fortunes and feelings of two girls. The one, Caroline Helstone, is a clergyman's daughter, neglected – not maltreated – by her unobservant father [sic], a harsh courageous man, whose right place would have been the army and not the church. The other is Shirley Keeldar, heiress and lady paramount of the district. The one is tender, the other is sparkling: both suffer from the malady of unrest and dissatisfaction, – on the prevalence of which among women of the nineteenth century so many protests have been issued, so many theories of 'emancipation' have been set forth. In both the desolateness and the fever are assuaged by one and the same master-enchanter – Love. Early in the tale they form a close and confidential friendship, – and for a while the reader is requested to believe that they attach themselves to the same object. This, however, the Critic could not for a passing instant accept. He perceived that Caroline Helstone's deep and quiet attachment for Gérard Moore, the mill-owner, and Shirley Keeldar's open and avowed pleasure in his society, were fruits which grew on a pair of trees widely apart and totally different: and it was no surprise to see the trouble dissolve like a mist, and the knot disentangled without threads or hearts being broken. The expedient, however, by which this is effected is most improbable ... The three curates who open the play and appear as Chorus, after the fashion of the three Anabaptists in Meyerbeer's *Prophète* [1849] – are hit off cleverly enough; and Mr. Donne's display of contempts and fine language, by way of astounding the Yorkshire heiress into admiration, is a good bit of comedy in its hard, dry way. Mr. Helstone, though a sketch, is a character. Gérard Moore, the mill-owner, is somewhat of an incompatibility, more closely resembling a hero cut out by a lady's scissors than one engraved by 'her master's' etching-needle. His occupation, however, and the locality and epoch of the tale (the close of the long war) give rise to some forcible scenes: – and the attack on the mill by the frame-breakers is among the number. Louis, the tutor, is yet another study of the proud, silent, but ardent student whose wooing was better sung by Mrs. Browning in her 'Ladye Geraldine's Courtship'[1] than it is *said* here.

We have still to group together a few objections and characteristics. The tale moves languidly and cumbrously. There is too much time given to mere conversations ... Tea, buns, catechisms and samplers

[1] In *Poems*, 1844.

are excellent things, – but not in the least picturesque; and in this story, which is in no respect a *good-boy* book, their introduction becomes grotesque. – The dialogue, though forcible, is at once too abrupt and too rhetorical ... The writer of *Shirley*, as in *Jane Eyre*, displays an intimate acquaintance with a peculiar district of the north of England, and a keen eye for sectarian peculiarities and differences. To close this notice – we do not think that *Shirley* is an advance upon *Jane Eyre*: – book which women will admire as very passionate and which men may regard as somewhat prosy.

27. Albany Fonblanque, from an unsigned review, *Examiner*

3 November 1849, 692-4

For Albany Fonblanque see No. 10. The authorship is indicated by Charlotte's letter to Williams of 5 November 1849:

The critic of the *Daily News* [No. 24] struck me as to the last degree incompetent, ignorant, flippant. A thrill of mutiny went ... through me ... [but] I am willing to be judged by the *Examiner* ... Fonblanque has power, he has discernment – I bend to his censorship; I am grateful for his praise; his blame deserves consideration; when he approves, I permit myself a modest emotion of pride. Am I wrong in supposing the critique to be written by Mr Fonblanque? But whether it is by him or Forster, I am thankful (*LL*, iii, 33),

and that to Ellen Nussey of 16 November 1849: 'the [review] in the *Examiner* is written by Albany Fonblanque, who is called the most brilliant political writer of the day, a man whose dictum is much thought of in London' (*LL*, iii, 37). The omitted passages include an outline of the story and extracts from 'The Valley of the Shadow of Death' (chapter 24) and 'The Rushedge Confessional' (chapter 30).

The peculiar power which was so greatly admired in *Jane Eyre* is not absent from this book. Indeed it is repeated, if we may so speak of anything so admirable, with too close and vivid a resemblance. The position of Shirley and her tutor is that of Jane and her master reversed. Robert and Louis Moore are not quite such social savages, externally, as Mr. Rochester; but in trifling with women's affections they are hardly less harsh or selfish, and they are just as strong in will and giant in limb. The heroines are of the family of Jane, though with charming differences, having wilful as well as gentle ways, and greatly desiderating 'masters'. The expression of motive by means of dialogue is again indulged to such minute and tedious extremes, that what ought to be developments of character in the speaker become mere exercitations of will and intellect in the author. And finally the old theme of tutors and governesses is pushed here and there to the tiresome point. The lesson intended is excellent; but works of art should be something more than moral parables, and should certainly embody more truths than one.

While we thus freely indicate the defects of *Shirley*, let us at the same time express, what we very strongly feel, that the freshness and lively interest which the author has contrived to impart to a repetition of the same sort of figures, grouped in nearly the same social relations, as in her former work, is really wonderful. It is the proof of genius. It is the expression of that intellectual faculty, or quality, which feels the beautiful, the grand, the humorous, the characteristic, as vividly after the thousandth repetition as when it first met the sense. We formerly compared the writer to Godwin, in the taste manifested for mental analysis as opposed to the dealing with events; and might have taken Lord Byron within the range of the comparison. As in *Jane Eyre*, so in *Shirley*, the characters, imagery, and incidents are not impressed from without, but elaborated from within. They are the reflex of the writer's peculiar feelings and wishes. In this respect alone, however, does she resemble the two authors named. She does not, like Godwin, subordinate human interests to moral theories, nor, like Byron, waste her strength in impetuous passion. Keen, intellectual analysis is her forte; and she seems to be, in the main, content with the existing structure of society, and would have everybody make the most of it.

As well in remarking on *Jane Eyre*, as in noticing other books from the same family, if not from the same hand, we have directed attention to an excess of the repulsive qualities not seldom rather coarsely indulged. We have it in a less degree in *Shirley*, but here it is. With a most delicate and intense perception of the beautiful, the writer combines a craving for stronger and rougher stimulants. She goes once again to the dales and fells of the north for her scenery, erects her 'confessionals' on a Yorkshire moor, and lingers with evident liking amid society as rough and stern as the forms of nature which surround them. She has a manifest pleasure in dwelling even on the purely repulsive in human character. We do not remember the same taste to the same extent in any really admirable writer, or so little in the way of playful or tender humour to soften and relieve the habit of harsh delineation. Plainly she is deficient in humour. In the book before us, what is stern and hard about Louis Moore is meant to be atoned by a dash of that genial quality. But while the disagreeable ingredient

is powerfully portrayed in action, the fascinating play of fancy is no
more than talked about.

Is there, indeed, in either of these books, or any of the writings which
bear the name of 'Bell,' one really natural, and no more than natural,
character – a character, we mean, in which the natural is kept within its
simple and right proportions? We suspect it would be hardly an exaggeration to answer this question in the negative. The personages to
whom Currer Bell introduces us are created by intellect, and are
creatures of intellect. Habits, actions, conduct are attributed to them,
such as we really witness in human beings; but the reflections and
language which accompany these actions, are those of intelligence
fully developed, and entirely self-conscious. Now in real men and
women such clear knowledge of self is rarely developed at all, and then
only after long trials. We see it rarely in the very young – seldom or
ever on the mere threshold of the world . . . It is impossible to imagine
that Shirley and her lover could have refined into each other's feelings
with such keen intellectual clearness as in the dialogues and interviews
detailed, yet remained ignorant so long of what it most behoved them
both to know. But even in the children described in this book we find
the intellectual predominant and supreme. The young Yorkes, ranging
from twelve years down to six, talk like Scotch professors of meta-
physics, and argue, scheme, vituperate, and discriminate, like grown up
men and women.

Yet in spite of this, and of the very limited number of characters and
incidents in this tale as in the former, the book before us possesses deep
interest, and an irresistible grasp of reality. There is a vividness and
distinctness of conception in it quite marvellous. The power of graphic
delineation and expression is intense. There are scenes which for
strength and delicacy of emotion are not transcended in the range of
English fiction. There is an art of creating sudden interest in a few
pages worth volumes of common-place description. Shirley does not
enter till the last chapter in the first volume, but at once takes the
heroine's place. Louis Moore does not enter till the last chapter of the
second volume, yet no one would dream of disputing with him the
character of hero.

Story there is none in *Shirley*. The principal continuous interest of
the book attaches to two brothers, and two girls with whom they are
in love . . . The staple of the three volumes is made up of the thinkings,
sayings, and doings of these four persons; presented to us less in the
manner of a continuous tale, in which incidents spring from character,

and reflections are suggested by incidents, than in a series of detached
and independent pictures, dialogues, and soliloquies, written or spoken.
So instinct with life, however, are these [scenes[. . . that the want of
continuity in the tale is pardoned. Tediousness is felt before the author's
purpose comes distinctly in view; but when it does, the interest
becomes enchaining. We could not lay down the third volume. We
may single out two of its chapters more especially – the 'Valley of the
Shadow of Death,' and the 'Rushedge Confessional' [chapters 24, 30] . . .

A host of subordinate characters . . . figure round the principal
persons, and appear or disappear as it suits the author's whim or convenience. Indeed by no means the least charm of the book consists in
the vigour and felicity with which these accessories are sketched. They
are hit off, mentally and bodily, with a startling force and reality.
Sometimes the mood they are conceived in is delightfully tender and
tolerant (as with the old maids, Miss Mann and Miss Ainley), sometimes placidly just (as with Hortense Moore, and those capital operative
sketches, Joe Scott and William Farren), but more often sarcastic to
the utmost extreme of the merciless (as with the Sympson family,
hardly redeemed by their gentle invalid boy, the wife and children of
Yorke, the wooden-legged Barraclough, and the curates of Whinbury,
Briarfield, and Nunnely).

The Rev. Mr. Mathewson Helstone, rector of Briarfield, one of the
most happily conceived and executed pictures in the book, claims
mention at more length . . . Wherever the rector makes his appearance, he is striking, characteristic, consistent. At home, cold, silent, and
unsympathising; in company, brilliant and vivacious; eager to seek
out danger, in high spirits when brought face to face with it, and making less powerful natures bend to his strong will; nothing can be better
done throughout . . .

Very characteristic is Yorke, too, in his way; and the contrast of
Helstone and Yorke with Robert Moore, so different, yet with so
much in common, all three so fearless, so strong in will, yet each so
individual, so marked out by his temper and the influence of his position and pursuits, is among the cleverest things in the book.

We can give little in the way of extract to illustrate the character of
Shirley. The minute, delicate, and brilliant traits would lose too much
in the transfer . . . Nevertheless in the predilection and general conclusions of the author of *Shirley* we will not pretend to concur. There
is a large and liberal tolerance in them, and a rational acquiescence in
the inevitable tendencies of society. But this acquiescence we suspect to

be reluctant. There is a hankering, not to be suppressed, after the fleshpots of Egypt – a strong sympathy with Toryism and High Church. The writer sees clearly that they are things of the past, but cannot help regretting them. The tone assumed to the dissenters and manufacturers is hardly fair. Their high qualities are not denied, but there is a disposition to deepen the shadows in delineating them. There is cordiality when the foibles of rectors and squires are laughed at, but when the defects of the commercial class are touched there is bitterness. The independence and manlier qualities of even that class are nevertheless appreciated, and some truths are told, though told too sharply, by which they may benefit. The views of human nature which pervade the volumes, notwithstanding the taste for dwelling on its harsher features already adverted to, are healthy, tolerant, and encouraging. A sharp relish for the beauties of external nature, no mean power of reproducing them, and occasional glimpses of ideal imagination of a high order, are visible throughout. The writer works upon a very limited range of rather homely materials, yet inspires them with a power of exciting, elevating, pleasing, and instructing, which belongs only to genius of the most unquestionable kind.

We have not hesitated to speak of the writer as a woman. We doubted this, in reading *Jane Eyre*; but the internal evidence of *Shirley* places the matter beyond a doubt.

28. From an unsigned review, *Spectator*

3 November 1849, xxii, 1043-5

See No. 9. The omitted passages include extracts describing the curates at tea with the Helstones (chapter 7), Robert Moore's treatment of William Farren (chapter 8) and the attitude of the trading classes to the war (chapter 20). The selection is in keeping with the reviewer's preference for the historical and social aspects of the novel.

In several respects this 'tale' exhibits a considerable improvement upon the novels that under the name of Bell with several prefixes have excited so much attention. There is less coarseness than was displayed in all of them, somewhat less questionable propriety than appeared in the best of them, *Jane Eyre*, and nothing of the low and almost disgusting characters and circumstances that disfigured the rest. *Shirley* has more variety of persons, and in a certain sense more of actual life than was found in *Jane Eyre*; but in essentials we observe little difference. That part which forms the *story* of the novel still depends less upon incidents than upon metaphysical delineation of character, executed with more power than skill or naturalness; a sort of ingrained rudeness – an absence of delicacy and refinement of feeling – pervades the book; and above all, we have small sympathy with either the principal or the subordinate characters. It would seem as if the writer's mind had a peculiarity which defeated its genius, compelling it to drop something distasteful into every idiosyncracy, that increases in proportion to the importance of the character to the fiction. The only exceptions to this are two old maids and a clergyman, who rarely appear, and who do nothing. These faults coexist with great clearness of conception, very remarkable powers of delineation both of internal emotion and outward scenes, much freshness of topic, scenery, and composition, with a species of vigour, which rather resembles the galvanic motions of a 'subject' than the natural movements of life. But Currer Bell has yet to learn, that in art the agreeable is as essential as the powerful, and that the reader's attention must be attracted, not forced.

The scene of *Shirley* is laid in Yorkshire, towards the close of the war against Napoleon, when the Imperial Decrees and the British Orders in Council were creating apprehension amongst the clothiers, distress among the workmen, and Jacobinical principles generally. To paint this state of society is one object of the tale, and, we think, the most successfully attained; though the generality of the characters have so strong a dash of the repelling, as well as of a literal provincial coarseness, that the attractive effect is partly marred by the ill-conditioned nature of the persons, whether it be the author's fault or Yorkshire's. The sketches of the workmen, the masters, the dignified clergy, the curates, the Dissenters, and the various persons who forty years ago went to make up the society of an obscure place in York-shire, are done with a somewhat exaggerated style, and coloured too much by the writer's own mind, but possessing rude vigour and harsh truth. The darkest part of the political night, immediately preceding the dawn, had raised peace-at-any-price people then, and enables the writer to give a present interest to the past in some of the general remarks . . .

The mode by which life and continuous interest is given to what would otherwise have been a series of provincial sketches, is by two love tales; but neither of a sufficiently large or pleasing kind . . .

Whether broad cloth and bankruptcy, or the marriage of a poor lover to a rich wife, are proper moving elements of fiction, may be doubted. Trade, in its money-making aspect, appeals to no lofty emotion, if it does not rather suggest the reverse. A bankruptcy or a legacy may be a means of inducing ill or good fortune, but it is only to be mentioned and dismissed. The meanness attaching to a fortune-hunter seems to have established as an unalterable canon that the hero's wealth should precede his formal declaration of love: he achieves greatness, but comes into property by luck or succession towards the 'finis.' This ill choice of subjects in *Shirley* is not counterbalanced by felicity of treatment. Robert Moore, out of the factory, is a self-satisfied melo-dramatic coxcomb 'half soft and half savage'; in the factory, he is a hard and mercenary man, his objects being too much sunk and his means too much presented. Caroline Helstone is marred by weakness and by an unfeminine display of her feelings. Louis Moore, though well drawn, and well sustained up to a certain point, flags at the critical moment, and, to make a bad thing worse, writes down the whole account of his wooing autobiographically. Indeed, this part is a sort of reverse of Mr. Rochester and Jane Eyre, and that of Caroline and Robert is a repetition of what is rarely attractive itself – a metaphysical love tale.

These circumstances render the incidental sketches, or scenes that are not directly connected with the love affairs, the most agreeable parts of the book.

29. William Howitt, from an unsigned review, *Standard of Freedom*

10 November 1849, 11

William Howitt (1792–1879), the prolific Quaker author, was also editor of *Howitt's Journal*, which had carried a favourable review of *Jane Eyre* (20 November 1847, xi, 333–4). For the authorship see Charlotte's letter to Williams of 15 November 1849, in which she discusses the newspaper reviews:

I have received . . . the *Globe, Standard of Freedom, Britannia, Economist* and *Weekly Chronicle* [No. 30] . . . from the tone of the Newspapers it seems that those who were most charmed with *Jane Eyre* are the least pleased with *Shirley* . . . while those who spoke disparagingly of *Jane Eyre* – like *Shirley* a little better . . . But . . . the fiat . . . does not depend on Newspapers – except . . . such . . . as the *Examiner* [No. 27] – the monthlies and the Quarterlies will pronounce it . . . Still . . . notice has on the whole been favourable: that in the *Standard of Freedom* was very kindly expressed – and coming from a dissenter – William Howitt – I wonder thereat (*LL*, iii, 35).

Howitt was among the first (with *The Economist* of the same date) to compare *Shirley* with *Mary Barton*. Shortly afterwards Charlotte received her first letter from Mrs Gaskell (which 'brought tears to my eyes') and sent her in return a copy of *Shirley* (*LL*, iii, 40; *Letters of Mrs Gaskell* (1966), 93). The omitted passages give an account of the historical setting and the principal characters.

The public will warmly welcome another work from the author of *Jane Eyre*, and it will not be disappointed. If any one could doubt, in reading *Jane Eyre*, that the author was a woman, that doubt will be dissipated in the perusal of *Shirley*. The hand of a woman is unmistakeably impressed on the present brilliant production, but it is a woman endowed not only with the finest and, we trust, the most tender sensibilities of her sex, but with the intellectual power of a man.

Shirley is essentially a story of English life. It combines those various features and characters that can alone be found meeting in English country life. The landed gentry, the clergy, and the wealthy manufacturers, all mingling, and giving their various colours, interests, and piquancy to the scene. We observe in *Shirley* evident traces of the author's admiration of *Mary Barton*. The impression is clear and strong, but does not for a moment detract from the originality of *Shirley*. The two authors, though kindred in the qualities of mind – great vigour, freshness, comprehension of individual character, and independence of feeling – regard life from two very different points of view. The author of *Mary Barton* lays her scene in the heart of the great manufacturing town; the author of *Shirley* in the country; and both introduce the struggles of master manufacturers and their work-people; but the author of *Mary Barton* is obviously more at home amongst the 'hands,' the author of *Shirley* amongst the masters. We are brought into close contact with the masses by Mrs. Gaskell; we are placed similarly near to the employers by the author of *Shirley*; while both preserve a fine impartiality as regards the question at issue, and make you feel that it is not party but humanity that guides the pen. The author of *Shirley* is unquestionably, moreover, a church-woman; and while she does not hesitate, as a faithful delineator of manners, to smile at the foibles of individual clergymen – the curates of the book, for instance – she draws her principal characters of the clerical class in a manner that makes you respect them. Mr. Helstone and Mr. Cyril Hall are unlike as light and darkness, but both act on principles that to them are as sound as they are inseparable from their dispositions.

The story lies in the north of England, of which the author shows intimate knowledge. You find yourselves in the cloth-manufacturing districts of Yorkshire, towards the end of the great French war, when the continental system of Napoleon, and the 'Orders in Council' of the English Government, had driven the manufacturers to distraction. The masters have their warehouses full of goods that they cannot sell; and the workpeople are driven by their distress to the unprofitable excesses of riots and smashing of machinery.

Mr. Robert Moore, a master manufacturer, of Hollow's Mill, a Fleming by birth, though of English parentage and connexions, is at once embarrassed by the state of trade, and menaced by the workpeople for his unflinching opposition to their unreasonable demands. Near him resides Mr. Helstone, the clergyman of Briarfield, his relative, and his niece, Caroline Helstone. Shirley Keeldar, a young lady just of age, the possessor of an estate of a thousand a year, and of Robert

Moore's mill, has just come to reside also close by, at her old manor-house of Fieldhead. We have also a Mr. Hiram Yorke, another master manufacturer, a character rarely introduced into books, but not unfrequently to be found in such a neighbourhood. He is a regular Radical in politics; speaks in broad dialect, is of a rough, independent temper, yet is a man of polished education; has travelled, and has his house full of the richest works of art. Hiram Yorke is fond of Robert Moore, and hates the rector, Mr. Helstone, who is not only a stout old Tory, but once carried off the woman that Yorke was passionately attached to.

Besides these there are numbers of other characters, – we should say too many; the canvass is too much crowded with figures. Still the chief figures are strong, prominent, and original, and the interest soon settles round them. We do not mean to go into the story, it would injure the reader's pleasure in the perusal of the work; but we may say that the attack of Moore's mill by the mob, its defence by Moore, his nephew Helstone, and a detachment of soldiery, and the intricacies of love affairs between Moore and Caroline Helstone, and his brother Louis Moore and the heiress Shirley, furnish sufficient excitement of that kind.

Beyond the story, however, the delineations of character, and the management of the passions of the actors, display the hand of real genius, and the deep and searching glance of woman's intuition . . .

The fault of the book is in its too-extended dialogue; it does not advance but retards the development of the story. But the landscapes are so fresh, the people so living, the whole so abounding with a free, lifelike, and most genial spirit, that it will leave a lasting and delightful impression on the reader.

30. From an unsigned review, *Weekly Chronicle*

10 November 1849, 3

See No. 29. Representative in finding *Shirley* worthy but less enthralling than *Jane Eyre*. The omitted passages give a comprehensive account of the story, including a lengthy extract from the narrative of Robert Moore's rejection by Shirley (chapter 30).

Readers whose memory can go back over that long space in the life of a generation, to twenty-five years ago, may remember the rage which about that time existed for the novel, when the press teemed with productions in the legitimate three volumes, when the great reviews did not think it beneath their province to devote many pages to works now forgotten, and the circulating libraries were besieged by eager crowds, hungry for their chief intellectual pabulum. The novel was then the great public instructor. People went to Scott or [G.P.R.] James for their history, to Disraeli for their politics, to Bulwer, Hook, Grattan, and the silver-fork school, to learn the customs of society and the manners of the great; to Banim,[1] Griffin, or Crowe, to glean some information on the condition of Ireland; to Marryatt, and the rest of the sea-tribe, for the achievements of England's blue-jackets; and to Pierce Egan for glimpses at the prize-ring and the bloods of the nineteenth century. But we have changed all that, and a new novel no longer creates a universal sensation, or shakes the nervous system of society, as, according to the evening papers, was the wont twenty-five years ago. The Reform agitation, and the Anti Corn Law agitation, changes in the fashion of literature, the humourists, the Dickenses and the Thackerays, have all no doubt conspired for the decline of the legitimate novel, which now flourishes very little better than the legitimate drama. Perhaps the inundation of trash which was poured upon the world when novel-reading was the fashion, has, like many other evils, worked its own cure, and quenched the fever in a deluge

[1] See No. 63, p. 231, n. 2.

of milk and water. There are, however, works of fiction, which either expressing the want, the yearning, or the silent thoughts of the time, or speaking, like divine poetry, direct to the universal heart of man, will always find welcome and a permanent place at the hearth and in the study. Many such have been cast on the shore by the stream of Time, to be reverently preserved and cherished while the English language shall endure. The author of *Jane Eyre* and *Shirley* aspires to add to the store. The future will apply its own test – the present age seems disposed to accord this writer a place in the foremost ranks.

Rarely indeed does a first work achieve so high a reputation as was won by the autobiography of Jane Eyre. A new mind, unhackneyed and thoroughly original, spoke its own thoughts, developed its own experience, delineated human character, with singular power and truth ... *Shirley* will not greatly enhance the fame acquired by *Jane Eyre*, but will not detract from it. In the main characteristics, the two works have many points of resemblance: in both the incidents are made subordinate to character, but in the first there is greater individuality, intensity, and directness of purpose, while the interest of the second is weakened by being divided amongst too many. It is impossible to lay down *Jane Eyre* once taken up: the main thread of *Shirley* is carried through so many windings of trivial incident unconnected with the plot, that the reader will often grow weary of following it, at least through the first half of the tale. Every person helps the development of the plot in the one; characters are so crowded together, as to impede the action in the other. Still, *Shirley* is a remarkable book, with many of the characteristic excellencies of its predecessor, and it will repay those who have courage to cross the bridge of the first volume ...

There is intrinsic evidence in the book in favour of the rumour that the author is a woman. The female characters are all drawn with care, minuteness, and truth to nature, not equally apparent in the men; and the philosophy and opinions are such as we might expect from a woman. We have already remarked that too many persons are crowded together, hindering the progress of the story, and many of them, especially the three curates, are sadly in the way. Justice, however, requires us to state that the principal characters of the picture are prominent, commanding, and well painted, and the surrounding groups contain many figures worthy of separate study. On the whole *Shirley* is not unworthy of the reputation of the author of *Jane Eyre*.

31. From an unsigned review, *Britannia*

10 November 1849, 714–15

Exceptional in connecting 'Currer Bell's' narrative poems with her development as a novelist (see Introduction, p. 18). The omitted passages include detailed descriptions of 'tableaux' in the poems and quotations from the novel designed to illustrate the author's 'power in raising images to the eye and in picturing scenes', notably descriptions of Shirley's appearance and her visionary imagination (chapters 13, 36) and the portrayal of the Sympsons (chapter 26).

Some years ago there appeared in most modest guise a small volume of poems by Ellis, Currer, and Acton Bell. They were generally overlooked on their publication, yet they had a kind of merit of an uncommon kind, and contained some passages well calculated to fix themselves on the mind. The principal pieces bore the signature of Currer Bell, and, though the versification was none of the smoothest, evinced wonderful power in raising images before the eye and in picturing scenes. One of these poems [i.e. 'Gilbert'], we remember, consisted of several tableaux ... As a poem the piece had faults, but for power of portraiture and for that rare faculty of exhibiting in words the shadowy images of mental agony, confused yet clear, undeveloped yet fully conceived, a thought without sensible embodiment, it was almost unequalled. Less finished than some similar pieces by Hood, it had a deeper significance and more impressive mystery.

Some lines of a lighter kind displayed equal mastery in the art of word painting.

[discusses 'The Letter'].

In *Shirley* there is striking and delightful evidence of the same talent. Shirley Keeldar is a young lady, a Yorkshire heiress, with very independent notions, and a somewhat masculine style of thought, though her face and figure are delicate in the extreme. She has been named

Shirley from the failure of male issue, and it is her whim sometimes to assume mannish airs. Mr. Bell has exerted all his ability to render this character at once original and attractive, and he has perfectly succeeded. She is like no other heroine of romance ever drawn. Wilful, obstinate, proud, pettish, provoking, she has a soul capable of the purest and deepest passion, and all her singularities of manner and expression only serve to set off her genius. In contrast ... is another young girl, Caroline, of a softer and gentler nature. For a time the reader is left to suppose that their affections are fixed on the same man, Robert Moore, a Yorkshire manufacturer. We do not get an inkling of the truth, or of the real aim, of the book until the middle of the third volume ...

More than one half of the work has little or no connection with the main story, and, though we can never read long together without coming upon some vigorous passage, yet we have the disagreeable feeling that much of the matter we are wading through is purposeless, and had better have been omitted. It is probable that Mr. Bell will hereafter compose with more art. But, were his faults infinitely greater than they are, his originality of mind, and the triumphant beauty of his heroine's character, would at once secure for his book great and deserved popularity.

32. From an unsigned review, *Critic*

15 November 1849, 519–21

Charlotte wrote on 19 November 1849:

The *Sun*, the *Morning Herald* and the *Critic* came this morning. None of them expresses disappointment from *Shirley*, or on the whole compare her disadvantageously with *Jane*. It strikes me that those worthies – the *Athenaeum* [No. 26], *Spectator* [No. 28], *Economist* made haste to be first with their notices that they might give the tone, if so, their manoeuvre has not quite succeeded. The *Critic*, our old friend [see Nos 1, 8] is a friend still. Why does the pulse of pain beat in every pleasure? Ellis and Acton are referred to, and where are they? (*LL*, iv, 39).

The rest of the review quotes the detailed description of Shirley's day (chapter 22); the 'mysteries of the "Jew-basket"' (chapter 7); the description of the Sympson family (chapter 26); Shirley on masculine ideas about women (chapter 20); Charlotte's attack on the British 'mercantile classes' (chapter 10); and Shirley's pagan conception of Nature (chapter 17).

And who *is* Currer Bell? The question is asked again and again in every literary coterie in London, at every tea-table in the country. Who are the *three* Bells, who together published the volume of poems, by which the name was first introduced to the public? Are they three or one? Can the unromantic name of Bell be an assumed one? Each of the three Bells has adventured a novel, having a family resemblance, but not like the offspring of the same parent. Were the three novels really written by three different Bells, or is one Bell the author of all? Can this literary prodigy be a modern Cerberus, 'three gentlemen in one,' as Mrs. Malaprop has it? If they be three distinct individualisms, how comes it that three have contrived to keep their secret so well? Is it possible that such a family could exist anywhere in England without so remarkable a constellation of genius being famous in their locality, at least? But if there be not three, but one only, why are the works that issue under the name of Currer Bell, so superior to those that have been put forth under the names of the two other Bells? Then there is another mystification. *What* is Currer Bell, the author of *Jane Eyre*? Is it the name of man or woman? There was much in the story and treatment of *Jane Eyre* to lead to the conclusion that Currer is of the masculine gender, and there is much in *Shirley* too, that gives the same impression. But in *Shirley* there is a great deal more of evidence on the other side, so much, indeed, that we have come to the conclusion, spite of the numerous and weighty proofs to the contrary, that Currer Bell is a lady. The female heart is here anatomized with a minuteness of knowledge of its most delicate fibres, which could only be obtained by one who had her own heart under inspection. The emotions so wondrously described were never *imagined*: they must have been *felt*.

Shirley is not so interesting a novel as was *Jane Eyre*, that is to say, viewed as a *novel* or story. But it is very superior to it in every other respect. The authoress has bestowed wonderful pains upon its composition, and she has been rewarded accordingly. It has been slowly written, carefully digested, touched and retouched, reviewed and revised, corrected in manuscript and in proof, and in this respect it is a pattern to our modern novelists, who give their scribblings to the press with all their imperfections, as they flow from their gold pen, scarcely troubling themselves to amend defects in grammar or remedy tautologies. Currer Bell has written with a lofty consciousness of the duty of her vocation, which is, to do well what one undertakes to do ... This is the first merit which must strike every reader of *Shirley*, and it is the more obvious from its rarity.

But it has far higher claims than these. It is a masterly delineation of character, wrought with unrivalled skill, not produced by bold outlines and striking effects, but laboriously constructed of a thousand delicate traits, thrown out one by one until the entire figure is before us, mind and all, instinct with life, and impressing itself upon the memory as something real and tangible, as acquaintances who have played a part with us in the drama of life ...

In almost every page of *Shirley*, there are scattered also brilliant flashes of poetry and the utterances of a reflective mind, which almost assume the shape of aphorisms. These are so unlike the usual writings of a lady, they are so comprehensive in their views, so terse in their expression, that, but for other evidence to the contrary, we should have received them as conclusive testimony to the masculine gender of Currer Bell.

Shirley will be read by everybody, and therefore we are not going to mar the pleasure of a single reader by giving the very slightest insight into the plot. We will cite only, in illustration of some of our remarks, such passages as are beautiful in themselves, and throw no light upon the story.

33. Eugène Forçade, from an article, *Revue des deux mondes*

15 November 1849, tome 4, 714–35

Charlotte wrote to Williams on 22 November 1849:

It is reviving to hear what you have written discussed and analysed by a critic who is master of his subject ... I do not find that [Forçade] detects any coarseness in the work – it is for the smaller critics to find that out (*LL*, iii, 40–1),

and to Ellen Nussey on the same day:

The best critique which has yet appeared ... [Forçade] follows Currer Bell through every winding, discerns every point, discriminates every shade ... if I saw him, I would say 'you know me, Monsieur – I shall deem it an honour to know you'. I could not say so much to the mass of London critics ... My own Conscience I satisfy first ... if I further content and delight a Forçade, a Fonblanque [see No. 27] and a Thackeray my ambition had its ration (*LL*, iii, 42).

The passages omitted from this long article include general reflections on the current political troubles in France and a detailed account of the narrative in *Shirley*.

It is just a year since I was giving you an account of the novel which marked the debut of the author of *Shirley – Jane Eyre* [No. 21]. I remember it as a piece of literary treasure-trove. Reading *Jane Eyre* was the first intellectual pleasure I had enjoyed since that ugly February revolution. I liked the novel because one felt blowing through it a breath of youth, of something new and open, that freshness that rejoices the soul ... *Jane Eyre* was presented as an autobiography; but the author was unknown. Who was this Currer Bell? Was it a man or a woman, one person or a number of people? Some were quite sure it was a man: a woman could not have drawn the strong, harsh figure of Rochester. It was a syndicate of writers, according to others: books have appeared by Ellis and Acton Bell, and a volume of verse entitled the *Poems of Currer, Ellis and Acton Bell*. Some, better advised, supposed it to be a woman, wayward and spirited, who had done battle with life. The mystery and the rumours surrounding it seemed to herald the arrival of an English George Sand.

When an author's first book produces such a degree of excitement, his second work is awaited with impatient curiosity. The test is especially difficult in the case of authors like Currer Bell, whose first work is a work of passion ... As feeling, *Jane Eyre* had a poignant and ardent reality; as plot, it was constructed after the fashion of a castle in Spain. Those who are moved more by the truth of the characters and passions than by the likelihood of the events were therefore impatient to see whether, in his second book, Currer Bell would not correct the least regrettable of his faults at the expense of his better qualities.

There was another interest in the new novel awaited from Currer Bell. *Jane Eyre* bore the accent of revolt against certain social conventions and contained aspirations to independence which frightened conservative critics who saw them as a threat ... Those writers who stand guard over the traditional values of English society were harsh in their denunciation of these tendencies. *Jane Eyre* was reproached with having been intended as an attack on marriage and the social order ...

Here then are three questions for *Shirley* to answer: Is Currer Bell a woman? Does the quality of *Shirley* fulfil the promise of *Jane Eyre*? Is Currer Bell really one of those bold and rebellious spirits so rightly mistrusted by law-abiding citizens in these unquiet times?

In the first place, Currer Bell is a woman: this is definitively proved by *Shirley*. The novel abounds in female characters which only a woman could have touched in with such delicacy and variety. The cause of women is defended throughout the book with a conviction and a skill perfectly characteristic of those who are pleading their own cause. As a picture of society, the novel could have been called *Shirley, or the condition of women in the English middle-class* ...

I do not know Yorkshire, where Currer Bell has set *Shirley*; but though the area and the society do not appear to be of a kind likely to prove very attractive to a Frenchman, I would willingly spend a month there if I could see a chapter of *Shirley* enacted each day, if I could live among people as agreeable, original and curious as those with which Currer Bell has peopled his novel, and if I could be admitted to the lively, energetic, positive, poetic and fanciful conversations that fill the book . . .

All these scenes, all these figures, described with such minute precision, have their charm; but, according to French ideas at least, the diffuseness that this entails will always be a defect. I know that the simplest details of everyday life leave in the reticent mind poetic impressions that hang in the memory like Dutch interiors in a gallery . . . English novelists are in the habit of introducing such pictures into their work. From Richardson on, they have embroidered their simple tales on this abundant but monotonous canvas . . .

This time, Currer Bell has not relieved the tedium of the action with the gusts of passion that swept through *Jane Eyre*. There are fewer improbabilities in *Shirley*; there is more observation in the study of the characters, more skill in the handling of the scenes, more art perhaps in the style; too bad, it is a second novel; I prefer the first. Currer Bell has, however, retained one of the most piquant spices that enlivened his first book and has even increased the dose here and there: the moral freedom, the spirit of insubordination, the impulses of revolt against certain social conventions. The final passage of *Shirley* is an ironical challenge to those who censured the morality of *Jane Eyre*: 'The story is told. I think I now see the judicious reader putting on his spectacles to look for the moral. It would be an insult to his sagacity to offer directions. I only say, God speed him in the quest.' In telling the story of *Shirley*, we shall see for ourselves whether the book has a moral and whether the moral is defective; but first of all we may touch for a moment on the great crime with which Currer Bell will certainly be charged: his denigration of marriage. When you learn the extent of our author's peccadillo, you will certainly agree that a society frightened at so little can have small cause to fear for the security of its morals.

In our time, novelists in France have attacked marriage so fiercely, so consistently and from so many sides that it might well be wondered whether a French novel could be written in which marriage was respected. In England, there is not a single novel in which marriage has been treated with irreverence or bitterness. Are English morals therefore more pure than ours? Have English novelists, in their hearts, more veneration than our writers for the most sacred of social institutions? I will not attempt to discuss the question on this lofty plane: I will content myself with a simple literary observation. There is one difference between English novels and French novels which has gone almost unnoticed. English novels are set before marriage, French novels after. This difference is merely the counterpart of a difference in society itself. In France, a woman's personality, her freedom, her life, begin only with marriage; we know that in England, on the contrary, the conventions endow young girls with an independence of character, of will and behaviour, which tends rather to be curtailed when they marry. In both countries, marriage cuts the life of women in two: in England the age of romance for women ends with marriage, in France it begins. For Frenchwomen, marriage is the key to knowledge of the world, the exercise of responsibility, movement, adventure and the first desires and illusions that come with freedom. So it is that in our country one meets with more romantic young women than romantic young girls. In both countries the novel has naturally mirrored the romantic age of women. In England it takes the young girl up to the day of her marriage and consequently does not impinge directly upon marriage itself. In France, on the contrary, by the same token, the novel is set in marriage, it tears aside the veil of mystery and lays bare all the characteristics, all the wounds inflicted by marriage, it exacerbates all its vicissitudes and in so doing necessarily violates its sanctity and hastens the corruption of morals by overstimulated imaginings.

If, with the high quality of his mind and the vigour of his pen, Currer Bell . . . had written the drama or the dark comedy of conjugal union, if he had set his novel, as the French do, between salon and boudoir, between boudoir and alcove, I could understand the violent censure that greeted his protests against a few of the fatal bonds of marriage; but mere satirical shafts inspired at random by a particular situation do not deserve such severe treatment. Currer Bell has in no way altered the general order of the English novel. In *Shirley*, the old people complain about marriage, it is true, but the young marry just the same. Currer Bell could not have a better answer for his critics.

[continues with a detailed account of the narrative]

I said at the outset that the finest and most characteristic qualities of this book defied analysis. The drama, in fact . . . is made up of the thousand moral situations, the thousand infinitesimal feelings and sweet passions which slowly intertwine and grow out of the least incidents, the least contact between the characters in scenes of everyday life which are minutely etched. It must be understood that in literature of this type, the chief merit is the perfection of the detail, the fidelity with which the design is traced, the liveliness and variety of the style, the naturalness, fire, spirit and fantasy of the dialogue, in short a certain general grace which invites and retains the reader's attention in the familiar labyrinth through which he is led to the denouement. Currer Bell possesses these qualities in a high degree. His language has the freshness, the unexpectedness, the mixture of poetic fervour and positive firmness, the richness and precision, the boldness and strength which make his inspiration so original. It is a style that cheers the mind like something fresh, alert and sane. Except for the spontaneous impetus, the original vitality that courses through every line of *Jane Eyre*, the pure passion of the first novel which is not to be found again in *Shirley*, the qualities of his second book retain for Currer Bell the high place he instantly achieved among English novelists.

You will have been able at least, from the fragments I have quoted, to judge the spirit of *Shirley*. Those people who found fault with the fact that in *Jane Eyre* a rich gentleman married a governess will also find it highly revolutionary for a rich heiress to marry a schoolmaster. In England, and one can only envy the English for it, they are still concerned with scruples of this kind. There is really very little cause for alarm concerning the anger or bitterness shown by Currer Bell towards certain conditions of marriage . . . It would be less unjust to accuse Currer Bell of preaching a spirit of insubordination, the absolute legitimacy of desire and blind faith in freedom . . .

Currer Bell's morality seems to be inspired by a powerful and exuberant individualism. It is possible that this may contain the principle of a wrong and fatal tendency; but we in France are so little given to this type of exaggeration, we have erred so far in the other direction, that instead of blaming Currer Bell I could wish rather that he could communicate his fault to us.[1] Our vice is to have drained all personality by idiotic outbursts against individualism and by a stupid apotheosis of the equity, reason and power of the masses . . . If good comes out of evil, if one excess breeds its opposite, then it is time for us in France to defend the rights of the individual.

[1] See headnote to No. 21.

34. Catherine Winkworth, from a letter

5 December 1849

Letter to Eliza Paterson, from *Memorials of Two Sisters, Susanna and Catherine Winkworth*, ed. Margaret J. Shaen (1908, reprinted *LL*, iii, 55). The writer had recently learnt the identity of 'Currer Bell' from her friend Mrs Gaskell (see *The Letters of Mrs Gaskell* (1966), 93, and No. 29 above).

So you like *Shirley* better than *Jane Eyre*; so do I, in some points. In power and in descriptions of scenery, there is nothing in *Shirley* which seems to me to come up to some parts of *Jane Eyre*, but then there is nothing also in *Shirley* like the disagreeable parts of *Jane Eyre*. The book is infinitely more original and full of character than the ordinary run of novels – it belongs quite to a higher class – but it is also infinitely below such as *Mary Barton* and *Deerbrook*.[1] Caroline and Mr Helstone are thoroughly good characters. Shirley and Mrs Pryor are good ideas, but badly worked out – the rest seem to me all exaggerated – Oh, Hortense Moore should be excepted, she is good, too. The conversations seem to me astonishingly poor; here and there comes an eloquent speech, as in Shirley's conversation with Mr Yorke, but the stiffness and dryness of the whole book, its utter want of brilliancy of wit or humour, and the unhappy tone of all the meditations make it altogether painful. That is not, however, so much to be wondered at, when one knows that the author is herself threatened with consumption at this time, and has lost her two sisters, Ellis and Acton Bell, by it. Their real name is Brontë.

[1] Harriet Martineau's *Deerbrook* had appeared in 1839.

35. From an unsigned review, *The Times*

7 December 1849

Charlotte's distress on reading this is recorded in Mrs Gaskell's *Life* (chapter 18). She wrote to Ellen Nussey on 9 December 1849, 'The thundering *Times* has attacked me savagely' (*LL*, iii, 56), and to Williams on 19 March 1850:

The acrimony . . . has proved its own antidote . . . I think it has little weight up here in the North . . . the generous pride many of the Yorkshire people have taken in the matter has been such as to awake and claim my gratitude . . . The very curates, poor fellows! show no resentment (*LL*, iii, 89–90).

The omitted passages are written in the same style as the rest and incorporate extracts, chiefly from the love scenes, to illustrate the novel's dependence on improbability and exaggeration.

With all its faults, *Jane Eyre* was a remarkable production. The volumes were disfigured by coarseness; in the final development of the plot the craft of the bookmaker was more commendable than the subtle and fine working of the master; after the story had been told, pages and pages of unnecessary matter were forced upon the reader to complete three imperfect volumes, and to spoil two which could hardly be improved; yet, in spite of these and other obvious imperfections, *Jane Eyre* had as good a claim as any work of fiction to the esteem and approval of the novel-reading public of 1848. Freshness and originality, truth and passion, singular felicity in the description of natural scenery and in the analyzation of human thought, enabled this tale to stand boldly out from the mass of such compositions, and to assume its own place in the bright, but at the best evanescent, field of romantic literature. The early scenes of *Jane Eyre* are not to be surpassed . . .

Struck, however, as we could not but be by the raciness and ability of the work . . . we perused the last words of the story with the conviction that the second effort of the author would not surpass the first . . . The circulating libraries heave with the materials of which the third volume of *Jane Eyre* is composed; you may ransack the same mausoleums in vain for such living stuff as animates the other two. How is this, if it be not that the full heart having too soon told its tale had nothing more to offer ... Currer Bell, whomsoever that name may represent, during two thirds of her performance obeyed the impulses and necessities of her mind ... for the remaining third she was the mere bond slave of the book-sellers. Emboldened by triumph and eager to extend renown, she starts from the point at which she left off, and at the beginning of another winter presents us with ... a novel made up of third volumes, a book to be read upon the strength of the book that was formerly devoured ...

Shirley is very clever, as a matter of course. It could not be otherwise. The pencil that sketched Jane Eyre and filled up the broad outlines of Rochester's fine form, could not be worn down to the stump by one vigorous performance. The faculty of graphic description, the strong imagination, the fervid and masculine diction, the analytic skill, all remain visible as before, but are thrown away upon a structure that bears no likeness to actual life, and affords no satisfaction or pleasure to those who survey it. The story of *Shirley* may be told in a couple of pages, yet a more artificial and unnatural history cannot be conceived; and what is true of the plot is even more applicable to the dramatis personæ. The characters, from Miss Shirley Keeldar down to the smallest boy in the narrative, are manufactured for the occasion. As for Miss Shirley, her metaphysical acumen and argumentative prowess are beyond all praise, whilst the dialectics of the precocious 12 year old would do honour to John Stuart Mill himself.

[continues with a sardonic account of the main events of the story]

What can be more commonplace and puerile than all this? Caroline's illness, again, is conducted in the true spirit of melancholy mediocrity. She wastes away, she has a cough, a fever, she loses her appetite, her strength; it is difficult to say what is not the matter with her. Disappointed love never in its bitterest working perpetrated a hundredth part of the mischief it produced in the delicate frame of Caroline Helstone ... We confess that, looking upon the skeleton and withered form of Miss Helstone in bed, we could on no rational theory account for the abiding fever and the continued atrophy. Neither were we prepared for her magical recovery; she gets well as unaccountably as she falls ill. The violence of either process is overpowering, whilst the manner of her contrivance is really feebler than the patient herself. It is not with such sheer blotches of pain that Scott depicts nature and Fielding finds his way to the heart. It is not by such tricks of the trade that Jane Eyre won sympathy and sorrow for her sufferings.

Mark how Caroline Helstone gets suddenly well after she had been as suddenly carried to the very edge of the grave! . . . At the close of volume the first Shirley Keeldar, the owner of Mr. Moore's mill, a young heiress with a thousand-a-year, appears on the stage with her governess. Both are originals in a way. The former belongs to a class of heroines whom Shakespeare had in his eye when he drew Katherine and Beatrice; whom Scott immortalized in Diana Vernon . . . Miss Keeldar has much of the metal of the sterner sex beneath her soft skin, and asserts intellectual independence as woman's right. There is always danger in dealing with such delicate commodity . . . one awkward touch spoils the picture and yields a caricature. One of our first views of Miss Shirley is when she is standing 'quietly near a window looking at the grand cedar on her lawn and watching a bird on one of its lower boughs. Presently she begins to chirrup to the bird; soon her chirrup grows clearer; ere long she is whistling: the whistle strikes into a tune'; by and by she tells us that she intends to take instruction in the art of keeping accounts, and 'won't she prove a precious pupil!' Then she calls upon a young curate 'to evacuate a certain room,' for it is no place for him; she thinks it easy 'to palaver about the degradation of charity,' but thinks charity a wholesome practice nevertheless; she 'sees a newspaper every day, and two of a Sunday; she reads the leading articles and the foreign intelligence, and looks over the market prices; in short, she reads just what gentlemen read; she hates needlework, but is tenacious of her book, her study being the rug, her seat a foot stool, or perhaps only the carpet at the governess's feet.' . . .

It is necessary to add that a more subtle metaphysician, a more acute reasoner, a finer talker, and a more skilful tactitian, never existed than the lovely and fascinating Miss Keeldar, and the portrait, so accordant with all that we see and hear of in every day life, is complete.

The governess is a very different personage . . . But that Mrs. Pryor is called upon to effect a most important denouement in the history, we should be glad to spare ourselves all mention of her existence, for a drearier gentlewoman it has seldom been our lot to meet . . .

Caroline Helstone's love affair . . . is not the only one found in this book . . . Lovemaking, in one shape or another, is going on from the first page to the last, and as soon as one couple quits the scene another comes on to entertain the spectators with dialogues such as no mortal lovers ever spoke, or, we trust, ever will speak in Miss Currer Bell's books again . . .

Shirley was evidently written during the recent pestilence.[1] Our author has but one prescription for all her lovers. Louis Moore by accident hears that Miss Keeldar has a tender regard for his manufacturing brother, and, in spite of his 'gift to proceed peacefully,' he too is smitten with a fever and sent off to bed. Louis is more fortunate than Caroline. Instead of having a maundering old woman for his nurse, Shirley herself comes, angel-like if not maiden-like, to his couch. She brings him grapes, which he sternly refuses, because he says 'Mrs. Gill gives him toast and water, which he likes much better,' but he gets rapidly well nevertheless. No sooner does he rally than he sends for Miss Shirley to the school-room, bids her sit down close to him, 'to put back her hair,' and to listen to him whilst he repeats in French the exciting narrative of the marriage of Genius and Humanity. Having performed this task he talks in the usual magniloquent style for a page or two. Miss Keeldar does the same, and we are all left just as forward as we found ourselves before the fever came on . . .

Need we protract the story or proceed with extracts? Two marriages take place one fine day in August. Such, of course, is the end of a very simple story, which it has taken a thousand octavo pages to tell, and to tell most cumbrously and artificially . . . Indeed, the whole structure seems erected for the simple purpose of enabling these creatures of the author's brain – certainly not of our every-day world – to do nothing, but talk after the manner of such purely intellectual companions.

And it would be unjust to the fair authoress – for lady she is, let who will say to the contrary – if we did not allow that at times the talk is worthy of her genius and that gems of rare thought and glorious passion shine here and there throughout her volumes. But the infrequent brilliancy seems but to make more evident and unsightly the surrounding gloom. *Shirley* is not a picture of real life; it is not a work that contains the elements of popularity, that will grapple with the heart of mankind and compel its homage. It is a mental exercise that can bring its author no profit, and will not extend by the measure of an inch her previous well-deserved success. Millions understood her before – she may count by units those who will appreciate her now. *Jane Eyre* was not a pure romance, *Shirley* is at once the most high flown and the stalest of fictions.

---

[1] The cholera epidemic which broke out in 1847.

36. From an unsigned review,
Fraser's Magazine

December 1849, xl, 691–4

Probably written by W. G. Clark (1821–78), the Shakespearian scholar and founder of the Clark lectureship in English Literature at Trinity College, Cambridge; the authorship is suggested by the reference in A. F. Hort, *Letters of F. J. A. Hort* (1896), i, 147 (Clark was Hort's tutor). The review forms part of an article on 'New Novels' and notices along with *Shirley* Catherine Sinclair's *Sir Edward Graham; or, Railway Speculators*, Janet W. Wilkinson's *Hands not Hearts*, G. P. R. James's *The Woodman, A Romance* and Alexander Baillie Cochrane's *Ernest Vane*. Clark is representative in finding *Shirley* a disappointment after *Jane Eyre* (reviewed in *Fraser's* by G. H. Lewes; see No. 14). The omitted passages include a brief outline of the situation in the novel and various illustrative extracts.

For some time back there has been accumulating upon our table a mass of volumes in the post octavo form; got up in various ways according to the varying tastes of the publishers, though all equally marked with the generic and unmistakeable character of novelism. Over and over again we essayed to approach the heap, and over and over again our heart failed us . . . At last our eyes chanced to catch the neatly lettered back of *Shirley*, and the spell came over us.

Well do we remember how we took up *Jane Eyre* one winter's evening, somewhat piqued at the extravagant commendations we had heard, and sternly resolved to be as critical as Croker. But as we read on we forgot both commendations and criticism, identified ourselves with Jane in all her troubles, and finally married Mr. Rochester about four in the morning. So to us the announcement of another novel by the same hand was exciting. We refused an invitation for the 31st October, and shut ourselves up with *Shirley* – there were four of us, three volumes and the present writer – determined on a sleepless night. But, no, about eleven o'clock we began our habitual series of yawns, then lighted the bed-candle, went to bed, fell asleep, and did not resume *Shirley* even in our dreams. It was three days before we finished it. Not that it is a dull book by any means – indeed nearly every page contains something worth reading; but the story is deficient in connexion and interest. In *Jane Eyre* the reader accompanied the heroine throughout, saw with her eyes, heard with her ears, in short, lived over again one life, and regarded other persons and things from *one* point of view – the heroine's personality. On this ground an autobiography well done is sure of creating the most absorbing interest. But a story in the narrative form requires much more artistic skill in its construction. It is required to concentrate the interest upon one person or one group, while regarding that person or group, as well as the subordinate groups, *ab extra*. The threads of intrigue must be so crossed and interlaced as to form but one pattern. Otherwise the reader's mind will have to make a painful effort (a sort of squint) to see two or more distinct things at once. Again, care must be taken lest by too great elaboration in the details you diminish the prominence of your central group – like Maclise in his pictures. On that foot halts Sir Walter Scott himself. Who cares for Waverley, though the author does call him our hero? *Our* hero is the Baron of Bradwardine. Now in the book before us there are characters that occupy much more space than the eponymous of the tale. It might as well have been called *Caroline*, or *Helstone*, as far as that goes. Shirley, the heroine – for, masculine as the name sounds, Shirley is a woman – does not appear at all till the end of the first volume; and the hero only drops in at the end of the second. Besides, the stage is overcrowded with characters too insignificant to be named in the bills; some, mere sceneshifters and candle-snuffers, have no business to be there at all. Let us count up the *dramatis personæ*, those who are actually named, and have a *rôle* in the play. Over and above the four young people whose marriage, somehow or other, is the object of the book, we have the Yorke family, seven; the Sympsons, five; the Nunnelys, four; the Sykeses, eight (we believe); three vicars; three curates; three Methodist preachers; three old maids; one governess; one patiently suffering operative and family; five or six riotous ditto; besides gardeners, grooms, housekeepers, housemaids, &c. Nearly a hundred characters to be disposed of! it could not be done, even with the 'resources' of Covent Garden ...

The first volume will be unintelligible to most people, for it is half in French and half in broad Yorkshire. There are many who know 'Yorkshire,' and don't know French; and others, we fear, who know French and don't know Yorkshire. For our own part, we possess a decent knowledge of both, and we venture to pronounce that the French and the Yorkshire are both excellent. Most writers seem to imagine that they can produce a genuine Yorkshireman by cutting off the final consonant of every word he utters. Currer Bell's Yorkshiremen are not such Cockneyfied automata. Their thoughts are as provincial as their speech. We would bet a trifle that the author is a Yorkshirewoman; – Yorkshire, we are sure; woman, we think. Why not Miss Currer Bell as well as Miss Shirley Keeldar? She knows women by their brains and hearts, men by their foreheads and chests. She (we cannot help begging the question) depicts women often quaint and odd, but never unnatural, while the men are not unfrequently ranting mountebanks, who, instead of the toleration and applause the author claims for them, would infallibly, in real life, be 'cut' or kicked, or shut up in a madhouse. The author, then, is a woman. Moreover she is, or has been, a governess. She is always good on the topic of governesses, their rights and wrongs. Jane Eyre was (as all the world knows) a governess, so (we beg to inform the world) is Mrs. Pryor, and Caroline Helstone wants to be one. Again, she has a sympathy with the cognate class of private tutors. As in her former book she made the governess marry her 'master,' so, in the present, the tutor has a love affair with his lady pupil (we are not going to tell how it ends) . . .

With regard to the male characters, it is not so much of the original conception as of the working out of that conception, that we wish to complain. The rough sketch is often as correct as it is daring – psychologically faultless. Take, for example, Robert Gerard Moore, as the author first presents him to us, half English, half French, a bankrupt mill-owner and a thorough gentleman, a furious Radical who detests the mob, a man of taste and refinement with his heart and soul in the dyeing-vats, lavishly generous, yet ready to sell his love for gold. The author deserves credit for no common skill in combining, out of such dissonant elements, a harmonious whole. But would this being ever have spoken as he does in chap. v.? Would he have carried on a colloquy with Joe Scott, his foreman, in that Alexander-the-Great style? Surely not.

Take, again, the instance in [chapter 15]. Donne is a curate (no monster, be it remarked, only a fool fresh from college); he asks Miss

Shirley Keeldar for a subscription to some school. She gives five pounds.

[quotes the subsequent scene]

We could point out many other instances of violence and exaggeration; the little Yorkes, lads in their early teens, talk like Master Betterton on the stage. The little Miss Yorkes, too, have an Ossianic style of their own, and a marvellous acquaintance with Johnson's *Dictionary*. We rather suspect that the author is planning another novel on the fate and fortunes of the Yorke family. For all their ranting, we should like to hear more of them ... We may have led our readers to suppose that this is but a mediocre novel, a thing which *our* columns join gods and men in prohibiting. But, in truth, it is a good novel dashed with a fair human alloy of bad; and we, with the amiable instinct of our craft, have fixed on the weak part ... We like the book as a whole. On the whole, we like its spirit. The author does not, after the manner of some we could name, plead the cause of the poor by indiscriminate slander of the rich, nor advocate religious tolerance by a display of the bitterest sectarian hatred.

The character of Shirley is excellently conceived and well sustained. And how touching is the story of Caroline ...

We sympathize with the author's general charity, with her special love for the old country, the old Church, and the old Duke; we kindle with her fervid bursts of eloquence, and recognize the truth of her pictures from life.

As to the morality, it must be a very precise prude, indeed, who could ferret out an innuendo in *Shirley*.

37. Unsigned notice, *Church of England Quarterly Review*

January 1850, xxvii, 224–5

See Introduction, p. 26. Charlotte acknowledged on 3 January 1850, 'the receipt of the *Morning Chronicle* with a good review – and of the *Church of England Quarterly* and the *Westminster* [No. 38] with bad ones' (*LL*, iii, 63).

Our readers will, perhaps, remember that in our notice of the maiden work of this author, while we felt it to be our duty to impugn its tendency, we unhesitatingly admitted its talent: upon which, if we may judge by the various reviews that have come under our notice, there would not appear to be much difference of opinion. There was an originality and freshness about the former work which at once captivated the fancy and chained the attention, and to which its sudden popularity is chiefly attributable. We dealt with it in a somewhat more matter-of-fact manner, testing its merits by its tendency – a criterion which it especially becomes a periodical like our own to adopt. And if we were to measure the talent employed by the excitement produced, we should assign to the work before us a lower grade of intellectual merit than *Jane Eyre*: but the excitement created is a false standard, and we repudiate it accordingly. *Shirley*, inferior in point of interest to its predecessor, is written with equal power; while its moral tendency, as a whole, is not open to serious objection. There is occasionally an irreverent use of scriptural phrases and a wresting, to common-place purposes, the examples in Scripture history, which it is impossible to pass without grave condemnation. The author's acquaintance with religion is of the most superficial description; or, if its truths are in his heart, they do not, from any evidence furnished by the pages before us, find their way to his lips. There is a vagueness about his expressions on religious subjects which leaves us in doubt if he have any defined notions of religion at all. The first chapter introduces us to three curates, whom we can readily imagine to be types of the working clergy of a bye-gone day; but, we believe, happily without parallel in our own times: and, therefore, we will not quarrel with our author on the fidelity of their portraiture; but he might as well have left them to rest in their graves for any benefit, in the way of example, their resuscitation is likely to effect. Beyond what we have stated, we have nothing to object to the *tendency* of these volumes; while, on the other and brighter side, there is much to commend in the way of powerful and picturesque writing which takes them out of, and above, the category of the novels of the day. The female characters are sketched with a delicacy for which we look in vain in his former work: indeed, the absence of it is the *blot* of *Jane Eyre*: and, while the interest of the story is generally well sustained, the *dénouement* is veiled with greater tact than is usually employed in modern fictions. The great master in this rare art was Banim[1] – it was the characteristic of every story he wrote – and even the great Sir Walter, unequalled in every other attribute of a good novelist, was behind the romancist of the sister island in this particular. If the popularity of *Shirley* be less than that of *Jane Eyre*, we shall grieve for the taste of the public, because it deserves more. If *Shirley* have less of sparkle it has not less of power, while it enlists the purer sympathies of our nature, instead of appealing to its baser passions: and this constitutes the distinction between the former and the present production of Currer Bell.

[1] See No. 63, p. 231, n. 2.

83. Unsigned notice, *Westminster Review*

January 1850, lii, 407–19

See No. 37. Preceded by a review of Bulwer Lytton's *The Caxtons. A Family Picture* (1849).

Shirley is a novel which has floated into circulation on the popularity of its predecessors. *Jane Eyre* was a remarkable production. There was originality in its construction, skill in the delineation of character, and great artistic power in the development of a plot – in itself a simple one, but wrought up to scenes of breathless interest. Moreover, it touched, although with great delicacy, upon certain ethical problems which were certain to lead to controversy, and which at once compelled every one to read the book who would take any part in the evening discussions of a lady's drawing-room. *Shirley* is nothing of this: it has a merit of its own; but must be regarded as a feeble effort – the effort, however, of a writer who shows in every page that she could do better if she would, but has been only half inspired by her subject. She tells us, in her preface, that we are not to expect a thrilling narrative, and she keeps her word. The character and incidents of the first volume fade from the memory before we have fairly got to the end; and, what is more provoking, in the third, when our attention ought to be at least fairly aroused, we can lay down the book in the middle of a chapter, – and go to sleep. This failure arises from the interest being too much diffused. The *dramatis personæ* are numerous, and many of them of no assistance to the plot; while in *Jane Eyre* the interest was concentrated upon the heroine and Mrs Rochester. *Shirley* begins with an extravagant portraiture of three young curates (very much in the nature of a caricature, but without bitterness), who, after supplying the materials of a few chapters, are quietly dropped, as of no further use to the author. Then we have two heroines where one would suffice – sweetness and gentleness in the person of Caroline Helston, and fire and animation in the person of Shirley – the latter a clever heiress, cleverly drawn. Both these ladies are in love with two brothers, without knowing it. One of the brothers is in the same predicament; and the other, who is intended as the soul of honour, only just escapes the condemnation of the reader as a bashful blockhead. When, in the *dénouement*, they all get comfortably married, we are glad that they have at last found out the state of each other's minds, but wonder they did not sooner make the same discovery.

Shirley is to some extent a reminiscence of *Mary Barton*.[1] The tale, like *Mary Barton*, is laid in the manufacturing districts, and the wrongs and rights of mill-owners and their operatives form the subsidiary parts of the story. In treating of these questions, a discriminating and a kindly spirit is evinced, with a manifold desire to heal the antagonism of classes; and we are glad to notice generally this great improvement in modern works of fiction.

[1] See No. 29.

39. G. H. Lewes, from an unsigned review, *Edinburgh Review*

January 1850, xci, 153–73

The review by George Lewes which provoked Charlotte's cele-brated outburst (exact date unknown), 'I can be on guard against my enemies, but God deliver me from my friends!' (*LL*, iii, 67). See Introduction, pp. 7, 24 and also her letter to Williams on 10 January 1850: '[The review] is very brutal and savage. I am not angry with Lewes, but I wish in future he would leave me alone, and not write what makes me feel so cold and sick' (*LL*, iii, 66). Lewes's views about the restricted achievement of women as creative artists have their own interest as an indication of current attitudes. He returned to the subject of women's special giftedness in writing novels in his 'The Lady Novelists' written for the *Westminster Review* in 1852 (vol. lviii, 129–41), that is in the year in which he first came to know George Eliot, whose career as a novelist owed much to his initial encouragement.

Men in general, when serious and not gallant, are slow to admit woman even to an equality with themselves; and the prevalent opinion certainly is that women are inferior in respect of intellect . . . We very much doubt, however, whether sufficient data exist for any safe or confident decision. For the position of women in society has never yet been – perhaps never can be – such as to give fair play to their capa-bilities. It is true, no doubt, that none of them have yet attained to the highest eminence in the highest departments of intellect. They have had no Shakespeare, no Bacon, no Newton, no Milton, no Raphael, no Mozart, no Watt, no Burke. But while this is admitted, it is surely not to be forgotten that these are the few who have carried off the high prizes to which millions of men were equally qualified by their training and education to aspire, and for which, by their actual pursuits, they may be held to have been contending; while the number of women who have had either the benefit of such training, or the incitement of such pursuits, has been comparatively insignificant . . .

The grand function of woman, it must always be recollected, is, and ever must be, Maternity . . . consequently for twenty years of the best years of their lives – those very years in which men either rear the grand fabric or lay the solid foundations of their fame and fortune – women are mainly occupied by the cares, the duties, the enjoyments and the sufferings of maternity. During large parts of these years, too, their bodily health is generally so broken and precarious as to incapacitate them for any strenuous exertion; and, health apart, the greater portion of their time, thoughts, interests, and anxieties ought to be, and generally are, centered in the care and the training of their children. But how could such occupations consort with the intense and unremitting studies which seared the eyeballs of Milton, and for a time unsettled even the powerful brain of Newton? High art and science always require the whole man; and never yield their great prizes but to the devotion of a life . . .

If it be said that these considerations only apply to wives and mothers, and ought not to carry along with them any disqualification of virgins or childless widows, the answer is, that as Nature qualifies and apparently designs all women to be mothers, it is impossible to know who are to escape that destiny, till it is too late to begin the training necessary for artists, scholars, or politicians. On the other hand, too much stress has, we think, been laid on man's superiority in physical strength . . . It should be remembered that, in the great contentions of man with man, it has not been physical strength which has generally carried the day; and . . . it is precisely in that art which demands least employment of physical force, viz. – music, that the apparent inferiority of women is most marked and unaccountable . . . it is an art that is cultivated by all women who have the least aptitude for it; and in which, as far as mere taste and execution are concerned, many more women than men are actually found to excel. But, as composers, they have never attained any distinction. They have often been great, indeed, as performers . . .

It is in literature, however, that women have most distinguished themselves; and probably because hundreds have cultivated literature, for one that has cultivated science or art. Their list of names in this department is a list that would rank high even among literary males. Madame de Stael was certainly as powerful a writer as any man of her age or country; and whatever may be the errors of George Sand's opinions, she is almost without a rival in eloquence, power, and invention.[1] Mrs Hemans, Miss Edgeworth, Miss Baillie, Miss Austen, Mrs Norton, Miss Mitford, Miss Landon, are second only to the first-rate men of their day; and would probably have ranked even higher, had they not been too solicitous about male excellence, – had they not often written from the man's point of view, instead of from the woman's . . . women have too often thought but of rivalling men. It is their boast to be mistaken for men, – instead of speaking sincerely and energetically as women. So true is this, that in the department where they have least followed men, and spoken more as women, – we mean in Fiction, – their success has been greatest. Not to mention other names, surely no man has surpassed Miss Austen as a delineator of common life? Her range, to be sure, is limited; but her art is perfect. She does not touch those profounder and more impassioned chords which vibrate to the heart's core – never ascends to its grand or heroic movements, nor descends to its deeper throes and agonies; but in all she attempts she is uniformly and completely successful.

It is curious too, and worthy of a passing remark, that women have achieved success in every department of fiction but that of humour. They deal, no doubt, in sly humorous touches often enough; but the broad provinces of that great domain are almost uninvaded by them . . . Compare Miss Austen, Miss Ferriar, and Miss Edgeworth, with the lusty mirth and riotous humour of Shakespeare, Rabelais, Butler, Swift, Fielding, Smollett, or Dickens and Thackeray. It is like comparing a quiet smile with the 'inextinguishable laughter' of the Homeric gods! So also on the stage, – there have been comic actresses of incomparable merit, lively, pleasant, humorous women . . . but they have no comic energy . . .

But we . . . fear our readers may have been wondering how we have wandered away . . . from the theme which seemed to be suggested by the title of the work now before us. The explanation and apology is, that we take Currer Bell to be one of the most remarkable of female writers; and believe it is now scarcely a secret that Currer Bell is the pseudonym of a woman. An eminent contemporary, indeed, has employed the sharp vivacity of a female pen to prove 'upon irresistible evidence' that *Jane Eyre* must be the work of a man.[2] But all that 'irresistible evidence' is set aside by the simple fact that Currer Bell is a woman. We never, for our own parts, had a moment's doubt on the subject. That Jane herself was drawn by a woman's delicate hand, and

[1] See Introduction, pp. 23–4.
[2] A reference to the review in the *Quarterly* (No. 22).

that Rochester equally betrayed the sex of the artist, was to our minds so obvious, as absolutely to shut our ears to all the evidence which could be adduced by the erudition even of a marchande des modes ... The fair and genious critic was misled by her own acuteness in the perception of details; and misled also in some other way, and more uncharitably, in concluding that the author of *Jane Eyre* was a heathen educated among heathens, – the fact being, that the authoress is the daughter of a clergyman!

This question of authorship ... helped to keep up the excitement about *Jane Eyre*; but, independently of that title to notoriety, it is certain that, for many years, there had been no work of such power, piquancy, and originality. Its very faults were faults on the side of vigour; and its beauties were all original. The grand secret of its success, however – as of all genuine and lasting success – was its reality. From out the depths of a sorrowing experience, here was a voice speaking to the experience of thousands. The aspects of external nature, too, were painted with equal fidelity ... Faults enough the book has undoubtedly: faults of conception, faults of taste, faults of ignorance, but in spite of all, it remains a book of singular fascination. A more masculine book, in the sense of vigour, was never written. Indeed that vigour often amounts to coarseness, – and is certainly the very antipode to 'lady like.'

This same over-masculine vigour is even more prominent in *Shirley*, and does not increase the pleasantness of the book ... Power it has unquestionably, and interest too, of a peculiar sort; but not the agreeableness of a work of art ... Nature speaks to us distinctly enough, but she does not speak sweetly. She is in her stern and sombre mood, and we see only her dreary aspects.[1]

Shirley is inferior to *Jane Eyre* in several important points. It is not quite so true; and it is not so fascinating. It does not so rivet the reader's attention, nor hurry him through all obstacles of improbability, with so keen a sympathy in its reality. It is even coarser in texture, too, and not unfrequently flippant; while the characters are almost all disagreeable, and exhibit intolerable rudeness of manner. In *Jane Eyre* life was viewed from the standing point of individual experience; in *Shirley* that standing point is frequently abandoned, and the artist paints only a panorama of which she, as well as you, are but spectators. Hence the unity of *Jane Eyre* in spite of its clumsy and improbable contrivances, was great and effective: the fire of one passion fused the

[1] But see John Skelton in his review of 1857, p. 340 below.

discordant materials into one mould. But in *Shirley* all unity, in consequence of defective art, is wanting. There is no passionate link; nor is there any artistic fusion, or intergrowth, by which one part evolves itself from another. Hence its falling-off in interest, coherent movement, and life. The book may be laid down at any chapter, and almost any chapter might be omitted. The various scenes are gathered up into three volumes, – they have not grown into a work. The characters often need a justification for their introduction; as in the case of the three Curates, who are offensive, uninstructive, and unamusing. That they are not inventions, however, we feel persuaded. For nothing but a strong sense of their reality could have seduced the authoress into such a mistake as admitting them at all. We are confident she has seen them, known them, despised them; and therefore she paints them! although they have no relation with the story, have no interest in themselves, and cannot be accepted as types of a class, – for they are not Curates but boors: and although not inventions, we must be permitted to say that they are not true. Some such objections the authoress seems indeed to have anticipated; and thus towards the close of her work defends herself against it. 'Note well! wherever you present the actual simple truth, it is somehow always denounced as a lie: they disown it, cast it off, throw it on the parish; whereas the product of your imagination, the mere figment, the sheer fiction, is adopted, petted, proper, sweetly natural' [chapter 37]. Now Currer Bell, we fear, has here fallen into a vulgar error ... Truth is never rejected, unless it be truth so exceptional as to stagger our belief; and in that case the artist is wrong to employ it, without so preparing our minds that we might receive it unquestioned. The coinage of imagination, on the other hand, is not accepted because it departs from the actual truth, but only because it presents the recognised attributes of our nature in new and striking combinations. If it falsify these attributes, or the known laws of their associations, the fiction is at once pronounced to be monstrous, and is rejected. Art, in short, deals with the broad principles of human nature, not with idiosyncracies: and, although it requires an experience of life both comprehensive and profound, to enable us to say with confidence, that 'this motive is unnatural,' or 'that passion is untrue,' it requires no great experience to say 'this character has not the air of reality; it may be copied from nature, but it does not look so.' Were Currer Bell's defence allowable, all criticism must be silenced at once. An author has only to say that his characters are copied from nature, and the discussion is closed. But though the portraits may be like the oddities from whom they are copied, they are faulty as works of art, if they strike all who never met with these oddities, as unnatural . . .

Again we say that *Shirley* cannot be received as a work of art. It is not a picture; but a portfolio of random sketches for one or more pictures. The authoress never seems distinctly to have made up her mind as to what she was to do; whether to describe the habits and manners of Yorkshire and its social aspects in the days of King Lud, or to paint a character, or to tell a love story. All are by turns attempted and abandoned; and the book consequently moves slowly, and by starts – leaving behind it no distinct or satisfactory impression. Power is stamped on various parts of it; power unmistakeable, but often mis-applied. Currer Bell has much yet to learn, – and, especially, the discipline of her own tumultuous energies. She must learn also to sacrifice a little of her Yorkshire roughness to the demands of good taste: neither saturating her writings with such rudeness and offensive harshness, nor suffering her style to wander into such vulgarities as would be inexcusable – even in a man. No good critic will object to the homeliness of natural diction, or to the racy flavour of conversa-tional idiom; but every one must object to such phrases as 'Miss Mary, getting up the steam in her turn, now asked,' etc., or as 'making hard-handed worsted spinners cash up to the tune of four or five hundred per cent.,' or as 'Malone much chagrined at hearing him pipe up in most superior style;' all which phrases occur within the space of about a dozen pages, and that not in dialogue, but in the authoress's own narrative. And while touching on this minor, yet not trivial point, we may also venture a word of quiet remonstrance against a most in-appropriate obtrusion of French phrases. When Gerard Moore and his sister talk in French, which the authoress translates, it surely is not allowable to leave scraps of French in the translation. A French word or two may be introduced now and then on account of some peculiar fitness, but Currer Bell's use of the language is little better than that of the 'fashionable' novelists. To speak of a grandmother as *'une grand'-mere,'* and of treacle as *'melasse,'* or of a young lady being angry as *'courroucée,'* gives an air of affectation to the style strangely at variance with the frankness of its general tone.

We scarcely know what to say to the impertinence which has been allowed to mingle so largely with the manners, even of the favourite actors in this drama. Their frequent harshness and rudeness is something which startles on a first reading, and, on a second, is quite inexplicable. Is this correct as regards Yorkshire, or is the fault with the artist? In one place she speaks with indignant scorn of those who find fault with Yorkshire manners; and defies the 'most refined of cockneys to presume' to do such a thing. 'Taken as they ought to be,' she assures us, 'the majority of the lads and lasses of the West Riding are gentlemen and ladies, every inch of them: and it is only against the weak affectation and futile pomposity of a would-be aristocrat that they ever turn mutinous.' This is very possible; but we must in that case strongly protest against Currer Bell's portraits being understood to be resemblances; for they are, one and all, given to break out and misbehave themselves upon very small provocation. The manner and language of Shirley towards her guardian passes all permission. Even the gentle, timid, shrinking Caroline enters the lists with the odious Mrs Yorke, and the two ladies talk at each other, in a style which, to southern ears, sounds both marvellous and alarming. But, to quit this tone of remonstrance, – which after all is a compliment, for it shows how seriously we treat the great talents of the writer, – let us cordially praise the real freshness, vividness, and fidelity, with which most of the characters and scenes are depicted.

[quotes the description of a rainy night from the opening of chapter 2, and from chapter 13 Caroline's images of the sea]

Similar power is manifested in the delineation of character: her eye is quick, her hand certain. With a few brief vigorous touches the picture starts into distinctness. Old Helstone, the copper-faced little Cossack parson, straight as a ramrod, keen as a kite; Yorke, the hard, queer, clever, parson-hating, radical-Gentleman; the benevolent Hall; the fluttering, good, irresolute Mrs Pryor; the patient, frugal, beneficent old maid, Miss Ainley; Hortense and Moore, and the Sympson family, – are all set with so much life before us, that we seem to see them moving through the rooms and across the moor . . .

The two heroes of the book, however, – for there are two – are not agreeable characters; nor are they felicitously drawn. They have both something sordid in their minds, and repulsive in their demeanour . . . A hero may be faulty, erring, imperfect; but he must not be sordid, mean, wanting in the statelier virtues of our kind. Rochester was far more to be respected than this Robert Moore! Nor is Louis Moore much better. On any generous view of life there is almost as much sordidness in his exaggerated notions of Shirley's wealth, and of the distance it creates between his soul and hers, as there is in Robert's direct and positive greed of the money . . .

The heroines are more lovable. Shirley, if she did not occasionally . . . display something in her behaviour, which, with every allowance for Yorkshire plainness, does imply want of breeding . . . would be irresistible . . . But if Shirley is, on the whole, a happy creation, Caroline Helstone, though sometimes remarkably sweet and engaging, is – if we may venture to say so – a failure. Currer Bell is exceedingly scornful on the chapter of heroines drawn by men. The cleverest and acutest of our sex, she says, are often under the strangest illusions about women – we do not read them in their true light; we constantly misapprehend them, both for good and evil.[1] Very possible. But we suspect that female artists are by no means exempt from mistakes quite as egregious when they delineate their sex; nay, we venture to say, that Mrs Pryor and Caroline Helstone are as untrue to the universal laws of our common nature as if they had been drawn by the clumsy hand of a male . . .

Mrs Pryor . . . belies the most indisputable laws of our nature, in becoming an unnatural mother, – from some absurd prepossession that her child must be bad, wicked, and the cause of anguish to her, because it is pretty! . . . Really this is midsummer madness! Before the child had shown whether its beauty did conceal perversity, the mother shuts her heart against it! Currer Bell! if under your heart had ever stirred a child, if to your bosom a babe had ever been pressed, – that mysterious part of your being, towards which all the rest of it was drawn, in which your whole soul was transported and absorbed, – never could you have imagined such a falsehood as that! It is indeed conceivable – under some peculiar circumstances, and with peculiar dispositions – that the loathing of the wife for the husband, might extend to the child, because it was the husband's child; the horror and hate being so intense as to turn back the natural current of maternal instincts; but to suppose that the mere beauty and 'aristocratic' air of an infant could so wrest out of its place a woman's heart, – supposing her not irretrievably insane, – and for eighteen years keep a mother from her child, is to outrage all that we know of human nature.[2]

Not quite so glaring, and yet very glaring, is the want of truth in Caroline . . . any one examining *Shirley* as a work of art, must be struck with want of keeping in making the gentle, shy, not highly cultivated Caroline talk from time to time in the strain of Currer Bell herself rather than in the strain of Helstone's little niece. We could cite several examples: the most striking perhaps is that long soliloquy at

---

[1] See chapter 20, 'If men could see us as we really are . . .'
[1] See Introduction, p. 24.

pages 269–274 of the second volume [chapter 10], upon the condition of women, – in which Caroline takes a leaf out of Miss Martineau's book. The whole passage, though full both of thought and of eloquence, is almost ludicrously out of place. The apostrophes to the King of Israel, to the fathers of Yorkshire, and to the men of England, might have rounded a period in one of the authoress's own perorations; but to introduce them into a soliloquy by Caroline Helstone is an offence at once against art and against nature ... A grave error, – one implying greater forgetfulness of dramatic reality and probability, – is the conduct of Caroline in her love for Moore. The mystery kept up between the two girls is the trick of a vulgar novelist. Shirley must have set Caroline's mind at rest; must have said, 'Don't be unhappy about Moore and me; I have no love for him – nor he for me.' Instead of this, she is allowed to encourage the delusion which she cannot but perceive in Caroline's mind; but what is more incredible still, Caroline – who believes that Moore loves Shirley and will marry her – never once feels the sharp and terrible pang of jealousy! ... a girl like Caroline ... might be willing even to submit in silence to the torture of her disappointment ... and a fine theme might this have afforded for some profound psychological probings ... But Caroline Helstone merely bows her head in meekness, and loves and clings to Shirley all the more; never has even a moment's rebellion against her, and behaves like pattern young ladies in 'good' books!

We have been more than once disturbed by what looked like wilful departures from probability in this novel ... we are willing to allow the imagination full sweep; but we demand, that into whatever region it carries us, it must be at least consistent: if we are to travel into fairy land, it must be in a fairy equipage, not in a Hansom's cab ... Thus in the second volume there is a really remarkable tirade about Milton's Eve: as an eloquent rhapsody we can scarcely admire it too much, but to be asked to believe that it was offered in a quiet conversation between two young ladies, destroys half our pleasure. Let the reader judge for himself.

[quotes chapter 18, 'The grey church, and greyer tombs ... if we are both silent']

Then, again, there is Louis Moore writing long narratives in his note-book. What he writes is often striking; and had the authoress only thought of making him keep a journal, probability would have been sufficiently saved. But, instead of that, she obliges him to sit down in Shirley's room, draw out a note-book, and proceed to write very circumstantially, for our benefit, what every one feels he would never have written at all ... All that Louis Moore writes might have been better told by the authoress, without subterfuge. We may make the same remark as to Robert Moore's confession of his scene with Shirley. Its effect would be far truer. The attack on the Mill, too, instead of being described in the natural course of the narrative, is told us in snatches of dialogue between the two girls; who, in utter defiance of all vraisemblance, are calm spectators of that which they could not have seen. It is scarcely worth while to point out the several details in this scene, which betray a female and inexperienced hand. Incident is not the forte of Currer Bell. If her invention were in any degree equal to her powers of execution, (with a little more judgment and practice,) she would stand alone among novelists; but in invention she is as yet only an artisan, not an artist.

As a proof of this poverty of invention we may refer again to the singular awkwardness of making Moore confess to Yorke the interview he had had with Shirley, and the terms on which he had offered to marry her. The scene is unquestionably very powerful; but it loses much of its power by the mode in which it is presented. Had it been narrated in the due course of the story, as in any other writer's hands, it would have been, perhaps, the most striking scene in the book. Such as it is, we give it, as another specimen of the peculiar character and ability displayed in it.

[chapter 30, 'I looked at her Yorke ... And thus we were severed']

Did space permit, we would gladly quote the anagnorisis of Mother and Daughter, – in its simple, humble, thrilling naturalness one of the most touching and feminine scenes in our literature; or that wild, imaginative, and original picture of the Mermaid, which shows the writer to have the true poetic power – the power, namely, of creating new life out of old materials.

[quotes chapter 13, 'I suppose you expect to see mermaids... she dives']

Our closing word shall be one of exhortation. Schiller, writing to Goethe about Madame de Stael's *Corinne* [1807] says, 'This person wants every thing that is graceful in a woman; and, nevertheless, the faults of her book are altogether womanly faults. She steps out of her sex – without elevating herself above it.' This brief and pregnant criticism is quite as applicable to Currer Bell: for she, too, has genius enough to create a great name for herself; and if we seem to have insisted too gravely on her faults, it is only because we are ourselves sufficiently her admirers to be most desirous to see her remove these blemishes from her writings, and take the rank within her reach. She has extraordinary power – but let her remember that '*on tombe du côté où l'on penche!*'

40. Tom Arnold, from a letter

15 August 1851

Unpublished letter to his sister Mary from Hobart Town, New Zealand (now in the Alexander Turnbull Library, Wellington). Charlotte first met Mrs Arnold and Matthew Arnold in December 1850 (see headnote to No. 89). The family's early interest in her work is indicated by William Arnold's unpublished letter of 1 August 1848 to his mother from India: 'Lying on the bed behind me is a man called Cavenagh, reading *Jane Eyre*, the book you were all talking about when I left home [i.e. at the beginning of 1848], which I have just got hold of and am going to read.' For Matthew Arnold on *Villette* see No. 53.

You speak, or rather Mother speaks, of having met Miss Brontë. I have read *Jane Eyre* and *Shirley* and like both, the first perhaps the best. Shirley is ill put together, as if the plot had been very imperfectly pre-arranged, so that some portions of it are not in keeping with the whole. But 'Caroline' is very sweet and attractive, nor do I by any means dislike 'Shirley'. A bracing North-Country air of power and simplicity united prevails in both books. After I had read (in August last year) the first two chapters of *Jane Eyre*, I felt certain that the writer was a woman, and from the North; and no rumour to the contrary – and there were many – could move me.

VILLETTE

The novel was ready to appear early in January, but publication was delayed until 28 January to give Mrs Gaskell's *Ruth* 'the start in the papers, daily and weekly, also ... leave free to her all the February magazines' (*LL*, iv, 34). In spite of this precaution, and although Charlotte felt 'comparisons to be odious' (*LL*, iv, 34), parallels were frequently drawn between her work and Mrs Gaskell's and in some cases the two novels were reviewed together (see Nos 55, 56).

41. Harriet Martineau, from an unsigned review, *Daily News*

3 February 1853, 2

For Charlotte's angry reaction to this review by Harriet Martineau see Introduction, pp. 27-8. See also her letter to George Smith of 7 February 1853:

Undoubtedly written by Miss Martineau ... I have received a letter from her precisely to the same effect ... Her letter only differs ... in being severe to the point of injustice; her eulogy is also more highly wrought (*LL*, iv, 44),

and that to Harriet Martineau (date unknown) in reply to her objections to the handling of love in *Villette*:

I know what *love* is as I understand it; and if man or woman should be ashamed of feeling such love, then there is nothing right, noble, faithful, truthful, unselfish in this earth (*LL*, iv, 42).

The ruptured friendship did not prevent Harriet Martineau from paying a warm tribute to Charlotte in her obituary notice (No. 88).

Everything written by 'Currer Bell' is remarkable. She can touch nothing without leaving on it the stamp of originality. Of her three books, this is perhaps the strangest, the most astonishing, though not the best. The sustained ability is perhaps greater in *Villette* than in its two predecessors, there being no intervals of weakness, except in the form of a few passages, chiefly episodical, of over-wrought writing, which, though evidently a sincere endeavour to express real feeling, are not felt to be congenial, or very intelligible, in the midst of so much that is strong and clear. In regard to interest, we think that this book will be pronounced inferior to *Jane Eyre* and superior to *Shirley*. In point of construction it is superior to both; and this is a vast gain and a great encouragement to hope for future benefits from the same hand which shall surpass any yet given. The whole three volumes are crowded with beauties – with the good things for which we look to the clear sight, deep feeling and singular, though not extensive, experience of life which we associate with the name of 'Currer Bell'. But under all, through all, over all, is felt a drawback, of which we were anxious before, but which is terribly aggravated here – the book is almost intolerably painful. We are wont to say, when we read narratives which are made up of the external woes of life, such as may and do happen every day, but are never congregated in one experience – that the author has no right to make readers so miserable. We do not know whether the right will be admitted in the present case, on the ground of the woes not being external; but certainly we ourselves have felt inclined to rebel against the pain, and, perhaps on account of protraction, are disposed to deny its necessity and truth. With all her objectivity, 'Currer Bell' here afflicts us with an amount of subjective misery which we may fairly remonstrate against; and she allows us no respite – even while treating us with humour, with charming description and the presence of those whom she herself regards as the good and gay. In truth, there is scarcely anybody that is good – serenely and cheerfully good, and the gaiety has pain in it. An atmosphere of pain hangs about the whole, forbidding that repose which we hold to be essential to the true presentment of any large portion of life and experience. In this pervading pain, the book reminds us of Balzac; and so it does in the prevalence of one tendency, or one idea, throughout the whole conception and action. All the female characters, in all their thoughts and lives, are full of one thing, or are regarded by the reader in the light of that one thought – love. It begins with the child of six years old, at the opening – a charming picture – and it closes with it at the last page; and, so dominant is this idea – so incessant is the writer's tendency to describe the need of being loved, that the heroine, who tells her own story, leaves the reader at last under the uncomfortable impression of her having either entertained a double love, or allowed one to supersede another without notification of the transition. It is not thus in real life. There are substantial, heartfelt interests for women of all ages, and under ordinary circumstances, quite apart from love: there is an absence of introspection, an unconsciousness, a repose in women's lives – unless under peculiarly unfortunate circumstances – of which we find no admission in this book; and to the absence of it, may be attributed some of the criticism which the book will meet from readers who are not prudes, but whose reason and taste will reject the assumption that events and characters are to be regarded through the medium of one passion only.

And here ends all demur. We have thought it right to indicate clearly the two faults in the book, which it is scarcely probable that anyone will deny. Abstractions made of these, all else is power, skill and interest. The freshness will be complete to readers who know none but English novels. Those who are familiar with Balzac may be reminded, by the sharp distinction of the pictured life, place and circumstance, of some of the best of his tales: but there is nothing borrowed; nothing that we might not as well have had if 'Currer Bell' had never read a line of Balzac – which may very likely be the case.[1] As far as we know, the life of a foreign *pension* (Belgian, evidently) and of a third-rate capital, with its half provincial population and proceedings, is new in purely English literature; and most lifelike and spirited it is. The humour which peeps out in the names – the court of Labassecour, with its heir-apparent, the Duc of Dindoneau – the Professors Boissec and Rochemorte – and so forth – is felt throughout, though there is not a touch of lightheartedness from end to end. The presence of the heroine in that capital and *pension* is strangely managed; and so is the gathering of her British friends around her there; but, that strangeness surmounted, the picture of their lives is admirable. The reader must go to the book for it; for it fills two volumes and a half out of the three. The heroine, Lucy Snowe, tells her own story. Every

[1] In her letter to George Smith of 7 February 1853 Charlotte angrily denied having read Balzac, but in fact she had been introduced to his work in 1850 by G. H. Lewes; see her letter to him of 17 October 1850, 'Balzac was for me quite a new author, and in making his acquaintance, through ... *Modeste Mignon* and *Illusions Perdues* ... by-and-by I seemed ... to discover with delight where his force lay ... still ... I like George Sand better ... her brain is larger – her heart warmer' (*LL*, iii, 172–3).

reader of *Jane Eyre* will be glad to see the autobiographical form returned to. Lucy may be thought a younger, feebler sister of Jane.
There is just enough resemblance for that – but she has not Jane's
charm of mental and moral health, and consequent repose. She is in a
state of chronic nervous fever for the most part; is usually silent and
suffering; when she speaks, speaks in enigmas or in raillery, and now
and then breaks out under the torture of passion; but she acts admirably
– with readiness, sense, conscience and kindliness. Still we do not wonder that she loved more than she was beloved, and the love at last
would be surprising enough, if love could ever be so. Perhaps Pauline
and her father are the best-drawn characters in the book, where all are
more or less admirably delineated. We are not aware that there is one
failure.

A striking peculiarity comes out in the third volume, striking from
one so large and liberal, so removed from ordinary social prejudices
as we have been accustomed to think 'Currer Bell'. She goes out of
her way to express a passionate hatred of Romanism. It is not the calm
disapproval of a ritual religion, such as we should have expected from
her, ensuing upon a presentment of her own better faith. The religion
she envokes is itself but a dark and doubtful refuge from the pain which
impels the invocation; while the Catholicism on which she enlarges
is even virulently reprobated. We do not exactly see the moral necessity for this (there is no artistical necessity) and we are rather sorry for
it, occurring as it does at a time when catholics and protestants hate
each other quite sufficiently; and in a mode which will not affect
conversion. A better advocacy of protestantism would have been to
show that it can give rest to the weary and heavy laden; whereas it
seems to yield no comfort in return for every variety of sorrowful
invocation. To the deep undertone of suffering frequent expression is
given in such passages as this – beautiful in the wording but otherwise
most painful.

[quotes chapter 24, 'Now a letter like that . . . soothe or comprehend
him']

We cannot help looking forward still to other and higher gifts from
this singular mind and powerful pen. When we feel that there is no
decay of power here and think what an accession there will be when
the cheerfulness of health comes in with its bracing influence, we trust
we have only to wait to have such a boon as *Jane Eyre* gives us warrant
to expect, and which 'Currer Bell' alone can give.

42. From an unsigned review, *Examiner*

5 February 1853, 84-5

Possibly by Albany Fonblanque or John Forster; see Nos 10, 27.
Charlotte wrote to George Smith on 7 February 1853:

I ought to be ... very thankful [for the reviews] ... That in the *Examiner*
is better than I expected, and that in the *Literary Gazette* [No. 43] is as good
as any author can look for. Somebody also sent me the *Nonconformist*
with a favourable review (*LL*, iv, 44).

This novel amply sustains the fame of the author of *Jane Eyre* and
Shirley as an original and powerful writer. Though the plot is very
slight, and the whole work if it had been one-fourth shorter might still
have filled the orthodox three volumes, the pleasure it affords to the
reader never flags. The men, women, and children who figure throughout it, have flesh and blood in them. All are worked out heartily, in
such a way as to evince a very keen spirit of observation on the author's
part, and a fine sense of the picturesque in character. There is not an
actor in the story, from M. Paul in the foreground who fills chapters,
to Rosine the portress at a *Pensionnat de Demoiselles* who fills paragraphs, whom any reader can regard as a mere thing of words. Often
with humour, and always with skill and truth, the people with whom
we have to do here are presented to us, so that we know them, mind
and body, and recognise out of our own daily experience the fitness of
each body for the kind of mind that dwells in it ...

The one defect of the book, a similar defect to those which we have
had occasion to point out in its predecessors, will be to most people as
apparent as its many and extraordinary merits. We touch upon it with
respect, because we find it difficult to disconnect from it a feeling of the
bitterness of experience actually undergone, and that a real heart
throbs at such times under the veil of Lucy Snowe. We do not know
that it is so, but the world brings much trial to many of us, and if the
author be numbered among those who have been sorely tried, she
may feel that she has cause to accuse fate, to account happiness an

accident of life to some who are more fortunate than others, to lapse occasionally into a tone of irony a little harder than is just and now and then to give vent to a little morbid wail. Her faith seems to be expressed in this passage –

'Oh, Doctor John – I shudder at the thought of being liable to such an illusion! It seemed so real. Is there no cure? – no preventive?'

'Happiness is the cure – a cheerful mind the preventive: cultivate both.'

No mockery in this world ever sounds to me so hollow as that of being told to *cultivate* happiness. What does such advice mean? Happiness is not a potato, to be planted in mould, and tilled with manure. Happiness is a glory shining far down upon us out of Heaven. She is a divine dew which the soul, on certain of its summer mornings, feels dropping upon it from the amaranth bloom and golden fruitage of Paradise.

'Cultivate happiness!' I said briefly to the doctor: 'do *you* cultivate happiness? How do you manage?'

'I am a cheerful fellow by nature: and then ill-luck has never dogged me. Adversity gave me and my mother one passing scowl and brush, but we defied her, or rather laughed at her, and she went by.'

'There is no cultivation in all this.' [chapter 22]

Now it is quite certain that if anybody be wedded to the theory that 'happiness is a glory shining far down upon us out of heaven' and that it 'is not a potato', to be cultivated, he or she, after a day of severe trouble, may sit down and wait for the far glory, and wait and wail until the end of life. Exertion is the indispensable condition of all healthy life, mental or bodily; sluggish despondency is nothing but disease. The social and moral faculties improve by cultivation, like the intellectual; we need never forget griefs, but we can break ourselves, if we please, of any habit of keeping our old sorrows obstinately in the gangway of our thoughts, in opposition to the active efforts made by nature, our good housekeeper, to put them carefully and tenderly aside in places where they may be seen without being perpetually tumbled over. The grievers have always their answer ready . . . They say with a sigh, 'Ah, you do not know. *You* never have been tried as we have.' . . . We do not include wholly the author of *Villette* among these wailers, for there is nothing sullen in her composition; she bears no ill-will to the world about her; she paints men and women no worse than they are, but on the whole perhaps rather better; she is prompt to detect good qualities that lie concealed. Except one selfish and vain Parisian governess, there is nobody depicted in *Villette* who is not rather a good person than otherwise. The majority are pleasant and love-worthy people; vanities are mocked, but in a fair, just way; and there is much more smile than heartache in the entire story. But Lucy Snowe deals now and then in needlessly tragical apostrophes. Every now and then, in a determined way, some dirge to the burden of 'I can't be happy' sounds from within; and in the last page of the book, when happiness is placed within her reach, and it was in the power of the disposing author of the book to close her story with a charming satisfying picture, which she really does elaborately paint, – she daubs her brush across it, and upon the last page spoils it all for no artistic purpose whatsoever, and to the sure vexation of all lookers-on.

In the next edition of *Villette* we should like very much to see the last page altered, and to find all the apostrophes expunged, together with all passages written in the same key as the following:

[quotes from chapter 12, 'I did long, achingly . . . repellent as she too often is']

The omission of such passages as this would be extremely easy, and would save readers the pains of skipping them, which they will inevitably do after experience of one or two. They are in no way necessary to the story, and are out of harmony with the true, large spirit of humour and good feeling, which prevails, except at these odd and occasional times, throughout the book.

We now turn gladly to the abundant charms and pleasures of this delightful novel.

[quotes extensively, including descriptions of Paulina, Ginevra Fanshawe and Paul Emanuel]

We might . . . have gone on quoting thus through a great number of columns, for we desire heartily to commend this novel in the way that it is best commended – by examples of its quality . . . Reserving the objection that we have already made, we can praise *Villette* as a most pleasant, a most admirably written novel, everywhere original, everywhere shrewd, and, at heart, everywhere kindly.

43. From an unsigned review, *Literary Gazette*

5 February 1853, 123–5

See No. 42. The omitted passages outline the story, giving substantial extracts from the account of Paulina's childhood (chapters 1–3) and Mrs Marchmont's story (chapter 4).

We had occasion a fortnight since to regret that the authoress of *Mary Barton* should peril her reputation by publishing a novel so thoroughly commonplace as *Ruth*, and we confess to taking up *Villette* with some apprehension that it might afford us a similar cause of regret. *Shirley* had not sustained its author's fame, and it would have grieved us to find that she had a second time fallen short of the standard of *Jane Eyre*. But the perusal of a few chapters sufficed to dispel the apprehension, and we laid down the book with the conviction that the warmest admirers of *Jane Eyre* – in which class we rank ourselves – will find in it a most satisfactory confirmation of Currer Bell's genius. This book would have made her famous, had she not been so already. It retrieves all the ground she lost in *Shirley*, and it will engage a wider circle of admirers than *Jane Eyre*, for it has all the best qualities of that remarkable book, untarnished, or but slightly so, by its defects.

There is throughout a charm of freshness which is infinitely delightful . . . The thoughts are the writer's own thoughts, – the words fit the very sentiment to be expressed with a nicety and a force which at once delight and surprise. The characters are types of classes; but each so thoroughly individualized, that the reader sees them, and enters into their peculiarities as if actually in contact with them . . . The incidents may not be very striking, nor the plot very cunningly masked, but neither are hackneyed, and we are too much engaged with the mental history of the various actors to feel any deficiency on this score. Brain and heart are both held in suspense by the fascinating power of the writer; and when we lay down the book we feel that we have derived from it a large addition to the stock of persons and images which are henceforth to be permanently remembered.

The form of the story, as in *Jane Eyre*, is autobiographical ... The elements of the characters are the same – great sensibility, great natural lovingness, and great independence, subdued by misfortune, and constrained to the severest self-control by the necessity of circumstances. Both are void of personal attractions, both subject to the emotions of love in an unusual degree, and both attract and are attracted by ugly men, through the influence of nearly the same qualities. Here, however, the resemblance ceases, and the circumstances into which Lucy Snowe is thrown are so entirely different from those of Jane Eyre; and the man she loves – M. Paul Emanuel, Professor of Literature – so unlike Mr. Rochester, that the common points of resemblance do not press unpleasantly upon the reader ...

It is not in the story, as we have already indicated, that the strength of this book lies. The experiences of a friendless girl as governess in a boarding-house at Brussels, which is obviously the *Villette* of the book, afford no great scope for exciting incident; but they furnish full play for that masterly delineation of character and analysis of emotion in which the writer excels. The characters are not numerous, but they are all new. The mistress of the boarding-house, Madame Beck, – with her catlike tread, her ever-wakeful eye, her composure, which no crisis can ruffle – is such a creation as only the hand of original genius could successfully portray. All the nice shades which secure respect, and almost liking, amidst so much to excite aversion, are touched by the delicacy of an observer whose eye and pencil no characteristic can escape ... These qualities are indeed conspicuous through all the characters. They are all of that mingled yarn which life presents – none all good, none all bad – and we therefore take them into our acquaintance as if we had known them. The impression left upon the mind by the heroine herself is precisely of this description. To few will she appear, on first acquaintance, loveable. There is a hardness and cold self-possession upon the surface of her character, somewhat repelling; and it is only when you see, by degrees, into its depths, when she flashes upon you revelations of emotion and suffering akin to the deepest you have yourself experienced, and when you feel what a glow of tenderness and loving-kindness is burning under the unattractive and frigid exterior, that you admit her into your heart. But when you do see these things, and can estimate the severity of the trial which she undergoes and overcomes, your respect and your affection are both at her disposal, though you may feel no desire to dispute with M. Paul Emanuel the possession of such a mistress. It is with the same sort of judgment that we regard all the other characters, thinking of them as real people, whom we have known, nor can we better express our admiration of the novelist's genius than by this admission. When she wearies, if she wearies at all, for a more deliberate perusal may suggest different considerations, it is in carrying her analysis of character upon occasion somewhat too far, and in dwelling too long upon the not peculiarly attractive qualities of M. Paul Emanuel, as displayed in his prelections at Madame Beck's seminary and elsewhere. These qualities in particular are dwelt upon with a lover's fondness, which, as such fondness will, rather tires those who do not partake it. Still the authoress may contend, and with some show of reason, that this detail is needful to give full effect to the good qualities of M. Emanuel, with which his fierce and domineering temper contrasts, and to make the reader accept him more cordially at the last. However this may be, cordially we do accept him, and it is, therefore, with a spirit for which we scarcely can forgive the authoress that we are left in doubt whether he returns in safety from Guadaloupe, to share with his demure fiery-souled bride in that charming house on the boulevard, to which we are introduced, and which was so daintily furnished by his thoughtful love.

This book is one to which we are disposed so heartily to recommend our readers, that it is of less moment, perhaps, we should illustrate our opinion by extracts. Indeed no extracts could give an adequate idea of its excellence. It must be read continuously, – we had almost said, studied, before its finest qualities can be appreciated. Premising this, we select a few passages, which may with least injury be detached from the context . . .

Currer Bell has lost none of that power of vividly describing natural objects and phenomena which distinguished *Jane Eyre*. With a few masterly touches, she can place a landscape living before you . . .

Of description this authoress is wisely sparing, but we never read one of her descriptions that we do not long for more. This book contains a few that are as good as Turner's to the mind's eye.

It would be easy to point out defects in the book, as, for example, the introduction of a phantom nun, who turns out to be a phantom of the Fitz-fulke kind, or some other improbable incident. The feelings of her heroine are also at times strained to an unnecessary pitch, and needless pain is inflicted by the uncertainty in which we are left as to M. Emanuel's death at the close.

Some traces, too, of the coarseness which occasionally disfigured

Currer Bell's former books still remain; but, viewed as a whole, there is so obvious an advance in refinement without loss of power, that it would be invidious to qualify the admiration with which *Villette* has inspired us by dwelling upon minor faults.

44. From an unsigned review, *Spectator*

12 February 1853, 155–6

See Introduction, p. 22.

Villette is Brussels, and Currer Bell might have called her new novel 'Passages from the Life of a Teacher in a Girls' School at Brussels, written by herself.' Of plot, strictly taken as a series of coherent events all leading to a common result, there is none; no more, at least, than there would be in two years of any person's life who had occupations and acquaintances, and told us about them. Of interesting scenes, and of well-drawn characters, there is, on the other hand, abundance; and these, though they fail to stimulate the curiosity of the reader like a well-constructed plot, sustain the attention, and keep up a pleasant emotion, from the first page to the last.

All the emotions excited by art are pleasant, even though their subject-matter be in itself painful; otherwise we should have hesitated in applying the term to the emotions caused by this book. For while the characters are various, happily conceived, and some of them painted with a truth of detail rarely surpassed, the centre figure – the girl who is supposed to write the book – is one who excites sympathies bitter-sweet, and in which there is little that is cheerful or consoling. Like Jane Eyre in her intense relish for affection, in her true-heartedness, in her great devotion to the small duties of her daily life, there is nothing about her of the real inward strength that made Jane's duties something of a compensation for the affection denied her. If it were not too harsh a word to be used of so good a girl as Miss Lucy Snowe, one might almost say that she took a savage delight in refusing to be comforted, in a position indeed of isolation and hardship, but one still that a large experience of mankind and the miseries incident to the lot of humanity would hardly pronounce to be by comparison either a miserable or a degraded lot. But this book, far more than *Jane Eyre*, sounds like a bitter complaint against the destiny of those women whom circumstances reduce to a necessity of working for their living by teaching, and who are debarred from the exercise of those affections which are indeed the crown of a woman's happiness, but which it is unwise and untrue to make indispensable to a calm enjoyment of life and to an honourable and useful employment of it. Nor do we think that the morbid sensibility attributed to Lucy Snowe is quite consistent with the strength of will, the daring resolution, the quiet power, the discretion and good sense, that are blended with it in Currer Bell's conception. Still less, perhaps, is such a quality, involving as it does a constant tormenting self-regard, to be found in common with clear insight into the characters and motives of others, and with the habit of minute observation, which, resulting in admirable and clear delineation, makes Lucy Snowe's autobiography so pleasant a book in all respects except the spasms of heart-agony she is too fond of showing herself in – we will not venture to hint of showing herself off in, for there is a terrible feeling of reality about them, which seems to say that they are but fictitious in form, the transcripts of a morbid but no less real personal experience.

But for this one fault in the central character – and even this may be true to nature, though to that exceptional nature which would prevent many persons from recognizing its truth – we have nothing but praise to bestow upon the characterization of this book . . . Mrs. Bretton and her son Dr. John, Madame Beck the mistress of the pensionnat at Brussels, M. Paul Emanuel professor of belles lettres, M. Home de Bassompierre and his charming little daughter, worthless pretty Ginevra Fanshawe, – we shall henceforth know them as if we had lived among them; and, bad or good, they are people worth knowing, for the skill of the painter if not for their own qualities. But the curious thing is, that the morbid feeling so predominant in the writer – the hunger of the heart which cannot obtain its daily bread, and will not make-believe that a stone is bread – does not in the least reflect itself upon these characters. They are as distinctly drawn, as finely appreciated, as if the soul of the writer were in perfect harmony with itself and with the world, and saw men and things with the correct glance of science, only warmed and made more piercing by a genial sympathy. It may therefore be conjectured, that the mind of Miss Lucy Snowe in writing the book had changed from the mood in which she passed through the scenes described in it; that a great calm had settled down upon the heart once so torn by storms; that a deep satisfaction, based upon experience and faith, had succeeded to the longing and distress of those earlier days.

Faith is indeed a very prominent feature in Miss Snowe's mind; more a religious than a theological faith; more a trust, a sentiment, and a hope, than a clearly-defined belief that could be stated in propositions. But truth is another feature, and she will not sacrifice truth to faith. When her experience is blank misery, she does not deny it, or slur it over, or belie it by shamming that she is happy. While her eyes turn upward with the agony that can find no resting-place on earth, she indulges no Pagan or Atheistical despair . . . She seems to think that the destiny of some human beings is to drink deep of this cup, and that no evasions, no attempts to make it out less bitter than it is, will turn aside the hand of the avenging angel, or cause that cup to be taken away one moment the sooner. We doubt the worldly philosophy of this view, as much as we are sure that it is not in any high sense Christian. It may, however, be a genuine effusion from an overstrained endurance – a sort of introverted Stoicism, which gives to the sufferer the strength of non-resistance and knowing the worst.

The characters that will most charm the readers of this book must be those of Miss de Bassompierre and M. Paul Emanuel; though the former is nearly as perfect as mortals ever can be; and the latter one of the oddest but most real mixtures of the good and disagreeable, of the generous and the little . . . The relation between this M. Paul and Lucy Snowe will recall both Rochester and Jane Eyre and Louis and Shirley; though the differences are striking, and the characters themselves have little resemblance. But all three positions have those elements in common which show them to be familiar to the writer, and favourable, in her opinion, for drawing out the characteristic points of her heroes and heroines . . .

The style of *Villette* has the same characteristics that distinguished Currer Bell's previous novels, – that clearness and power which are the result of mastery over the thoughts and feelings to be expressed, over the persons and scenes to be described. When the style becomes less pleasing, it is from an attempt to paint by highly figurative language the violent emotions of the heart. This is sometimes done at such length, and with so much obscurity from straining after figure and allusion, as to become tedious and to induce skipping.

45. G. H. Lewes, from an unsigned review, *Leader*

12 February 1853, 163–4

Lewes had founded the *Leader* with Thornton Hunt in 1850. His review expresses his renewed enthusiasm after his disappointment over *Shirley* (see No. 39 and Introduction, p. 24) and his obvious desire to assure the author that she is to be accepted thankfully '*as* she is'. What he calls his '*pièces justicatives*' include passages describing Paulina as a child (chapter 3), Lucy at Miss March- mont's (chapter 4), Reubens's 'Cleopatra' (chapter 19), Rachel (chapter 23), shorter extracts under the headings 'The Heart's Struggles', 'Physical and Moral Pain' and 'The Value of Rank and Station' (chapters 17, 24, 27), and, as an example of Charlotte's poetic style, lines on Paulina ('Her eyes were the eyes . . . as she grew in years' (chapter 24)). For Lewes's second review of *Villette*, see No. 55.

In Passion and Power – those noble twins of Genius – Currer Bell has no living rival, except George Sand. Hers is the passionate heart to feel, and the powerful brain to give feeling shape; and that is why she is so original, so fascinating. Faults she has, in abundance; they are so obvious, they lie so legible on the surface, that to notice them with more insistance than a passing allusion is the very wantonness of criticism. On a former occasion, and in another place, we remon- strated with her on these said faults, but we now feel that the lecture was idle. Why wander delighted among the craggy clefts and snowy solitudes of the Alps, complaining at the want of verdure and of flowers? In the presence of real Power why object to its not having the quiet lineaments of Grace? . . .

One may say of Currer Bell that her genius finds a fitting illustration in her heroes and heroines – her Rochesters and Jane Eyres. They are men and women of deep feelings, clear intellects, vehement tempers, bad manners, ungraceful, yet loveable persons. Their address is brusque, unpleasant, yet individual, direct, free from shams and conventions of all kinds. They outrage 'good taste', yet they fascinate. You dislike them at first, yet you learn to love them. The power that is in them makes its vehement way right to your heart. Propriety, ideal outline, good manners, good features, ordinary thought, ordinary speech, are not to be demanded of them. They are the Mirabeaus of romance;[1] and the idolatry of a nation follows the great gifts of a Mirabeau, let 'Propriety' look never so 'shocked'. It is the triumph of what is sterling over what is tinsel, of what is essential to human worth over what is collateral . . .

Villette has assuredly many faults, and novel readers, no less than critics, will have much to say thereon. More adroit 'construction', more breathless suspense, more thrilling incidents, and a more moving story, might easily have been manufactured by a far less active, inventive, passionate writer; but not such a book. Here, at any rate, is an *original book*. Every page, every paragraph, is sharp with *individuality*. It is Currer Bell speaking to you, not the Circulating Library reverberating echos. How *she* has looked at life, with a saddened, yet not vanquished soul; what *she* has thought, and felt, not what she thinks others will expect her to have thought and felt; *this* it is we read of here, and this it is which makes her writing welcome above almost every other writing. It has held us spell-bound.

Descending from generals to particulars, let us say that, considered in the light of a novel, it is a less interesting story than even *Shirley*. It wants the unity and progression of interest which made *Jane Eyre* so fascinating; but it is the book of a mind more conscious of its power. *Villette* is meant for Brussels. The greater part of the scenes pass in the Netherlands, not unhappily designated as *Labassecour*. People will wonder why this transparent disguise was adopted. We conjecture

---

[1] The colourful career of Honoré-Gabriel de Riquetti, Comte de Mirabeau, revolutionary orator and statesman, had been a topic of conversation since the publication of John Store Smith's *Mirabeau: A Life History* (1848). Charlotte first read this in June 1848 (see her letter thanking George Smith for sending a copy, *LL*, ii, 222) and in 1850 received another copy as a gift from the author (*LL*, iii, 81, 126).

that it was to prevent personal applications on the reader's part, and also to allow the writer a greater freedom as to details. The point is, however, very unimportant . . .

The story begins in England. Charming indeed the picture of Mrs Bretton's house, and the little love affair between Polly, a quaint child of six, and Graham, a youth of sixteen, who pets her as boys sometimes pet children. We hear this child objected to, and called 'unnatural'. To our experience, the child's character is perfectly consonant, and the only thing we could wish in the delineation is that which we miss in *all* portraits of quaint precocious children, – viz., a more vivid recollection of the childlike nonsense and whimsicality which *accompany* the demonstrations of feeling and intelligence . . . We purposely abstain from giving any hint of a story all will read; our extracts shall be *pièces justicatives* . . .

46. From an unsigned review, *Athenaeum*

12 February 1853, 186–8

See Charlotte's letter to George Smith on 16 February 1853 on 'the general tone of the notices so far':

My father seems pleased with them, and so am I . . . I must not tell you what I think of such reviews as that in the *Athenaeum*, lest you pronounce me fastidious and exacting (*LL*, iv, 46).

The review incorporates several extracts to illustrate the book 'as a work of Art and of power', including descriptions of the concert and of 'Vashti's' acting (chapters 20, 23) and scenes with Paul Emanuel (much admired by the reviewer for their vitality), notably from 'Monsieur's Fête' (chapter 29).

So curious a novel as *Villette* seldom comes before us, – and rarely one offering so much matter for remark. Its very outset exhibits an indifference to certain precepts of Art, singular in one who by artistic management alone interests us in an unpromising subject. *Villette* is a narrative of the heart-affairs of the English instructress and the Belgian professor of literature in a school at Brussels, – containing no combinations so exciting as those that in its author's memoirs of another teacher, *Jane Eyre*, rivetted some readers and shocked others. Yet, thrilling scenes there might have been in it had our authoress pleased. The *Benedick* to whom Lucy Snowe is *Beatrice* is a devout Roman Catholic educated by Jesuits. During a considerable portion of the story we are led to expect that the old well-thumbed case of conscience is going to be tried again, – and that having dealt with a Calvinistic missionary in *Jane Eyre*, Currer Bell is about to draw a full-length picture of a disciple of Loyola in *Villette*. But the idea is suggested – not fulfilled. Our authoress is superior to the nonsense and narrowness that call themselves religious controversy. She allows the peril of the position to be felt, – without entering on the covert rancour, the imperfect logic, and the inconclusive catastrophe which distinguish such polemics when they are made the theme of fiction. – We fancied, again, from certain indications, that something of supernatural awe and terror were to be evoked: – but as a sequel to these, Currer Bell has fairly turned round upon herself with a mockery little short of sarcasm. – The tale is merely one of the affections. It may be found in some places tedious, in some of its incidents trivial, – but it is remarkable as a picture of manners. A burning heart glows throughout it, and one brilliantly distinct character keeps it alive. – The oldest man, the sternest, and the most scientific, who is a genuine novel-reader, will find it hard to get out of Madame Beck's school when he has once entered there with Lucy Snowe, and made acquaintance with the snappish, choleric, vain, child-like, and noble-hearted arbiter of her destiny, M. Paul Emanuel.

Thus far we have had to recognize the artist's hand . . . We must now return to the fault . . . To adopt a musical phrase, the novel begins out of the key in which it is composed. In its first chapters interest is excited for a character who disappears during a large part of the story, and who returns to it merely as a second-rate figure. A character in truth, and not a caricature, is the little Paulina . . . We hoped that Currer Bell was going to trace out the girlhood, courtship, and matrimony of such a curious, elvish mite. Instead of this, towards the middle of the first volume the narrator steps into the part of heroine, with an inconsequence and abruptness that suggest change of plan after the tale was undertaken. From this point, we are once again invited to follow the struggles and sufferings of a solitary woman, – to listen to the confessions of a heart famishing for excitement and sympathy – at last finding Love, not 'among the rocks,' but in the midst of storm and contradiction. Currer Bell will be surprised to be told, that the burden of her Pindaric concerning 'Woman's mission' is virtually identical with that sarcastic and depreciating proverb (born among bachelor monks) which ranged Man's helpmate with the ass and the walnut-tree, as 'three things that do nothing rightly if not beaten'. But such is the case. – From the moment when M. Paul Emanuel begins to insult Miss Lucy Snowe, we give up her heart as gone . . . We know that the right man has only now come, and that the match when made will be one after Currer Bell's own heart. The recurrence of the same argument (with unimportant variations) in this writer's three novels would form a good thesis for a lecture in any court of Love where 'the sex' is honoured, not with Arcadian phrases, but with grave and simple truth. Fever, discontent, distress existing in a heart full of tenderness and a head guided by conscientiousness . . . of such material is composed the strange pathetic, painful revelation of Woman's nature thrice offered by a woman. Such a phase may – and possibly does – belong to our times. It may be inevitable that the tendency of female authorship should lean towards defence rather than deprecation: – but by perpetually setting it forth, the chances of healing, calming, strengthening, setting free, and placing aright the sufferer are not increased ... Currer Bell can bring off her heroine in triumph ... can find her a respectable shelter, without the slightest previous prospect, the first day that an unknown stranger sets foot in a foreign land, – can pilot her home through illuminated Brussels on a gala night without a rough word said to her, – can reward the frank declaration of her breaking heart by as frank reply, 'with healing on its wings.' But we fear that such sequences are to be found rather in the artist's chambers of faëry imagery than on the pages of Reality's record. Her books will drive many minds out among the breakers, – they will guide few to sure havens. Her talk is of duty, – her predilections lie with passion.

Enough of this homily, – necessary as it has seemed at a juncture when every poetess seems bent on being a preacher and a prophetess also. – Let us endeavour to justify our praise of *Villette* as a work of Art and of power, by an extract or two. But good illustrative passages such as are susceptible of being detached are hard to find in this novel. The confidential and intimate minuteness of its imaginary writer's confessions – the fragmentary way in which they stop, to be resumed at some later period, or to be eked out by collateral disclosures, – while they give to *Villette* the semblance of a real record, render its scenes more than ordinarily unmanageable. – An episodical passage or two tempt us ...[1]

By Lucy Snowe's notes of other experiences in which the irascibility, vanity, violence and childishness of this exigent little foreigner are relieved by traits of truth, simplicity, kindliness and self-sacrifice, her hero is brought before us with a vividness and a consistency rare even in male delineations of male characters so complex. Without precisely sympathizing, we are made to understand how in her case curiosity brings on fear, – and fear, respect, – and respect, confidence, – and confidence, affection. But there are 'lions in the path,' – a he-jesuit and a she-jesuit. The latter is Madame Beck, the school-mistress, – whose character also is one of the truest portraitures of foreign humanity by an English writer with which we are acquainted. Little less excellent,

[1] Concludes with Lucy's account of Paul Emanuel's fête.

in their secondary sphere, are, Graham Bretton, with his benign, warm, honourable worldliness (on account of that worldliness alone falling short of perfection), and Miss De Bassompierre – the little Paulina of the first chapters, in whom (as we have said) and not in the ill-looking and impassioned imaginary narrator, we had hoped to find the heroine of this novel. – To conclude, *Villette* is a book which will please much those whom it pleases at all. Allowing for some superfluity of rhetoric used in a manner which reminds us of the elder Miss Jewsbury – and for one or two rhapsodies, which might have been 'toned down' with advantage, – this tale is much better written than *Shirley*, the preceding one by its authoress.

47. From an unsigned review, *Critic*

15 February 1853, xii, 94–5

The rest of the review consists of an outline of the story and three extracts headed 'Miss Genevra Fanshawe', 'Monsieur Paul' and 'The Little Paulina' (chapters 9, 14, 1).

The present season has given us the largest and the richest supply of new novels[1] that has issued from the press during a similar period of time within our critical memory, which now extends over ten years. Every novelist of reputation has produced a fiction: few have failed to sustain the reputation previously achieved, and some have added to it. Among these latter we may class Miss Brontë, *alias* Currer Bell.

Not that *Villette* is so interesting a novel as *Jane Eyre*. Like *Shirley*, its claims to distinction are not in its story, but in its admirable delineations of character, in its powerful descriptions, in its wholesome vein of sentiment, in its spirit and vigour, and in the charm of a style that never grows tame and never permits the attention of the reader to flag

[1] Among them Catherine Gore's *The Dean's Daughter: or the days we live in* (1853), also reviewed here.

for a moment. We are aware that it was not to these qualities so much as to the attractions of its story that *Jane Eyre* owed its popularity; and if either *Shirley* or *Villette* had preceded instead of following that famous fiction, we doubt if it would have succeeded, for the vast majority of novel readers are certainly more moved by an exciting tale than by any amount of ability in the telling of it. But, fortunately for Miss Brontë, she made popularity by a plot, and she maintains her fame by good writing. Many who read the first for the story now read for the name of the writer; because not to have read is to be out of the fashion. Nevertheless we know that with some of these (and, we doubt not with more than choose to avow it) neither *Shirley* nor *Villette* are favourites; rather, they are voted heavy: the fact is, that they are *too good* – there is too much substance and thought in them for people who read novels for the story, skipping the dialogues and reflections.

Happily, our critical duty is to judge the novelist by a higher standard than that which tries the title to circulating-library popularity: it is our pleasant task to review the new novels as literary compositions, as the productions of artists, and as works of art; and therefore it is often our agreeable duty to praise highly what is not popular, and our painful one to find fault with what the young ladies and gentlemen in a quadrille declare to be charming.

Upon *Villette* we, at least, have no difficulty in pronouncing an opinion. Tried as a production of the intellect, it is entitled to take a very high place in the literature of fiction. It has not the thousand times repeated conventionalities of a commonplace novel, either in plot, or character, or incident, or dialogue; it is manifestly the offspring of an original and inventive mind, accustomed to think for itself. There is no 'bald, disjointed chat' in these pages; no mere words; none of the tinkling brass of phrase-makers; no swelling periods that enter the ear and die there, because they are sound only. For Miss Brontë has a full mind – she expresses its impulses, and utterances, and thoughts, because they are in her, and must come forth of her. She does not determine to write something, and then sit down and rack her brain for something to write about; but she has something in her mind which she wants to say, and therefore she writes. This difference in the origin of books can always be traced in them by an eye accustomed to criticism. The full mind is visible in the full page – we mean not the page of packed type, but of closely packed ideas – every sentence containing a thought: no words wasted; no endeavour to eke out paragraphs, pages, or volumes, with mere verbiage.

So it was with *Shirley*; so it is with *Villette*. The reader must enter upon it with purpose to peruse for the enjoyment of the telling of the story rather than for the story itself. Thus prepared he will not be disappointed. He will find entertainment, and even profit, in every page; he will see character nicely conceived and powerfully depicted; he will discover much quiet humour, a lively wit, brilliant dialogue, vivid description, reflections that are both new and true, sentiment wholesomely free from cant and conventionality, and bursts of eloquence and poetry flashing here and there. But if he cares not for all these attractions, and wants an exciting and absorbing plot, he must not send for *Villette*.

48. George Eliot, letters

February and March 1853

Letters to Mrs Bray of 15 February and 12 March 1853, from *The Letters of George Eliot* (1954), ii, 87, 92. See also No 17.

15 February:

I am only just returned to a sense of the real world about me, for I have been reading *Villette*, a still more wonderful book than *Jane Eyre*. There is something almost preternatural in its power ...

12 March:

Villette – *Villette* – have you read it?

49. From an unsigned notice, *Guardian*

23 February 1853, 128–9

Linked by Charlotte with the *Christian Remembrancer* as one of the 'organs of the High Church' whose hostility she had provoked (see No. 54). She wrote to Williams on 9 March 1853:

Thank you for the *Eclectic Review* [No. 50] and the *Guardian* . . . I *must* see such [notices] as are *un*satisfactory and hostile . . . in these I best read public feeling and opinion . . . the poor Guardian critic has a right to lisp his opinion that Currer Bell's female characters do not realise his notion of ladyhood – and even 'respectfully to decline' the honour of an acquaintance with 'Jane Eyre' and 'Lucy Snowe' (*LL*, iv, 50–1).

Currer Bell has a style and feelings of her own: the style strong, clear, lively, sometimes passionate and eloquent, often declamatory and exaggerated; her feelings vehement and deep, but stern and masculine in their character and modes of expression. Suppressed emotion and unreturned affection, desolate and misunderstood characters, the miseries of semi-servile situations, and the loneliness of minds out of harmony with the position in which their lot is cast – these are the elements of her pathos, and the subjects which she finds her chief vocation in depicting. Mannerism there certainly is about her, and an unpleasant mannerism, from the somewhat cynical and bitter spirit in which she conceives her tales. It may be the world has dealt hardly with her; it may be that in her writings we gather the honest and truthful impressions of a powerful but ill-used nature; that they are the result of affections thrown back upon themselves, and harshly denied their proper scope and objects. But so it is, that, in spite of their ability, they are not pleasant reading, and though their teaching may be necessary, it is too uniformly painful, and too little genial, to be accepted by the generality as unmingled truth. It is part of the same character that she should be wanting in refinement, and that even her best characters, those she wishes to be models of purity and grace, are represented by her as consenting to situations and adopting practices

no really high-minded and virtuous person would consent to. Especially this is the case with her women, who can never be accepted as
real ladies. In the same spirit of self-reliance and scornful superiority
to what she considers weak prejudice, we have differences in religion
treated as immaterial, and Christianity itself degraded from a revealed
system of doctrine to a loose sentiment or feeling, without objective
truth of any kind, and released from the disagreeable trammels of any
positive belief . . . Lucy Snowe, the supposed writer of the story,
glories in attending all kinds of public worship except the Roman, as
if it was a matter of pure indifference, and it was the mark of a weak
mind to insist upon such puerile distinctions. These faults – and faults
like these, moral as well as artistic – at present prevent Currer Bell
from attaining to that excellence which her powers might enable her
to reach; and from the perusal of these volumes we fear that she is by
no means on the road towards correcting them . . .

The characters, in description at least, are capital; not pleasant, not
very interesting in themselves, with the exception of M. Paul, the fiery,
eccentric, but self-denying and really heroic professor, yet painted
with the hand of a master, and full of life and vigour. Take for example
this portrait of Madame Beck.

[quotes the description in chapter 8]

Dr. John's mother, a true, warm-hearted, and decided woman
(next to M. Paul the pleasantest person in the book), Paulina in her
way (though the most striking part of her portrait is the chapter on
her childhood), and, above all, M. Paul, are really good. The latter is
a creation, and a character on which we can repose with satisfaction;
his fiery and passionate disposition is so beautifully mingled and con-
trasted with traits romantic and delicate generosity. He is a character
to laugh at, but to love and respect with all one's heart at the same
time. We cannot help feeling he deserved a better fate than to become
engaged to Lucy Snowe, and to be drowned at sea (as we understand
the somewhat mysterious conclusion) before he could be married to
her. Lucy Snowe herself is *Jane Eyre* over again; both are reflections of
Currer Bell; and for the reasons above given, though we admire the
abilities of these young ladies, we should respectfully decline (ungallant
critics that we are) the honour of their intimate acquaintance . . .

50. From an unsigned review, *Eclectic Review*

March 1853, n.s. v, 305–20

See No. 49. The Nonconformist *Eclectic Review* was founded in 1805 and edited by the bookseller and hymn writer Josiah Conder (died 1855). The mingling of praise and condemnation is in keeping with the uneasy tone of many of its literary reviews. The omitted passages record narrative details.

The tale we have analyzed requires from us some critical observations, not only for its own sake, but also as a type of a class. The observation of Horace upon poetry may be applied with truth to fiction – that its great object is to charm and please, and that if it fails of this it is to literature what discordant music is to a convivial entertainment, which would be agreeable enough without any music at all ... In the work before us there is so much to admire that it is not agreeable to take exceptions, and yet the application of Horace's rule discloses one cardinal shortcoming. With all its talent as a composition it fails to please as a fiction ...

In the first place, then, the characters are not such as are calculated to interest the sympathies and the heart of the reader ... Dr. John Graham Bretton is certainly intelligent, vivacious, humane, and affectionate, but Mrs. Bretton is too much a woman of the world. She lacks tenderness even to her protégé, the heroine; indeed, her whole nature seems absorbed in that pride in her son which looks too much like a sort of secondary selfishness to awaken a deeper feeling than complacency ... Paulina again, while she is most uninteresting as a child, excites no very impassioned interest at eighteen, owing to a strong-minded control of her affections, which contrasts a little with a fretful petulance that spoils both the dignity and the amiability of her character. Of Ginevra Fanshawe it is enough to say that she is a sort of Cleopatra in her way, selfish and sensuous, and equally destitute of faith and feeling. Nor can we, with every desire to do so, fall in love with the heroine herself. She is sensible, clever, and somewhat emotional, but she lacks enthusiasm and deep womanly love ... we desiderate in vain those characteristics which have so often charmed us in the heroines of the Waverley Novels, and which have made Flora Macdonald, Julia Mannering, and many others, as real personages, to our imaginations, as if they had been the living objects of an unsuccessful but unforgotten love ... Professor Emanuel Paul, as the husband of the heroine, must, we suppose, on all the laws of fiction, be considered as the hero. But what a hero! A short, bustling, angry schoolmaster, between forty and fifty years of age; vain, passionate, and imperious, and who designates as his chief treasure the pair of spectacles that suits his defective eyesight; – a Jesuit, and of course a spy, whose highest glory is the most prominent exhibition of his person in a public assembly; a man who makes young ladies tremble before him in class, and seriously protests that he will hang the housemaid if she dares again to venture into his class-room to announce that Mademoiselle Somebody is wanted for a music lesson in another apartment ... There are some writers who invest even the bad with a sort of heroic sublimity, from the colossal pre-eminence of their wickedness. Milton's Satan, Shakespeare's Lady Macbeth, and a thousand others, will occur to the reader as illustrations of our meaning. But even about the defects in the characters of our author there is a tame negativeness ...

And yet, after all, it is the plot alone that is defective; the development of the characters, comparatively insipid as they are, is achieved with a degree of talent, the triumph of which is rendered the more remarkable by comparison with the poverty and scantiness of the material. The plot itself lacks incident, it contains few of what the dramatists call *situations*, and is chiefly transacted in a girls' boarding school. Hence the work mainly consists of dialogue, and although this is sustained with all the vivacity of an unquestionably powerful pen, yet it tires by its sameness. The greatest master of fiction that ever wrote would have fatigued his readers if he had dwelt upon crochet, guardchains, cookery, and dress, and all the vapid details of a girls' school room. In a word, that Currer Bell possesses distinguished talents, and that delicacy of touch which none but a female writer can give, we most cheerfully concede; but the plan of her fictions is not equal to their execution. If a bolder hand were to strike her outline, and to develop the plot with her own admirable discrimination of light and shade, we think she would produce a work far more worthy of her talents than any with which the public has yet associated her fictitious name.

51. Thackeray, letters

March and April 1853

Letters to Lucy Baxter (11 March 1853), Mrs Carmichael-Smyth (25–28 March 1853) and Mrs Bryan Proctor (4 April 1853) from *The Letters and Private Papers of W. M. Thackeray*, ed. Gordon N. Ray (1947), iii, 232–3, 248, 252. Mrs Bryan Proctor wrote to Thackeray on 8 March 1853:

Villette . . . is an excellently written book – but a very disagreeable one. She turns every one . . . 'the seamy side out' – So plain a person must see all things darkly – but the book is like a fine dutch picture. The painting is as minute and delicate (*ibid.*, 231).

To Lucy Baxter, 11 March 1853:

So you are all reading *Villette* to one another – a pretty amusement to be sure – I wish I was a hearing of you and a smoakin of a cigar the while. The good of *Villette* in my opinion Miss is a very fine style; and a remarkably happy way (which few female authors possess) of carrying a metaphor logically through to its conclusion. And it amuses me to read the author's naive confession of being in love with 2 men at the same time; and her readiness to fall in love at any time. The poor little woman of genius! the fiery little eager brave tremulous homely-faced creature! I can read a great deal of her life as I fancy in her book, and see that rather than have fame, rather than any other earthly good or mayhap heavenly one she wants some Tomkins or another to love her and be in love with. But you see she is a little bit of a creature without a penny worth of good looks, thirty years old I should think,[1]

[1] Charlotte was nearly thirty-seven (born 21 April 1816).

buried in the country, and eating up her own heart there, and no Tomkins will come. You girls with pretty faces and red boots (and what not) will get dozens of young fellows fluttering about you – whereas here is one a genius, a noble heart longing to mate itself and destined to wither away into old maidenhood with no chance to fulfil the burning desire.

To Mrs Carmichael-Smyth, 25–28 March 1853:

I have been reading *Villette* and *My Novel*[1] – I think the latter is very dexterously brewed and bottled small beer, and *Villette* is rather vulgar – I don't make my *good* women ready to fall in love with two men at once, and Miss Brontë would be very angry with me and cry fie if I did.

To Mrs Bryan Proctor, 4 April 1853:

That's a plaguey book that *Villette*. How clever it is – and how I don't like the heroine.

[1] Bulwer Lytton's *My Novel* was published 1853.

52. Eugène Forçade, from a review, *Revue des deux mondes*

15 March 1853, tome 1, 1084–96

Reviews first *Villette* and then Lady Georgina Fullerton's *Lady Bird* (1853) under the heading 'Un Roman Protestant et un Roman Catholique en Angleterre'. The article opens by referring to the increasing number of women writers and identifies both authors (naming 'Currer Bell' as 'Miss Bronty'). No comment by Charlotte is recorded (for her earlier warm approval of Forçade see Nos 21, 33). She may have taken exception to the personal details in the review and to Forçade's emphasis on her sex; see, for instance, her attitude to G. H. Lewes's commentary on *Shirley* (No. 39 and Introduction, pp. 7, 26).

There could not, in fact, be a more complete and piquant contrast than that presented by *Villette* and *Lady-Bird*, by the talent of Currer Bell and the talent of Lady Fullerton ... Currer Bell has chosen to place her novels in a middle-class setting, she seeks out the grey and arid realities of life, she traces the events in ill-shaped, mediocre, laborious existences; she is a middle-class writer. Without being pretentious, Lady Fullerton selects her heroes and unfolds her adventures in the brilliant surroundings of high society; she remains, in spite of her religious aims, a 'society' novelist. Currer Bell's manner is harsh, tormented, a little uncouth; the author of *Villette* is scrupulous as to details, though abrupt and fanciful in her arrangement of them; her narrative is full of abrupt transitions, the scenes of her drama are arranged with a skill disguised beneath a contempt for the conventional and the commonplace; and by the artful use of combination and contrast, this author is able to lend a strange and romantic colour to the most common occurrences of everyday life. Lady Fullerton has none of these premeditated singularities ...

Currer Bell's sentences are wayward and broken; her language is, in the English phrase, more idiomatic, that is to say more Anglo-

Saxon in its vocabulary and phraseology. Lady Fullerton's periods are smooth, harmonious and flowing; her language and phrasing are closer to the spirit of the French language. Even more striking is the difference between the natures and the moral aims of these two distinguished women. Currer Bell has a mixture of restrained passion and irony, a kind of virile power; the struggles she delights in are those in which the individual, alone and thrown entirely on his own resources, has only his own inner strength to rely upon . . . she preaches with Titanic pride the moral power of the human soul; her books contain vigour and originality, never tears; she surprises, she interests, but she does not soften us; she is protestant to the last fibre of her being. Lady Fullerton, on the other hand, is a feminine soul; she is of the company of those who have been pierced with the sword of religious feeling.

[continues with a detailed résumé of the narrative in *Villette*]

. . . Such is the outline of this long novel. From a literary point of view, the qualities that distinguish it are precisely what defy analysis. It is the minutely depicted scenes that endow the characters with a living and piquant reality; it is the author's technique that enhances with a personal touch and with unexpected and original handling the most apparently common subjects. It is the fiery spirit of the mind and the pen, that bursts through the deliberately prosaic nature of the incidents and situations.

53. Matthew Arnold, from a letter

14 April 1853

Letter to Mrs Forster, from *Letters of Matthew Arnold*, 1848–88, ed. G. W. Russell (1895), 29. For his feeling in 1855 see No. 89, and for other comments by members of the Arnold family, No. 40.

Why is *Villette* disagreeable? Because the writer's mind contains nothing but hunger, rebellion and rage, and therefore that is all she can, in fact put into her book. No fine writing can hide this thoroughly, and it will be fatal to her in the long run. *My Novel*[1] I have just finished. I have read it with great pleasure, though Bulwer's nature is by no means a perfect one either, which makes itself felt in his book.

[1] See Thackeray's letters, No. 51, p. 198 above.

54. Anne Mozley, from an unsigned review, *Christian Remembrancer*

April 1853, n.s. xxv, 401–43

Anne Mozley (1809–91) was a regular contributor to this Anglican periodical, which was edited by her brother, James Bowling Mozley, later (1871) Regius Professor of Divinity at Oxford; she edited his letters (1855) and those of J. H. Newman (1891). Her analysis of *Villette* is frequently shrewd and pays it the compliment of serious analysis and, as indicated below, extensive quotation from the text. Her criticisms spring from a bias against Charlotte's individual religious and personal temper (see Introduction, p. 27). Charlotte wrote to Margaret Wooler on 13 April 1853:

Currer Bell's remarks on Romanism have drawn down on him the condign displeasure of the High Church Party – which displeasure has been unequivocally expressed through their principal organs the *Guardian* [No. 49], the *English Churchman* and the *Christian Remembrancer* . . . this must be borne . . . I can suffer no accusation to oppress which is not supported by the inward evidence of Conscience and Reason (*LL*, iv, 58).

Charlotte's resolve did not prevent her from later writing a letter to the editor (dated 18 July 1853) protesting against insinuations in the review concerning her preference for a secluded life (*LL*, iv, 79). The letter was published by the *Christian Remembrancer* in 1857 in its review of Mrs Gaskell's *Life*; see No. 100.

***

After threading the maze of harrowing perplexities thus set forth by Lady Georgiana . . . it is, we own, a relief to turn to the work-day world of *Villette*. The rough winds of common life make a better atmosphere for fiction than the stove heat of the 'higher circles.' Currer Bell, by hardly earning her experience, has, at least, won her knowledge in a field of action where more can sympathise; though we cannot speak of sympathy, or of ourselves as in any sense sharing in it,

without a protest against the outrages on decorum, the moral perversity, the toleration of, nay, indifference to vice which deform her
first powerful picture of a desolate woman's trials and sufferings –
faults which make *Jane Eyre* a dangerous book, and which must leave
a permanent mistrust of the author on all thoughtful and scrupulous
minds. But however alloyed with blame this sympathy has necessarily
been, there are indications of its having cheered her and done her
good. Perhaps ... she has been the better for a little happiness and
success, for in many important moral points *Villette* is an improvement
on its predecessors. The author has gained both in amiability and propriety since she first presented herself to the world, – soured, coarse,
and grumbling; an alien, it might seem, from society, and amenable
to none of its laws.

We have said that Currer Bell has found life not a home, but a
school ... She may, indeed, be considered the novelist of the school-
room ... because, as the scholastic world would seem to have been
the main theatre of her experience – as here have been excited, in
herself, many a vivid thought and keen interest – she chooses that others
shall enter it with her. She will not condescend to shift the scene ...
what has interested her, she means shall interest them: nor are we
losers by the obligation. It cannot be denied that hitherto the art of
teaching has cast a suspicion of coldness and dryness over its professors:
it should not be so; it is unfair to an honourable profession, which
should at least be cheered by sympathy in its irksome labours. In these
days of educational enthusiasm the prejudice ought to be done away.
Currer Bell seems to regard it as the mission of her genius to effect
this: her clear, forcible, picturesque style gives life to what our fancies
thought but a vegetating existence. Not that she wishes to represent
life in the schoolroom as happy; far from it; but she shows us that
life does not stagnate there in an eternal round of grammar and dictionary – in a perpetual infusion of elementary knowledge; and
wherever it can be shown to flow freely and vigorously, wherever the
mind has scope and the heart and emotions free play, there we can find
interest and excitement. *Villette* must be considered the most scholastic
of the series. In *Jane Eyre* we have the melancholy experience of the
Clergy-daughters' school, and her own subsequent position as governess; in *Shirley* we have the heart-enthralling tutor, and the heiress
falling in love as she learns her French and writes her copy-books
under the assumed austerity of his rule, – a wrong state of things, we
need not say: but in *Villette* almost the whole corps of the drama is

furnished for the *Pensionnat de Demoiselles*. The flirting beauty of a school-girl; the grave, thoughtful young English teacher, with her purely intellectual attractions; Madame, the directress, the presiding genius; the little French professor of *Belleslettres*, for the hero, and the classes and large school-garden for the scenes. Even the outer-world hero, Graham, comes in as the physician of the establishment, and is entangled by the school-girl beauty; though it is his business to introduce us sometimes to the world beyond the walls, which now and then affords a refreshing change.

Nor does she gain the point of interesting us by ignoring any professional peculiarity which belongs to the science of teaching. Even the writer (for it is an autobiography) is, we see clearly, in look and air the 'teacher' she describes herself: her manner affected and influenced by her position. The consciousness of being undervalued, the longings for some one to care for her leading to some undignified results, the necessary self-reliance, the demure air, the intellect held in check, but indemnifying itself for the world's neglect and indifference by the secret indulgence of an arrow-like penetration, – all are portrayed; and for the hero – what can be more like a professor and less like a standard hero than M. Paul Emanuel? a character in the highest degree fresh and original, but in no sense calculated to attract a lady's fancy except in scenes where the world of male society is shut out as it is in large female assemblies, – in schools, convents, and, according to the satirist, old maid coteries, – in all of which a very small amount of heroic qualities are often found enough to constitute a man a hero . . .

. . . The defect of the plot is a want of continuity. In fact, the style is rather that of an autobiography – and, perhaps, excusable as adopting that form – than a novel. Persons are introduced in the beginning who have no share in the conduct of the story; adventures are given, which begin and end in themselves. The whole episode of Miss Marchmont is of this nature. At the end of it we find our heroine – she would not give herself this ambitious title – friendless and penniless, except for the £15 which remain from her salary as Miss Marchmont's companion. The spirit of adventure rises with the need for exertion. She goes to London, and from thence sails to Bouemarine, the sea-port of Labassecour, to seek her fortune in a foreign land; and here commences the scholastic part of the story, for on board she meets with Ginevra Fanshawe, a girl of seventeen on her way to Madame Beck's establishment at Villette . . .

Madame Beck's establishment is conducted on the system of surveillance which some have thought necessary to good education, – a system of which she is complete mistress, being addicted to arts which are usually supposed to be practised only by the detective police of some tyrannical power, but which the present writer traces to the influence of Roman Catholicism in the countries where it prevails.

There is probably prejudice, but there may be also valuable information, in her picture of even a good foreign school.

[quotes from chapter 8 Madame Beck's disciplinary system and Lucy's first introduction to her pupils]

We believe that this peculiar aspect, these eyes, and hard unblushing brows [i.e. of Lucy's pupils], are to be found in our island, under the same circumstances as foster them in Labassecour. Wherever girls and young women, for any purpose, are brought in great numbers together, and allowed to associate in wild unrestrained companionship, the same thing may be observed. Girls, we believe, are not suited to congregate in large numbers together: they lose their charm, the softness, and the bloom, and many of the precious things these flowery words typify, under such training. To such an exterior corresponds the following view of heart and principle. We give it with no means ourselves of verifying the truth of so awful a charge; nor are we told how the naive confession ever reached the author's Protestant ears: –

To do all parties justice, the honest aboriginal Labassecouriennes had an hypocrisy of their own too, but it was of a coarse order, such as could deceive few. Whenever a lie was necessary for their occasions, they brought it out with a careless ease and breadth, altogether untroubled by the rebuke of conscience. Not a soul in Madame Beck's house, from the scullion to the directress herself, but was above being ashamed of a lie; they thought nothing of it; to invent might not be precisely a virtue, but it was the most venial of faults. 'J'ai menti plusieurs fois,' formed an item of every girl's and woman's monthly confession; the priest heard unshocked, and absolved unreluctant. If they had missed going to Mass, or read a chapter of a novel, that was another thing; these were crimes whereof rebuke and penance were the unfailing meed [chapter 9].

Reflecting upon this extraordinary moral perversity, the English teacher once ventured to remonstrate, and to express her views of the relative depravity of the two sins – a lie, or an occasional omission in Church going. . . . We are not at all proud of her as a representative of our reformed faith; and believe there might be much better reason for this than she would be willing to allow. We own we should be sorry to subject any child of ours to the teaching and insinuations of the mind here pictured; whose religion is without awe, – who despises and sets down every form and distinction she cannot understand, – who rejects all guides but her Bible, and at the same time constantly quotes and plays with its sacred pages, as though they had been given to the world for no better purpose than to point a witticism or furnish an ingenious illustration.

[continues with further details of the narrative]

We have left the Professor for the duties of the story; it is fit now to return to him ... the following episode will give our reader a better notion of M. Emanuel than any further description. It could not be shortened without being spoiled, which must be our excuse for its length. Our authoress shines in such scenes. Her accuracy and truth of detail, the bright playful enjoyment of her own success, her power of seizing the point, of bringing minds in contact, of showing what vivid moments there are in scenes apparently trivial, if only a quick eye and graphic pen can catch the evanescent spirit, and give it consistency, are all delightful. Can our readers doubt that this scene is no invention, but in some modification or other has actually occurred.

[quotes the episode with Monsieur Paul which opens chapter 27]

We do not wonder, with such skill in turning this fiery little temper, that Miss Lucy found herself attracted towards the possessor of it ... With all his absurdities, M. Paul is a man of great ability, almost of genius. We are conscious of his real power while we laugh at him. It is a sort of simplicity and humility, an avowed contempt for his own dignity, which shows so prominently his vanity and other weak points. We are disposed in the end to adopt the writer's conclusion, that it is his nerves that are irritable, not his temper. His religion, too, after the fashion of his country, is a very real and genuine feature. We quite acquiesce in her content to have him as he is, without any attempt to make him like herself. He had been educated by a Jesuit, and is still most dutiful at confession, having to go through some tribulations on account of his predilection for the English heretic, whom he endeavours in vain to convert by laying persuasive brochures in her way, which she treats with true Protestant contempt. Childlike in his faith, he is also pure in life, and the soul of honour; in all these points being in happy contrast with his brother professors. Some romantic acts of

generosity and self-denial, which come out towards the end of the
story, have not truth enough about them to match with his very true
character; and in the same way the scenes of love-making in the end,
between him and Lucy, have a very apocryphal air . . .

The moral purpose of this work seems to be to demand for a certain
class of minds a degree of sympathy not hitherto accorded to them; a
class of which Lucy Snowe is the type, who must be supposed to
embody much of the authoress's own feelings and experience, all
going one way to express a character which finds itself unworthily
represented by person and manner, conscious of power, equally and
painfully conscious of certain drawbacks, which throw this superiority
into shade and almost hopeless disadvantage. For such she demands
room to expand, love, tenderness, and a place in happy domestic life.
But in truth she draws a character unfit for this home which she yearns
for. We want a woman at our hearth;[1] and her impersonations are
without the feminine element, infringers of modest restraints, despisers
of bashful fears, self-reliant, contemptuous of prescriptive decorum;
their own unaided reason, their individual opinion of right and wrong,
discreet or imprudent, sole guides of conduct and rules of manners, –
the whole hedge of immemorial scruple and habit broken down and
trampled upon. We will sympathise with Lucy Snowe as being father-
less and penniless, and are ready, if this were all, to wish her a husband
and a fire-side less trying that M. Paul's must be, unless reformed
out of all identity; but we cannot offer even the affections of our
fancy (right and due of every legitimate heroine) to her unscrupulous,
and self-dependent intellect – to that whole habit of mind which,
because it feels no reverence, can never inspire for itself that one
important, we may say, indispensable element of man's true love.

One suggestion we would make in parting with these two ladies – a
question applicable to other scrutinizers of the female bosom – whether,
indeed, they are consulting the interests of the sex, for which they contend so earnestly, by betraying – what gallantry is slow to credit – that
women give away their hearts unsought as often as they would have us
believe? So long as men wrote romance, that heart was described as an
all-but-impregnable fortress . . . But now that our fair rivals wield the
pen, the tables are turned . . . They show us the invader greeted from
afar – invited, indeed, within the walls. They betray the castle to have
been all the while wanting a commander, the heart an owner. If it were
indeed so, would the prize won on such easy terms be thought so much

[1] See p. iii, n.

worth the having? Would this 'more than willingness' satisfy the inherent love of difficulty and of achievement in man's nature? But, happily, the question need not seriously be asked. A restless heart and vagrant imagination, though owned by woman, can have no sympathy or true insight into the really feminine nature. Such cannot appreciate the hold which a daily round of simple duties and pure pleasures has on those who are content to practise and enjoy them. They do not know the power of home over the heart – how it asserts its sway against new and more enthralling interests. Those who own such influences will still be difficult to win. Nor can we promise the aspirant to their favour any such eloquent, unsought avowals as the maidens of modern romance succeed so well in. He must be content to wait for the genial influences of a new home, to unthaw reserve; for trial, to prove constancy; and time and sorrow, to develop the full force, the boundless resources, of a pure, unselfish affection.

55. G. H. Lewes, 'Ruth' and 'Villette', Westminster Review

April 1853, ii, 485–91

From an unsigned review written by G. H. Lewes and judged 'unsatisfactory' by George Eliot, who was then editor of the *Westminster Review* (*The George Eliot Letters*, ii, 93). The rest of the article peters out into a random repetition of points made in his earlier review for the *Leader* (No. 45), but his attempt to compare *Villette* with Mrs Gaskell's *Ruth* prompted him to introduce the reflections about art and morality which are reproduced here.

Should a work of Art have a moral? In other words, must the Artist, during creation, keep the wandering caprices of his fancy within the limits of some didactic formula? The question has been often, but somewhat confusedly, debated. It has been seen, on the one hand, that the merely didactic tale frustrates, in a great measure, its own objects: the reader resents having his pill gilded – resents having the leaves of a religious tract slipped in between the pages of a novel; and in the spirit of reaction, it has been said that the Artist has nothing to do with morality. On the other hand, there are people whose first question is, What is the moral? What does this prove? Hegel has said very truly, that 'there is a moral in every work of art, but it depends on him that draws it.' George Sand . . . makes a decided stand against this moral requisition, and both in her own person, and vicariously for all other novelists, declares that 'art can prove nothing, nor should it be expected to prove anything'. She says that readers have always wished to see vice punished and virtue rewarded; and that, in this respect, she is one of the public. But poetical justice proves nothing either in a story or in a drama. When vice is not punished on the stage or in a book – as it very often is not in life – this does not prove that vice is unhateful and unworthy of punishment; for a narrative can prove nothing. If the vessel which carried 'Paul and Virginia' had not been wrecked, would it have proved that chaste love is always crowned with happiness? And because this vessel goes to the bottom with the interesting heroine, what does *Paul and Virginia* prove? It proves that youth, friendship, love, and tropics are beautiful things, when Bernardin de Saint Pierre describes them. If 'Faust' were not led away and vanquished by the devil, would it prove that the passions were weaker than reason? And because the devil is stronger than the philosopher, does it prove that philosophy can never vanquish the passions? What does 'Faust' prove? It proves that science, human life, fantastic images, profound, graceful or terrible ideas, are wonderful things, when Goethe makes out of them a sublime and moving picture. So far George Sand; but this does not meet the question. Although a narrative is not a demonstration, and cannot be made one; although, therefore, in the strict sense of the word, Art proves nothing; yet it is quite clear that the details of a narrative may be so grouped as to satisfy the mind like a sermon. It is an exhortation, if you like, not a demonstration, but it does not the less appeal to our moral sense. What does a sermon prove? And can a sermon prove anything? Yet, by appealing to the moral sense, it works its purposes. The debaters of this question seem to leave out of view the fact that in fiction as in real life, while our emotions are excited by the narrative, and, so to speak, by the physical accidents of the story, our moral sense requires to be gratified; and the meaning of poetical justice is, that the satisfaction required by this moral sense should be furnished in the conclusion of the story. If we hear of an actual injustice done upon earth, remaining unpunished, we are indignant and dissatisfied ... Precisely the same feeling is left in our minds when poetical justice is violated. In a fiction, we are angry with the author for not doing what our moral sense demands should be done. When the incidents of the story, besides exciting our interest, run along moral lines, and call up *tableaux vivant* of just retribution, and the happy terminations of worthy lives, then not only is that faculty gratified to which fiction more immediately appeals, but the moral sense is also gratified ...

Now, in the question of the moral as respects fiction, it is quite clear, from French practice more than any other, that without formally inculcating any immoral dogma, the writer may very successfully produce an immoral effect. Who can mistake the immoral moral which breathes through the pages of Eugène Sue?[1] Who can mistake the foregone conclusion employed in his selection of main incidents and characters? in his flattery of the people, which consists in making the virtuous poor, and the vicious rich; linking together, as in necessary connexion, virtue and dirty hands, maculate consciences and immaculate linen? On the other hand, there is no mistaking the moral influence of good novels; even when no specific formula can be appended to the closing chapter. The novel may carry its moral openly on its very title-page, through all its conclusions; or, it may carry within it, not one but many moral illustrations, naturally arising out of the way the incidents are grouped, and the way the characters express themselves.

These two forms of moral are illustrated in *Ruth* and *Villette*, two works by our most popular authoresses. *Ruth* has a moral carried in the story; not preached, but manifested. It is a story of seduction ... Turning from *Ruth* to *Villette*, the contrasts meet us on all sides. Never were two women's books more unlike each other. There is a moral too in *Villette*, or rather many morals, but not so distinctly a *morale en action*. It is a work of astonishing power and passion. From its pages there issues an influence of truth as healthful as a mountain breeze. Contempt of conventions in all things, in style, in thought, even in the art of story-telling, here visibly springs from the independent originality of a strong mind nurtured in solitude. As a novel, in the ordinary

---

[1] Marie-Joseph ['Eugène'] Sue (1804–75), prolific popular novelist. His best known works in the 1840s and 1850s include *Les Mystères de Paris* (1842–3), *Le Juif Errant* (1844–5) and *Les Mystères du Peuple* (1849–56).

sense of the word, *Villette* has few claims; as a book, it is one which, having read, you will not easily forget. It is quite true that the episode of Miss Marchmont, early in the first volume, is unnecessary, having no obvious connexion with the plot or the characters; but with what wonderful imagination is it painted! Where shall we find such writing as in that description of her last night, wherein the memories of bygone years come trooping in upon her with a vividness partaking of the last energy of life? It is true also that the visit to London is unnecessary, and has many unreal details. Much of the book seems to be brought in merely that the writer may express something which is in her mind; but at any rate she has something in her mind, and expresses it as no other can . . .

We could go on quoting and commenting through several pages, for indeed it is . . . the utterance of an original mind. In this world, as Goethe tells us, 'there are so few voices, and so many echoes;' . . . so few persons thinking and speaking for themselves, so many reverberating the vague noises of others. Among the few stands *Villette*. In it we read the actual thoughts and feelings of a strong, struggling soul; we hear the cry of pain from one who has loved passionately, and who has sorrowed sorely. Indeed, no more distinct characteristic of Currer Bell's genius can be named, than the depth of her capacity for all passionate emotions. Comparing *Villette* with *Ruth*, in this respect, we are comparing sunlight with moonlight, passion with affection; and there is no writer of our day, except George Sand, who possesses the glory and the power which light up the writings of Currer Bell. She has not the humour, so strong and so genial, of Mrs. Gaskell. There are, occasionally, touches approaching to the comic in *Villette*, but they spring mostly from fierce sarcasm, not from genial laughter. Ginevra Fanshaw is 'shown up' in all her affectations and careless coquetry, but there is something contemptuous in the laugh, nothing sympathetic. Nor has Currer Bell any tendency towards the graceful, playful, or fanciful. There is more of Michael Angelo than of Raffaelle in her drawing; more of Backhuysen than of Cuyp; more of Salvator Rosa[1] than of Claude.

[1] See p. 224, n.

56. 'Villette' and 'Ruth', Putnam's Monthly Magazine

May 1853, i, 535-9

From an unsigned review. The reviewer goes on to discuss *Ruth* as a 'sad and sweet story' which 'contrasts strangely with the gusty tumult of *Villette* . . . It is more simple, more concentrated, more intense' and has 'a rare unity'. He finds in conclusion that:

Villette is written from a conscious study of character, *Ruth* from a profound sympathy with it. *Villette* is a joyful cry of conscious power from the heart of the struggle, *Ruth* is a tear, washing the eyes clear, so that they see the way out of it. They are both admirable and remarkable novels.

The whole force of English romance-writing has been deployed during the last six months. Dickens, Thackeray, and Bulwer, the chiefs of that department of literature, have been in full play, and Miss Brontë (*Jane Eyre*), Mrs. Gaskell (*Mary Barton*), Mrs. Marsh, Mrs. Gore, Miss Julia Kavanagh, and lesser ladies, have advanced almost simultaneously, and platoon-wise, discharged each a new novel. They have all, at least, achieved what Frenchmen, with their facile flattery, call a *succès d'estime*. A *succès*, by the bye, with which no man nor woman was ever known to be content. We are not sure that Thackeray's *Henry Esmond* [1852] was more ardently anticipated, than Miss Brontë's *Villette*. *Jane Eyre* – a novel with a heroine neither beautiful nor rich, an entirely abnormal creation among the conventional heroines – came directly upon *Vanity Fair, a Novel without a hero* [1847–8], and made friends as warm, and foes as bitter, as that noted book. *Shirley* disappointed. It is in fact overshadowed by its predecessor. But now, after six years, *Villette* appears, and takes rank at once with *Jane Eyre*, displaying the same vigor – the same exuberant power – the same bold outline – the same dramatic conception – and the same invincible mastery and fusion of elements usually considered repugnant to romance. The great success of *Jane Eyre* as a work of art, and apart from the interest of the story, which is very great, consists in its rejection of all the stage-appointments of novels – all the Adonis-Dukes and Lady Florimels in satin boudoirs, which puerile phantoms still haunt the pages of Bulwer (although he is rapidly laying them) and the remorseless [G.P.R.] James, and are, of course, the staple of the swarm of 'the last new novels' which monthly inundate the circulating libraries in England. The author takes the reader among a crowd of ordinary human beings, and declares proudly, 'Here you shall find as much romance and thrilling interest, as in the perfumed purlieus of palaces.' . . .

This *actuality* is the very genius and spirit of modern English fiction, and this is its humane and prodigious triumph. The democratic principle has ordered romance to descend from thrones and evacuate the palace. Romance is one of the indefeasible 'rights of man.' Disraeli's Young Duke and Bulwer's Harley L'Estrange and Pelham are tailor's blocks and fashion-plates. Give us *men*, scarred and seamed as you please, that we may feel the thrill of sympathy: and learn, if we may, from their thought and action, how we should think and act. Discrown the 'Lady Arabella' and the 'haughty Countess' sacred in satin from warm emotion, give us no 'impossible she,' but,

> A creature not too bright and good
> For human nature's daily food.[1]

So cries the age, with stentorian lungs. And they come . . . We open our novels and there is our life mirrored, – dimly sometimes, and insufficiently – but not impossibly nor incredibly.

This *actuality* we conceive to be the healthy principle of contemporary fiction. We will not now stop to say that it may very easily run, on the right hand, into a want of that sufficient stimulus which belongs to 'ideal' portraitures, and which, by the charm of an almost fabulous virtue, allures us to excellence; and on the left, into that sermonizing and romance of reform which is the quick destruction of story-telling. No man bidden to a feast of fiction expects to sit down to a sermon . . . If the novelist do really hold the mirror up to nature, he need not fear that any delicate reader will too finely scent a moral. But if he attempt to pin the moral to the picture, – to say that Johnny being good had a gooseberry tart and naughty Tommy was put into a dark closet, – he simply assumes an accident as a consequent . . . The tart theory is not true. If goodness were always served with gooseberry sauce, who would be bad?

[1] Wordsworth's 'She was a Phantom of Delight . . .' (1807), ll. 17–18.

Thackeray is the most ponderous protestant against this nursery and primer view of human nature and human life, and close upon him, comes Miss Brontë. Jane Eyre was a governess, and a strongminded woman. She was by no means the lady with whom Harley L'Estrange in or out of *My Novel*[1] would ever fall in love. There were great doubts whether she knew how to dress, and none at all that she had no 'style.' . . . She was a woman bullied by circumstances and coping bravely with a hard lot, and finally proving her genuine force of character by winning the respect and love of a man who had exhausted the world and been exhausted by it; . . . Of course a novel of this kind, full of the truthful and rapid play of character, and from which rustling silks and satins are rigorously excluded – except once, when they sweep, cloud-like, down the stairs, in one of the most picturesque passages of the book – has no interest for those who are snuffing in the air for perfumes . . .

Villette has the same virtues. It is a novel of absorbing interest as a story. It is somewhat less severe than *Jane Eyre*. Paulina is a strain of grace and tenderness that does not occur in the other book. Paul has many traits like Rochester. Lucy Snowe is a governess like Jane Eyre herself – neither very young, nor lovely, nor fascinating, as we can easily see from the impression she makes upon Grahame Bretton. He is such a hero as daily experience supplies. We have all seen many Grahame Brettons, free, joyous natures, bounding through life; and therefore we are the better for meeting him in *Villette* . . .

When Paul first comes upon the stage, the reader does not like him. He has, however, like Rochester, the fascination of power, and when, later in the book, that power is developed, not grotesquely, but nobly, the reader smiles, and willingly puts Lucy's hand in Paul's . . . The skill of the treatment is shown in the gradual melting of the dislike of Paul, until it is entirely replaced by esteem; and this, by no means which seem forced, and which are not quite naturally and easily evolved from character and circumstance. The difficulty with the book as a work of art is, that the interest does not sufficiently concentrate upon the two chief figures. Grahame and Paulina are disproportionately interesting. In fact, we are not sure that most readers are not more anxious to marry Grahame than to follow the destiny of Lucy Snowe. There is a pause over his marriage, and a glance into the future, which properly belong only to the close of the book, and which materially affect the sequence of interest.

[1]See p. 198, n.

Yet it is a legitimate novel, a story told for the pleasure of telling it, with only such moral as is necessarily contained in the circumstances – a cheerful, inspiring confidence in integrity and valor. The book overflows with exuberant power. Its scenery is vivid and grim, like the pictures in *Jane Eyre*. But it is also more ambitious in style, and more evidently so, which is a great fault. The personifications of passion are unnatural, and clumsily patched upon the tale. They are the disagreeable rents in the scenery, making you aware that it is a drama, and not a fact; that it is an author writing a very fine book, and not scenes of life developing themselves before you. To be désillusioné in this manner is disagreeable. The finest passages in the book are the descriptions of the dreary vacation. The portrait of Rachel is sketched in the lurid gloom of the French melo-dramatic style. It partakes of the fault of the personification to which we alluded. *Villette* has less variety, but more grace than *Jane Eyre*. It is quite as bold, original, and interesting, allowing always for the fact that we have had the type in the earlier book.

THE NOVELS OF 'ELLIS AND ACTON BELL', 1847-8

WUTHERING HEIGHTS (1847)
and *AGNES GREY* (1847)

57. Unsigned notice, *Spectator*

18 December 1847, xx, 1217

See Introduction, pp. 15, 22, 31.

An attempt to give novelty and interest to fiction, by resorting to those singular 'characters' that used to exist everywhere, but especially in retired and remote country places. The success is not equal to the abilities of the writer; chiefly because the incidents are too coarse and disagreeable to be attractive, the very best being improbable, with a moral taint about them, and the villainy not leading to results sufficient to justify the elaborate pains taken in depicting it. The execution, however, is good: grant the writer all that is requisite as regards matter, and the delineation is forcible and truthful.

Wuthering Heights occupies two volumes: the third is filled out by a tale called *Agnes Grey*; which is not of so varied or in its persons and incidents of so extreme a kind as the first story; but what it gains in measure is possibly lost in power. We know not whether the names of

Ellis Bell and Acton Bell, which appear on the titlepages of this publication, have any connexion with Currer Bell, the editor of *Jane Eyre*; but the works have some affinity. In each, there is the autobiographical form of writing; a choice of subjects that are peculiar without being either probable or pleasing; and considerable executive ability, but insufficient to overcome the injudicious selection of the theme and matter.

58. Unsigned review, *Athenaeum*

25 December 1847, 1324-5

Probably by H. F. Chorley; see No. 7 and Introduction, pp. 18, 32.

Here are two tales so nearly related to *Jane Eyre* in cast of thought, incident and language as to excite some curiosity. All three might be the work of one hand, – but the first issued remains the best. In spite of much power and cleverness; in spite of its truth to life in the remote nooks and corners of England *Wuthering Heights* is a disagreeable story. The Bells seem to affect painful and exceptional subjects: – the misdeeds and oppressions of tyranny – the eccentricities of 'woman's fantasy.' They do not turn away from dwelling on those physical acts of cruelty which we know to have their warrant in the real annals of crime and suffering, – but the contemplation of which taste rejects. The brutal master of the lonely house on 'Wuthering Heights' – a prison which might be pictured from life – has doubtless had his prototype in those uncongenial and remote districts where human beings, like the trees, grow gnarled and dwarfed and distorted by the inclement climate; but he might have been indicated with far fewer touches, in place of so entirely filling the canvas that there is hardly a scene untainted by his presence. It was a like dreariness – a like unfortunate selection of objects – which cut short the popularity of Charlotte Smith's novels[1] – rich though they be in true pathos and faithful descriptions of Nature. Enough of what is mean and bitterly painful and degrading gathers round every one of us during the course of his pilgrimage through this vale of tears to absolve the Artist from choosing his incidents and characters out of such a dismal catalogue; and if the Bells, singly or collectively, are contemplating future or frequent utterances in Fiction, let us hope that they will spare us further interiors so gloomy as the one here elaborated with such dismal minuteness [i.e. in *Wuthering Heights*]. In this respect *Agnes Grey* is more acceptable to us, though less powerful. It is the tale of a governess who undergoes much that is the real bond of a governess's endurance: – but the new victim's trials are of a more ignoble quality than those which awaited *Jane Eyre*. In the household of the Bloomfields the governess is subjected to torment by Terrible Children (as the French have it); in that of the Murrys she has to witness the ruin wrought by false indulgence on two coquettish girls, whose coquetries jeopardize her own heart's secret. In both these tales there is so much feeling for character, and nice marking of scenery, that we cannot leave them without once again warning their authors against what is eccentric and unpleasant. Never was there a period in our history of Society when we English could so ill afford to dispense with sunshine.[2]

[1] Charlotte Smith (1749–1806) was the author of *Elegiac Sonnets and other Essays* (1784; 9th edn 1800) and of many equally popular novels, notably *Emmeline, or the Orphan of the Castle* (1788), *Celestina* (1792), *The Old Manor House* (1793).

[2] See Introduction, p. 32.

59. From an unsigned review of *Wuthering Heights, Examiner*

January 1848, 21–2

One of the five reviews found in Emily's desk. For the others see Nos 60, 61, 63, 67. The reviewer (perhaps A. W. Fonblanque or John Forster; see No. 10) recognized Emily's talent and took offence at Charlotte's failure to acknowledge this in her 1850 preface; see No. 82.

This is a strange book. It is not without evidences of considerable power: but, as a whole, it is wild, confused, disjointed, and improbable; and the people who make up the drama, which is tragic enough in its consequences, are savages ruder than those who lived before the days of Homer. With the exception of Heathcliff, the story is confined to the family of Earnshaw, who intermarry with the Lintons; and the scene of their exploits is a rude old-fashioned house, at the top of one of the high moors or fells in the north of England. Whoever has traversed the bleak heights of Hartside or Cross Fell, on his road from Westmoreland to the dales of Yorkshire, and has been welcomed there by the winds and rain on a 'gusty day,' will know how to estimate the comforts of Wuthering Heights in wintry weather.

[quotes the opening paragraphs of the novel]

Heathcliff may be considered as the hero of the book, if a hero there be. He is an incarnation of evil qualities; implacable hate, ingratitude, cruelty, falsehood, selfishness, and revenge. He exhibits, moreover, a certain stoical endurance in early life, which enables him to 'bide his time,' and nurse up his wrath till it becomes mature and terrible; and there is one portion of his nature, one only, wherein he appears to approximate to humanity. Like the Corsair, and other such melodramatic heroes, he is

Linked to one virtue and a thousand crimes;[1]

[1] Byron's *The Corsair* (1814) iii, 864: 'Linked with one virtue, and a thousand crimes . . .'

and it is with difficulty that we can prevail upon ourselves to believe in the appearance of such a phenomenon, so near our own dwellings as the summit of a Lancashire or Yorkshire moor.

It is not easy to disentangle the incidents and set them forth in chronological order. The tale is confused, as we have said, notwithstanding that the whole drama takes place in the house that we have described, and that the sole actors are the children of Earnshaw, by birth or adoption, and their servants.

[outlines the story]

We are not disposed to ascribe any particular intention to the author in drawing the character of Heathcliff, nor can we perceive any very obvious moral in the story. There are certain good rough dashes at character; some of the incidents look like real events; and the book has the merit, which must not be undervalued, of avoiding commonplace and affectation. The language, however, is not always appropriate[1] and we entertain great doubts as to the truth, or rather the *vraisemblance* of the main character. The hardness, selfishness, and cruelty of Heathcliff are in our opinion inconsistent with the romantic love that he is stated to have felt for Catherine Earnshaw. As Nelly Dean says, 'he is as hard as a whinstone.' He has no gratitude, no affection, no liking for anything human except for one person, and that liking is thoroughly selfish and ferocious. He hates the son of Hindley, which is intelligible enough; but he also hates and tyrannizes over his own son and the daughter of his beloved Catherine, and this we cannot understand.

We have said that there are some good dashes at character.

[quotes from chapter 5 descriptions of Cathy's appearance and behaviour]

From what we have said, the reader will imagine that the book is full of grim pictures. Here is one.

[quotes from chapter 29 Heathcliff's account of opening Catherine Linton's coffin eighteen years after her death]

If this book be, as we apprehend it is, the first work of the author, we hope that he will produce a second, – giving himself more time in its composition than in the present case, developing his incidents more carefully, eschewing exaggeration and obscurity, and looking steadily

[1] See Introduction, p. 29, and No. 65.

at human life, under all its moods, for those pictures of the passions that he may desire to sketch for our public benefit. It may be well also to be sparing of certain oaths and phrases, which do not materially contribute to any character, and are by no means to be reckoned among the evidences of a writer's genius. We detest the affectation and effeminate frippery which is but too frequent in the modern novel, and willingly trust ourselves with an author who goes at once fearlessly into the moors and desolate places, for his heroes; but we must at the same time stipulate with him that he shall not drag into light all that he discovers, of coarse and loathsome, in his wanderings, but simply so much good and ill as he may find necessary to elucidate his history – so much only as may be interwoven inextricably with the persons whom he professes to paint. It is the province of an artist to modify and in some cases refine what he beholds in the ordinary world. There never was a man whose daily life (that is to say, *all* his deeds and sayings, entire and without exception) constituted fit materials for a book of fiction. Even the figures of the Greeks (which are

In old marbles ever beautiful)[1]

were without doubt selected from the victors in the ancient games, and others, by Phidias and his scholars, and their forms and countenances made perfect before they were thought worthy to adorn the temple of the wise Athena.

The only book which occurs to us as resembling *Wuthering Heights* is a novel of the late Mr Hooton's,[2] a work of very great talent, in which the hero is a tramper or beggar, and the *dramatis personae* all derived from humble and middle life; but which, notwithstanding its defects, we remember thinking better in its peculiar kind than anything that had been produced since the days of Fielding.

---

[1] Keats's *Endymion* (1818) i, 319.
[2] Charles Hooton's novels include *Adventures of Bilberry Hurland* (1836), *Colin Clink* (1841) and *Launcelot Wedge* (1849).

60. From an unsigned review of *Wuthering Heights, Britannia*

15 January 1848, 42–3

One of the five reviews found in Emily's desk; see No. 59 and Introduction, p. 18. The account of the story (omitted below) is detailed and incorporates substantial quotations.

There are scenes of savage wildness in nature which, though they inspire no pleasurable sensation, we are yet well satisfied to have seen. In the rugged rock, the gnarled roots which cling to it, the dark screen of overhanging vegetation, the dank, moist ground and tangled network of weeds and bushes, – even in the harsh cry of solitary birds, the cries of wild animals, and the startling motion of the snake as it springs away scared by the intruder's foot, – there is an image of primeval rudeness which has much to fascinate, though nothing to charm, the mind. The elements of beauty are found in the midst of gloom and danger, and some forms are the more picturesque from their distorted growth amid so many obstacles. A tree clinging to the side of a precipice may more attract the eye than the pride of a plantation.

The principle may, to some extent, be applied to life. The uncultured freedom of native character presents more rugged aspects than we meet with in educated society. Its manners are not only more rough but its passions are more violent. It knows nothing of those breakwaters to the fury of tempest which civilized training establishes to subdue the harsher workings of the soul. Its wrath is unrestrained by reflection; the lips curse and the hand strikes with the first impulse of anger. It is more subject to brutal instinct than to divine reason.

It is humanity in this wild state that the author of *Wuthering Heights* essays to depict. His work is strangely original. It bears a resemblance to some of those irregular German tales in which the writers, giving the reins to their fancy, represent personages as swayed and impelled to evil by supernatural influences.[1] But they give spiritual identity to

---

[1] One of the earliest attempts to relate Emily's novel to German romantic tales. See Introduction, p. 32.

evil impulses, while Mr. Bell more naturally shows them as the natural offspring of the unregulated heart. He displays a considerable power in his creations. They have all the angularity of misshapen growth, and form in this respect a striking contrast to those regular forms we are accustomed to meet with in English fiction. They exhibit nothing of the composite character. There is in them no trace of ideal models. They are so new, so wildly grotesque, so entirely without art, that they strike us as proceeding from a mind of limited experience, but of original energy, and of a singular and distinctive cast.

In saying this we indicate both the merits and faults of the tale. It is in parts very unskilfully constructed: many passages in it display neither the grace of art nor the truth of nature, but only the vigour of one positive idea, – that of passionate ferocity. It blazes forth in the most unsuitable circumstances, and from persons the least likely to be animated by it. The author is a Salvator Rosa with his pen.[1] He delineates forms of savage grandeur when he wishes to represent sylvan beauty. His Griseldas are furies, and his swains Polyphemi. For this reason his narrative leaves an unpleasant effect on the mind. There are no green spots in it on which the mind can linger with satisfaction. The story rushes onwards with impetuous force, but it is the force of a dark and sullen torrent, flowing between high and rugged rocks.

It is permitted to painting to seize one single aspect of nature, and, as the pleasure arising from its contemplation proceeds partly from love of imitation, objects unattractive in themselves may be made interesting on canvass. But in fiction this kind of isolation is not allowed. The exhibition of one quality or passion is not sufficient for it. So far as the design extends it must present a true image of life, and if it takes in many characters it must show them animated by many motives. There may be a predominant influence of one strong emotion, perhaps that is necessary to unity of effect, but it should be relieved by contrasts, and set off by accessories. *Wuthering Heights* would have been a far better romance if Heathcliff alone had been a being of stormy passions, instead of all the other characters being nearly as violent and destructive as himself. In fiction, too, as the imitation of nature can never be so vivid and exact as in painting, that imitation is insufficient of itself to afford pleasure, and when it deals with brutal subjects it becomes positively disgusting. It is of course impossible to prescribe rules for either the admission or the rejection of what is shocking and

[1] *Atlas* (No. 63) makes the same comparison. Salvator Rosa (1615–73) was admired in England for the energy and picturesque grandeur of his landscapes.

dreadful. It is nothing to say that reality is faithfully followed. The aim of fiction is to afford some sensation of delight. We admit we cannot rejoice in the triumph of goodness – that triumph which consists in the superiority of spirit to body – without knowing its trials and sufferings. But the end of fictitious writings should always be kept in view: and that end is not merely mental excitement, for a very bad book may be very exciting. Generally we are satisfied there is some radical defect in those fictions which leave behind them an impression of pain and horror. It would not be difficult to show why this is, and must be, the case, but it would lead us into deeper considerations than are appropriate to this article.

Mr. Ellis Bell's romance is illuminated by some gleams of sunshine towards the end which serve to cast a grateful light on the dreary path we have travelled. Flowers rise over the grave of buried horrors. The violent passions of two generations are closed in death, yet in the vision of peace with which the tale closes we almost fear their revival in the warped nature of the young survivors.

Heathcliff is the central character of the piece. He is a gipsy foundling, and has been adopted from a feeling of benevolence – though of a rough and eccentric kind – by a country gentleman. At the time the book opens, this Heathcliff, then past the middle of life, has the estate of his benefactor, together with a neighbouring property.

[outlines the story]

It is difficult to pronounce any decisive judgment on a work in which there is so much rude ability displayed, yet in which there is so much matter for blame. The scenes of brutality are unnecessarily long and unnecessarily frequent; and as an imaginative writer the author has to learn the first principles of his art. But there is singular power in his portraiture of strong passion. He exhibits it as convulsing the whole frame of nature, distracting the intellect to madness, and snapping the heart-strings. The anguish of Heathcliff on the death of Catherine approaches to sublimity.

We do not know whether the author writes with any purpose; but we can speak of one effect of his production. It strongly shows the brutalizing influence of unchecked passion.[1] His characters are a commentary on the truth that there is no tyranny in the world like that which thoughts of evil exercise in the daring and reckless breast.

Another reflection springing from the narrative is that temper is

[1] Agrees with G. H. Lewes's reading in 1850 (No. 83, p. 292).

often spoiled in the years of childhood. 'The child is father of the man.' The pains and crosses of its youthful years are engrafted in its blood, and form a sullen and a violent disposition. Grooms know how often the tempers of horses are irremediably spoiled in training. But some parents are less wise regarding their children. The intellect in its growth has the faculty of accommodating itself to adverse circumstances. To violence it sometimes opposes violence, sometimes dogged obstinacy. The consequence in either case is fatal to the tranquillity of life. Young Catherine Linton is represented as a naturally sensitive, high-spirited, amiable girl; subjected to the cruel usage of her brutal stepfather, she is roused to resistance, and answers his curses with taunts, and his stripes with threatenings. Released from his tyranny, a more gracious spirit comes over her, and she is gentle and peaceful.

There are some fine passages scattered through the pages. Here is a thought on the tranquillity of death.

[Nelly Dean's reflections on death, chapter 16]

Of Joseph, the old sullen servant of Heathcliff, it is quaintly said, that he was 'the sourest-hearted pharisee that ever searched a Bible to rake all the blessings to himself and fling all the curses to his neighbours.'

The third volume of the book is made up of a separate tale relating the fortunes of a governess. Some characters and scenes are nicely sketched in it, but it has nothing to call for special notice. The volumes abound in provincialisms. In many respects they remind us of the recent novel of *Jane Eyre*. We presume they proceed from one family, if not from one pen.

The tale to which we have more particularly alluded is but a fragment, yet of colossal proportion, and bearing evidence of some great design. With all its power and originality, it is so rude, so unfinished, and so careless, that we are perplexed to pronounce an opinion on it, or to hazard a conjecture on the future career of the author. As yet it belongs to the future to decide whether he will remain a rough hewer of marble or become a great and noble sculptor.

61. From an unsigned review, *Douglas Jerrold's Weekly Newspaper*

15 January 1848, 77

One of the five reviews found in Emily's desk (see No. 59). Unusual in quoting from *Agnes Grey* as well as from *Wuthering Heights*.

Two of these volumes contain a tale by Mr. Ellis Bell, called *Wuthering Heights*, and the third volume is devoted to another story, told in an autobiographical form, by Mr. Acton Bell, and is entitled *Agnes Grey*.

Dissimilar as they are in many respects, there is a distinct family likeness between these two tales; and, if our organ of comparison be not out of order, we are not far wrong in asserting that they are not so much like each other, as they are both like a novel recently published under the editorship of Mr. Currer Bell, viz., *Jane Eyre*. We do not mean to say that either of the tales now before us is equal in merit to that novel, but they have somewhat of the same fresh, original, and unconventional spirit; while the style of composition is, undoubtedly, of the same north-country, Doric school; it is simple, energetic, and apparently disdainful of prettinesses and verbal display.

Of *Agnes Grey*, much need not be said, further than this, that it is the autobiography of a young lady during the time she was a governess in two different families; neither of which is a favourable specimen of the advantages of home education. We do not actually assert that the author must have been a governess himself, to describe as he does the minute torments and incessant tediums of her life, but he must have bribed some governess very largely, either with love or money, to reveal to him the secrets of her prison-house, or, he must have devoted extraordinary powers of observation and discovery to the elucidation of the subject. In either case, *Agnes Grey* is a tale well worth the writing and the reading. The heroine is a sort of younger sister to *Jane Eyre*; but inferior to her in every way. The following is, we imagine, a truthful picture of an interior.

[quotes from chapter 3, 'However, by dint of great labour ... Remember that, Mrs Bloomfield!']

Wuthering Heights is a strange sort of book, – baffling all regular criticism; yet, it is impossible to begin and not finish it; and quite as impossible to lay it aside afterwards and say nothing about it. In the midst of the reader's perplexity the ideas predominant in his mind concerning this book are likely to be – brutal cruelty, and semi-savage love. What may be the moral which the author wishes the reader to deduce from his work, it is difficult to say; and we refrain from assigning any, because to speak honestly, we have discovered none but mere glimpses of hidden morals or secondary meanings. There seems to us great power in this book but a purposeless power, which we feel a great desire to see turned to better account. We are quite confident that the writer of *Wuthering Heights* wants but the practised skill to make a great artist; perhaps, a great dramatic artist. His qualities are, at present, excessive; a far more promising fault, let it be remembered, than if they were deficient. He may tone down, whereas the weak and inefficient writer, however carefully he may write by rule and line, will never work up his productions to the point of beauty in art. In *Wuthering Heights* the reader is shocked, disgusted, almost sickened by details of cruelty, inhumanity, and the most diabolical hate and vengeance, and anon come passages of powerful testimony to the supreme power of love – even over demons in the human form. The women in the book are of a strange fiendish-angelic nature, tantalizing, and terrible, and the men are indescribable out of the book itself. Yet, towards the close of the story occurs the following pretty, soft picture, which comes like the rainbow after a storm.

[quotes from chapter 32, 'Both doors and lattices were open ... refuge in the kitchen']

We strongly recommend all our readers who love novelty to get this story, for we can promise them that they never have read anything like it before. It is very puzzling and very interesting, and if we had space we would willingly devote a little more time to the analysis of this remarkable story, but we must leave it to our readers to decide what sort of book it is.

62. Unsigned notice, *New Monthly Magazine*

January 1848, lxxxii, 140

Ellis Bell and Acton Bell appear in the light of two names borrowed to represent two totally different styles of composition and two utterly opposed modes of treatment of the novel, rather than to indicate two real personages.

They are names coupled together as mysteriously in the literary, as the sons of Leda are in the asterial world; and there is something at least gained by being mysterious at starting. *Wuthering Heights*, by Ellis Bell, is a terrific story, associated with an equally fearful and repulsive spot. It should have been called *Withering* Heights, for any thing from which the mind and body would more instinctively shrink, than the mansion and its tenants, cannot be easily imagined. 'Wuthering,' however, as expressive in provincial phraseology of 'the frequency of atmospheric tumults out of doors' must do, however much the said tumults may be surpassed in frequency and violence by the disturbances that occur in doors. Our novel reading experience does not enable us to refer to any thing to be compared with the personages we are introduced to at this desolate spot – a perfect misanthropist's heaven.

Agnes Grey, by Acton Bell, is a story of quite a different character. It is a simple tale of a governess's experiences and trials of love, borne with that meakness, and met by that fortitude, that ensure a final triumph. It has one advantage over its predecessor, that while its language is less ambitious and less repulsive, it fills the mind with a lasting picture of love and happiness succeeding to scorn and affliction, and teaches us to put every trust in a supreme wisdom and goodness.

63. From an unsigned review, *Atlas*

22 January 1848, 59

One of the five reviews found in Emily's desk; see No. 59. Contains one of the rare references in the reviews of 1847–8 to the Brontës' poems.

About two years ago a small volume of poems by 'Currer, Acton, and Ellis Bell' was given to the world. The poems were of varying excellence; those by Currer Bell, for the most part, exhibiting the highest order of merit; but, as a whole, the little work produced little or no sensation, and was speedily forgotten. Currer, Acton, and Ellis Bell have now all come before us as novelists, and all with so much success as to make their future career a matter of interesting speculation in the literary world.

Whether, as there is little reason to believe, the names which we have written are the genuine names of actual personages – whether they are, on the other hand, mere publishing names, as is our own private conviction – whether they represent three distinct individuals, or whether a single personage is the actual representative of the 'three gentlemen at once' of the title-pages – whether authorship of the poems and the novels is to be assigned to one gentleman or to one lady, to three gentlemen or three ladies, or to a mixed male and female triad of authors – are questions over which the curious may puzzle themselves, but are matters really of little account. One thing is certain; as in the poems, so in the novels, the signature of 'Currer Bell' is attached to pre-eminently the best performance. We were the first to welcome the author of *Jane Eyre* as a new writer of no ordinary power.[1] A new edition of that singular work has been called for, and we do not doubt that its success has done much to ensure a favourable reception for the volumes which are now before us.

Wuthering Heights is a strange, inartistic story. There are evidences in every chapter of a sort of rugged power – an unconscious strength –

[1] See No. 5.

230

which the possessor seems never to think of turning to the best advantage. The general effect is inexpressibly painful. We know nothing in the whole range of our fictitious literature which presents such shocking pictures of the worst forms of humanity. *Jane Eyre* is a book which affects the reader to tears; it touches the most hidden sources of emotion. *Wuthering Heights* casts a gloom over the mind not easily to be dispelled. It does not soften; it harasses, it extenterates. There are passages in it which remind us of the *Nowlans* of the late John Banim[1] but of all pre-existent works the one which it most recalls to our memory is the *History of Mathew Wald*.[2] It has not, however, the unity and concentration of that fiction; but is a *sprawling* story, carrying us, with no mitigation of anguish, through two generations of sufferers – though one presiding evil genius sheds a grim shadow over the whole, and imparts a singleness of malignity to the somewhat disjointed tale. A more natural story we do not remember to have read. Inconceivable as are the combinations of human degradation which are here to be found moving within the circle of a few miles, the *vraisemblance* is so admirably preserved; there is so much truth in what we may call the *costumery* (not applying the word in its narrow acceptation) – the general mounting of the entire piece – that we readily identify the scenes and personages of the fiction; and when we lay aside the book it is some time before we can persuade ourselves that we have held nothing more than imaginary intercourse with the ideal creations of the brain. The reality of unreality has never been so aptly illustrated as in the scenes of almost savage life which Ellis Bell has brought so vividly before us.

The book sadly wants relief. A few glimpses of sunshine would have increased the reality of the picture and given strength rather than weakness to the whole. There is not in the entire *dramatis personæ* a single character which is not utterly hateful or thoroughly contemptible. If you do not detest the person, you despise him; and if you do not despise him, you detest him with your whole heart. Hindley, the brutal, degraded sot, strong in the desire to work all mischief, but impotent in his degradation; Linton Heathcliff, the miserable, drivelling coward, in whom we see selfishness in its most abject form; and Heathcliff himself, the presiding evil genius of the piece, the tyrant father of an

---

[1] John Banim (1798–1842), 'the Scott of Ireland', novelist, dramatist and poet, published *The Nowlans* (1826) as a contribution to *Tales by the O'Hara Family*, second series (first series 1825). 'The O'Hara Family' was a pseudonym adopted by John Banim and his brother Michael (see Introduction, p. 9).

[2] *The History of Matthew Wald. A Novel* (1824) by J. G. Lockhart.

imbecile son, a creature in whom every evil passion seems to have reached a gigantic excess – form a group of deformities such as we have rarely seen gathered together on the same canvas. The author seems to have designed to throw some redeeming touches into the character of the brutal Heathcliff, by portraying him as one faithful to the 'idol of his boyhood' – loving to the very last – long, long after death had divided them, the unhappy girl who had cheered and brightened up the early days of his wretched life. Here is the touch of nature which makes the whole world kin – but it fails of the intended effect. There is a selfishness – a ferocity in the love of Heathcliff, which scarcely suffer it, in spite of its rugged constancy, to relieve the darker parts of his nature. Even the female characters excite something of loathing and much of contempt. Beautiful and loveable in their childhood, they all, to use a vulgar expression, 'turn out badly.' Catherine the elder – wayward, impatient, impulsive – sacrifices herself and her lover to the pitiful ambition of becoming the wife of a gentleman of station. Hence her own misery – her early death – and something of the brutal wickedness of Heathcliff's character and conduct; though we cannot persuade ourselves that even a happy love would have tamed down the natural ferocity of the tiger. Catherine the younger is more sinned against than sinning, and in spite of her grave moral defects, we have some hope of her at the last.

Wuthering Heights is not a book the character of which it is very easy to set forth in extract; but the following scene in which Catherine and Heathcliff – the lovers of early days each wedded to another – are the actors, will afford a glimpse of Ellis Bell's power.

[quotes from chapter 15 the last meeting of Heathcliff and Catherine]

This is at least forcible writing; but, to estimate it aright, the reader . . . must not fancy himself in a London mansion; but in an old north-country manor-house, situated on 'the dreary, dreary moorland,'[1] far from the haunts of civilised men. There is, at all events, keeping in the book – the groups of figures and the scenery are in harmony with each other. There is a touch of Salvator-Rosa in all.[2] *Agnes Grey* is a story of very different stamp. It is a tale of every day life, and though not wholly free from exaggeration (there are some detestable young ladies in it), does not offend by any startling improbabilities. It is more

---

[1] Tennyson's 'Locksley Hall' (1842), 40: 'O the dreary, dreary moorland! – O the barren, barren shore . . .'
[2] See *Britannia* (No. 60, p. 224).

level and more sunny. Perhaps we shall best describe it as a somewhat coarse imitation of one of Miss Austin's [sic] charming stories. Like *Jane Eyre*, it sets forth some passages in the life of a governess; but the incidents, wound up with the heroine's marriage to a country clergyman, are such as might happen to anyone in that situation of life, and, doubtless, have happened to many. There is a want of distinctness in the character of Agnes, which prevents the reader from taking much interest in her fate – but the story, though lacking the power and originality of *Wuthering Heights*, is infinitely more agreeable. It leaves no painful impression on the mind – some may think it leaves no impression at all. We are not quite sure that the next new novel will not efface it, but *Jane Eyre* and *Wuthering Heights* are not things to be forgotten. The work of Currer Bell is a great performance; that of Ellis Bell is only a promise, but it is a colossal one.

64. From an unsigned notice of *Wuthering Heights*, *Literary World*

April 1848, 243

The New York *Literary World* (1847–53), edited by Evert and George Duyckink (who were friendly among others with Hawthorne and Melville), was always more favourably disposed towards the Brontës than many other American periodicals: see also No. 74 and compare Nos 65, 66, 69.

The extraordinary popularity of *Jane Eyre* will give this book a reputation which it would not, perhaps, have otherwise acquired for itself. Few of those who read that work will find in this a worthy successor, for, although possessing far more strength and power in its darker portions, yet it lacks the relief necessary to make it as pleasing as *Jane Eyre*. It is 'a dark tale darkly told;' a book that seizes upon us with an iron grasp, and makes us read its story of passions and wrongs whether we will or no. Fascinated by strange magic we read what we dislike, we become interested in characters which are most revolting to our feelings, and are made subject to the immense power, of the book, – a rough, shaggy, uncouth power that turns up the dark side of human nature, and deals with unbridled passions and hideous inhumanities. In the whole story not a single trait of character is elicited which can command our admiration, not one of the fine feelings of our nature seems to have formed a part in the composition of its principal actors; and yet, spite of this, spite of the disgusting coarseness of much of the dialogue, and the improbabilities and incongruities of the plot, we are spell-bound, we cannot choose but read. As a specimen of the whole character of the book the following extract will, we think, give a fair estimate of its various peculiarities, its coarse feeling, its unnatural characters, and its dark fascination.

[quotes from chapter 15 the account of Heathcliff's last meeting with Catherine]

The book, throughout, is characterised by the same mind whose peculiarities of thought and expression are stamped upon the work of 'Currer Bell', but we know not by what authority our worthy American publishers have explicitly named it as being by the author of *Jane Eyre*, in as much as in the English advertisement *Wuthering Heights* purports to be by '*Ellis* Bell'. A third work of similar style and character has just appeared abroad entitled *Agnes Grey*, by '*Acton* Bell'.[1]

---

[1] 'Acton Bell' is apparently assumed to be the author of all the 'Bell' novels in the *Literary World*'s review of *The Tenant of Wildfell Hall* (No. 74).

65. G. W. Peck, from an unsigned review of *Wuthering Heights*, *American Review*

June 1848, vii, 572–85

An exceptionally lengthy review initialled by George Washington Peck (1817–59), author, journalist and music critic, who wrote regularly for this periodical during 1847–50; his other literary articles include discussions of Longfellow, Dana, Cooper, Poe and Charles Lamb. It is perhaps worth adding that his own career was, like Emily Brontë's, cut short by tuberculosis. His analysis of *Wuthering Heights* is an odd mixture of shrewdness, enthusiasm and moral disapproval, and contains discerning comment on the book's mixture of brilliance and naïveté together with the most detailed of the various attacks made on its so-called 'coarse' language (see Introduction, p. 29). His explanation of this 'coarseness' in terms of what he sees to be a certain kind of snobbery on the part of the author is unique, and if wide of the mark in some respects is highly suggestive in others. Among the omitted passages style and a number of incidental reflections on contemporary American manners and morals.

Respecting a book so original as this, and written with so much power of imagination, it is natural that there should be many opinions. Indeed, its power is so predominant that it is not easy after a hasty reading to analyze one's impressions so as to speak of its merits and demerits with confidence. We have been taken and carried through a new region, a melancholy waste, with here and there patches of beauty; have been brought in contact with fierce passions, with extremes of love and hate, and with sorrow that none but those who have suffered can understand. This has not been accomplished with ease, but with an ill-mannered contempt for the decencies of language, and in a style which might resemble that of a Yorkshire farmer who should have endeavored to eradicate his provincialism by taking lessons of a London footman. We have had many sad bruises and tumbles in our journey, yet it was interesting, and at length we are safely arrived at a happy conclusion.

The first feeling with which we turn back to recall the incidents passed through, is one of uneasiness and gloom; even the air of summer, so reviving to city dwellers, does not dispel it. To write or think about the tale, without being conscious of a phase of sadness, is impossible . . .

We shall take for granted that a novel which has excited so unusual an attention, has been or will soon be in the hands of most of our readers of light literature, shall therefore write rather *from* than *upon* it. We will not attempt an outline of the story; it is so void of events that an outline would be of small assistance to any who have not read it, and would only be tedious to those who have. It is a history of two families during two generations, and all transpires under their two roofs . . .

If we did not know that this book has been read by thousands of young ladies in the country, we should esteem it our first duty to caution them against it simply on account of the coarseness of the style . . .

The book is original; It is powerful; full of suggestiveness. But still it is *coarse* . . . Setting aside the profanity, which if a writer introduces into a book, he offends against both politeness and good morals, there is such a general roughness and savageness in the soliloquies and dialogues here given as never should be found in a work of art . . . It would indicate that the writer was not accustomed to the society of gentlemen, and was not afraid, indeed, rather gloried, in showing it . . .

A person may be unmannered from want of delicacy of perception, or cultivation, or ill-mannered intentionally. The author of *Wuthering Heights* is both. His rudeness is chiefly real but partly assumed . . . The following is put into the mouth of a young boy telling how his playmate was bitten by a bulldog: –

The devil had seized her ankle, Nelly; I heard his abominable snorting. She did not yell out – no! She would have scorned to do it, if she had been spitted on the horns of a mad cow. I did, though; *I vociferated curses enough to annihilate any fiend in Christendom*; and I got a stone and thrust it between his jaws, and tried with all my might to cram it down his throat. [chapter 6]

Afterwards he tells how she was taken care of in the parlour of the Lintons: –

The curtains were still looped up at one corner, and I resumed my station as spy, because, if Catherine had wished to return, I *intended shattering their great glass panes to a million fragments*, unless they let her out.

She sat on the sofa quietly, Mrs. Linton took off the gray cloak of the dairy maid which we had borrowed for our excursion – shaking her head, and *expostulating* with her, I suppose; she was a young lady, and they made a distinction between her treatment and mine. Then the woman servant brought a basin of warm water, and washed her feet, and Mr. Linton mixed a tumbler of negus, and Isabella emptied a plateful of cakes into her lap, and Edgar stood gaping at a distance. Afterward, they dried and combed her beautiful hair, and gave her a pair of *enormous* slippers, and wheeled her to the fire; and I left her, as merry as she could be, dividing her food between the little dog and Skulker, whose nose she pinched as he ate, and kindling a spark of spirit in the vacant blue eyes of the Lintons – *a dim reflection from her own enchanting face – I saw they were full of stupid admiration; she is so immeasurably superior to them* – to everybody on earth; is she not, Nelly? . . . [chapter 6]

These are examples of simple vulgarity, or want of a refined perception. Their occurring in a work written with so much strength, that in reading hastily, one hardly notices them (and thousands such) as blemishes, does not redeem them.

In another place the author finds an old diary, which, according to his dates, must have been written by a little imperfectly educated girl in the very year of the Declaration of American Independence: –

An immediate interest kindled within me for the unknown Catherine, and I began forthwith to decipher her faded hieroglyphics.

'An awful Sunday!' commenced the paragraph beneath. 'I wish my father were back again. Hindley is a *detestable substitute* – his conduct to Heathcliff is *atrocious* – H. and I are going to rebel – we took our *initiatory step* this evening.' [chapter 3]

All these instances may be observed to be not only vulgar, but vulgar in a peculiar way. They savour, to use a word which is the only one in the language that will express the thing, of *snobbishness* . . .

To one variety of the English snob may be traced a certain, peculiar, easy fluency of expression, which has its counterpart also in the American. This peculiarity seems to be founded in a desire to assimilate the language of strong emotion to that of mercantile correspondence, and manifests itself in an eloquence which resembles that of business circulars.

But as business correspondence is intended to conceal emotion, it forms a poor model for style, and hence it is particularly the duty of critics to be on the alert to detect its presence and expose it. The words and parts of sentences italicized in the above extracts, have a tang of Mantalini and Chawls Yellowplush . . .[1]

But the taint of vulgarity with our author extends deeper than mere snobbishness; he is rude, because he prefers to be so. In the outset he represents himself as a misanthropist, and confesses to a degree of reserve which it would puzzle a psychologist to explain . . .

It is evident that the author has suffered, not disappointment in love, but some great mortification of pride. Possibly his position in society has given him manners that have prevented him from associating with those among whom he feels he has intellect enough to be classed, and he is thus in reality the misanthropist he claims to be. Very likely he may be a young person who has spent his life, until within a few years, in some isolated town in the North of England. It is only by some such supposition that his peculiarities of style and thought can be accounted for. He is one who is evidently unfamiliar with, and careless of acquiring, the habits of refined society.

But the writer's disposition to be coarse is, perhaps, still more clearly shown by examples like the following: –

I was surprised to see Heathcliff there also. He stood by the fire, his back toward me, just finishing a stormy scene to poor Zillah, who ever and anon interrupted her labor to pluck up the corner of her apron, and heave an indignant groan.

'And you, you worthless —' he broke out as I entered, turning to his daughter-in-law, and employing an epithet as harmless as duck, or sheep, but generally represented by a dash .[chapter 4 (the narrator is Lockwood)]

Had the writer been simply, unconsciously coarse, he would, in this instance, have said, 'slut' or 'bitch,' without advertising to the harmlessness of the word. But by alluding to its harmlessness, he at once uses it, and offers a defence of it. This as plainly evinces a conscious determination to write coarsely, as if he had quoted and defended a passage from Rabelais. He knew the word to be a low word, though not an immodest one, and he determined to show his bold independence by using and defending it . . .

The influence which this book cannot but have upon manners, must be bad. For the coarseness extends farther than the mere style; it extends *all through*; and the crude style and rude expressions are too much in

---

[1] On Mantalini see p. 114, n. Thackeray's *The Yellowplush Correspondence and Mr Yellowplush's Ajew* are of 1837–8.

keeping with the necessary situations. It deals constantly in exaggerated extremes of passion. From the beginning to the end, there is hardly a scene which does not place the actors in the most agonizing or antagonizing predicament possible ...

Catherine's election of Linton and her reasons for it, as it is the main incident of the story, may be most properly taken to examine the *naturalness* of the passion.

[quotes from chapter 9]

But is this natural passion? Would the most imperious, impetuous and wayward young lady that can be imagined, ever have reasoned with herself, situated as she was, in the manner here represented? ... Let any of our young gentlemen readers look fairly and honestly into their own hearts and ask themselves, whether ... they could argue the question in their minds in this manner: 'Here is one young lady whom I love as I do my own soul; I cannot live without her; nothing on earth shall separate us. But at the same time I cannot marry her, because we should be poor; I will, therefore, take this other rich one, who likes me well enough, in order that it may be better "in a pecuniary point of view" for my real love!' We do not ask if any young man would *act* on such grounds, but only if he can fancy a state of mind, in which he could for an instant seriously *propose* to himself to act thus ... But it will be urged, and the author, with a great deal of tact, endeavors to make it so appear, that poor Cathy was unconscious of the nature of her love for Heathcliff: she had been brought up with him; they had played together all their lives; a kind of sisterly feeling for him was all that she was actually conscious of.

This is more unnatural than the other ... The physical condition of our bodies, the changes which take place on arriving at an age proper for marriage, do not allow of the ignorance which our author requires us to suppose in his heroine, not only in this place, but especially after Heathcliff's absence and return, when she is the wife of Linton and about to become a mother ... Could Mrs. Linton, after Heathcliff's return, desire his presence without being conscious that her feelings towards him were such as his presence would only render more intolerable, unless, as the author leaves us no room to suppose, she meant to be untrue to her husband? We think that when any one considers the matter, he will find in what we have said above, a very plain explanation of what has been talked of as a puzzling character ... there is in these characters an absence of all that natural desire which should accompany love. They are abstract and bodiless. Their love is feline; it is tigerish.

Yet the work is carried on with such power that it excites a sense of shame to turn back to many of its most 'thrilling' scenes, and reflect that we were able to read them with so little disgust . . . The characters are drawn with dramatic force and made to seem alive, yet when we lay the book aside, they collapse, they die, they vanish; and we see that we have been cheated with illusory semblances. The children know too much about their minds and too little about their bodies; they understand at a very early age all the intellectual and sentimental part of love, but the 'bloom of young desire' does not warm their cheeks. The grown-up characters are the mere tools of fixed passions. Their actions and sayings are like those of monomaniacs or persons who have breathed nitrous oxide. When they hate, they swear and fight and pull out each other's hair. When they are grieved they drink themselves to madness . . . Agony is heaped on agony, till the deficient mass topples down headlong. The fancy gives out, and like a tired hound, rushes reeling to the conclusion.

Yet with all this faultiness, *Wuthering Heights* is, undoubtedly, a work of many singular merits. In the first place it is not a novel which deals with the shows of society, the surfaces and conventionalities os life. It does not depict men and women guided merely by motivef intelligible to simplest observers. It lifts the veil and shows boldly the dark side of our depraved nature. It teaches how little the ends of life in the young are rough hewn by experience and benevolence in the old. It goes into the under-current of passion, and the rapid hold it has taken of the public shows how much truth there is hidden under its coarse extravagance.

Next to the merit of this novel as a work of thought and subtle insight, is its great power as a work of the imagination. In this respect it must take rank very high, if not among the highest. It is not flowingly written; the author can hardly be an easy writer. Yet he has the power, with all his faults of style, of sometimes flashing a picture upon the eye, and the feeling with it, in a few sentences. The snow-storm which occurs in the second and third chapters of the first volume, is an example . . .

The dialogue is also singularly effective and dramatic. The principal characters all talk alike; yet they stand before us as definite as so many individuals . . .

That the book is original all who have read it need not be told. It is *very* original. And this is the reason of its popularity. It comes upon a sated public [as] a new sensation. Nothing like it has ever been written before; it is to be hoped that in respect of its faults, for the sake of good manners, nothing will be hereafter. Let it stand by itself, a coarse, original, powerful book, – one that does not give us true characters, but horridly striking and effective ones. It will live a short and brilliant life, and then die and be forgotten ... Poor Cathy's ghost will not walk the earth forever; and the insane Heathcliff will soon rest quietly in his coveted repose.

We are not aware that anything has been written upon the rank that ought to be assigned to such works as *Wuthering Heights* in fictitious literature. In conversation we have heard it spoken of by some as next in merit to Shakespeare for depth of insight and dramatic power; while others have confessed themselves unable to get through it. But all agree that it affects them somewhat unpleasantly. It is written in a morbid phase of the mind, and is sustained so admirably that it communicates this sickliness to the reader. It does in truth lay bare some of the secret springs of human action with wonderful clearness; but still it dissects character as with a broad-axe – chops out some of the great passions, sets them together and makes us almost believe the combinations to be real men and women. It abounds in effective description, is very individual, and preserves the unity of its peculiar gloomy phase of mind from first to last. Yet the reader rises from its conclusion with the feeling of one passing from a sick chamber to a comfortable parlour, or going forth after a melancholy rain, into a dry, clear day.

Now if the rank of a work of fiction is to depend solely on its naked imaginative power, then this is one of the greatest novels in the language. Not one of Walter Scott's resembles it in assuming a peculiar and remote mood of feeling, and carrying it through two volumes in spite of the most staring faults and extravagances ... Even after his most tragic novel, the *Bride of Lammermoor*, the regret which we feel is not of that uneasy kind which the soul struggles to shake off; we do not feel as if we had been reading a horrible murder in the Newgate Calendar ... Yet few men are really more individual than he ... Only he is never *designedly* or *consciously* individual ... we will recur to the question, as to what rank ought to be assigned to such works as *Wuthering Heights*. We have said, what all who have read it know, that it was original ... A certain personal phase, not a pleasant one, is assumed and carried through it with great power. But this phase must have been conscious to the writer. He must have been designedly original. He must have set to his work with some such feeling towards the world, as he would probably think well expressed by the words, 'There! take *that*, and see how you like it!'

No truly great artist ever desired to place himself before the world in that attitude. The pride of genuine nobleness is more humble. It does not condescend to don the motley and please the general with fantastic tricks. In a word, *that originality which is conscious to the writer, is not genuine*, and it is soon found out and disliked. Herein we fear that the author of *Wuthering Heights* has some unsound timbers in him ...

All that is really great and good in this book, might have been given in a better style, without its revolting pictures. Indeed, the writer might have been personal and peculiar, and melancholy even, if he had so pleased, provided his greatest solicitude had been to please the reader. As it is, admirable as is his power, he must be ranked not among the first writers of fiction. His book has the air rather of an *exposé* of his life-suffering, to use a Germanism, than a purely ideal composition.

66. Unsigned notice of *Wuthering Heights*, *Graham's Magazine*

July 1848, 60

See No. 64 and Introduction, p. 32.

This novel is said to be by the author of *Jane Eyre*, and was eagerly caught at by a famished public, on the strength of the report. It afforded, however, but little nutriment, and has universally disappointed expectation. There is an old saying that those who eat toasted cheese at night will dream of Lucifer. The author of *Wuthering Heights* has evidently eaten toasted cheese. How a human being could have attempted such a book as the present without committing suicide before he had finished a dozen chapters, is a mystery. It is a compound of vulgar depravity and unnatural horrors, such as we might suppose a person, inspired by a mixture of brandy and gunpowder, might write for the edification of fifth-rate blackguards. Were Mr. Quilp[1] alive we should be inclined to believe that the work had been dictated by him to Lawyer Brass, and published by the interesting sister of that legal gentleman.

67. Unidentified review of *Wuthering Heights*

c. 1847

See Introduction, p. 31. The origin of the review has not been traced. It is reproduced by Charles Simpson in his *Emily Brontë* (1929), 172–9, from the cutting found in Emily's desk and now lodged at Haworth Parsonage Museum. For the other reviews found with it see No. 59.

This is a work of great ability, and contains many chapters, to the production of which talent of no common order has contributed. At the same time, the materials which the author has placed at his own disposal have been but few. In the resources of his own mind, and in his own manifestly vivid perceptions of the peculiarities of character – in short, in his knowledge of human nature – has he found them all. An antiquated farm-house, a neighbouring residence of a somewhat more pretending description, together with their respective inmates, amounting to some half a dozen souls in each, constitute the material and the personal components of one of the most interesting stories we have read for many a long day. The comfortable cheerfulness of the one abode, and the cheerless discomfort of the other – the latter

[1] In Dickens's *The Old Curiosity Shop* (1841).

being less the result of a cold and bleak situation, old and damp rooms, and (if we may use the term) of a sort of 'haunted house' appearance, than of the strange and mysterious character of its inhabitants – the loves and marriages, separations and hatreds, hopes and disappointments, of two or three generations of the gentle occupants of the one establishment, and the ruder tenants of the other, are brought before us at a moment with a tenderness, at another with a fearfulness, which appeals to our sympathies with the truest tones of the voice of nature; and it is quite impossible to read the book – and this is no slight testimony to the merits of a work of the kind – without feeling that, if placed in the same position as any one of the characters in any page of it, the chances would be twenty to one in favour of our conduct in that position being precisely such as the author has assigned to the personages he has introduced into his domestic drama. But we must at once impose upon ourselves a task – and we confess it is a hard one – we must abstain (from a regard to the space at our disposal) from yielding to the temptation by which we are beset to enter into that minute description of the plot of this very dramatic production to which such a work has an undoubted claim. It is not every day that so good a novel makes its appearance; and to give its contents in detail would be depriving many a reader of half the delight he would experience from the perusal of the work itself. To its pages we must refer him, then; there will he have ample opportunity of sympathising, – if he has one touch of nature that 'makes the whole world kin' – with the feelings of childhood, youth, manhood, and age, and all the emotions and passions which agitate the restless bosom of humanity. May he derive from it the delight we have ourselves experienced, and be equally grateful to its author for the genuine pleasure he has afforded him.

68. Charlotte Brontë on 'Ellis' and 'Acton'

1847-8

Letters to W. S. Williams of 21 December 1847, 15 February 1848, 14 August 1848 (*LL*, ii, 165, 189, 244-5).

21 December 1847:

You are not far wrong in your judgment respecting *Wuthering Heights* and *Agnes Grey*. Ellis has a strong, original mind, full of strange though sombre power. When he writes poetry that power speaks in language at once condensed, elaborated, and refined, but in prose it breaks forth in scenes which shock more than they attract. Ellis will improve, however, because he knows his defects. *Agnes Grey* is the mirror of the mind of the writer.

15 February 1848:

I should much . . . like to take that quiet view of the 'great world' you allude to . . . Ellis, I imagine, would soon turn aside from the spectacle in disgust. I do not think he admits it as his creed that 'the proper study of mankind is man' – at least not the artificial man of cities. In some points I consider Ellis somewhat of a theorist: now and then he broaches ideas which strike my sense as much more daring and original than practical; his reason may be in advance of mine, but certainly it often travels a different road. I should say Ellis will not be seen in his full strength till he is seen as an essayist . . .

14 August 1848:

You say Mr Huntingdon [in *The Tenant of Wildfell Hall*] reminds you of Rochester. Does he? Yet there is no likeness between the two; the foundation of each character is entirely different. Huntingdon is a specimen of the naturally selfish, sensual, superficial man, whose one merit of a joyous temperament only avails him while he is young and healthy, whose best days are his earliest, who never profits by experience, who is sure to grow worse the older he grows. Mr Rochester has a thoughtful nature and a very feeling heart; he is neither selfish nor self-indulgent; he is ill-educated, misguided; errs, when he does err, through rashness and inexperience: he lives for a time as too many other men live, but being radically better than most men, he does not like that degraded life and is never happy in it. He is taught the severe lessons of experience and has sense to learn wisdom from them. Years improve him; the effervescence of youth foamed away, what is really good in him still remains. His nature is like wine of a good vintage, time cannot sour, but only mellows him. Such at least was the character I meant to portray.

Heathcliff, again, of *Wuthering Heights* is quite another creation. He exemplifies the effects which a life of continued injustice and hard usage may produce on a naturally perverse, vindictive, and inexorable disposition. Carefully trained and kindly treated, the black gipsy-cub might possibly have been reared into a human being, but tyranny and ignorance made of him a mere demon. The worst of it is, some of his spirit seems breathed through the whole narrative in which he figures: it haunts every moor and glen, and beckons in every fir-tree of the Heights.

69. E. P. Whipple on *Wuthering Heights* from 'Novels of the Season', *North American Reveiw*

October 1848, cxli, 354–69

For the commentaries in the same review on *Jane Eyre* and *The Tenant of Wildfell Hall* see Nos 20, 75. Charlotte wrote to Williams on 22 November 1848:

The *North American Review* is worth reading; there is no mincing the matter there. What a bad set the Bells must be! What appalling books they write! Today, as Emily appeared a little easier, I thought the *Review* would amuse her, so I read it aloud to her and Anne. As I sat between them . . . I studied the two ferocious authors. Ellis, the 'man of uncommon talents, but dogged, brutal, and morose', sat leaning back in his easy-chair drawing his impeded breath as he best could, and looking, alas! piteously pale and wasted . . . he smiled half-amused, and half in scorn as he listened. Acton . . . smiled too, dropping . . . a single word of calm amazement to hear his character so darkly portrayed. I wonder what the reviewer would have thought of his own sagacity could he have beheld the pair as I did. Vainly, too, might he have looked round for the masculine partner in the firm of 'Bell & Co'. How I laugh in my sleeve when I read the solemn assertion that *Jane Eyre* was written in partnership, and that it 'bears the marks of more than one mind and one sex' (*LL*, ii, 287).

The truth is, that the whole firm of Bell & Co. seem to have a sense of the depravity of human nature peculiarly their own. It is the yahoo, not the demon, that they select for representation; their Pandemonium is of mud rather than fire.

This is especially the case with Acton Bell [sic], the author of *Wuthering Heights*, *The Tenant of Wildfell Hall*, and, if we mistake not, of certain offensive but powerful portions of *Jane Eyre*. Acton, when left together to his own imaginations, seems to take a morose satisfaction in developing a full and complete science of human brutality. In *Wuthering Heights* he has succeeded in reaching the summit of this laudable ambition. He appears to think that spiritual wickedness is a combination of animal ferocities, and has accordingly made a compendium of the most striking qualities of tiger, wolf, cur, and wild-cat, in the hope of framing out of such elements a suitable brute-demon to serve as the hero of his novel. Compared with Heathcote [sic], Squeers is considerate and Quilp humane. He is a deformed monster, whom the Mephistopheles of Goethe would have nothing to say to, whom the Satan of Milton would consider as an object of simple disgust, and to whom Dante would hesitate in awarding the honour of a place among those whom he has consigned to the burning pitch. This epitome of brutality, disavowed by man and devil, Mr. Acton Bell attempts in two whole volumes to delineate, and certainly he is to be congratulated on his success. As he is a man of uncommon talents, it is needless to say that it is to his subject and his dogged manner of handling it that we are to refer the burst of dislike with which the novel was received. His mode of delineating a bad character is to narrate every offensive act and repeat every vile expression which are characteristic. Hence, in *Wuthering Heights*, he details all the ingenuities of animal malignity, and exhausts the whole rhetoric of stupid blasphemy, in order that there may be no mistake as to the kind of person he intends to hold up to the popular gaze. Like all spendthrifts of malice and profanity, however, he overdoes the business. Though he scatters oaths as plentifully as sentimental writers do interjections, the comparative parsimony of the great novelists in this respect is productive of infinitely more effect. It must be confessed that this coarseness, though the prominent, is not the only characteristic of the writer . . . he aims further to exhibit the action of the sentiment of love on the nature of the being whom his morbid imagination has created. This is by far the ablest and most subtle portion of his labours, and indicates that strong hold upon the elements of character, and that decision of touch in the delineation of the most evanescent qualities of emotion, which distinguish the mind of the whole family. For all practical purposes, however, the power evinced in *Wuthering Heights* is power thrown away. Nightmares and dreams, through which devils dance and wolves howl, make bad novels.

THE TENANT OF WILDFELL HALL

Summer 1848

70. From an unsigned review, *Spectator*

8 July 1848, xxi, 662–3

The volumes of fiction that some time since appeared under the name of Bell, with three several prænomens, had such a generic resemblance to one another that several reviewers remarked it. The first and most striking affinity was of substance. Each of the Bells selected the singular both in character and incident. The persons were such as are formed by a natural peculiarity of disposition, influenced by an equal peculiarity of circumstances, or produced by strong passions running their course unrestrained in the freedom of a remote country place, at a time which permitted greater liberty to individual will or caprice than is vouchsafed even to brutal and isolated squireens in these days. The composition – not mere diction, but the arrangement of the incidents and persons, as well as the style of the things themselves – was extreme and wild; seeking to base effects on the startling, without much regard either to probability or good taste. A rough vigour characterized the whole batch of Bells; but Currer Bell, the author or editor of *Jane Eyre*, exhibited rather the most cultivated taste and decidedly the most literary skill.

Nearly one half of *The Tenant of Wildfell Hall*, by Acton Bell, forms a sort of setting to the main story, and is pitched in a more natural key than the author's previous novel, though not without occasional roughness. In escaping from his extreme and violent manner, however, he loses somewhat of his strength and interest. There is nature, undoubtedly; but it is of a common kind. The daily life of a young and self-sufficient gentleman farmer and his family, with the characters and gossip of his neighbourhood, are scarcely enough to sustain the reader for a volume, even with the addition of the aforesaid farmer's love for the mysterious tenant of Wildfell Hall.

The tale of this lady, which she has written down apparently for her lover to read, is a story of suffering in married life, arising from the licentiousness, drunkenness, and downright blackguardism of her husband and his associates. She is provoked by his profligacy, disgusted by his habits, and surrounded by tempting gallants; and scenes founded on such subjects form the narrative of the tale, till she secretly escapes, and takes refuge near her brother; whom Gilbert Markham, the farmer lover, has mistaken for a favoured swain, and ferociously assaulted. In due time Mr. Huntingdon the husband dies: his widow's possession of property causes a considerable delay in the denouement; but it comes at last.

The Tenant of Wildfell Hall, like its predecessor, suggests the idea of considerable abilities ill applied. There is power, effect, and even nature, though of an extreme kind, in its pages; but there seems in the writer a morbid love for the coarse, not to say the brutal; so that his level subjects are not very attractive, and the more forcible are displeasing or repulsive, from their gross, physical, or profligate substratum. He might reply, that such things are in life: and probably glimpses of such a set as Huntingdon and his friends are occasionally caught in Doctors Commons cases, and tradition pictures such doings as not very rare in the early part of George the Third's reign, – although Mr. Bell paints them as contemporary. Mere existence, however, as we have often had occasion to remark, is not a sufficient reason for a choice of subject: its general or typical character is a point to consider, and its power of pleasing must be regarded, as well as its mere capabilities of force or effect. It is not only the subject of this novel, however, that is objectionable, but the manner of treating it. There is a coarseness of tone throughout the writing of all these Bells, that puts an offensive subject in its worst point of view, and which generally contrives to dash indifferent things.

From the nature of the work, any scene from *The Tenant of Wildfell Hall* will be of rather a broad kind. The following exhibits a Mr. Hargrave, having worked himself up to a phrensy in making love to Mrs. Huntingdon, suddenly surprised by the husband and friend.

[quotes chapter 39, 'I never saw a man so terribly excited . . . "I will. Blast me, if I don't."' (the text follows the first edition)]

71. From an unsigned review, *Athenaeum*

July 8 1848, 670–1

Probably by H. F. Chorley; the authorship is suggested by the continuity with the review in this periodical of *Wuthering Heights* and *Agnes Grey* (No. 58). See Introduction, pp. 33–4.

The three Bells, as we took occasion to observe when reviewing *Wuthering Heights* [No. 58] ring in a chime so harmonious as to prove that they have issued from the same mould. The resemblance borne by their novels to each other is curious. *The Tenant of Wildfell Hall* must not hope to gain the popularity of her elder sister *Jane Eyre*, – but the blood of the family is in her veins. A short extract will sufficiently prove this [quotes the opening scene] . . .

The reader is by this time curious to get a peep of 'the tenant' of such a wild abode: being convinced that, since

> Vague mystery hangs about these desert places,

she must be a Lady with 'a history.' But not a line or passage of this shall be divulged in the *Athenæum*, – however tempted to lengthen our lecture on family likeness. With regard to one point, however, we cannot remain silent: – The Bells must be warned against their fancy for dwelling upon what is disagreeable. The brutified estate of Mr. Huntingdon might have been displayed within a smaller compass in place of being elaborated with the fond minuteness of a Jan Steen. The position of the wife with regard to her husband's paramour is, on the other hand, treated with a sort of hard indifference, – natural enough, it may be, but not in harmony with the impressions of the Lady which we have been invited to entertain. Were the metal from this Bell foundry of baser quality than it is it would be lost time to point out flaws and take exceptions. As matters stand, our hints may not be without their use to future 'castings:' nor will they be unpalatable, seeing that they are followed by our honest recommendation of *Wildfell Hall* as the most interesting novel which we have read for a month past.

72. From Anne Brontë's preface to the second edition

22 July 1848

Attached to the second edition; see Introduction, p. 34. Both Charlotte and W. S. Williams thought it 'sensible' (see No. 77).

While I acknowledge the success of the present work to have been greater than I anticipated, and the praises it has elicited from a few kind critics to have been greater than it deserved, I must also admit that from some other quarters it has been censured with an asperity which I was as little prepared to expect, and which my judgment, as well as my feelings, assures me is more bitter than just. It is scarcely the province of an author to refute the arguments of his censors and vindicate his own productions; but I may be allowed to make here a few observations with which I would have prefaced the first edition, had I foreseen the necessity of such precautions against the misapprehensions of those who would read it with a prejudiced mind or be content to judge it by a hasty glance.

My object in writing the following pages was not simply to amuse the Reader; neither was it to gratify my own taste, nor yet to ingratiate myself with the Press and the Public: I wished to tell the truth, for truth always conveys its own moral to those who are able to receive it. But as the priceless treasure too frequently hides at the bottom of a well, it needs some courage to dive for it, especially as he that does so will be likely to incur more scorn and obloquy for the mud and water into which he has ventured to plunge, than thanks for the jewel he procures . . .

As the story of *Agnes Grey* was accused of extravagant overcolouring in those very parts that were carefully copied from the life, with a most scrupulous avoidance of all exaggeration, so, in the present work, I find myself censured for depicting *con amore*, with 'a morbid love of the coarse, if not of the brutal,' those scenes which, I will venture to say, have not been more painful for the most fastidious of my critics to read than they were for me to describe. I may have gone too far; in which case I shall be careful not to trouble myself or my readers in the same way again; but when we have to do with vice and vicious characters, I maintain it is better to depict them as they really are than as they would wish to appear. To represent a bad thing in its least offensive light is, doubtless, the most agreeable course for a writer of fiction to pursue; but is it the most honest, or the safest? Is it better to reveal the snares and pitfalls of life to the young and thought-less traveller, or to cover them with branches and flowers? Oh, reader! if there were less of this delicate concealment of facts – this whispering, 'Peace, peace,' when there is no peace, there would be less of sin and misery to the young of both sexes who are left to wring their bitter knowledge from experience.

I would not be understood to suppose that the proceedings of the unhappy scapegrace, with his few profligate companions I have here introduced, are a specimen of the common practices of society – the case is an extreme one, as I trusted none would fail to perceive; but I know that such characters do exist, and if I have warned one rash youth from following in their steps, or prevented one thoughtless girl from falling into the very natural error of my heroine, the book has not been written in vain . . .

One word more, and I have done. Respecting the author's identity, I would have it to be distinctly understood that Acton Bell is neither Currer nor Ellis Bell, and therefore let not his faults be attributed to them . . . As to whether the name be real or fictitious, it cannot greatly signify to those who know him only by his works. As little, I should think, can it matter whether the writer so designated is a man, or a woman, as one or two of my critics profess to have discovered . . . I am satisfied that if a book is a good one, it is so whatever the sex of the author may be. All novels are, or should be, written for both men and women to read, and I am at a loss to conceive how a man should permit himself to write anything that would be really disgraceful to a woman, or why a woman should be censured for writing anything that would be proper and becoming for a man.

73. From an unsigned review, *Examiner*

29 July 1848, 483–4

Possibly written by the same reviewer as Nos 59 and 82.

The authors of *Jane Eyre*, *Wuthering Heights*, *Agnes Grey* and *The Tenant of Wildfell Hall* are evidently children of the same family. They derive their scenes from the same country; their associations are alike; their heroines are for the most part alike, three being thrown upon their own talents for self-support, and two of them being all-enduring governesses; and their heroes also resemble each other, in aspect, and temper, almost in habits. We have, once or twice, entertained a suspicion that all the books that we have enumerated might have issued from the same source; sent forth at different seasons, in different states of mind or humour, or at different periods or elevations of the intellect, – *Jane Eyre* having been achieved at the culminating point. At all events, the writers are of the same stock, have undoubted marks of family resemblance, and are, in fact,

> Matched in mouth like Bells,
> Each under each.

The Bells are of a hardy race. They do not lounge in drawing-rooms or boudoirs. The air they breathe is not that of the hot-house, or of perfumed apartments: but it whistles through the rugged thorns that shoot out their prickly arms on barren moors, or it ruffles the moss on the mountain tops. Rough characters, untamed by contact with towns or cities; wilful men, with the true stamp of the passions upon them; plain vigorous Saxon words, not spoiled nor weakened by bad French or school-boy Latin; rude habits; ancient residences – with Nature in her great loneliness all around; – these – with the gray skies or sunset glories above – are the elements of their stories, compounded and reduced to shape, in different moods and with different success.

From all this, it will be observed that Currer, Acton, and Ellis Bell, whatever may be their defects otherwise, are not common-place writers. Their characters are not faint or tawdry copies of other characters which have already wearied us, and which have oppressed the pages of novelists, month after month, for the last thirty years. They have bone and sinew about them; animal life peeps out in every form; and the phraseology, although sometimes tedious enough, is rarely conventional. On these accounts, we are disposed to give a full and overflowing measure of praise to writers, who in assuming to portray nature have been wise and sincere enough to go back to their original; and we earnestly recommend them as examples to other labourers in the same path.

The story called *The Tenant of Wildfell Hall* is very inartificially constructed. The main part of the tale consists of a recital or journal made by a certain Mrs Graham, the mysterious tenant for the time being of the Hall, and the subject of innumerable slanderous hints and inuendos on the part of the restless gossips of a remote village. The lady herself, whose charms have disturbed the tranquillity of a very rough Cymon, by name Gilbert Markham, turns out to be a Mrs Huntingdon, and to be unhappily married; and it is not until the author very judiciously kills the first husband that the fortune of Gilbert the hero emerges out of the troubles which have hung about him, and his happiness is finally consummated.

There are two distinct series of character in the book: the one being the inhabitants of the village in the neighbourhood of Wildfell Hall; the other, less rural and far more ambitiously sketched; the friends and acquaintance who surround the heroine in her native county, and tend to illustrate her conduct in the earlier and later portions of her life. For she is 'Tenant of Wildfell Hall' during some months only, when she has been forced to fly from a drunken, vicious, and tyrannical husband; and there is in fact no connection whatever between the two sets of dramatis personæ, except the very slender link which the heroine herself presents, by passing from one place to the other.

To say the truth, there is no very intense excitement in any part of the book. Just at the time when we begin to feel some interest about Markham and the lady, we are thrown back upon her previous history, which occupies a full half of the three volumes before us. This is a fatal error: for, after so long and minute a history, we cannot go back and recover the enthusiasm which we have been obliged to dismiss a volume and half before.

Nevertheless, there are some distinct markings of character. In the village, besides the ordinary gabble of women who have nothing else to do but to slander their neighbour, there is an outline of a pompous parson, who seems drawn from life. The ladies are less original; and the general tone of all the conversations in this part of the story – except only when the wilfulness or ferocity of the hero intervenes – are tedious and commonplace. We are reminded occasionally of the minute gossip in which Miss Austin [sic] occasionally indulged, but with less of that particular quality which her dialogues invariably possessed, of illustrating the characters of the speakers.

Owing to the faulty construction of the tale, it is scarcely possible to analyze it, for the information of the reader . . .

The following extracts will put the reader in possession of all that is necessary for him to know respecting Mr Arthur [sic] Huntingdon.

[quotes the description of Helen's portrait of Henry Huntingdon (chapter 5); her first introduction to him (chapter 16); his scrutiny of her drawings (chapter 18)]

She eventually marries this vulgar coxcomb, who introduces her to some of his associates, – a set of drunken savages, such as we do not remember to have heard of as having been tolerated for many years, within the pale of civilized society . . . There is something touching in the renovation of Lord Lowborough, who rises from his ruin, and abandons himself, heart and soul, to a heartless beauty, one Annabella Wilmot, who on her part despises and deserts him for the more ostentatious Huntingdon, already the husband of Helen. The infidelity of the parties is discovered by the heroine, who overhears a conversation between them, and who thereupon withdraws herself from the society of her husband (whose excesses of all sorts increase daily), and finally flies, with her child, from his residence, to seclude herself at Wildfell Hall, under the assumed name of Mrs Graham . . .

The volumes afford few extracts. Here is a description, however, of Wildfell Hall, which is not very unlike the house inhabited by the wild people of *Wuthering Heights*.

[quotes Gilbert Markham's account, 'I left the more frequented regions . . . departed occupants' (chapter 2)]

There is a drunken scene of considerable power in the second volume, but we do not know that we should edify any of our readers by extracting it. We therefore forbear, and turn to gentler matters. The husband of Helen dies, as we have said, but Markham is ignorant of the sentiments of the beautiful widow, respecting whom he has received no tidings; and therefore, restless and unhappy, he wanders about her residence – hears of her great wealth – and, poor himself, is too proud to announce himself to her. They meet, however, by accident, and, after a few of those little misunderstandings which only enhance the happiness that succeeds and clears them away, the lovers are united, and the narrative ends. Here is a short love passage; and with this we must conclude our extracts.

[quotes from the closing chapter the scene between Helen and Gilbert, 'She remained in silence . . . my worldly goods']

74. From an unsigned review, *Literary World*

12 August 1848

See No. 64 and Introduction, pp. 29, 34.

There is no longer a doubt that the public is threatened with an infinite series of novels of a new class, which will be strung on, like the knotted tail of a kite, to the popular work *Jane Eyre* . . . The mind that conceived them is one of great strength and fervor, but coarse almost to brutality. Its owner may be descended from a jarl or a sea-king; but though his name be written on the roll of Battle-Abbey, there is a leaven of intense vulgarity in his very fibre that no washings of heraldry can ever efface. But we mean not to be offensively severe on this trait – we only want his American readers to recognise it while doing just homage to his genius. The *reality* of these writings makes them seize upon the public mind; and already there is the liveliest discussion about their principles, when in fact the danger from their diffusion lies much nearer the surface. For good taste supplies the *antennæ* or feelers as to what is right with half the world, and if that be perverted the weaker part at least are sure to go wrong.

Let us illustrate. The delightful tales of Hogg, the Ettrick shepherd, are full of grossness; but these tell for nothing with the reader of education. 'Tis a man of genius whom he knows to have been originally low in his associations, describing scenes of social life through his own peculiar appointed medium of viewing them. But in the novels of Acton Bell the public mind is fixed as yet only upon the *genius* of the writer: his pictures of nature are unsurpassed, and his pictures of life being almost equally vivid, we take his delineations of the better classes of society in the north of England with the same confidence that we accord to his delineations of scenery. And yet what a set of boorish cubs, nauseating profligates, and diabolical ruffians, does he present us, as specimens of the social life, whether immediately around him, or among the gay and far-descended, with whose habits and peculiarities he claims to be more or less familiar! In *Wuthering Heights*, all his far-descended demi-noblesse of the north of England would be out of place in a decent American kitchen. And in his last book the beautiful tenant of Wildfell Hall, the heiress of parks and villas, and the belle of a London season, marries a boor, whom the writer describes as lacking either spirit, generosity, or language to make a full apology to her invalid brother, whom he has nearly beaten to death by mistake; and this caitiff ditcher, who should have been passed out of the window with a farm-yard fork, the writer makes his hero; because he can talk sentiment, and criticise pictures, loves poetry, and has something more than a peasant's meteorological observation of the influence of the weather on the landscape.

But it may be said, 'there is a good deal of human nature about the whole thing.' There is the blindness of the critic! It is the writer's genius which makes his incongruities appear natural. When or where was there such a state of society, such a jumble of character and manners as he describes. His London Buck, Mr. Huntingdon, belongs to the squirearchy period of Smollett and Fielding's novels – the wife of the profligate to the sentimental, progress women of the present era. His 'Gilbert Markham' has the intelligence of a country gentleman that might have flourished in some pleasant hamlet on the North river; but he commits an assault and battery upon 'the squire' that would have wrought an indictment wherever our country squires are to be found; while his very apology, if it did not provoke a call for pistols and coffee in the party outraged, would have insured his being set ashore from a Mississippi steamboat as unfit to associate with the cabin passengers. Such gross incongruities of character do undoubtedly exist in individuals the world over; but can this sort of half-civilization, half-brutification, be characteristic of English society in any portion of that highly artificial country? Is it customary to find the combination of the boor and the bravo (both male and female by the way) in hereditary possession of long-descended estates like Wuthering Heights? Is it characteristic of 'English Respectabilities' – the landholders, common law men, or gig-keeping classes – to unite manners and principles like those of Huntingdon to property and position like his – or intelligence and taste like that of Markham to his clownishness?

We shrewdly suspect these books to be written by some gifted and retired woman, whose principal notions of men are derived from other books; or who, taking some walking automaton of her native village for a model, throws in certain touches of rascality, of uncouthness or boisterousness, to make her lay figures animated and, as she thinks, masculine. If any one chooses to study her male characters, it will be found that all that is good or attractive about them is or might be womanish, while all that is bad relishes either of the flash English novel, or of the melodramas of Kotzebue's day.

But what, then, do we leave this writer as the secret of her power? – It is comprised in vigor of thought, freshness and naturalness of expression, and remarkable reality of description. No matter how untrue to life her scene or character may be, the vividness and fervor of her imagination is such that she instantly *realizes* it. And herein lies the undoubted test – the distinctive power – the often sad gift of genius, viz. the thorough sympathy with, the living in, the intense realization of the creations of its own fancy. There are many thoroughly matter of fact scenes in these books so literally depicted that we read them only as faithful transcripts of the writer's experience; yet these very scenes are not unlikely to originate just as much in the conceptions of fancy as any others. You cannot detect the *jointing* on of the real to the unreal, in a writer of genius, from the simple fact that the images of the latter are often more vivid to his own mind than the actual pictures drawn by the former. But you may trace his identities through the medium of his tastes, natural or conventional. If these are coarse he will certainly betray himself at some time, like the cat who, endowed as a princess, instinctively betrayed the royal dignity, when a mouse at the foot of the throne called out her feline propensities.

The work before us, although infinitely inferior to, yet in some respects greatly resembles *Jane Eyre*: not alone in manner of thinking, but in the execution. Like its predecessor, it is an autobiography . . .

the reader will discover a strong family likeness to the plot of *Jane Eyre*, which purports to be written by a brother of the author. It may be curious to point out some few additional proofs of this resemblance. In both, the heroines, so soon as troubles thicken around them, take to the open country under an assumed name, like Rosalind and Celia, in the Forest of Arden, where they keep themselves concealed, and suffer hardships. Certainly, they ought to have had a legal adviser to show them the use of their country's laws. And so in style does this likeness exist. Every one remembers, in *Jane Eyre*, how beautifully, in a few words, a whole landscape is presented to the reader – aye, and more than that – how cunningly or how magically the author conveys the scene he (or she) describes to the mind's eye, so as not only to impress it with the mere view, but to speak, as it were, to the imagination, to the inner sense, as is ever the case with the Poetry as the Painting of real genius. This same mysterious word-painting is one of the features of the present tale.

[quotes from chapter 5 descriptions of the heroine's paintings, from chapter 7 the walk to the sea, and from chapter 52 the winter landscape surrounding Wildfell Hall]

We have yet a few remarks to add before taking leave of these works. We have at the opening of this article expressed our sense of the author's views of life and society in sufficiently decided terms. But after placing him (or her) in about the same social position as the rarely endowed author of the Queen's Wake; and accounting for many coarsenesses upon the same score that every one excuses them in the prose tales of the Ettrick Shepherd, we do not believe one word in the charge of immorality so often brought against these books. An aberration of taste, an ignorance of society, must by no means be confounded with a departure from principle ... We are told that no woman, unless divested of all those finer sensibilities that constitute the chief graces of her heart, could possibly comport herself towards any man as do the heroines before us, Helen and Jane. Again we doubt all this ... we contend that it was not possible for Jane Eyre, loving as she did with all the nervous tension of which the heart is capable, to act otherwise than she did ... In tracing her career, the heroine tells truthfully everything that would interest the reader, however much the cool head of worldly calculation or of self-complacent inexperience may sneer at or condemn it. Who does not cry Amen to the indignant malison Jane Eyre denounces against her devilish aunt? ...

It is sheer nonsense to say that . . . the ceremonials of society – that wholesome framework of conventionality which makes the common sense of the many in times past and present, the stay and support against which the weak and the bewildered may always lean with safety . . . must always *inevitably* interfere between the earthly – perhaps the eternal happiness of two beings whose destiny is wound up in each other! Prims and Prudes may decry passages exhibiting the heart as it is, but as honest Jack Falstaff says, 'Is not the truth the truth;' what more can we say? However objectionable these works may be to crude minds which cannot winnow the chaff of vulgarity from the rich grain of genius which burdens them, very many, while enjoying their freshness and vigor, will gladly hail their appearance, as boldly and eloquently developing blind places of wayward passion in the human heart, which it is far more interesting to trace than all the bustling lanes and murky alleys through which the will-o'-wisp genius of Dickens has so long led the public mind.

75. E. P. Whipple from 'Novels of the Season' *North American Reveiw*

October 1848, cxli, 354–69

See Nos 20 and 69.

The Tenant of Wildfell Hall is altogether a less unpleasing story than its immediate predecessor [*Wuthering Heights*], though it resembles it in the excessive clumsiness with which the plot is arranged, and the prominence given to the brutal element of human nature. The work seems a convincing proof, that there is nothing kindly or genial in the author's powerful mind, and that, if he continues to write novels, he will introduce into the land of romance a larger number of hateful men and women than any other writer of the day. Gilbert, the hero,

seems to be a favorite with the author, and to be intended as a specimen of manly character; but he would serve as the ruffian of any other
novelist. His nature is fierce, proud, moody, jealous, revengeful, and
sometimes brutal. We can see nothing good in him except a certain
rude honesty; and that quality is seen chiefly in his bursts of hatred and
his insults to women. Helen, the heroine, is doubtless a strong-minded
woman, and passes bravely through a great deal of suffering; but if
there be any lovable or feminine virtues in her composition, the author
has managed to conceal them. She marries a profligate, thinking to
reform him; but the gentleman, with a full knowledge of her purpose,
declines reformation, goes deeper and deeper into vice, and becomes
at last as fiendlike as a very limited stock of brains will allow. This is
a reversal of the process carried on in *Jane Eyre*; but it must be admitted
that the profligate in *The Tenant of Wildfell Hall* is no Rochester. He is
never virtuously inclined, except in those periods of illness and feebleness which his debaucheries have occasioned, thus illustrating the old
proverb, –

When the devil was sick, the devil a monk would be,
When the devil was well, the devil a monk was he.

He has almost constantly by him a choice coterie of boon companions, ranging from the elegant libertine to the ferocious sensualist,
and the reader is favored with exact accounts of their drunken orgies,
and with numerous scraps of their profane conversation. All the
characters are drawn with great power and precision of outline, and
the scenes are as vivid as life itself. Everywhere is seen the tendency of
the author to degrade passion into appetite, and to give prominence to
the selfish and malignant elements of human nature; but while he
succeeds in making profligacy disgusting, he fails in making virtue
pleasing. His depravity is total depravity, and his hard and impudent
debauchees seem to belong to that class of reprobates whom Dr. South
considers 'as not so much born as damned into the world.' The reader
of Acton Bell gains no enlarged view of mankind, giving a healthy
action to his sympathies, but is confined to a narrow space of life, and
held down, as it were, by main force, to witness the wolfish side of his
nature literally and logically set forth. But the criminal courts are not
the places in which to take a comprehensive view of humanity, and the
novelist who confines his observation to them is not likely to produce
any lasting impression, except of horror and disgust.

76. From an unsigned review, *Sharpe's London Magazine*

August 1848, vii, 181-4

Sharpe's was unfavourably disposed towards the Brontës in their lifetimes, though it printed a well-meaning article on Charlotte in 1855 (see Introduction, p. 37). Its review of *Shirley* (1850, ii, 370-3) castigated the novel for its morbidity and exaggeration and recommended instead the 'genteel' life depicted by Jane Austen and Maria Edgeworth. Charlotte wrote to her father at the time (4 June 1850): 'Mr Smith says it is of no consequence whatever in a literary sense. Sharpe, the proprietor, was an apprentice of Mr Smith's father' (*LL*, iii, 117). The periodical was founded in 1845 as 'a journal of entertainment and instruction for general reading' and edited 1847-52 by 'Frank Fairleigh' (Francis E. Smedley).

Several novels have lately appeared before the public, purporting to be written by three brothers, Currer, Ellis, and Acton Bell. Of these works, *Jane Eyre*, by Currer Bell, is the best known, and deservedly the most popular. We say deservedly, for though it has great faults, it has still greater merits. Such is by no means the case with the work now before us; indeed, so revolting are many of the scenes, so coarse and disgusting the language put into the mouths of some of the characters, that the reviewer to whom we entrusted it returned it to us, saying it was unfit to be noticed in the pages of *Sharpe*; and we are so far of the same opinion, that our object in the present paper is to warn our readers, and more especially our lady-readers, against being induced to peruse it, either by the powerful interest of the story, or the talent with which it is written. Did we think less highly of it in these particulars, we should have left the book to its fate, and allowed it quietly to sink into . . . insignificance . . . Yet we consider the evils which render the work unfit for perusal (for we go that length in regard to it,) to arise from a perverted taste and an absence of mental refinement in the writer, together with a total ignorance of the usages of good society, rather than from any systematic design of opposing the cause of religion and morality. So far from any such intention being apparent, the moral of the tale is excellent, and the author we should imagine a religious character, though *he* (for, despite reports to the contrary, we *will* not believe any woman could have written such a work,) holds one doctrine, to which we shall more particularly allude hereafter, for which we fear he can find no sufficient authority in Scripture . . .

Up to more than two-thirds of the first volume, there is little to find fault with, much to praise. The character of Gilbert is cleverly drawn, original, yet perfectly true to nature; that of Helen, interesting in the extreme; and the scenes between them, though occasionally too warmly coloured, life-like and engrossing, while the description of village society is sufficiently amusing to afford relief to the more serious business of the novel. With the commencement of the journal, however, the faults . . . begin to develop themselves . . . Throwing off the slight restraint which his evanescent passion for Helen had placed him under, Mr. Huntingdon speedily resumes his dissipated habits; his absences from home become more and more protracted, the scenes on his return each time less endurable, till at length, losing all sense of decency and proper feeling, he fills his house with his profligate associates, and carries on a *liaison* with a married woman, beneath the roof which shelters his outraged wife. When we add, that the scenes which occur after the drinking bouts of these choice spirits are described with a disgustingly truthful minuteness, which shows the writer to be only too well acquainted with the revolting details of such evil revelry, we think we need scarcely produce further proof of the unreadableness of these volumes.

Let us turn from this hateful part of the subject to the . . . noble fortitude with which [Helen] endures the lot her self-willed rashness has brought upon her; the long suffering affection, inducing her to hope against hope, as she tries in vain to reclaim her worthless husband; the brutal insults to which she is exposed while pursuing her labour of love . . .

The only thing which in the slightest degree affords Helen consolation under these harrowing circumstances, is her belief (which, from the way in which it is mentioned, we cannot but conclude to be that of the writer also,) in the doctrine of universal final salvation – the wicked are to pass through purifying penal fires, but all are to be saved at last. The dangerous tendency of such a belief must be apparent to any one who gives the subject a moment's consideration; and it becomes scarcely necessary, in order to convince our readers of the madness of trusting to such a forced distortion of the Divine attribute of mercy, to add that this doctrine is alike repugnant to Scripture, and in direct opposition to the teaching of the Anglican Church.

One word as to the authorship of this novel. At the first glance we should say, none but a man could have known so intimately each vile, dark fold of the civilized brute's corrupted nature; none but a man could make so daring an exhibition as this book presents to us. On the other hand, no man, we should imagine, would have written a work in which all the women, even the worst, are so far superior in every quality, moral and intellectual, to all the men; no man would have made his sex appear at once coarse, brutal, and contemptibly weak, at once disgusting and ridiculous. There are, besides, a thousand trifles which indicate a woman's mind, and several more important things which show a woman's peculiar virtues. Still there is a bold coarseness, a reckless freedom of language, and an apparent familiarity with the sayings and doings of the worst style of *fast* men, in their worst moments, which would induce us to believe it impossible that a woman could have written it. A possible solution of the enigma is, that it may be the production of an authoress assisted by her husband, or some other *male* friend: if this be not the case, we would rather decide on the whole, that it is a man's writing.

In taking leave of the work, we cannot but express our deep regret that a book in many respects eminently calculated to advance the cause of religion and right feeling, the moral of which is unimpeachable and most powerfully wrought out, should be rendered unfit for the perusal of the very class of persons to whom it would be most useful, (namely, imaginative girls likely to risk their happiness on the forlorn hope of marrying and reforming a captivating rake,) owing to the profane expressions, inconceivably coarse language, and revolting scenes and descriptions by which its pages are disfigured.

77. From an unsigned review, 'Mr Bell's New Novel', *Rambler*

September 1848, iii, 65–6

See Introduction, p. 34. Charlotte speaks for herself and Anne in her letter to W. S. Williams of September 1848:

We are very much obliged to you for sending the notice from the *Rambler*. It is indeed acting the part of a true friend to appraise an author faithfully of what opponents say [see No. 49] . . . Defects there are both in *Jane Eyre* and *Wildfell Hall* which it will be the authors' wisdom and duty to endeavour to avoid in future. Other points there are to which they deem it incumbent on them freely to adhere, whether such adherence bring popularity or unpopularity, praise or blame. The standard heroes and heroines of novels are personages in whom I could never from childhood upwards take an interest, believe to be natural, or wish to imitate . . . Were I obliged to copy any former novelist, even the greatest, even Scott, in anything, I would not write. Unless I have something of my own to say, and a way of my own to say it in, I have no business to publish. Unless I can look beyond the greatest Masters, and study Nature herself, I have no right to paint. Unless I can have the courage to use the language of Truth in preference to the jargon of Conventionality, I ought to be silent.

I am glad you have seen and approve of the preface to the Second Edition of *Wildfell Hall* [No. 72]; I, too, thought it sensible (*LL*, ii, 254–5).

The names of Acton Bell, Currer Bell, and Ellis Bell, are now pretty generally recognised as mere *noms de guerre* in the literary world. The novels lately published by these supposed individuals, or at least those which have the names of the first two of the three, are too palpably the work of one hand to deceive even the unpractised critic; while few eople would doubt that that hand belonged to a woman, and, as we suspect, a Yorkshirewoman. *Jane Eyre* is the best known of all the tales bearing the *Bell* designation; and the last that has come forth from the same source is the story whose title is *The Tenant of Wildfell Hall*. These two are, indeed, so strikingly alike in sentiment, style, and general modes of thought, that the criticisms which apply to one of them are almost equally applicable to the other.

That the author is a clever and vigorous writer, the popularity of *Jane Eyre* is a fair proof. She has also a certain marked tone of mind, which has impressed itself upon her books, and rendered them more individual and characteristic than the ordinary run even of clever novels. And for the sake of the morals of the novel-reading public, we hope that this their peculiar feature has been the real cause of their attractiveness to many readers; and not that truly offensive and sensual spirit which is painfully prominent both in *Jane Eyre* and in the tale now before us . . .

Jane Eyre is, indeed, one of the coarsest books which we ever perused. It is not that the *professed* sentiments of the writer are absolutely wrong or forbidding, or that the odd sort of religious notions which she puts forward are much worse than is usual in popular tales. It is rather that there is a certain perpetual *tendency* to relapse into that class of ideas, expressions, and circumstances, which is most connected with the grosser and more animal portion of our nature; and that the detestable morality of the most prominent character in the story is accompanied with every sort of palliation short of unblushing justification. The heroine, who tells the story, and who certainly is made to paint herself and her companions with very considerable force and skill, is as utterly unattractive and unfeminine a specimen of her sex as the pen of novelist ever drew.

The Tenant of Wildfell Hall is also a species of autobiography. One third of the story is told by the hero, a kind of gentleman farmer, whose morals, religion, cultivation, and talents, are about on a par with those of Jane Eyre herself; and the other two thirds consist of the diary of the lady with whom he falls in love, not knowing that, though living in solitude, she is really married to a living husband. Throughout the whole book, there does not appear a single character who has the power to interest the sympathies of the reader. All are commonplace, vulgar, rough, brusque-mannered personages, whatever their supposed station in life; while the scenes which the heroine relates in her diary are of the most disgusting and revolting species. She is married to a man of family and fortune, to whom she chose to link herself against the wishes of her friends, and who speedily turns out a sensual brute of the most intolerable kind, and treats her with every indignity, insult, and ill-usage which can be conceived, short of actual personal violence. Her diary is the record of what she endured at his hands, and details with offensive minuteness the disgusting scenes of debauchery, blasphemy, and profaneness, in which, with a herd of boon companions, he delighted to spend his days. By and by, of course, he dies, and the authoress gives us one of those pictures of a death-bed which are neither edifying, nor true to life, nor full of warning to the careless and profligate. In the end, the hero and heroine marry, after a courtship conducted with that peculiar bluntness and roughness of conduct and language which is the characteristic of all this writer's creations.

Nevertheless, on the whole, we should say that *The Tenant of Wildfell Hall* is not so *bad* a book as *Jane Eyre*. There is not such a palpable blinking of the abominable nature of the morality of its most prominent characters. The hero and heroine are people of decent intentions; and though the same offensive element of interest (so to call it) occurs in both of the tales, and in each our sympathies are unwittingly engaged for an attachment formed by a married person before death had dissolved the first contracted bond; yet the subject of this second passion in the last published story is more conscious of its real nature than in its predecessor. The religious sentiments which the authoress puts into the mouth of her heroines are either false and bad, or so vague and unmeaning as to add to the unreality of the scenes, without in any way redeeming their blots, as uncalled-for and unhealthy representations of the viler phases of human life. In a word, unless our authoress can contrive to refine and elevate her general notions of all human and divine things, we shall be glad to learn that she is not intending to add another work to those which have already been produced by her pen.

We hardly know where to find an extract suitable for quotation, by way of illustration of our criticisms, and shall content ourselves with the sketch of one of the least disagreeable individuals who figure in the story [the Reverend Michael Millward, chapter 1].

78. Charles Kingsley, from an unsigned review, *Fraser's Magazine*

April 1849, xxxix, 417–32

From Charles Kingsley's aiticle, 'Recent Novels', listed by Mrs M. F. Farrand Thorp in the bibliography attached to her *Charles Kingsley* (1937). The authorship is of considerable interest, since Kingsley's view of the Brontës is usually judged by his initially unfavourable response to *Shirley*; see Introduction, pp. 19–20, and No. 96. The other novels discussed in the review include Harrison Ainsworth's *The Lancashire Witches* (1849), Marmion Savage's *My Uncle the Curate* (1849), and Mrs Gaskell's *Mary Barton* (1848). The arguments pursued are in keeping with Kingsley's Christian Socialist views, as the opening paragraphs indicate.

To get a hearing the people's novelist must succeed in 'strong writing.' That is the secret of the enormous influence of French novels, and George Sand is now successfully turning it to account in enforcing *her* morality and politics. If England ever sees, which Heaven grant she may, a Christian George Sand, this feature of her style must not be watered down into smooth respectability.

It is very easy for refined tastes, sated with literature of every species, to cry out against the horrible and exaggerated. It is very easy for comfortable folks, who have nothing to do but to receive their dividends, pay their visits, drive from exhibition to exhibition, and sit down in a comfortable arm-chair among prints and statuettes, and take out of their shelves what book they fancy most, to think that the minds of the working-classes will thrive on the same sober stuff as their own. They may as well expect a navigator to work on water-gruel, instead of beefsteaks and porter. Let those who have never seen try, at least, to imagine the circumstances under which the majority of the working-classes pass their dull lives from dawn to dusk – the stifling shop, the crowded and pestilential work-room, the noisy and dust-grimed manufactory; let them think of the thousands to whom poor Hood's immortal song will apply, –

> Work! work work!
> Seam, and gusset, and band –
> Band, and gusset, and seam –
> Till over the buttons I fall asleep,
> And sew them on in a dream.

And then let them consider, whether it does not require excitants somewhat 'above proof strength' to keep their minds even in a healthy state of movement. The taste for horrible fictions among the working-classes is really Nature's own craving for her proper medicine. To the educated man such literature might be perniciously enervating; though all barristers and statesmen will tell us, that in proportion to the dull severity of its professional labours does the mind require intervals of frivolous and even fantastic amusement . . .

A people's novel of a very different school is *The Tenant of Wildfell Hall*. It is, taken altogether, a powerful and an interesting book. Not that it is a pleasant book to read, nor, as we fancy, has it been a pleasant book to write; still less has it been a pleasant training which could teach an author such awful facts, or give courage to write them. The fault of the book is coarseness – not merely that coarseness of subject which will be the stumbling-block of most readers, and which makes it utterly unfit to be put into the hands of girls; of that we do not complain. There are foul and accursed undercurrents in plenty, in this same smug, respectable, whitewashed English society, which must be exposed now and then; and Society owes thanks, not sneers, to those who dare to shew her the image of her own ugly, hypocritical visage. We must not lay Juvenal's coarseness at Juvenal's door, but at that of the Roman world which he stereotyped in his fearful verses. But the world does not think so. It will revile Acton Bell for telling us, with painful circumstantiality, what the house of a profligate, uneducated country squire is like, perfectly careless whether or not the picture be true, only angry at having been disturbed from its own self-complacent doze . . .

It is true, satirists are apt to be unnecessarily coarse. Granted; but are they half as coarse, though, as the men whom they satirise? That gnat-straining, camel-swallowing Pharisee, the world, might, if it chose, recollect that a certain degree of coarse-naturalness, while men continue the one-sided beings which they are at present, may be necessary for all reformers, in order to enable them to look steadily and continuously at the very evils which they are removing. Shall we despise the surgeon because he does not faint in the dissecting-room? Our Chadwicks and Southwood Smiths would make but poor sanitary reformers if their senses could not bid defiance to sulphuretted hydrogen and ammonia. Whether their nostrils suffer or not, ours are saved by them: we have no cause to grumble. And even so with 'Acton Bell.'

But taking this book as a satire, and an exposure of evils, still all unnecessary coarseness is a defect, – a defect which injures the real usefulness and real worth of the book. The author introduces, for instance, a long diary, kept by the noble and unhappy wife of a profligate squire; and would that every man in England might read and lay to heart that horrible record. But what greater mistake, to use the mildest term, can there be than to fill such a diary with written oaths and curses, with details of drunken scenes which no wife, such as poor Helen is represented, would have the heart, not to say the common decency, to write down as they occurred? Dramatic probability and good feeling are equally outraged by such a method. The author, tempted naturally to indulge her full powers of artistic detail, seems to have forgotten that there are silences more pathetic than all words.

A cognate defect, too, struck us much; the splenetic and bitter tone in which certain personages in the novel are mentioned, when really, poor souls, no deeds of theirs are shewn which could warrant such wholesale appellations as 'brute' and 'demon.' One is inclined sometimes to suspect that they are caricatures from the life, against whom some private spite is being vented; though the author has a right to reply, that the whole novel being the autobiography of a young gentleman farmer, such ferocities are to be charged on him, not on her. True, but yet in his mouth as much as in any one's else they want cause for them to be shewn, according to all principles of fiction; and if none such exists on the face of the story, it only indicates a defect in the youth's character which makes his good fortune more improbable. For the book sets forth how the gallant Gilbert wins the heart, and after her husband's death, the hand of the rich squire's well-born and highly-cultivated wife.

Now we do not complain of the 'impossibility' of this. *Ne me dites jamais ce bête de mot*, as Mirabeau[1] said. Impossible? Society is full of wonders; our worst complaint against fiction-mongers is, that they

[1] See above, p. 185 n.

are so tame, so common-place, so shamefully afraid of wonders, . . .
But the novelist, especially when he invents a story, instead of merely
giving dramatic life to one ready made, which is the Shakspearian, and,
as we suspect, the higher path of art, must give some internal and
spiritual probability to his outward miracles; and this, we think, Acton
Bell has in this case failed to do. We cannot see any reason why
Gilbert Markham, though no doubt highly attractive to young ladies
of his own calibre, should excite such passionate love in Helen, with
all her bitter experiences of life, her painting, and her poetry, her deep
readings and deep thoughts – absolutely no reason at all, except the
last one in the world, which either the author or she would have
wished, namely, that there was no other man in the way for her to
fall in love with. We want to see this strange intellectual superiority
of his to the general run of his class (for we must suppose some such);
and all the characteristics we do find, beyond the general dashing,
manful spirit of a young farmer, is a very passionate and somewhat
brutal temper, and, to say the least, a wanton rejection of a girl to
whom he has been giving most palpable and somewhat rough proofs
of affection, and whom he afterwards hates bitterly, simply because
she rallies him on having jilted her for a woman against whose character there was very possible ground for suspicion. This is not to be
counterbalanced by an occasional vein of high-flown sentimentalism in
the young gentleman (and that, too, not often) when he comes in contact with his lady-love. If the author had intended to work out the
noble old Cymon and Iphigenia myths, she ought to have let us see
the gradual growth of the clown's mind under the influence of the
accomplished woman; and this is just what she has not done. Gilbert
Markham is not one character oscillating between his old low standard
and his higher new one, according as he comes in contact with his own
countrified friends or his new lady-love, but two different men, with
no single root-idea of character to unite and explain the two opposite
poles of his conduct . . . The puffs inform us that the book is very like
Jane Eyre. To us it seems to have exaggerated all the faults of that
remarkable book, and retained very few of its good points. The superior *religious* tone in which alone it surpasses *Jane Eyre* is, in our eyes,
quite neutralised by the low *moral* tone which reigns throughout.

Altogether, as we said before, the book is painful. The dark side of
every body and every thing is dilated on; we had almost said, revelled
in . . . The author has not had the tact which enabled Mr. Thackeray,
in *Vanity Fair*, to construct a pleasing whole out of most unpleasing

materials, by a harmonious unity of parts, and, above all, by a tone of tender grace and solemn ironic indignation, in the midst of all his humour, spreading over and softening down the whole; – that true poetic instinct, which gives to even the coarsest of Fielding's novels and Shakspeare's comedies, considered as wholes, a really pure and lofty beauty. The author has not seen that though it is quite fair to write in a melancholy, or even harsh key, and to introduce accidental discords, or even sounds in themselves disagreeable, yet that this last must be done only to set off by contrast the background of harmony and melody, and that the key of the whole must be a correct and a palpable one; it must not be buried beneath innumerable occasional flats and sharps; above all, we must not, as in *The Tenant of Wildfell Hall*, with its snappish fierceness, be tortured by a defective chord, in which one false note is perpetually recurring; or provoked by a certain flippant, rough staccato movement throughout, without softness, without repose, and, therefore, without dignity. We advise the author, before the next novel is taken in hand, to study Shakspeare somewhat more carefully, and see if she★ cannot discover the secret of the wonderful harmony with which he, like Raphael, transfigures the most painful, and, apparently, chaotic subjects.

★ We have spoken of the author in the feminine gender, because, of whatever sex the name 'Acton Bell' may be, a woman's pen seems to us indisputably discernible in every page. The very coarseness and vulgarity is just such as a woman, trying to write like a man, would invent, – second-hand and clumsy, and not such as men do use; the more honour to the writer's heart, if not to her taste.

79. Charlotte Brontë on Anne Brontë

September 1850

From the 'Biographical Notice' printed in the second edition of *Wuthering Heights* and *Agnes Grey*. Charlotte wrote to much the same effect in her letter to W. S. Williams, 15 September 1850:

Wildfell Hall it hardly seems to me desirable to preserve. The choice of subject in that work is a mistake ... Blameless in deed and almost in thought, there was from her very childhood a tinge of religious melancholy in her mind ... I have found amongst her papers mournful proofs that such was the case (*LL*, iii, 156).

The Tenant of Wildfell Hall by Acton Bell, had likewise an unfavourable reception. At this I cannot wonder. The choice of subject was an entire mistake. Nothing less congruous with the writer's nature could be conceived. The motives which dictated this choice were pure, but, I think, slightly morbid. She had, in the course of her life, been called on to contemplate, near at hand and for a long time, the terrible effects of talents misused and faculties abused; hers was naturally a sensitive, reserved, and dejected nature; what she saw sank very deeply into her mind; it did her harm. She brooded over it till she believed it to be a duty to reproduce every detail (of course with fictitious characters, incidents, and situations) as a warning to others. She hated her work, but would pursue it. When reasoned with on the subject, she regarded such reasonings as a temptation to self-indulgence. She must be honest; she must not varnish, soften, or conceal. This well-meant resolution brought on her misconstruction and some abuse, which she bore, as it was her custom to bear whatever was unpleasant, with mild, steady patience. She was a very sincere and practical Christian, but the tinge of religious melancholy communicated a sad shade to her brief, blameless life.

Part II

The Brontës in the 1850s

80. Sydney Dobell on 'Currer Bell' and *Wuthering Heights, Palladium*

September 1850, 161–75

An unsigned review by Sydney Dobell, reprinted in *The Life and Letters of Sydney Dobell*, ed. E. Jolly (1878). See Introduction, pp. 29, 33.

Sydney Dobell (1824–1874), then in his late twenties, had recently published his dramatic poem 'The Roman'. Charlotte wrote to James Taylor (of Smith, Elder) on 5 September 1850:

The article ... is one ... over which an author rejoices ... I am counselled to wait and watch. D.V., I will do so ... I need not say how I felt the remarks on *Wuthering Heights*... they are true, they are discriminating, they are full of late justice ... Whoever the author ... may be, I remain his debtor (*LL*, iii, 154).

Charlotte had learnt his identity from Harriet Martineau by 16 October 1850 (*LL*, iii, 171), and in December sent him a copy of the 1850 edition of *Wuthering Heights* and *Agnes Grey* with a letter asking him to let her know whether he still doubted the authorship of the novels (*LL*, iii, 187; for his reply see *LL*, iii, 217–19). The article is somewhat florid in style and has been severely cut.

Who is Currer Bell? is a question which has been variously answered ... A year or two ago, we mentally solved the problem thus: Currer Bell is a woman. Every word she utters is female. Not feminine, but female ... Though she spoke in thunder, and had the phrase and idiom of Achilles, she cannot *think* in a beard ... Placing in an assumed order of production (though not of publication) the novels called *Wuthering Heights, Wildfell Hall, Jane Eyre*, and *Shirley*, as the works of one author under sundry disguises, we should have deemed, a few days since, that an analysis of the first (and, by our theory, the earliest) of these was the amplest justice she could at present receive. Opening, however, the third edition of *Jane Eyre*, published before the appearance of *Shirley*, we find a preface in which all other works are disclaimed. A *nom de guerrist* has many privileges, and we are willing to put down to a *double entendre* all that is serious in this disclaimer. That any hand but that which shaped *Jane Eyre* and *Shirley* cut out the rougher earlier statues, we should require more than the evidence of our senses to believe. That the author of *Jane Eyre* need fear nothing in acknowledging these yet more immature creations of one of the most vigorous of modern idiosyncracies, we think we shall shortly demonstrate.

Laying aside *Wildfell Hall*, we open *Wuthering Heights*, as at once the earlier in date and ruder in execution. We look upon it as the flight of an impatient fancy fluttering in the very exultation of young wings; sometimes beating against its solitary bars, but turning, rather to exhaust, in a circumscribed space, the energy and agility which it may not yet spend in the heavens – a youthful story, written for oneself in solitude, and thrown aside till other successes recall the eyes to it in hope. In this thought let the critic take up the book; lay it down in what thought he will, there are some things in it he can lay down no more.

That Catherine Earnshaw – at once so wonderfully fresh, so fearfully natural – new, 'as if brought from other spheres,' and familiar as the recollection of some woeful experience – what can surpass the strange compatibility of her simultaneous loves; the involuntary art with which her two natures are so made to co-exist, that in the very arms of her lover we dare not doubt her purity; the inevitable belief with which we watch the oscillations of the old and new elements in her mind, and the exquisite truth of the last victory of nature over education, when the past returns to her as a flood, sweeping every modern landmark from within her, and the soul of the child, expanding, fills the woman? Found at last, by her husband, insensible on the breast of her lover, and dying of the agony of their parting, one looks back upon her, like that husband, without one thought of accusation or absolution; her memory is chaste as the loyalty of love, pure as the air of the Heights on which she dwelt.

Heathcliff *might* have been as unique a creation. The conception in his case was as wonderfully strong and original, but he is spoilt in detail. The authoress has too often disgusted, where she should have terrified, and has allowed us a familiarity with her fiend which has ended in unequivocal contempt. If *Wuthering Heights* had been written as lately as *Jane Eyre*, the figure of Heathcliff, symmetrised and elevated, might have been one of the most natural and most striking portraits in the gallery of fiction.

Not a subordinate place or person in this novel, but bears more or less the stamp of high genius. Ellen Dean is the ideal of the peasant playmate and servant of 'the family.' The substratum in which her mind moves is finely preserved. Josephus, as a specimen of the sixty years' servitor of 'the house,' is worthy a museum case. We feel that if Catherine Earnshaw bore her husband a child, it must be that Cathy Linton, and no other. The very Jane Eyre, of quiet satire, peeps out in such a paragraph as this: – 'He told me to put on my cloak, and run to Gimmerton for the doctor and the parson. I went, through wind and rain, and brought one, the doctor, back with me: the other said, *he would come in the morning*' [chapter 5]. What terrible truth, what nicety of touch, what 'uncanny' capacity for mental aberration in the first symptoms of Catherine's delirium. 'I'm not wandering; you're mistaken, or else I should believe you really *were* that withered hag, and I should think I *was* under Penistone Crag: and I'm conscious it's night, and there are two candles on the table making the black press shine like jet' [chapter 12]. What an unobtrusive, unexpected sense of *keeping* in the hanging of Isabella's dog.

The book abounds in such things. But one looks back at the whole story as to a world of brilliant figures in an atmosphere of mist; shapes that come out upon the eye, and burn their colours into the brain, and depart into the enveloping fog. It is the unformed writing of a giant's hand; the 'large utterance' of a baby god.[1] In the sprawlings of the infant Hercules, however, there must have been attitudes from which the statuary might model. In the early efforts of unusual genius, there are not seldom unconscious felicities which maturer years may look back upon with envy. The child's hand wanders over the strings. It cannot combine them in the chords and melodies of manhood; but its separate notes are perfect in themselves, and perhaps sound all the sweeter for the Æolian discords from which they come.

We repeat, that there are passages in this book of *Wuthering Heights* of which any novelist, past or present, might be proud. Open the first volume at the fourteenth page, and read to the sixty-first. There are few things in modern prose to surpass these pages for native power. We cannot praise too warmly the brave simplicity, the unaffected air of

[1] Keats's 'Hyperion' (1820), ll. 50–1,

> . . . Oh how frail
> To that large utterance of the early Gods ! . . .

intense belief, the admirable combination of extreme likelihood with the rarest originality, the nice provision of the possible even in the highest effects of the supernatural, the easy strength and instinct of keeping with which the accessory circumstances are grouped, the exquisite but unconscious art with which the chiaroscuro of the whole is managed, and the ungenial frigidity of place, time, weather, and persons, is made to heighten the unspeakable pathos of one ungovernable outburst.

The *thinking-out* of some of these pages – of pp. 52, 53, and 60 [the sequence of events from the opening of chapter 2 to Lockwood's settling for the night in the kitchen (chapter 3)] – is the masterpiece of a poet, rather than the hybrid creation of the novelist . . . in the memory of those whose remembrance makes *fame*, the images in these pages will live – when every word that conveyed them is forgotten – as a recollection of *things heard and seen*. This is the highest triumph of description.

We are at a loss to find anywhere in modern prose . . . in the same space, such wealth and such economy, such apparent ease, such instinctive art. *Instinctive* art; for, to the imaginative writer, all art that is not instinctive is dangerous. All art that is the result of the application of principles, however astutely those principles be applied – though it be even *ars celare artem* – smacks not of the artist but the artisan. Let no man think to improve in his working by any knowledge that can be taken up or laid down at will, any means or appliances from without . . . If this authoress had *published* any novel before *Jane Eyre*, *Jane Eyre* would not have been the moral wonder which it is, and will for many years remain. If *Jane Eyre* had met with a less triumphant *furore* of review, *Shirley* would have been a worthier successor. To say that an artist is *spoilt* by criticism, is to disprove his right to the title; to say that he is, for the present, maimed and disabled by it, may be to bear the highest witness to his intrinsic genius – and this witness we bear to Currer Bell. When Currer Bell writes her next novel, let her remember, as far as possible, the frame of mind in which she sat down to her first. She cannot now commit the faults of that early effort; it will be well for her if she be still capable of the virtues. She will never sin so much against consistent keeping as to draw another Heathcliff; she is too much *au fait* of her profession to make again those sacrifices to machinery which deprive her early picture of any claim to be ranked as a work of art. Happy she, if her next book demonstrate the unimpaired possession of those powers of insight that instinctive obedience to the nature within her, and those occurrences of infallible inspiration, which astound the critic in the young author of *Wuthering Heights*. She will not let her next dark-haired hero babble away the respect of his reader and the awe of his antecedents; nor will she find another house-keeper who remembers two volumes *literatim*. Let her rejoice if she can again give us such an elaboration of a rare and fearful form of mental disease – so terribly strong, so exquisitely subtle – with such nicety in its transitions, such intimate symptomatic truth in its details, as to be at once a psychological and medical study. It has been said of Shakspeare, that he drew cases which the physician might study; Currer Bell has done no less. She will not, again, employ her wonderful pencil on a picture so destitute of moral beauty and human worth. Let her exult, if she can still invest such a picture with such interest. We stand painfully before the portraits; but our eyes are drawn to them by the irresistible ties of blood relationship. Let her exult, if she can still make us weep with the simple pathos of that fading face, which looked from the golden crocuses on her pillow to the hills which concealed the old home and the churchyard of Gimmerton. 'These are the earliest flowers at the Heights,' she exclaimed. 'They remind me of thaw-winds, and warm sunshine, and nearly-melted snow. Edgar, is there not a south wind, and is not the snow almost gone?' – 'The snow is quite gone down here, darling,' replied her husband; 'and I only see two white spots on the whole range of moors. The sky is blue, and the larks are singing, and the becks and brooks are all brimful. Cath-erine, last spring, at this time, I was longing to have you under this roof; now, I wish you were a mile or two up those hills: the air blows so sweetly, I feel that it would cure you.' – 'I shall never be there but once more,' said the invalid, 'and then you'll leave me, and I shall remain foɪ ever. Next spring, you'll long again to have me under this roof, and you'll look back, and think you were happy to-day' [chapter 13]. Let Currer Bell prize the young intuition of character which dictated Cathy's speech to Ellen. [Catherine's speech in chapter 10, ' "The event of this evening has reconciled me . . . I'm an angel" '] There is a deep, unconscious philosophy in it. There are minds, whose crimes and sorrows are not so much the result of intrinsic evil as of a false position in the scheme of things, which clashes their energies with the arrangements of surrounding life. It is difficult to cure such a soul from *within*. The point of view, not the eye or the landscape, is in fault. Move *that*, and, as at the changing of a stop, the mental machine assumes its proper relative place, and the powers of discord become, in the same measure, the instruments of harmony. It was a fine instinct which saw this. Let Currer Bell be passing glad if it is as vigorous now as then; and let her thank God if she can now draw the apparition of the 'Wanderer of the Moor.'

Any attempt to give, in a review, a notion of *Jane Eyre*, would be injustice both to author and reviewer; and, fortunately for both, is now unnecessary. Few books have been, and have deserved to be, so universally read, and so well remembered. We shall not now essay even an analysis of the work itself, because we have in this article fixed our eyes rather upon the author than the reader; and whatever absolute superiority we may discover in *Jane Eyre*, we find in it only further evidence of the same producing qualities to which *Wuthering Heights* bears testimony. Those qualities, indurated by time, armed by experience, and harmonised by the natural growth of a maturing brain, have here exhibited, in a more favourable field, and under stronger guidance, the same virtues and the same faults. In *Shirley*, on the other hand, we see the same qualities – with feebler health, and under auspices for the time infelicitous – labouring on an exhausted soil. Israel is at work, indeed; but there is a grievous want of straw, and the groan of the people is perceptible. The book is misnamed *Shirley*. Caroline Helstone, the child of nature, should yield no pre-eminence to Shirley Keeldar, the daughter of circumstance. The character of the one is born of womanhood; that of the other, of 'Fieldhead, and a thousand a year.' Kant's formula, inefficient in morals, is sometimes useful in criticism. 'Canst thou will thy maxim to be law universal?' Place Caroline Helstone where you will, she is still exquisitely sweet, and, in element, universally true. To make Shirley Keeldar repulsive, you have only to fancy her poor.[1] This absence of intrinsic heroism in the heroine, and some shortcomings on the part of the authoress – a consciousness of the reader, an evident effort, and an apparent disposition to rest contented with present powers, opinions, and mental status – would do much to damp the hopes of a critic, were they not the mere indications of overwork, and of a brain not yet subsided from success. One eloquent and noble characteristic remains to her unimpaired. Her mission is perpetually remembered. In that reconstruction of society – that redistribution of the elements of our con-

[1] Shirley Keeldar was partly intended as a representation of Emily as she might have been 'had she been placed in health and prosperity' (*Life*, chapter 18; Haworth edition, 414). See Mary Robinson, 'We recognise Charlotte's sister; but not the author of *Wuthering Heights* . . . Sydney Dobell spoke a bitter half-truth' (*Emily Brontë* (1833), 210, 213).

ventional systems, which all eyes can see already at work ... there will be needed, and will arise, some great novelist as a chief apostle. There is much work here which the poets cannot do, and which the ungifted *may* not do. The poets, when they are prophets, should speak only to the highest minds. The giftless should not speak to any ... We believe that, among other high callings, this evangelism has fallen to Currer Bell, and we bid her God speed in her grand work.

WUTHERING HEIGHTS and *AGNES GREY*

1850 edition

---

81. Charlotte Brontë on *Wuthering Heights*

1850

Attached with her 'Biographical Notice' to the second edition of
Wuthering Heights and *Agnes Grey*.

I have just read over *Wuthering Heights*, and, for the first time, have
obtained a clear glimpse of what are termed (and, perhaps, really are)
its faults; have gained a definite notion of how it appears to other
people – to strangers who knew nothing of the author; who are
unacquainted with the locality where the scenes of the story are laid;
to whom the inhabitants, the customs, the natural characteristics of
the outlying hills and hamlets in the West-Riding of Yorkshire are
things alien and unfamiliar.

To all such *Wuthering Heights* must appear a rude and strange
production. The wild moors of the north of England can for them
have no interest; the language, the manners, the very dwellings and
household customs of the scattered inhabitants of those districts, must
be to such readers in a great measure unintelligible, and – where
intelligible – repulsive. Men and women who, perhaps, naturally very
calm, and with feelings moderate in degree, and little marked in kind,
have been trained from their cradle to observe the utmost evenness of
manner and guardedness of language, will hardly know what to make
of the rough, strong utterance, the harshly manifested passions, the
unbridled aversions, and headlong partialities of unlettered moorland
hinds and rugged moorland squires, who have grown up untaught and
unchecked, except by mentors as harsh as themselves. A large class of
readers, likewise, will suffer greatly from the introduction into the

pages of this work of words printed with all their letters, which it has become the custom to represent by the initial and final letter only – a blank line filling the interval. I may as well say at once that, for this circumstance, it is out of my power to apologize; deeming it, myself, a rational plan to write words at full length. The practice of hinting by single letters those expletives with which profane and violent persons are wont to garnish their discourse, strikes me as a proceeding which, however well meant, is weak and futile. I cannot tell what good it does – what feeling it spares – what horror it conceals.

With regard to the rusticity of *Wuthering Heights*, I admit the charge, for I feel the quality. It is rustic all through. It is moorish, and wild, and knotty as a root of heath. Nor was it natural that it should be otherwise; the author being herself a native and nursling of the moors. Doubtless, had her lot been cast in a town, her writings, if she had written at all, would have possessed another character. Even had chance or taste led her to choose a similar subject, she would have treated it otherwise. Had Ellis Bell been a lady or a gentleman accustomed to what is called 'the world,' her view of a remote and unreclaimed region, as well as of the dwellers therein, would have differed greatly from that actually taken by the homebred country girl. Doubtless it would have been wider – more comprehensive: whether it would have been more original or more truthful is not so certain. As far as the scenery and locality are concerned, it could scarcely have been so sympathetic: Ellis Bell did not describe as one whose eye and taste alone found pleasure in the prospect; her native hills were far more to her than a spectacle; they were what she lived in, and by, as much as the wild birds, their tenants, or as the heather, their produce. Her descriptions, then, of natural scenery, are what they should be, and all they should be.

Where delineation of human character is concerned, the case is different. I am bound to avow that she had scarcely more practical knowledge of the peasantry amongst whom she lived, than a nun has of the country people who sometimes pass her convent gates. My sister's disposition was not naturally gregarious; circumstances favoured and fostered her tendency to seclusion; except to go to church or take a walk on the hills, she rarely crossed the threshold of home. Though her feeling for the people round was benevolent, intercourse with them she never sought; nor, with very few exceptions, ever experienced. And yet she knew them: knew their ways, their language, their family histories; she could hear of them with interest, and talk of them with detail, minute, graphic, and accurate; but *with* them, she rarely exchanged a word. Hence it ensued that what her mind had gathered of the real concerning them, was too exclusively confined to those tragic and terrible traits of which, in listening to the secret annals of every rude vicinage, the memory is sometimes compelled to receive the impress. Her imagination, which was a spirit more sombre than sunny, more powerful than sportive, found in such traits material whence it wrought creations like Heathcliff, like Earnshaw, like Catherine. Having formed these beings, she did not know what she had done. If the auditor of her work when read in manuscript, shuddered under the grinding influence of natures so relentless and implacable, of spirits so lost and fallen; if it was complained that the mere hearing of certain vivid and fearful scenes banished sleep by night, and disturbed mental peace by day, Ellis Bell would wonder what was meant, and suspect the complainant of affectation. Had she but lived, her mind would of itself have grown like a strong tree, loftier, straighter, wider-spreading, and its matured fruits would have attained a mellower ripeness and sunnier bloom; but on that mind time and experience alone could work: to the influence of other intellects, it was not amenable.

Having avowed that over much of *Wuthering Heights* there broods 'a horror of great darkness;'[1] that, in its storm-heated and electrical atmosphere, we seem at times to breathe lightning, let me point to those spots where clouded daylight and the eclipsed sun still attest their existence. For a specimen of true benevolence and homely fidelity, look at the character of Nelly Dean; for an example of constancy and tenderness, remark that of Edgar Linton. (Some people will think these qualities do not shine so well incarnate in a man as they would do in a woman, but Ellis Bell could never be brought to comprehend this notion: nothing moved her more than any insinuation that the faithfulness and clemency, the long-suffering and loving-kindness which are esteemed virtues in the daughters of Eve, become foibles in the sons of Adam. She held that mercy and forgiveness are the divinest attributes of the Great Being who made both man and woman, and that what clothes the Godhead in glory, can disgrace no form of feeble humanity.) There is a dry saturnine humour in the delineation of old Joseph, and some glimpses of grace and gaiety animate the younger Catherine. Nor is even the first heroine of the name destitute of a

---

[1] Genesis 15:12.

certain strange beauty in her fierceness, or of honesty in the midst of perverted passion and passionate perversity.

Heathcliff, indeed, stands unredeemed; never once swerving in his arrow-straight course to perdition, from the time when 'the little black-haired, swarthy thing, as dark as if it came from the Devil,' was first unrolled out of the bundle and set on its feet in the farm-house kitchen, to the hour when Nelly Dean found the grim, stalwart corpse laid on its back in the panel-enclosed bed, with wide-gazing eyes that seemed 'to sneer at her attempt to close them, and parted lips and sharp white teeth that sneered too.'

Heathcliff betrays one solitary human feeling, and that is *not* his love for Catherine, which is a sentiment fierce and inhuman: a passion such as might boil and glow in the bad essence of some evil genius; a fire that might form the tormented centre – the ever-suffering soul of a magnate of the infernal world: and by its quenchless and ceaseless ravage effect the execution of the decree which dooms him to carry Hell with him wherever he wanders. No; the single link that connects Heathcliff with humanity is his rudely confessed regard for Hareton Earnshaw – the young man whom he has ruined; and then his half-implied esteem for Nelly Dean. These solitary traits omitted, we should say he was child neither of Lascar nor gipsy, but a man's shape animated by demon life – a Ghoul – an Afreet.

Whether it is right or advisable to create beings like Heathcliff, I do not know: I scarcely think it is. But this I know; the writer who possesses the creative gift owns something of which he is not always master – something that at times strangely wills and works for itself. He may lay down rules and devise principles, and to rules and principles it will perhaps for years lie in subjection; and then, haply without any warning of revolt, there comes a time when it will no longer consent 'to harrow the vallies, or be bound with a band in the furrow' – when it 'laughs at the multitude of the city, and regards not the crying of the driver'[1] – when, refusing absolutely to make ropes out of sea-sand any longer, it sets to work on statue-hewing, and you have a Pluto or a Jove, a Tisiphone or a Psyche, a Mermaid or a Madonna, as Fate or Inspiration direct. Be the work grim or glorious, dread or divine, you have little choice left but quiescent adoption. As for you – the nominal artist – your share in it has been to work passively under dictates you neither delivered nor could question – that would not be uttered at your prayer, nor suppressed nor changed at your caprice.

[1] Job 39:10, 7.

If the result be attractive, the World will praise you, who little deserve praise; if it be repulsive, the same World will blame you, who almost as little deserve blame.

Wuthering Heights was hewn in a wild workshop, with simple tools, out of homely materials. The statuary found a granite block on a solitary moor: gazing thereon, he saw how from the crag might be elicited a head, savage, swart, sinister; a form moulded with at least one element of grandeur – power. He wrought with a rude chisel, and from no model but the vision of his meditations. With time and labour, the crag took human shape; and there it stands colossal, dark, and frowning, half statue, half rock: in the former sense, terrible and goblin-like; in the latter, almost beautiful, for its colouring is of mellow grey, and moorland moss clothes it; and heath, with its blooming bells and balmy fragrance, grows faithfully close to the giant's foot.

82. From an unsigned review, *Examiner*

21 December 1850, 815

See Nos 59, 73. Charlotte wrote to Ellen Nussey on 27 December 1850:

The *Examiner* is very sore about my Preface, because I did not make it a special exception in speaking of the mass of critics. The soreness is unfortunate and gratuitous, for in my mind I certainly excepted it. Another paper shows painful sensitiveness on the same account (*LL*, iii, 191–2).

In a preface to this volume the author of *Jane Eyre* partially lifts the veil from a history and mystery of authorship which has occupied the Quidnuncs of literature for the last two years. The substance of what we are told we shall repeat as briefly as we may . . .

The character of Anne is strongly discriminated from that of Emily by the earnest survivor who loved both alike. What in the one was fortitude, in the other was patience; what in the one rested on her own inward sense of what was right, appears to have been upheld in the other by a faith as unwavering, though somewhat morbidly indulged, in the hopes and promises of religion. So sustained, Anne does not seem to have shrunk from the lowliest duties of self-denial laid upon her by her lot, or from practice of the most patient social virtues; while the virtues of Emily, though not less self-denying, appear rather to show themselves akin to those bleak solitudes of Yorkshire moors in whose liberty and independence she had nurtured her own. Their loving sister sums up what she says of both by the remark that for strangers they were nothing, and for superficial observers less than nothing; but for those who had known them all their lives in the intimacy of close relationship, they were genuinely good and truly great. 'This notice,' she adds, 'has been written, because I felt it a sacred duty to wipe the dust off their gravestones, and leave their dear names free from soil.'

So ends their brief, sad story. And if the sister who shared with them in these struggles and disappointments of genius, and excelled them in its instant manifestation and acceptance, may not thus lift their names to the level of her own success, she has at least fairly challenged for them dead, more honourable recognition than she believes to have fallen to them living. She has done her best to reverse what she holds to have been the unjust judgment of the critics who coldly disapproved or harshly misrepresented their productions. She has wiped off this dust, and freed them from this soil.

But let us not overstate Currer Bell's censure of the critical neglect by which her sisters suffered. She makes one exception . . . to 'the general rule of criticism' [i.e. Sydney Dobell's commentary, No. 80 above] . . .

The 'general rule of criticism' is a phrase somewhat startling in connection with the wondrous unanimity of critical judgments on *Jane Eyre*; and there is another passage in the preface, where Currer Bell speaks of the assumed names of herself and her sisters, in which a yet stronger feeling of the same sort perhaps unconsciously escapes. 'We had a vague impression that authoresses are liable to be looked on with prejudice; we had noticed how critics sometimes use for their chastisement the weapon of personality, *and for their reward, a flattery which is not true praise.*' Poor hapless critics! But nothing of this kind should surprise a writer who has had the most moderate experience of the thankless vocation. Whether it be censure contemptuously rejected as unworthy, or praise condescendingly received as not worthy enough, the reviewer's fate knows very little variation. Nor be it ours to say that he may not for the most part be worthy of it, and find himself justly in the position of the old lady in the fable whose ear was bitten off by her son at the gallows, for having refused to hear the truth of him, encouraged him in his extravagant courses, and (as Currer Bell expresses it) rewarded him with a flattery which was not true praise. But to the particular case recorded in this volume we have a word or two, on our own poor behalf, to plead in arrest of judgment.

The authors of *Wuthering Heights* and the *Tenant of Wildfell Hall* were not unjustly or contemptuously treated in the columns of the *Examiner*. We do not lay claim to the mene-tekel-upharsin powers assigned to the critic of 'keen vision and fine sympathies' singled out by Currer Bell as having alone done justice to her sister, and who appears to have done his somewhat tardy justice so recently as last September in a journal called the *Palladium*. We dare say, judging from the tone of the extracted criticism prefixed to the volume, that our style of handling these things would seldom come up to the mark of Currer Bell's rejoicing. But it is right to mention notwithstanding, that reviews of the works in question by no means depreciatory appeared in this journal almost instantly on the appearance of the tales respectively named, and that we did not wait till

'deaf the closed ear and mute the tuneful tongue,'

before we gave expression to the praise which both Ellis and Acton Bell seemed fairly to challenge at our hands. Lengthy reviews with very copious extracts were given of both, at the opening of 1848 and in the summer of the same year.

Wuthering Heights we characterized as a strange but powerful book, containing good 'rough dashes at character,' the impress of 'real events,' and 'no commonplace or affectation.' We said that it had forcibly reminded us of a book which we remembered thinking 'better in its peculiar kind than anything that had been produced since the days of Fielding.' And of its faults we spoke thus:

[see No. 59, 'If this book be, as we apprehend it is, the first work of the author . . . fit materials for a book of fiction']

We shall also perhaps be forgiven if we reproduce the remarks with which we opened our criticism of the *Tenant of Wildfell Hall*.

[see No. 73, 'The authors of *Jane Eyre, Wuthering Heights* . . . other labourers in the same path']

Was this scant or grudging praise? Did it refuse to recognize the 'immature but very real powers' of these young and struggling authors? Did it 'misunderstand' or 'misrepresent' them.

If so, Currer Bell must herself share the reproach, for the language in which she speaks of her sister Emily's early habits and associations, as explaining what was faulty as well as what was excellent in her writings, does not materially differ from this which has just been quoted. For ourselves we have nothing to add to it – neither praise to retract, nor censure to explain. We have only most unfeignedly to deplore the blight which fell prematurely on such rich intellectual promise, and to regret that natures so rare and noble should so early have passed away.

83. G. H. Lewes, from an unsigned review, *Leader*

28 December 1850, 953

See Introduction, pp. 29–30, and No. 94.

There are various points of interest in this republication, some arising from the intrinsic excellence of the works themselves, others from the lustre reflected on them by *Jane Eyre*. The biographical notice of her two sisters is plainly and touchingly written by Currer Bell. With their early struggles in authorship thousands will sympathize.

[quotes from the 'Biographical Notice']

Critics, we are told, failed to do them justice. But to judge from the extracts given of articles in the *Britannia* and *Atlas*, the critics were excessively indulgent, and we take it the great public was the most recalcitrant, and would *not* be amused with these strange wild pictures of incult humanity, painted as if by lurid torchlight, though painted with unmistakeable power – the very power only heightening their repulsiveness. The visions of madmen are not more savage, or more remote from ordinary life. The error committed is an error in art – the excessive predominance of shadows darkening the picture. One cannot dine off condiments, nor sup off horrors without an indigestion.

And yet, although there is a want of air and light in the picture we cannot deny its truth; sombre, rude, brutal, yet true. The fierce ungoverned instincts of powerful organizations, bred up amidst violence, revolt, and moral apathy, are here seen in operation; such brutes we should all be, or the most of us, were our lives as insubordinate to law; were our affections and sympathies as little cultivated, our imaginations as undirected. And herein lies the moral of the book, though most people will fail to draw the moral from very irritation at it.

Curious enough it is to read *Wuthering Heights* and *The Tenant of Wildfell Hall*, and remember that the writers were two retiring, solitary, consumptive girls! Books, coarse even for men, coarse in language and coarse in conception, the coarseness apparently of violence and uncultivated men – turn out to be the productions of two girls living almost alone, filling their loneliness with quiet studies, and writing these books from a sense of duty, hating the pictures they drew, yet drawing them with austere conscientiousness! There is matter here for the moralist or critic to speculate on.

That it was no caprice of a poor imagination wandering in search of an 'exciting' subject we are most thoroughly convinced. The three sisters have been haunted by the same experience. Currer Bell throws more humanity into her picture; but Rochester belongs to the Earnshaw and Heathcliff family. Currer Bell's riper mind enables her to paint with a freer hand; nor can we doubt but that her two sisters, had they lived, would also have risen into greater strength and clearness, retaining the extraordinary power of vigorous delineation which makes their writings so remarkable.

The power, indeed, is wonderful. Heathcliff, devil though he be, is drawn with a sort of dusky splendour which fascinates, and we feel the truth of his burning and impassioned love for Catherine, and of her inextinguishable love for him. It was a happy thought to make her love the kind, weak, elegant Edgar, and yet without lessening her passion for Heathcliff. Edgar appeals to her love of refinement, and goodness, and culture; Heathcliff clutches her soul in his passionate embrace. Edgar is the husband she has chosen, the man who alone is fit to call her wife; but although she is ashamed of her early playmate she loves him with a passionate abandonment which sets culture, education, the world, at defiance. It is in the treatment of this subject that Ellis Bell shows real mastery, and it shows more genius, in the highest sense of the word, than you will find in a thousand novels.

Creative power is so rare and so valuable that we should accept even its caprices with gratitude. Currer Bell, in a passage on this question, doubts whether the artist can control his power; she seems to think with Plato (see his argument in the *Ion*), that the artist does not possess, but is possessed. . . . [See No. 81, pp. 287–8]

This is so true that we suppose every writer will easily recall his sensation of being 'carried away' by the thoughts which in moments of exaltation possessed his soul – will recall the headlong feeling of letting the reins slip – being himself as much astonished at the result as any reader can be. There is at such time a *momentum* which propels the mind into regions inaccessible to calculation, unsuspected in our calmer moods.

The present publication is decidedly an interesting one. Besides the two novels of *Wuthering Heights* and *Agnes Grey* it contains the biographical notices already spoken of, and a selection from the poems left by both sisters. We cannot share Currer Bell's partiality for them; in no one quality distinguishing poetry and prose are they remarkable; but although their poetic interest is next to nought they have a biographical interest which justifies their publication. The volume is compact, and may be slipped into a coat pocket for the railway, so that the traveller may wile away with it the long hours of his journey in grim pleasure.

From an unsigned review, *Athenaeum*

28 December 1850, 1368–9

Charlotte wrote to James Taylor on 15 January 1851:

The only notices that I have seen of the new edition of *Wuthering Heights* were those in the *Examiner* [No. 82] the *Leader* [No. 83] and the *Athenaeum*. That in the *Athenaeum* somehow gave me pleasure; it is quiet but respectful – so I thought, at least (*LL*, iii, 200).

Perhaps written by H. F. Chorley; see No. 7.

Female genius and female authorship may be said to present some peculiarities of aspect and circumstance in England, which we find associated with them in no other country. Among the most daring and original manifestations of invention by Englishwomen, – some of the most daring and original have owed their parentage, not to defying *Britomarts* at war with society, who choose to make their literature match with their lives, – not to brilliant women figuring in the world, in whom every gift and faculty has been enriched, and whetted sharp, and encouraged into creative utterance, by perpetual communication with the most distinguished men of the time, – but to writers living retired lives in retired places, stimulated to activity by no outward influence, driven to confession by no history that demands apologetic parable or subtle plea. This, as a characteristic of English female genius, we have long noticed: – but it has rarely been more simply, more strongly, some will add more strangely, illustrated than in the volume before us.

The lifting of that veil which for a while concealed the authorship of *Jane Eyre* and its sister-novels, excites in us no surprise. It seemed evident from the first prose pages bearing the signatures of Currer, Ellis, and Acton Bell, that these were *Rosalinds* – or a *Rosalind* – in masquerade: – some doubt as to the plurality of persons being engendered by a certain uniformity of local colour and resemblance in choice of subject, which might have arisen either from identity, or from joint peculiarities of situation and of circumstance. – It seemed no less evi-

dent . . . that the writers described from personal experience the wild
and rugged scenery of the northern parts of this kingdom; and no
assertion or disproval, no hypothesis or rumour, which obtained
circulation after the success of *Jane Eyre*, could shake convictions that
had been gathered out of the books themselves . . . In the prefaces and
notices before us, we find that the Bells were three sisters: – two of
whom are no longer amongst the living. The survivor describes their
home . . . [and] the story of the authorship of these singular books . . .

Though the particulars be little more than the filling-up of an outline
already clearly traced and constantly present whenever those characteristic tales recurred to us, – by those who have held other ideas with
regard to the authorship of *Jane Eyre* they will be found at once curious
and interesting from the plain and earnest sincerity of the writer. She
subsequently enters on an analysis and discussion of *Wuthering Heights*
as a work of Art: – in the closing paragraph of her preface to that novel
insinuating an argument, if not a defence, the urgency of which is not
sufficiently admitted by the bulk of the world of readers.

[quotes 'Whether it is right or advisable to create beings like Heathcliff
. . . at your caprice'; see above, p. 287]

It might have been added, that to those whose experience of men
and manners is neither extensive nor various, the construction of a
self-consistent monster is easier than the delineation of an imperfect
or inconsistent reality – with all its fallings-short, its fitful aspirations,
its mixed enterprises, and its interrupted dreams. But we must refrain
from further speculation and illustration: – enough having been given
to justify our characterizing this volume, with its preface, as a more
than usually interesting contribution to the history of female authorship
in England.

85. From an unsigned review, *Eclectic Review*

February 1851, 5th series, 223–7

For the prevailing temper of the reviews in this periodical see No. 50. The omitted passages include details from Charlotte's 'Biographical Notice'.

We purpose dealing rather with the Biographical Notice prefixed to this volume, than with the two works which it contains. There are various reasons for this. It is sufficient to say that the former interests us deeply, which the latter do not; and that the present is its first appearance, whereas the *Fictions* it prefaces are already somewhat known to the public. Not that we shall wholly omit to record our judgment, more particularly on *Wuthering Heights*; but our special business is with the 'Notice' now supplied by Currer, rather than with the productions of Ellis and Acton Bell. Our readers are, doubtless, aware of the questions which have been raised respecting the authorship of *Jane Eyre* and *Shirley*, with that of their predecessors reprinted in the volume on our table. Whether these works were the productions of a gentleman or a lady, and whether their authorship was single or threefold, have been mooted with considerable interest in some literary circles, and have sometimes been pronounced on with a dogmatism which would have been amusing, had it not indicated a sad lack of modesty and intelligence. Though the internal evidence of the works is strongly favorable to the hypothesis of a female authorship, there is, nevertheless, a certain masculine air about their style, a repudiation of conventionalisms, and a bold, nervous, cast of thought and action, which suggests the presence of the other sex. Slight inaccuracies in some matters of female dress are, moreover, alleged in proof of their being the production of a masculine pen.

These considerations, however, avail little against the general complexion and air of the works in question. It appears to us impossible to read them without feeling that their excellences and faults, their instinctive attachments and occasional exaggerations, the depths of their tenderness and their want of practical judgment, all betoken the authorship of a lady. In their perusal, we are in the company of an intelligent, free-spoken, and hearty woman, who feels deeply, can describe with power, has seen some of the rougher sides of life, and, though capable of strong affection, is probably wanting in the 'sweet attractive grace' which Milton so beautifully ascribes to Eve.

As to the other point which had been mooted, it is marvellous, we confess, that a doubt should ever have existed. That either of the works now before us should be attributed to the same writer as *Jane Eyre* and *Shirley*, is one of the strangest blunders of criticism with which we ever met. It is true there is talent in them, and that too of an order – we refer more particularly to *Wuthering Heights* – similar in its general character to what those works display. Yet the points of distinction are numerous, and of a character which ought to have precluded doubt. . . .

Jane Eyre was instantaneously popular; but not so the productions of Ellis and Acton Bell. We are not surprised at this. . . . The successful work was attractive as well as talented, while *Wuthering Heights* – we know little of *Agnes Grey* – is one of the most repellent books we ever read. With all its talent – and it has much – we cannot imagine its being read through from any fascination in the tale itself. The powers it displays are not only premature, but are misdirected. The characters sketched are, for the most part, dark and loathsome, while a gloomy and sombre air rests on the whole scene, which renders it anything but pleasing . . .

The sorrowful tale unfolded in this biographical notice . . . has much literary interest, but to us it is yet far more interesting in the picture it exhibits of domestic harmony and love, broken in upon and shaded by the presence of 'the king of terrors.' Such scenes are of frequent occurrence, though it rarely happens that a sisterhood is linked by such mental sympathies and literary engagements as distinguished Ellis, Acton, and Currer Bell. May the survivor combine, with her intellectual occupations, the faith and devotion which stand in intimate connexion with 'joys unspeakable and divine!'

Of *Wuthering Heights*, we must say a word before closing. We have already indicated our opinion; but it is due to our readers and to ourselves that we should state somewhat more fully the grounds of our judgment. That the work has considerable merit we admit. The scenery is laid in the North, the bleak, moorish, wild, character of which is admirably preserved. Ellis Bell was evidently attached to her native hills. She was at home amongst them; and there is, therefore, a vividness and graphic power in her sketches which present them actually before us. So far we prefer no complaint, but the case is different with the *dramatis personae*. Such a company we never saw grouped before; and we hope never to meet with its like again. Heathcliff is a perfect monster, more demon than human. Hindley Earnshaw is a besotted fool, for whom we scarce feel pity; while his son Hareton is at once ignorant and brutish, until, as by the wand of an enchanter, he takes polish in the last scene of the tale, and retires a docile and apt scholar. The two Catherines, mother and daughter, are equally exaggerations, more than questionable in some parts of their procedure, and absurdly unnatural in the leading incidents of their life. Isabella Linton is one of the silliest and most credulous girls that fancy ever painted; and the enduring affection and tenderness of her brother Edgar are so exhibited as to produce the impression of a feeble rather than of a virtuous character. Of the minor personages we need say nothing, save that, with slight exceptions, they are in keeping with their superiors.

As the characters of the tale are unattractive, so the chief incidents are sadly wanting in probability. They are devoid of truthfulness, are not in harmony with the actual world, and have, therefore, but little more power to move our sympathies than the romances of the middle ages, or the ghost stories which made our granddames tremble.

86. Elizabeth Barrett Browning, letters

1850-3

Letters from Florence to Miss Mitford of 9 January and 18 February 1850; to Mrs James of 2 April 1850; to Mr Westwood of September 1853; from *The Letters of Elizabeth Barrett Browning*, ed. Frederic G. Kenyon (1897), 1, 432, 435, 442; ii, 139.

9 January 1850:

Plainly *Jane Eyre* was by a woman. It used to astound me when sensible people said otherwise.

18 February 1850:

I certainly don't think that the qualities, half savage and half free-thinking, expressed in *Jane Eyre* are likely to suit a model governess or schoolmistress; and it amuses me to consider them in that particular relation.

2 April 1850:

I have read *Shirley* lately; it is not equal to *Jane Eyre* in spontaneousness and earnestness . . . I found it heavy, I confess, though in the mechanical part of the writing – the compositional *savoir faire* – there is an advance.

September 1853:

If you can read novels, and you have too much sense not to be fond of them, read *Villette*. The scene of the greater part of it is in Belgium, and I think it a strong book.

87. D. G. Rossetti, from a letter

1854

Letter to William Allingham, 19 September 1854, from *Letters of Dante Gabriel Rossetti*, ed. O. Doughty and R. J. Wahl (1965) i, 224. Rossetti retained his enthusiasm for *Wuthering Heights*; see William Allingham's diary-entry recording Rossetti's tastes and opinions, 19 September 1867, '*Wuthering Heights* is a Koh-i-noor among novels, *Sidonia the Sorceress* a stunner' (*William Allingham's Diary*, ed. Geoffrey Grigson (1967) 163). Rossetti anticipates Walter Pater in bringing together Meinhold's *Sidonia* and *Wuthering Heights* (see No. 114).

I've been greatly interested in *Wuthering Heights*, the first novel I've read for an age, and the best (as regards power and sound style) for two ages, except *Sidonia*[1]. But it is a fiend of a book, an incredible monster, combining all the stronger female tendencies from Mrs Browning to Mrs Brownrigg.[2] The action is laid in Hell, – only it seems places and people have English names there. Did you ever read it?

[1] *Sidonia the Sorceress*, by Johann Wilhelm Meinhold (1797–1851); translated into English in 1844 (see p. 445, n.).
[2] Elizabeth Brownrigg, midwife, hanged in 1767 for murdering Mary Clifford, a workhouse apprentice.

88. Harriet Martineau, obituary of Charlotte Brontë, *Daily News*

April 1855

Reprinted in *Biographical Sketches*, 1869.

'Currer Bell' is dead! The early death of the large family of whom she was the sole survivor prepared all who knew the circumstances to expect the loss of this gifted creature at any time: but not the less deep will be the grief of society that her genius will yield us nothing more. We have three works from her pen which will hold their place in the literature of our country; and, but for her frail health, there might have been three times three, – for she was under forty – and her genius was not of an exhaustible kind. If it had been exhaustible, it would have been exhausted some time since. She had every inducement that could have availed with one less high-minded to publish two or three novels a year. Fame waited upon all she did; and she might have enriched herself by very slight exertion: but her steady conviction was that the publication of a book is a solemn act of conscience – in the case of a novel as much as any other kind of book. She was not fond of speaking of herself and her conscience; but she now and then uttered to her very few friends things which may, alas! be told now, without fear of hurting her sensitive nature; things which ought to be told in her honour. Among these sayings was one which explains the long interval between her works. She said that she thought every serious delineation of life ought to be the product of personal experience and observation of a normal, and not of a forced or special kind. 'I have not accumulated, since I published *Shirley*,' she said, 'what makes it needful for me to speak again, and, till I do, may God give me grace to be dumb!' She had a conscientiousness which could not be relaxed by praise or even sympathy – dear as sympathy was to her sensitive nature. She had no vanity which praise could aggravate or censure mortify. She calmly read all adverse reviews of her books, for the sake of instruction; and when she could not recognize the aptness of criticism, she was more puzzled than hurt or angry. The common flatteries which wait upon literary success she quizzed with a charming grace; and any occasional severity, such as literary women are favoured with at the beginning of their course, she accepted with a humility which was full of dignity and charm. From her feeble constitution of body, her sufferings by the death of her whole family, and the secluded and monotonous life she led, she became morbidly sensitive in some respects; but in her high vocation, she had, in addition to the deep intuitions of a gifted woman, the strength of a man, the patience of a hero, and the conscientiousness of a saint. In the points in which women are usually most weak – in regard to opinion, to appreciation, to applause, – her moral strength fell not a whit behind the intellectual force manifested in her works. Though passion occupies too prominent a place in her pictures of life, though women have to complain that she represents love as the whole and sole concern of their lives, and though governesses especially have reason to remonstrate, and do remonstrate, that their share of human conflict is laid open somewhat rudely and inconsiderately and sweepingly to social observation, it is a true social blessing that we have had a female writer who has discountenanced sentimentalism and feeble egotism with such practical force as is apparent in the works of Currer Bell. Her heroines love too readily, too vehemently, and sometimes after a fashion which their female readers may resent; but they do their duty through everything, and are healthy in action, however morbid in passion.

How admirable this strength is – how wonderful this force of integrity – can hardly be understood by any but the few who know the story of this remarkable woman's life. The account of the school in *Jane Eyre* is only too true. The 'Helen' of that tale is – not precisely the eldest sister, who died there – but more like her than any other person. She is that sister, 'with a difference.' Another sister died at home soon after leaving school, and in consequence of its hardships; and 'Currer Bell' (Charlotte Brontë) was never free while there (for a year and a half) from the gnawing sensation or consequent feebleness of downright hunger; and she never grew an inch from that time. She was the smallest of women; and it was that school which stunted her growth. As she tells us in *Jane Eyre*, the visitation of an epidemic caused a total change and radical reform in the establishment, which was even removed to another site. But the reform came too late to reverse the destiny of the doomed family of the Brontës.

These wonderful girls were the daughters of a clergyman who, now very aged and infirm, survives his wife and all his many children. The name Brontë (an abbreviation of Bronterre) is Irish and very ancient. The mother died many years ago, and several of her children. When the reading world began to have an interest in their existence, there were three sisters and a brother living with their father at Haworth, near Keighley, in Yorkshire. The girls had been out as governesses – Charlotte, at Brussels, as is no secret to the readers of *Villette*. They rejoiced to meet again at home Charlotte, Emily, and Ann[e] ('Currer,' 'Ellis,' and 'Acton'). In her obituary notice of her two sisters 'Currer' reveals something of their process of authorship, and their experience of failure and success. How terrible some of their experience of life was, in the midst of the domestic freedom and indulgence afforded them by their studious father, may be seen by the fearful representations of masculine nature and character found in the novels of Emily and Ann. They considered it their duty, they told us, to present life as they knew it; and they gave us *Wuthering Heights* and *The Tenant of Wildfell Hall*. Such an experience as this indicates is really perplexing to English people in general; and all that we have to do with it is to bear it in mind when disposed to pass criticism on the coarseness which, to a certain degree, pervades the works of all the sisters,[1] and the repulsiveness which makes the tales by Emily and Ann really horrible to people who have not iron nerves.

Jane Eyre was naturally and universally supposed to be Charlotte herself; but she always denied it, calmly, cheerfully, and with the obvious sincerity which characterized all she said. She declared that there was no more ground for the assertion than this. She once told her sisters they were wrong – even morally wrong – in making their heroines beautiful, as a matter of course. They replied that it was impossible to make a heroine interesting on other terms. Her answer was, 'I will prove to you that you are wrong. I will show you a heroine as small and plain as myself who shall be as interesting as any of yours.' 'Hence, *Jane Eyre*,' she said in telling the anecdote; 'but she is not myself, any further than that.' As the work went on the interest deepened to the writer. When she came to 'Thornfield' she could not stop. Being short-sighted to excess, she wrote in little square paper books, held close to her eyes, and (the first copy) in pencil. On she went, writing incessantly for three weeks; by which time she had carried her heroine away from Thornfield, and was herself in a fever, which compelled her to pause. The rest was written with less vehe-

[1] See Introduction, p. 28.

mence, and more anxious care. The world adds, with less vigour and
interest. She could gratify her singular reserve in regard to the publication of this remarkable book. We all remember how long it was
before we could learn who wrote it, and any particulars of the writer,
when the name was revealed. She was living among the wild Yorkshire
hills, with a father who was too much absorbed in his studies to notice
her occupations, in a place where newspapers were never seen (or
where she never saw any), and in a house where the servants knew
nothing about books, manuscripts, proofs, or the post. When she told
her secret to her father, she carried her book in one hand, and an
adverse review in the other, to save his simple and unworldly mind
from rash expectations of a fame and fortune which she was determined
should never be the aims of her life. That we have had only two novels
since shows how deeply grounded was this resolve.

Shirley was conceived and wrought out in the midst of fearful
domestic griefs. Her only brother, a young man of once splendid
promise which was early blighted, and both her remaining sisters, died
in one year. There was something inexpressibly affecting in the aspect
of the frail little creature who had done such wonderful things, and
who was able to bear up, with so bright an eye and so composed a
countenance, under such a weight of sorrow, and such a prospect of
solitude. In her deep mourning dress (neat as a quaker's), with her
beautiful hair, smooth and brown, her fine eyes blazing with meaning, and her sensible face indicating a habit of self-control, if not of
silence, she seemed a perfect household image - irresistibly recalling
Wordsworth's description of that domestic treasure. And she was this.
She was as able at the needle as the pen. The household knew the
excellence of her cookery before they heard of that of her books. In so
utter a seclusion as she lived in - in those dreary wilds, where she was
not strong enough to roam over the hills,[1] in that retreat where her
studious father rarely broke the silence - and there was no one else
to do it; in that forlorn house, planted on the very clay of the churchyard, where the graves of her sisters were before her window; in such
a living sepulchre her mind could not [but] prey upon itself; and how
it did suffer, we see in the more painful portions of her last novel -
Villette. She said, with a change in her steady countenance, that she
should feel very lonely when her aged father died. But she formed new
ties after that. She married; and it is the old father who survives to
mourn her. He knows, to his comfort, that it is not for long. Others

[1] Obviously an error. See Mrs Gaskell's *Life*, chapter 22 (Haworth edition, 485).

now mourn her, in a domestic sense; and, as for the public, there can be no doubt that a pang will be felt in the midst of the strongest interests of the day, through the length and breadth of the land, and in the very heart of Germany (where her works are singularly appreciated), France, and America[1] that the 'Currer Bell,' who so lately stole a shadow into the field of contemporary literature had already become a shadow again – vanishing from our view, and henceforth haunting only the memory of the multitude whose expectation was fixed upon her.

[1] Her novels also travelled to India and New Zealand; see Nos 18, 40.

89. Matthew Arnold, 'Haworth churchyard', *Fraser's Magazine*

May 1855, li, 527–30

Reprinted, in a revised form, in *Poems* 1877

The 'two ... Gifted women' (ll. 8–9) are Charlotte Brontë and Harriet Martineau, both of whom Arnold first met on 21 December 1850 (*LL*, iii, 198–200); the omitted stanzas celebrate Harriet Martineau who was thought in 1855 to be mortally ill. Arnold visited Haworth to inspect the Wesleyan School on 6 May 1852, but his description of the Brontës' graves (ll. 155–6) suggests that he did not visit the church or churchyard; see his letter to Mrs Gaskell of 1 June 1855:

I am almost sorry you told me about the place of their burial. It really seems to me to put the finishing touch to the strange cross-grained character of the fortunes of that ill-fated family that they should even be placed after death in the wrong, uncongenial spot (*Bulletin of the John Rylands Library*, xix (1935) 135–6).

For other references to the Brontës by members of the Arnold family see No. 40.

> Where, under Loughrigg, the stream
> Of Rotha sparkles, the fields
> Are green, in the house of one
> Friendly and gentle, now dead,
> Wordsworth's son-in-law, friend –   5
> Four years since, on a mark'd
> Evening, a meeting I saw.
>
> Two friends met there, two fam'd
> Gifted women. The one,
> Brilliant with recent renown.   10

Young, unpractis'd, had told
With a Master's accent her feign'd
History of passionate life:
The other, maturer in fame,
Earning, she too, her praise   15
First in Fiction, had since
Widen'd her sweep, and survey'd
History, Politics, Mind.

They met, held converse: they wrote
In a book which of glorious souls   20
Held memorial: Bard,
Warrior, Statesman, had left
Their names: – chief treasure of all,
Scott had consign'd there his last
Breathings of song, with a pen   25
Tottering, a death-stricken hand.

I beheld; the obscure
Saw the famous. Alas!
Years in number, it seem'd,
Lay before both, and a fame   30
Heighten'd, and multiplied power.
Behold! The elder, to-day,
Lies expecting from Death,
In mortal weakness, a last
Summons: the younger is dead. . . .   35

How shall we honour the young.   80
The ardent, the gifted? how mourn?
Console we cannot; her ear
Is deaf. Far northward from here,
In a churchyard high mid the moors,
Of Yorkshire, a little earth   85
Stops it for ever to praise.

Where, behind Keighley, the road
Up to the heart of the moors
Between heath-clad showery hills
Runs, and colliers' carts   90

Poach the deep ways coming down,
And a rough, grim'd race have their homes –
There, on its slope, is built
The moorland town. But the church
Stands on the crest of the hill,   95
Lonely and bleak; at its side
The parsonage-house and the graves.

See! in the desolate house
The childless father! Alas –
Age, whom the most of us chide,   100
Chide, and put back, and delay –
Come, unupbraided for once!
Lay thy benumbing hand,
Gratefully cold, on this brow!
Shut out the grief, the despair!   105
Weaken the sense of his loss!
Deaden the infinite pain!

Another grief I see,
Younger; but this the Muse,
In pity and silent awe   110
Revering what she cannot soothe,
With veil'd face and bow'd head,
Salutes, and passes by.

Strew with roses the grave
Of the early-dying. Alas!   115
Early she goes on the path
To the Silent Country, and leaves
Half her laurels unwon,
Dying too soon: yet green
Laurels she had, and a course   120
Short, yet redoubled by Fame.

For him who must live many years
That life is best which slips away
Out of the light, and mutely; which avoids
Fame, and her less-fair followers, Envy, Strife,   125
Stupid Detraction, Jealousy, Cabal,

Insincere Praises: – which descends
The mossy quiet track to Age.

    But, when immature Death
Beckons too early the guest   130
From the half-tried Banquet of Life,
Young, in the bloom of his days;
Leaves no leisure to press,
Slow and surely, the sweet
Of a tranquil life in the shade –   135
Fuller for him be the hours!
Give him emotion, though pain!
Let him live, let him feel, *I have liv'd.*
Heap up his moments with life!
Quicken his pulses with Fame!   140

    And not friendless, nor yet
Only with strangers to meet,
Faces ungreeting and cold,
Thou, O Mourn'd One, to-day
Enterest the House of the Grave.   145
Those of thy blood, whom thou lov'dst,
Have preceded thee; young,
Loving, a sisterly band:
Some in gift, some in art
Inferior; all in fame.   150
They, like friends, shall receive
This comer, greet her with joy;
Welcome the Sister; the Friend;
Hear with delight of thy fame.

    Round thee they lie; the grass   155
Blows from their graves toward thine.
She, whose genius, though not
Puissant like thine, was yet
Sweet and graceful: and She –
(How shall I sing her?) – whose soul   160
Knew no fellow for might,
Passion, vehemence, grief,
Daring, since Byron died,

That world-fam'd Son of Fire; She, who sank
Baffled, unknown, self-consum'd;   165
Whose too-bold dying song[1]
Shook, like a clarion-blast, my soul.

Of one too I have heard,
A Brother – sleeps he here? –
Of all his gifted race   170
Not the least-gifted; young,
Unhappy, beautiful; the cause
Of many hopes, of many tears.
O Boy, if here thou sleep'st, sleep well!
On thee too did the Muse   175
Bright in thy cradle smile:
But some dark Shadow came
(I know not what) and interpos'd.

Sleep, O cluster of friends,
Sleep! or only, when May,   180
Brought by the West Wind, returns
Back to your native heaths,
And the plover is heard on the moors,
Yearly awake, to behold
The opening summer, the sky,   185
The shining moorland; to hear
The drowsy bee, as of old,
Hum o'er the thyme, the grouse
Call from the heather in bloom:

Sleep; or only for this   190
Break your united repose.

[1] Arnold noted, in 1877, 'See the last verses by Emily Brontë in *Poems by Currer, Ellis and Acton Bell* [1846].' He was thinking of 'No coward soul is mine . . .', first published in Charlotte's memorial edition of 1850 with the note, 'The following are the last lines my sister ever wrote'. See, however, C. W. Hatfield's *The Complete Poems of Emily Jane Brontë* (1941), where the poem is dated 2 January 1846 and followed by two poems dated 14 September 1846 and 13 May 1848. The song was 'too bold' presumably because of its assertions in stanzas 1–3.

90. Margaret Oliphant, from an unsigned article, *Blackwood's Magazine*

May 1855, lxxvii, 557-9

From 'Modern Novelists – Great and Small', one of Mrs Oliphant's numerous journalistic surveys for *Blackwood's*. The article was prepared before Charlotte's death, but a farewell tribute was added at the close. The prolific Margaret Oliphant (1828–97) contributed to *Blackwood's*, from the 1850s onwards, many novels as well as articles; published monographs on Dante (1877) and Cervantes (1880); and produced among various other books a literary history of England (1882). For her views on the Brontës in the 1860s and 1880s see No. 105 and Introduction, pp. 41–2, and for Swinburne's comparison of her work with Charlotte's see No. 108.

Ten years ago we professed an orthodox system of novel-making. Our lovers were humble and devoted – our ladies were beautiful, and might be capricious if it pleased them; and we held it a very proper and most laudable arrangement that Jacob should serve seven years for Rachel, and recorded it as one of the articles of our creed; and that the only true-love worth having was that reverent, knightly, chivalrous true-love which consecrated all womankind, and served one with fervour and enthusiasm. Such was our ideal, and such our system, in the old halcyon days of novel-writing; when suddenly there stole upon the scene, without either flourish of trumpets or public proclamation, a little fierce incendiary, doomed to turn the world of fancy upside down. She stole upon the scene – pale, small, by no means beautiful – something of a genius, something of a vixen – a dangerous little person, inimical to the peace of society. After we became acquainted with herself, we were introduced to her lover. Such a lover! – a vast, burly, sensual Englishman, one of those Hogarth men, whose power consists in some singular animal force of life and character, which it is impossible to describe or analyse. Such a wooing! – the lover is rude, brutal, cruel. The little woman fights against him with courage and spirit – begins to find the excitement and relish of a new life in this struggle – begins to think of her antagonist all day long – falls into fierce love and jealousy – betrays herself – is tantalized and slighted, to prove her devotion – and then suddenly seized upon and taken possession of, with love several degrees fiercer than her own. Then comes the catastrophe which prevents this extraordinary love from running smooth. Our heroine runs away to save herself – falls in with another man almost as singular as her first love – and very nearly suffers herself to be reduced to marry this unloved and unloving wooer; but, escaping that risk, finally discovers that the obstacle is removed which stood between her and her former tyrant, and rushes back straightway to be graciously accepted by the blind and weakened Rochester. Such was the impetuous little spirit which dashed into our well-ordered world, broke its boundaries, and defied its principles – and the most alarming revolution of modern times has followed the invasion of *Jane Eyre*.

It is not to be wondered at that speculation should run wild about this remarkable production. Sober people, with a sober respect for womankind, and not sufficient penetration to perceive that the grossness of the book was such grossness as only could be perpetrated by a woman, contested indignantly the sex of the writer. The established authorities brought forth proofs in the form of incorrect costume, and errors in dress. Nobody perceived that it was the new generation nailing its colours to its mast. No one would understand that this furious love-making was but a wild declaration of the 'Rights of Woman' in a new aspect. The old-fashioned deference and respect – the old-fashioned wooing – what were they but so many proofs of the inferior position of the woman, to whom the man condescended with the gracious courtliness of his loftier elevation! The honours paid to her in society – the pretty fictions of politeness, they were all degrading tokens of her subjection, if she were but sufficiently enlightened to see their true meaning. The man who presumed to treat her with reverence was one who insulted her pretensions; while the lover who struggled with her, as he would have struggled with another man, only adding a certain amount of contemptuous brutality, which no man would tolerate, was the only one who truly recognized her claims of equality . . .

Here is your true revolution. France is but one of the Western Powers; woman is the half of the world. Talk of a balance of power which may be adjusted by taking a Crimea, or fighting a dozen battles

– here is a battle which must always be going forward – a balance of power only to be decided by single combat, deadly and uncompromising, where the combatants, so far from being guided by the old punctilios of the duello, make no secret of their ferocity, but throw sly javelins at each other, instead of shaking hands before they begin. Do you think that young lady is an angelic being, young gentleman? . . . Unhappy youth! . . . In her secret heart she longs to rush upon you, and try a grapple with you, to prove her strength and her equality. She has no patience with your flowery emblems. Why should *she* be like a rose or a lily any more than yourself? Are these beautiful weaklings the only types you can find of *her*? And this new Bellona steps forth in armour, throws down her glove, and defies you – to conquer her if you can. Do you like it, gentle love? – would you rather break her head and win, or leave her alone and love her? The alternative is quite distinct and unmistakable – only do not insult her with your respect and humility, for this is something more than she can bear.

These are the doctrines, startling and original, propounded by Jane Eyre; and they are not Jane Eyre's opinions only, as we may guess from the host of followers or imitators who have copied them. There is a degree of refined indelicacy possible to a woman, which no man can reach. Her very ignorance of evil seems to give a certain piquancy and relish to her attempts to realize it. . . . There are some conversations between Rochester and Jane Eyre which no *man* could have dared to give – which only could have been given by the overboldness of innocence and ignorance trying to imagine what it never could understand, and which are as womanish as they are unwomanly.

When all this is said, *Jane Eyre* remains one of the most remarkable works of modern times – as remarkable as *Villette*, and more perfect. We know no one else who has such a grasp of persons and places, and a perfect command of the changes of the atmosphere, and the looks of a country under rain or wind. There is no fiction in these wonderful scenes of hers. The Yorkshire dales, the north-country moor, the streets of Brussels, are illusions equally complete. Who does not know Madame Beck's house, white and square and lofty, with its level rows of windows, its green shutters, and the sun that beams upon its blinds, and on the sultry pavement before the door? How French is Paul Emmanuel and all his accessories! How English is Lucy Snowe! We feel no art in these remarkable books. What we feel is a force which makes everything real – a motion which is irresistible. We are swept on in the current, and never draw breath till the tale is ended. Afterwards we may disapprove at our leisure, but it is certain that we have not a moment's pause to be critical till we come to the end.

The effect of a great literary success, especially in fiction, is a strange thing to observe, – the direct influence it has on some one or two similar minds, and the indirect bias which it gives to a great many others. There is at least one other writer of considerable gifts, whose books are all so many reflections of *Jane Eyre*. We mean no disparagement to Miss Kavanagh,[1] but, from *Nathalie* to *Grace Lee*, she has done little else than repeat the attractive story of this conflict and combat of love or war – for either name will do. . . . We might perhaps trace the origin of this passion for *strength* further back than *Jane Eyre*; as far back, perhaps, as Mr Carlyle's idolatry of the 'Canning' – the king, man, and hero. But it is a sad thing, with all our cultivation and refinement, to be thrown back upon sheer blind force as our universal conqueror. Mr Carlyle's Thor, too, is a sweet-hearted giant, and bears no comparison to Mr Rochester and Mr John Owen. . . . These ladies, however, are not so solicitous to have some one who can conquer war or fortune, as to find some one who can subdue, and rule with a hand of iron – themselves. Nor is the *indirect* influence of this new light in literature less remarkable.

Mrs Gaskell, a sensible and considerate woman, and herself ranking high in her sphere, has just fallen subject to the same delusion. *North and South* is extremely clever, as a story; and, without taking any secondary qualification to build its merits upon, it is perhaps better and livelier than any of Mrs Gaskell's previous works; yet here are still the wide circles in the water, showing that not far off is the identical spot where Jane Eyre and Lucy Snowe, in their wild sport, have been casting stones; here is again the desperate, bitter quarrel out of which love is to come; here is love itself, always in a fury, often looking exceedingly like hatred, and by no means distinguished for its good manners, or its graces of speech.

---

[1] Julia Kavanagh (1824–1877), novelist and short-story writer, published *Nathalie: A Tale* (1850), *Daisy Burns: A Tale* (1853) and *Grace Lee: A Tale* (1855). She admired Charlotte, whom she met in summer 1850 (*LL*, iii, 118) and with whom she corresponded. Charlotte's comments on *Nathalie* and *Daisy Burns* appear at *LL*, iii, 203; iv, 51, and on *Madeleine: A Tale of Auvergne* (1848), which she especially liked, at *LL*, ii, 287.

91. From an unsigned article, 'Thackeray and Currer Bell', *Oxford and Cambridge Magazine*

June 1856, 328–32

Principally devoted to general reflections concerning the moral penetration found in the novels of Thackeray, whose *The New-comes* (1853–5), *Vanity Fair* (1847–8), *Our Street* (1848) and *The Perkins's Ball* [sic] (1847) are listed (in this order) at the head of the article before Charlotte's *Jane Eyre*, which is admired for its equally serious though differently weighed moral concerns. See Introduction, p. 21.

It is interesting to note how the same phase of society and feeling is reflected in different minds. . . . Who, for example, at first sight would accuse Thackeray and Currer Bell of any connection? And yet, at the bottom, the present time is viewed by both much in the same light. Hitherto, in all highly civilized nations a time has come, when the machinery and scaffolding of civilization have threatened to overgrow the building itself; a time, when prudence threatens to choke goodness, cleverness to trample on simplicity, affectation to lord it over nature and even over art; when interest blinds justice, worldly wisdom petrifies the heart, and etiquette poisons comfort; a time when the letter seems likely to swallow up the law, means to usurp the place of ends, and rules to make a clean sweep of reason; when honours are more coveted than worth, riches than happiness, power than affection; when clothes are for character, and hollow praise for genuine love – a time rich in the 'irony of fate.' Such in some respects seems to be our present phase. And far as Currer Bell and Thackeray seem apart, yet a deep hatred of this predominance of the husk over the kernel, of the letter over the spirit, of the essence over the accident, will, we think, be found to form the prevailing undercurrent of their works.

Jane Eyre by many has been looked upon as an immoral production, and Currer Bell as the treacherous advocate of contempt of established maxims and disregard of the regulations of society. Now this is precisely the fault which the Pharisees found with the teaching of the Saviour. Where indeed, we would ask, is the immorality of Jane Eyre, if not that, acting in the purity of her heart and the might of her integrity, she spurns the letter to give triumph to the spirit? ... Are there no strong hearts left? Because temptation has often triumphed, has singleness of purpose died out of the world, and may no one be calmly conscious of virtue to act and strength to resist? Jane Eyre is Currer Bell's answer to the question – and, viewed as a contrast to the disgusting cant of immorality lurking beneath tawdry finery and mock humility, may be considered no unimportant contribution to the characteristic delineations of our time. Her situations are often extremely forced; she revels in the depiction of freedom; but after all, she makes will triumph over temptation, exalting the spirit over the letter, nor is there anything in her descriptions which betrays more than the intense aspirations of a powerful moral sense and the eager desire to raise the weak and neglected of the earth to the independence of mind, without which, virtue is but a shadow. The noble conduct of the women, who, through evil report and good report, in spite of sneers and fears, within the last few months, left the comforts of an English home to bear consolation and kindness and care to our wounded beneath an eastern sun[1] – was in the true spirit of Jane Eyre.

We will quote the following passages from *Jane Eyre* and *Vanity Fair*, with a view to illustration, and also to compare the peculiarities of their authors. Jane is governess in Mr Rochester's family. His wife is mad. He loves Jane Eyre, and has just related to her the unfortunate circumstances, which in earlier life led him to contract an alliance with a woman he never did love.

[quotes from chapter 27 Jane Eyre's renunciation]

'*I care for myself. The more solitary, the more friendless, the more unsustained I am, the more I will respect myself.*' Becky Sharp respected herself in a very different manner.

As a contrast in artistic performance, in spirit and in style, with this we compare the following picture from *Vanity Fair*.

[quotes from chapter 37 Becky's flirtation with the Marquis of Steyne]

---

[1] I.e. those who travelled out to join Florence Nightingale in the Crimea (Turkey was evacuated by the British in July 1856).

But that the same spirit under the utmost difference of the outer garb, and the same hidden sympathy united the clergyman's daughter and the man of the world, may perhaps be seen from the following passages.

[quotes from Charlotte's 1847 dedication of *Jane Eyre* to Thackeray, 'Conventionality is not morality . . . between them']

These ideas under Mr Thackeray's pen assume the following shape.

[quotes from *The Newcomes*, chapter 28, 'Shame! What is shame? . . . Lord Abraham's arm']

And here it may not be out of place to point out a few particulars in which we conceive Currer Bell and Thackeray to agree and to disagree. Both satirize existing features of society; but Currer Bell, by describing what is not; Thackeray, by describing what is; the former by eliciting moral heroism from the depths of a nature apparently ordinary; the latter by divesting of heroism characters which might pass for heroic; the former by giving reins to an aspiration after plain unvarnished and inner truth of human action, which betrays her into exaggerations; the latter by coldly saying, 'there is high life for you, such as it is; pick out the good and steer clear of the evil, if you can;' – a spirit which occasionally leads him in spite of his benevolence and artistic impartiality beyond the boundaries of irony and satire into indiscriminate cynicism.

92. Elizabeth Gaskell on *The Professor*

August–October 1856

Letters to George Smith of 1 and 13 August 1856, to Emily Shaen of 7–8 September 1856, to George Smith of 2 October 1856, from *The Letters of Mrs Gaskell* (1966), 401, 403, 409–10, 417.

1 August 1856:

I have not seen the 'Professor' as yet, you must remember, so perhaps all my alarm as to the subject of it may be idle and groundless; but I am afraid it relates to M. Heger, even more distinctly & exclusively than *Villette* does. I have no doubt as to it's genius, & the immense sale it would command. As to its genius she hardly writes 2 lines on the commonest subject, in the most hasty manner, but what there is a felicity of expression, or a deep insight into the very heart of things quite separate & apart from any body else.

13 August 1856:

I have read the Professor, – I don't see the objections to its publication that I apprehended, – or at least only such, as the omissions of three or four short passages not altogether amounting to a page, – would do away with. I don't agree with Sir James [Kay Shuttleworth] that 'the publication of this book would add to her literary fame' – I think it inferior to all her published works – but I think it a very curious link in her literary history, as showing the *promise* of much that was afterwards realized. Altogether I decline taking any responsibility as to advising for or against it's publication ... the decision as to that must entirely rest with Mr Nicholls. Sir James has written to him by this day's post urging its publication. – I have also written to Mr N., saying pretty much what I have said to you above, – but rather expressing my opinion that Miss B. would not have liked Sir J. P K Shuttleworth to revise it – if indeed she would have liked any one to do so.

7–8 September 1856:

We carried off the Professor – that *first* novel, rejected by all the
publishers. This Sir James took away with him intending to read it
first & then forward to me. He wrote to me before he forwarded it,
praising it extremely – saying it would add to her reputation, – object-
ing to 'certain coarse & objectionable phrases' – but offering to *revise*
it, – 'and expunge & make the necessary alterations,' – & begging me
to forward his letter to Mr Smith. I dreaded lest the Prof: should
involve anything with M. Heger – I had heard her say it related to
her Brussels life, – & I thought if he were again brought before the
public, what would he think of me? I believed him to be too good to
publish those letters – but I felt that his friends might really with some
justice urge him to do so, – so I awaited the arrival of the Prof. . . .
with great anxiety. It does relate to the School; but not to M. Heger,
and Mme, or Madame Beck, is only slightly introduced; so on *that*
ground there would be no objection to publishing it. I don't think it
will *add* to her reputation, – the interest will arise from its being the
work of so remarkable a mind. It is an autobiography – of a *man* the
English Professor at a Brussels school, – there are one or two remarkable portraits – the most charming *woman* she ever drew, and a glimpse
of that woman as a mother – very lovely; otherwise little or no story;
& disfigured by more coarseness, – & profanity in quoting texts of
Scripture disagreeably than in any of her other works. However I had
nothing to do except to be a medium, – so I sent Sir J. P K S.'s letter
on to Mr Nicholls, & told him I was going to send a copy of it to Mr
Smith, if he had no objection; that I did not think so highly of the book
as Sir J P K S; although I thought that great public interest would be
felt in it, – that I thought that she herself having prepared it for the
press Sir J. P K S ought not to interfere with it – as, although to my
mind there certainly were several things that had better be expunged;
yet that he (Mr N) was, it seemed to me, the right person to do it[1]. . . .
Mr N. quite agreed with me, & wrote to Sir James declining his
proposal, saying privately to me that he feared Sir J. would be hurt
(he, Sir J., evidently wants to appear to the world in intimate connexion
with her,) but that 'knowing his wife's opinion on the subject, he
could not allow any such revisal,' but that he would himself look over
the Professor, and judge as well as he could with relation to the passages
Sir J. & I had objected to. So there it rests with Mr Nicholls, to whom

[1] But see Introduction, p. 16.

the MS of the Prof: was returned a fortnight ago. With regard to Mr Smith of course he jumped at the idea; whatever sum *I* fixed on as the price should be cheerfully paid – (I declined the responsibility – but said I thought it ought to be paid for like her other works in proportion to the length.) Would I edit it? (No! for several reasons.) When would the Life be ready. Michaelmas? The time of publishing the Prof: would have to be guided by that.

2 October 1856:

I believe, if Sir J. P K S had not suggested the publication I should not have done so. The Professor is curious as indicating strong character & rare faculties on the part of the author; but not interesting as a story. And yet there are parts one would not lose – a lovely female character – & glimpses of home & family life in the latter portion of the tale. – But oh! I wish Mr Nicholls wd have altered more! I fear from what you say he has left many little things *you* would & I would have taken out, as . . . neither essential to the characters or the story, & as likely to make her misunderstood. For I would not, if I could help it, have another syllable that could be called coarse to be associated with her name. Yet another *woman* of her drawing – still more a *nice* one still more a *married* one, ought to be widely interesting.

I think that, – placing myself in the position of a reader – instead of a *writer* – of her life, – I should feel my knowledge of her incomplete without seeing the *Professor*. I suppose biographers always grow to fancy everything about their subject of importance, but I *really* think that such is the case about her; that leaving all authorship on one side, her character as a woman was unusual to the point of being unique. I never heard or read of anyone who was for an instant, or in any respect, to be compared to her. And everything she did, and every word she said & wrote bore the impress of this remarkable character. I as my own reader should not be satisfied after reading the Memoir – (of which I may speak plainly enough for so much of it will consist of extracts from her own letters,) if I did not read her first work, – looking upon it as a phsychological [*sic*] curiosity. So again I think you are right, & that the Memoir must come first.

93. Peter Bayne on 'Ellis, Acton and Currer Bell', *Essays in Biography and Criticism*

1857

From *Essays in Biography and Criticism*, first series, 1857, 393–424.

Peter Bayne (1830–96), author and journalist, studied for the ministry, and edited the Edinburgh *Witness* in 1856 and the Presbyterian *Weekly Review* in 1862–5. He wrote at still greater length about the Brontës in his later study of 1881 (see No. 110), in which he speculated further about Emily Brontë's metaphysical beliefs. His preface (dated 'Berlin, April 18, 1857') records that the present essay was revised from an earlier version in 'an Edinburgh Magazine', the other essays (on Elizabeth Browning, Tennyson and Ruskin) being now published for the first time. Omitted passages contain for the most part biographical information and various personal reflections about literature and life.

The mind of Currer Bell was assuredly original; and when we add, that the genius by which it was characterized was accompanied by an earnestness which might be called religious, and turned, by a strong human sympathy, upon the general aspects and salient points of the age, it becomes a matter of serious moment to sum up the work she has done, and estimate the lesson she has taught us . . .

Perhaps our whole literary annals will show no more touching episode than that on which the leaf has just been turned by [her] death. It is our present purpose to treat chiefly of the works of this last, but we shall be pardoned for making allusion to her sisters.

Emily Brontë, author of *Wuthering Heights*, was, we have no hesitation in saying, one of the most extraordinary women that ever lived. We have felt strongly impelled to pronounce her genius more powerful, her promise more rich, than those of her gifted sister, Charlotte. For accepting this avowal, the reader will be somewhat prepared, by . . . the biographic notice, brief, but of thrilling interest, of her two sisters, given to the world by Currer Bell. . . .

The picture . . . vividly drawn of a frail form standing up undaunted in the scowl of death, should be kept before us as we turn to the work left us by Ellis Bell. It were a strange and surely a distempered criticism which hesitated to pass sentence of condemnation on *Wuthering Heights*. We have no such hesitation. Canons of art sound and imperative, true tastes and natural instincts, of which these canons are the expression, unite in pronouncing it unquestionably and irremediably monstrous. . . . If it is true that in every work of art, however displayed, we must meet the proofs of moderation, of calmness, of tempered and mastered power . . . this work must be condemned. On the dark brow and iron cheek of Heathcliff, there are touches of the Miltonic fiend; but we shrink in mere loathing, in 'unequivocal contempt,' from the base wretch who can use his cruelty as the tool of his greed, and whose cruelty itself is so unredeemed by any resistance or stimulant, as to expend itself on a dying son or a girl's poodle. There are things which the pen of history cannot be required to do more than touch on and pass by. . . . The whole atmosphere, too, of this fiction is distempered, disturbed, and unnatural. Fever and malaria are in the air. The emotions and the crimes are on the scale of madness; and, as if earthly beings, and feelings called terrestrial, were not of potency sufficient to carry on the exciting drama, there are dangerous, very ghostly personages, of the spectral order, introduced, and communings held with the spirit world which would go far to prove Yorkshire the original locality of spirit-rapping. All this is true, and no reader of the book will deem our mode of expressing it severe. Yet we have perfect confidence in pointing to *Wuthering Heights*, as a work containing evidence of powers it were perhaps impossible to estimate, and mental wealth which we might vainly attempt to compute. A host of Titans would make wild work, if directed by a child to overturn the mountains; a host of dwarfs would do little good or harm in any case; but bring your Titans under due command, set over them a judgment that can discern and command, and hill will rise swiftly over hill, till the pyramid is scaling the sky. The powers manifested in this strange book seem to us comparable to a Titan host; and we know no task beyond their might, had they been ruled by a severe taste and discriminating judgment. The mere ability to conceive and depict, with strength so unwavering and clearness so vivid, that wild group of characters, the unmeasured distance into which recedes all that is conventional, customary, or sentimental, the tremendous strength and maturity of the style, would be enough to justify our words. . . . It may be the wild,

and haggard pageantry of a dream at which we gaze, but it is a dream
we can never forget ... In the strength of the assertion, we overlook
its absurdity. Touching the character of Heathcliff, moreover, and,
with less expressness, of that of Cathy Earnshaw, we have a remark
to make, which will extend to certain of the characters of Currer Bell,
and which might, we think, go far to point out a psychological
defence ... of much that is extravagant and revolting in either case.
The power over the mind of what Mr Carlyle calls 'fixed idea,' is
well known; the possession of the whole soul by one belief or aim
produces strange and unaccountable effects, commingling strength and
weakness, kindness and cruelty, and seeming, at first sight, to compro-
mise the very unity of nature. Ellis Bell, in *Wuthering Heights*, deals
with a kindred, though somewhat different phenomenon. She has not
to do with intellect, but emotion. She paints the effects of one overmastering feeling, the maniac actings of him who has quaffed one
draught of maddening passion. The passion she has chosen is love. There
is still a gleam of nobleness, of natural human affection, in the heart
of Heathcliff in the days of his early love for Cathy, when he rushes
manfully at the bull-dog which has seized her, and sets himself, after
she is safe in Thrushcross Grange, on the window ledge, to watch how
matters go on.... But we watch that boyish heart, until, in the furnace
of hopeless and agonizing passion, it becomes as insensible to any tender
emotion, to any emotion save one, as a mass of glowing iron to trickling
dew. Heathcliff's original nature is seen only in the outgoing of his love
towards Cathy; there he is human, if he is frenzied; in all other cases,
he is a devil. As his nature was never good, as there were always in it
the hidden elements of the sneak and the butcher, the whole of that
semi-vital life which he retains towards the rest of the world is ignoble
and revolting. His sorrow has been to him moral death. With truly
diabolic uniformity, every exercise of power possible to him upon any
creature, rational or irrational, Cathy, of course, excepted, is made for
its torment. He seems in one half of his nature to have lost all sensibility, to be unconscious that human beings suffer pain. The great
agony of passion has burned out of his bosom the chords of sympathy
which linked him to his kind, and left him in that ghastly and fiendish
solitude, which it is awful to dream of as a possible element in the
punishment of hell. However frightful the love-scenes in the death
chamber of Cathy – and we suppose there is nothing at all similar to
these in the range of literature – we feel that we are in the presence of
a man. When we think on his early roamings with his lost and dying

love on the wild moors, we can even perceive, stealing over the heart, a faint breath of sympathy. But when he leaves the world of his real existence – the world of his love for Cathy, whether as a breathing woman, or as the wraith which he still loves on – we shrink from him as from a corpse, made more ghastly by the hideous movements of galvanism. Somewhat different is the effect of the same passion upon Cathy. Hers was originally a brave, beautiful, essentially noble nature; through all her waywardness, we love her still; and though her passion for Heathcliff costs her her life, it never scathes and sears her soul into a calcined crag like his. To the last, her heart and imagination can bear her to the wild flowers she used to gather amid the heath; strange and wraith-like as she grows in the storm of that resistless passion, we know full well that no mean, or cruel, or unwomanly thought could enter her breast. Viewed as a psychological study of this sort, a defence might, we say, be set up for the choice of these two characters; and when thus confessedly morbid, their handling will be allowed to be masterly. Nor can it be alleged that instances of similar passion, attended by like results, are not to be met with in real life. Madness, idiocy, and death, are acknowledged to follow misguided or hopeless affection. In the case both of Cathy and Heathcliff, there was unquestionably a degree of the first. But the defence can at best be partial, for, we submit, bedlam is no legitimate sphere of art. Of one thing, however, there can be no doubt. The girl's hand which drew Heathcliff and Cathy, which never shook as it brought out those lines of agony on cheek and brow, which never for a moment lost its strength and sweep in flourish or bravura, was such as has seldom wielded either pen or pencil.

We might descant at great length on the variety of power displayed in this extraordinary book; but we should leave it without conveying an idea, even partially correct, of its general character, if we omitted to notice those touches of nature's softest beauty, those tones of nature's softest melody, which are blended, so cunningly as to excite no sense of discord, with its general excitement and gloom.

[quotes from chapter 24 Catherine's image of heaven]

None but a free, and elastic, and loving nature could thus, with the inimitable touch of truth and reality, have heard, through the ear of that glad girl, in the joy-toned anthem of bird, and water, and rustling branch, the very music of heaven. The faithfulness of the picture, the perfect and effortless realization of the whole summer scene . . . is demonstration absolutely sufficient of that inborn love of nature's joy and beauty which never yet dwelt in a narrow or unworthy breast . . . There is a free, strong, graceful force in every line; there is no dallying, no second touch . . .

Ellis Bell's poetry . . . is characterized by strength and freshness, and by that original cadence, that power of melody, which, be it wild, or tender, or even harsh, was never heard before, and comes at first hand from nature, as her sign of the born poet. We have compared the poetry of the three sisters; and in spite of a prevailing opinion to the contrary, we scruple not to declare, that the clear result of our examination is the conclusion that Ellis Bell's is beyond measure the best.

But, after all, we must pronounce what has been left us by this wonderful woman, unhealthy, immature, and worthy of being avoided. *Wuthering Heights*, we repeat, belongs to the horror school of fiction, and is involved in its unequivocal and unexcepting condemnation . . . At the foot of the gallows, touches of nature's tenderness may be marked: in the pallid face of the criminal you may note workings of emotion not to be seen elsewhere. . . . But it admits not of question, that the general effect of such spectacles is brutalizing, and we would therefore without hesitation terminate their publicity. On exactly the same grounds, would we bid our readers avoid works of distempered excitement. Even when such are of the highest excellence in their class, as those of Ellis Bell and Edgar Poe, we would deliberately sentence them to oblivion. Their general effect is to produce a mental state alien to the calm energy and quiet homely feelings of real life; to make the soul the slave of stimulants, and those of the fiercest kind; and, whatever morbid irritability may for the time be fostered, to shrivel and dry up those sympathies which are the most tender, delicate, and precious. Works like those of Edgar Poe[1] and this *Wuthering Heights* must be plainly declared to blunt, to brutalize, and to enervate the mind. Of the poetry, also, of Ellis Bell, it must be said that it is not healthful. Its beauty is allied to that wild loveliness which may gleam on the hectic cheek, or move while it startles, as we listen to maniac ravings. And wherefore this unchanging wail, whence this perpetual and inexpressible melancholy, in the poems of one so young? What destiny is it with which this young heart so vainly struggles, and by which it is overcome? . . . Her genius was yoked with death. It never

---

[1] Poe had died in 1849. His eighth book, *Tales*, was published in 1845.

freed itself from the dire companionship, never rose into freedom and clearness. . . .[1]

Of Anne Brontë, known as Acton Bell, we have scarce a remark to make. In her life, too, sadness was the reigning element, but she possessed no such strong genius as her sister. . . . The last lines written by Acton Bell are so full of pathos, awaken a sorrow so holy and ennobling, and breathe a faith so strong and tranquil, that we cannot pass them by.

[quotes 'I hoped that with the brave and strong . . .']

It may well be doubted whether any more than a faint and mournful reminiscence of Ellis and Acton Bell will survive the generation now passing away. But the case is widely different with the eldest of the sisters. Currer Bell has won for herself a place in our literature from which she cannot be deposed. Her influence will long be felt, as a strong plastic energy, in the literature of Britain and the world. The language of England will retain a trace of her genius. . . .

The style of Currer Bell is one which will reward study for its own sake. Its character is directness, clearness, force. We could point to no style which appears to us more genuinely and nobly English. Prompt and business-like, perfectly free of obscurity, refining, or involution, it seems the native garment of honest passion and clear thought, the natural dialect of men that can work and will. Perhaps its tone is somewhat too uniform, its balance and cadence too unvaried. Perhaps, also, there is too much of the abruptness of passion. We should certainly set it far below many styles in richness, delicacy, calmness, and grace. But there is no writer whose style can be pronounced a universal model; and for simple narrative, for the relation of what one would hear with all speed, yet with a spice of accompanying pleasure, this style is a model . . .

The peculiar strength of Currer Bell as a novelist can be pointed out in a single word. It is that to which allusion was made in speaking of *Wuthering Heights*; the delineation of one relentless and tyrannizing passion. . . . As the victim lies on his rock, the whole aspect of the world changes to his eye. Ordinary pleasures and ordinary pains are impotent to engage the attention, to assuage the torment. . . . Such a passion is the love of Rochester for Jane, perhaps in a somewhat less degree, that of Jane for Rochester; such, slightly changed in aspect, is the passion

---

[1] For Bayne's later explanation see No. 110, pp. 424-6.

beneath which Caroline pines away, and that which convulses the brave bosom of Shirley. With steady and daring hand, Currer Bell depicts this agony in all its stages ... So perfect is the verisimilitude, nay, the truth of the delineation, that you cannot for a moment doubt that living hearts have actually throbbed with like passion. It is matter, we believe, of universal assent, that Currer Bell here stands almost alone among the female novelists of Britain ...

What positive lesson, we ask finally, moral or intellectual, did Currer Bell read to her age? The question can be simply and briefly answered. In her works, there is a universal assertion of rights and emotions stamped by the seal-royal of nature, against the usurpations of avarice and mode. The passion which is kindled really by nature, though the hearts in which it glows may be far asunder, shall burn its way, through station, through prejudice, through all obstacles that can oppose it, until the fires unite, and rise upwards in one white flame. The true love of Rochester for the governess he employs, the true love of the rich and brilliant Shirley for her tutor, must finally triumph: Nature and Custom contend, and the 'anarch old' goes down ...

There being, therefore, much of what is stirring and healthful in the works of Currer Bell, can we close with a declaration that the region in which her characters move is the highest and purest, and that she has solved, or hinted how we may solve, the social problems which at present confront the earnest and practical mind? We cannot. We must record our distinct and unalterable negative in either case. The truth she proclaims is one sided. Her scheme of life is too narrow. The pleasures and sufferings of existence do not all depend on one emotion though it be that of love, on one passion though itself be right. Her works are the ovation of passion. It may be true, it may be noble, it may be allied with principle, but Passion is ever the conqueror and king ... Who sees not more to be desired in the very anguish of the love of Caroline or Shirley, than in the blanched existence of Miss Ainley? Do we not mark St. John Rivers go away, joyless and marble-cold, on his high mission, while Passion welcomes back Jane to his burning, bliss-giving arms? Where Passion appears, all becomes real and alive: where Passion is not, the widest philanthropy, the holiest devotion, are powerless to confer happiness. And shall we thus crown Passion, and bend the knee before him? By no means. Passion, when alone, is essentially and ignobly selfish. Despite a barren kindness of heart, the existence of Rochester is utterly selfish. *His* luckless marriage, *his* impure love, *his* interesting sorrows, have eaten up the substance of his life. . . . If passion is the whole of love, it must debase and not ennoble.

When we speak of those practical problems, on which Currer Bell has touched, but which she has not solved, we refer specially to the dreary pictures she draws in *Shirley* of the social standing of woman. Marriage, we are told, is the one hope of the great majority of England's daughters, a hope destined in countless cases to be never realized. A youth of scheming inanity, deriving a faint animation from this hope, must face into a blighted and solitary age. The authority of a lady may be taken as conclusive of the state of the case here; but when we assent to her allegations, and paragraph after paragraph has impressed them on our minds, we have no more, by way of remedy, than a sentence of general and valueless exhortation to fathers to cultivate the minds of their daughters. There is nothing in the works of Currer Bell to assure us that any amount of cultivation will produce fresh and satisfying happiness, unless that one wish which she points to is gratified. She indicates no fields of pleasure accessible to all. She exhibits not the means of the cultivation she commends, and leaves us to guess the connection between culture and enjoyment. The hand of this gifted woman had power, we think, to paint a daughter of England gladdening and beautifying her existence, though the light of passion never rose upon her path. But this she has not done.

MRS GASKELL'S *THE LIFE OF CHARLOTTE BRONTË* (1857)

---

94. G. H. Lewes, letter

April 1857

Letter to Mrs Gaskell of 15 April 1857 from the Scilly Isles where he was staying with George Eliot; from *The George Eliot Letters* (1956), ii, 315–16. In the following year at Munich he and George Eliot read aloud *Wuthering Heights* in the evenings; see G. S. Haight, *George Eliot, a Biography* (1968), 258.

I have just finished your *Life of Charlotte Bronte* – which has afforded exquisite delight to my evenings on this remote patch of rock, round which the Atlantic roars, and dashes like a troop of lions, making a solitude almost equal to Haworth moors – quite equal, as far as any society I get here. If I had any public means of expressing my high sense of the skill, delicacy and artistic power of your Biography, I should not trouble you with this note. But it is a law of the literary organization that it must relieve itself in expression, and I discharge my emotion through the penny post; at least, such of it as was not discharged in wet eyes and swelling heart, as chapter after chapter was read.

The book will, I think, create a deep and permanent impression; for it not only presents a vivid picture of a life noble and sad, full of encouragement and healthy teaching, a lesson in duty and self-reliance; it also, thanks to its artistic power, makes us familiar inmates of an interior so strange, so original in its individual elements and so picturesque in its externals – it paints for us at once the psychological drama and the scenic accessories with so much vividness – that fiction has nothing more wild, touching, and heart-strengthening to place above it.

The early part is a triumph for you; the rest a monument for your friend. One learns to love Charlotte, and deeply to respect her. Emily has a singular fascination for me – probably because I have a passion for lions and savage animals, and she was une bête fauve[1] in power, splendour, and wildness. What an episode that death of hers! and how touching is Charlotte's search for the bit of heather which the glazed eyes could not recognize at last! And what a bit of the true religion of home is the whole biography!

I have nothing but thanks for the way you have managed my slight episode. There is however one thing I could have wished, – and perhaps in a second edition, if your own judgement goes that way, you might insert a phrase respecting the *Edinburgh* article,[2] intimating that it is *not* a disrespectful article to women, although maintaining that in the *highest* efforts of intellect women have not equalled men. Lord Jeffrey tampered with the article, as usual, and inserted some to me offensive sentences, but the main argument – as far as I recollect it – is complimentary to women, not disrespectful. As far as appears in this book I seem to have written an offensive article, not only one offensive on the personal ground but on the general ground. *Is* this so? And if not, would not a word from you intimate as much?

I am ashamed to trouble you with so small a matter; but as I did not object to Currer Bell's uncomplimentary passages appearing, you will not, I hope, think me oversensitive in wishing not to be misrepresented on a subject which I feel to be momentous.

---

[1] Louis Moore's phrase for Shirley (*Shirley*, chapter 29).
[2] See No. 39.

95. John Skelton, from an unsigned review, *Fraser's Magazine*

May 1857, lv, 569–82

By 'Shirley', i.e. Sir John Skelton (1831–97), author, essayist, and extensive reviewer, especially for *Blackwood's*. The first part of the review gives a detailed account of the biographical facts recorded in Mrs Gaskell's study. Reprinted in *Essays in History and Biography*, 1883. See Introduction, pp. 38–40.

A strange childhood! – out of which, through various schools and other harsh experiences, the Brontës grew up to man and woman's estate, and which explains a good deal in their subsequent history. They are the offspring of the moors; and after the sea – whose authority is supreme – the moorland has perhaps the strongest influence in forming and determining the character. All their lives the Brontës love these moors intensely. They look down from their bleak 'hills of Judea,' and wonder how the dwellers contrive to exist in the 'Philistine flats' beneath. The turbid waters of their 'beck' are more sacred than the Jordan's. In dreams, at Brussels they hear the Haworth harebells rustle in the wind. Emily cannot live away from them. She pines and sickens, and would die if she were not brought back and restored to their wild companionship. Everything they say or write is consecrated by this bleak communion. Their honey had the taste of the heath. The scent of the heather is as clearly traceable in their works as the smack of the salt sea in the architecture of the lagoons.

After passing through much uncongenial drudgery as teachers, both at home and on the Continent, the sisters in 1844, find themselves once more united in the quiet home among the hills. Throughout the intervening period, Charlotte has been silently amassing materials for future work. Nothing comes amiss to that observant and inventive brain. She notices every one with whom she is brought into contact – dissects and analyzes. The result is, that when she begins to write, her life is transcribed into her novels. The one is a daguerrotype of the other. The

scenes reviewers condemn as exaggerated, the characters they pronounce unnatural, are taken from personal experience. When you read
her life, you read *Jane Eyre*, *Shirley*, *Villette*, in fragments . . .

But no explanation can ever be quite exhaustive. The experience
can never entirely explain the work. For between lies the mystery of
Genius . . .

Vagueness, inaccuracy, slovenliness whether in mind or person, she
cannot tolerate. Sentiment and sentimental insincerity are repugnant to
the simple directness of her character. She was naturally and by education superstitious, and her mental conflicts would have driven many a
man into the cloister. But it is not so with her. She is deeply religious,
but never fanatical. She has the old Puritans' perfect confidence in
God's government; to her, as to them, the trials of life are divinely
appointed, and 'at the end of all exists the Great Hope;' but there is no
narrowness in her creed. She does not venture to attribute to the
Almighty in the government of his universe the partialities of a parish
bigot. It is indeed most interesting to find this girl, in her Yorkshire
solitudes, grasping, single handed, at doctrines to which our most
devout men are yet blindly striving, as they best can. The character
altogether is very complex, – cool yet vivid, affluent yet ascetic,
vehement yet sedate.

In 1844 the sisters . . . are again united, and recommence the interrupted occupations . . . The first fruit . . . is the advent from the
metropolis of a diminutive volume, *Poems by Currer, Ellis, and Acton
Bell.*

That modest little volume has an old charm for us, in its rude typography, plain binding, peculiar punctuation, and the date, 1846, on the
title page – just the year Sir Robert repealed the Corn Laws. For it
was when the country was in the last throes of that great conflict,
when Peel was winning victory for the people and defeat for himself,
and the barbed shafts of the Israelite[1] quivered every field-night under
the Minister's spotless shirt-front, that the poems of the three sisters
were given to the world, and permitted to pass unnoticed, as was
indeed to be looked for. Yet the book is one that might have riveted
attention even then, and must not now be forgotten.

For the poems are perfectly genuine – veritable utterances of the
women who wrote them. There is no poetic exaggeration, no false
sentiment, nor study of theatrical effect. They do not wanton with the
flowers of rhetoric. I do not believe that more than half a dozen

[1] Benjamin Disraeli.

metaphors occur throughout the volume. A Puritan could not be more conscientious in his intercourse with his crop-eared brethren, than these girls are in their poetic talk. The imagination is taken to task. The estimate of life is strictly subdued. They have worked out an experience for themselves, and with God's help they will stick to it. Their gravity of thought and chasteness of language contrast strikingly with the florid and exuberant ornamentation of our younger poets – the poets of the *Renaissance*.

And because of this entire genuineness they never imitate. There is no foreign music in their melody. One does not detect the influence of any other writer. Young poets are habitual plagiarists: but with this volume neither Byron, nor Scott, nor Tennyson, nor Browning has anything to do. The writers speak out plainly and calmly what they have felt themselves, and their thoughts assume without effort the poetic form to which they are most adapted.

They speak calmly, I say, yet we feel sometimes that this composure is enforced. There are deeps of passion underneath the passionless face. The estimate of life is studiously grave and sombre: but at times an intoxicating sense of liberty thrills their blood and the wild gladness of a Bacchante sparkles in their eyes:

> I'd die when all the foam is up,
> > The bright wine sparkling high,
> Nor wait till in the exhausted cup
> > Life's dull dregs only lie.[1]

There is the martyr's spirit, but there is the hero's too. They *will* not love nor hate over-much: but the throbbing of the wounded heart cannot be always restrained, and at times they are intensely bitter: –

> They named him mad and laid his bones
> > Where holier ashes lie,
> But doubt not that his spirit groans
> > In hell's eternity.

There are indications in Currer's contributions of that amazing intellectual force which a year afterwards was to move painfully every English heart: but as yet she has not learnt her strength. Her steps are restrained and embarrassed. She does not move freely. She touches life with the tips of her fingers, so to speak: her whole heart and soul have not yet been cast into her work.

[1] This and the following quotation are from, respectively, Charlotte's 'Passion' and 'Mementos'.

Yet most of the subjects are strangely chosen for girls, and such as a very marked and decided idiosyncrasy alone would have selected. In Acton's, indeed, there is more of the ordinary woman, mild, patient, devout, loving; and her poetry has little to distinguish it from the poetry of many women who acquire 'the faculty of verse.' But those of the other two are very different. In them there is none of the ordinary romance of girlhood. Their heroes are not the heroes of the ball-room, but of the covenant and the stake, – the warrior priest who can die for his faith; the patriot who, if it be for his country's gain, will steadfastly allow his honour to be soiled, and

> wait securely
> For the atoning hour to come;[1]

the worker who in his loneliness achieves the redemption of his people; the martyr with the thorny crown upon his brow, but with the peace of God and the hope of immortality in his heart. Success, the usual gauge applied by youth, is not with them the test of worth;

> The long war closing in defeat,
> Defeat serenely borne,[2]

is in their eyes the noblest fate that can be reserved for any man. So they do not pray for happiness, but for inward control, and the patience which endures to the end.

> Of God alone, and self-reliance,
> I ask for solace, – hope for aid.[3]

Praise, fame, friendship, the good word of the world, they do not covet; they can live without them; nay, resign them cheerfully if need be.

> There's such a thing as dwelling
> On the thought ourselves have nursed,
> And with scorn and courage telling
> The world to do its worst.

And these are the feelings expressed, not by strong men, but by two delicate women in their girlhood! The stern spirit of their northern

[1] From Charlotte's 'Preference'.
[2] From Emily's 'The evening passes fast away . . .'
[3] This and the following quotation are from, respectively, Charlotte's 'Frances' and 'Parting'.

hills and of the bleak Yorkshire moorland haunted their birthplace, and must have entered early into their souls.

Yet the book does not altogether lack the gentler graces of poetry. In the concise realism of Currer there is little indeed of that abstract and ethereal spirit men call the imagination; but it inspires the wild and plaintive music of many of Ellis's songs. Some of these are so perfect that we cannot understand why they are not widely known; certainly modern poetry has produced few lyrics more felicitous either in sentiment or expression than 'Remembrance.' How quaint and composed, and yet how plaintive, it is! The bereaved speaks calmly, but there is a passion of tears below.

[quotes in full 'Cold in the earth . . .']

The lyric entitled 'A Death Scene' . . . has a beauty of a peculiar kind.

[quotes in full, 'Oh Day! he cannot die . . .']

Here is a song which reminds us of one sung in *The Princess* [1847] . . .

[quotes in full 'There should be no despair for you . . .']

Though I do not think Currer's contributions quite equal to Ellis's, yet in some of them much sympathy for natural beauty is manifested. The wealth of affection which was so jealously watched in her intercourse with men and women, was permitted in the lonely presence of the hills to lavish itself unchecked. Here are Dawn, Twilight, and Night: –

> And oh! how slow that keen-eyed star
> Has tracked the chilly grey!
> What watching yet! how very far
> The morning lies away![1]

> That sunset! Look beneath the boughs
> Over the copse, – beyond the hills;
> How soft yet deep and warm it glows,
> And heaven with rich suffusion fills
> With hues where still the opal's tint
> Its gleam of prisoned fire is blent;
> Where flame through azure thrills![2]

[1] This is in fact from Emily's 'The moon is full this winter's night . . .'

[2] This and the following two quotations are from, respectively, Charlotte's 'The Wood', 'Stanzas', and 'Mementos'.

Pause in the lane, returning home;
   'Tis dusk it will be still:
Pause near the elm, a sacred gloom
   Its breezeless boughs will fill.
Look at that soft and golden light
   High in the unclouded sky;
Watch the last bird's belated flight
   As it flits silent by.

Nor would she leave that hill till night
Trembled from pole to pole with light.

I have spoken at length of this first volume, because we find in it, I think, the germ of much in their later and more mature works. It is little known; but the poems are so simple, genuine, and characteristic, that they must some time become popular.

Shortly after the arrival of the book of Poems at Haworth, *Wuthering Heights*, by *Ellis Bell*, or Emily Brontë, is sent to the printer.

Emily Brontë – the finer, we are afraid we must say the ideal, side of whose character is sketched in *Shirley* – is, I think, the most powerful of the Brontë family . . . Charlotte loved her with her whole heart; to her the implacable sister, is 'mine bonnie love;' but Emily never responds. She is stern, taciturn, untameable. Her logic is rigorous; but when she once forms an opinion, however extreme it may be, no logic can move her. She clings to it with stubborn tenacity. Her affections, such as they are are spent on her moorland home, and the wild animals she cherishes. The tawny bull-dog 'Keeper' is her special friend. But even 'Keeper' must be taught to obey that iron will, and he is taught in a way that he never forgets. On her death-bed she accepts no assistance – does not admit that she suffers even. Her death, Charlotte said afterwards, 'was very terrible. She was torn, conscious, panting, reluctant, yet resolute, out of a happy life.'

Wuthering Heights is not unworthy of its grim parentage. Emily's novel is not, perhaps, more powerful than her sister's; but we meet in it, I think, with more subtle diversities of character than we do in any of them. Charlotte Brontë's heroes are all broad and emphatic; marked types, not delicate suggestions. They are strong, passionate, generous, vindictive, as the case may be; but no attempt is made to explain conflicting motives, to assimilate complex passions. There is a certain immobility and hardness in the outline. They want the delicate tendernesses of the imagination, the gleams of barbaric poetry which lie deep buried under the swart brow of the Moor, or flash from the blue eyes of the Northman. Masculine, independent, impatient of the prose of life, they are, yet they are not poetic. There is nothing of the gipsy nature in them. They remain broad-featured, broad-shouldered Anglo-Saxons, even in their moments of dreariest independence. In Emily's we are conscious of something more. A volcano is beneath the flowers where we stand, and we cannot tell where it may burst. There is a refrain of fierce poetry in the men and women she draws – gleams of the gipsy savageness and of the gipsy tenderness. A strange fire, inherited from an Eastern kindred, lighted among Norland moors, burns in their eyes. They flutter on the confines between our love and our hate. Their caprice, their sullenness, their mercilessness, hurt and revolt us; but we cannot abandon them to perdition without a prayer that they may be saved. Heathcliff, the boy, is ferocious, vindictive, wolfish; but we understand the chain of fire that binds Cathy to him. There stands the brawny young Titan, with his blackened visage and unwashed hands and unkempt hair, as though he had come in hot haste from the infernal forge, sullen, resentful, no Christian virtue implanted in his heathenish soul, no English grace softening his obdurate visage; and yet, as he stands moodily in the presence of his fastidiousness, courtly, and well-bred rival, we feel that though his soul is the fouler, he is the greater, the more loveable of the two. He may be an imp of darkness at bottom – as is indeed most probable, considering his parentage – but he has come direct from the affluent heart of nature, and the hardy charm of her bleak hill-sides and savage moorlands rests upon the boy. On the boy only, however; for the man develops and degenerates; it is then a tiger-cat's passion, a ghoul's vindictiveness, a devil's remorse.

The elder Cathy, too, is very subtly conceived in her fire, and tenderness, and vanity, and perversity, and the untutored grace of her free moorland nature. The hardy half savage child, with her mocking spirit, and bleeding feet, and swart companion-imp, 'as dark almost as if it came from the devil,' scampering across the hills in gipsy-fashion, and scaring the meek maidens of the village with her elfish laughter; the wilful little vagrant who, in her dream of Heaven, breaks her heart with weeping to come back to earth, and wakens sobbing for joy because 'the angry angels have cast her out into the middle of the heath on the top of Wuthering Heights;' the perverse, fervent, untamed coquette, alternating between love and pride, hell and heaven, our admiration and our dread – unplummed depths of passion convulsing her soul, but with nothing mean or meagre in the whole of her burning heart, – excites a wonderful interest, retains it to the last, and gives to the *Catherine Linton* scrawled upon the nursery panel an eerie and fitful pathos. Her childish delight in arranging on her death-bed the lapwing, the mallard, and the moor-fowl's feathers – the wild birds she had followed with Heathcliff in their childish rambles across the moorland, – is sad and true as the 'coronet flowers' of Ophelia.[1] In that idle forgetfulness and tender confusion there is a genuine reminiscence of the Shakspearian madness. This richness and affluence of poetic life in which Emily invests the creations of her brain, these delicacies and subtleties of insight, are all the more striking, from the grave, sombre, and resolutely homely form in which her tale is narrated. She may describe abnormal characters; but, whatever they are, she describes them with startling genuineness.[2]

This was the only romance Emily ever wrote: a year after its publication she died. Those very grand and impressive lines were her last....[3]

Jane Eyre has been austerely condemned by austere critics. It is said that in it the interest depends on the terrible and the immoral, – two elements of interest which cannot be rightly appropriated by fiction. Admitting that the charge is true, we inquire – why not?

The old dramatists, at least, did not judge so; and the result was that they evoked 'high passions and high actions' which stir our hearts to the core. Where in modern tragedy, with its guarded touch and surface propriety, shall we find such an appeal to our deepest feelings, as – leaving Shakspeare altogether out of question – in Hieronimo's madness: –

> In truth it is a thing of nothing,
> The murder of a son or so;
> A thing of nothing, my lord;[4]

---

[1] See Introduction, p. 40.

[2] Skelton adds a substantial footnote on Joseph, the old retainer, with his Yorkshire brogue and inclement 'Calvinism', whom he takes to 'have been drawn from the life. The character is capitally sustained throughout . . .'. A liberal selection of extracts is made to illustrate Emily's portrayal of his speech and behaviour.

[3] Quotes in full 'No coward soul is mine . . .'. It was not Emily's last poem; see above, p. 310, n.

[4] This and the two following quotations are from, respectively, Kyd's *The Spanish Tragedy*, Ford's '*Tis Pity She's a Whore* and *The Broken Heart*.

in Annabella's –

> Forgive him, Heaven, and me, my sins. Farewell
> Brother unkind, unkind;

in Calantha's –

> Oh my lords!
> I but deceived your eyes with antick gesture.
> When one news straight came huddling on another –
> Of death, and death, and death; still I danced forward.
> But it struck home, and here, and in an instant.
> They are the silent griefs which cut the heartstrings.
> Let me die smiling.
> One kiss on these cold lips – my last; crack, crack,
> Argos now 's Sparta's king.

They looked terror and death, the momentous issues of life, fearlessly in the face; wherever the true tragic came out, there we find them. And they succeeded in impressing on us a sense of its greatness, its reality, its infinite capacities for grief or gladness, such as we now seldom obtain. Seldom, because we have become afraid of its sternness, and gloss it over; because very few of our poets dare to gauge boldly the perilous pains of the spirit, the great majority contenting themselves with saying pretty things at their fastidious leisure about sorrows which are as genuine as a pasteboard doll's; because, when a woman like Charlotte Brontë does try to evoke that mighty spirit of tragedy which lurks in the heart of every man she is told that she is creating the horrible, and breaking artistic statutes more immutable than those of the Medes and Persians . . .

But while we aver without hesitation that *Jane Eyre* is not an immoral book, we are ready to admit that those parts which have been censured are by no means blameless, when considered artistically. The confidence between Jane Eyre and Rochester is much too sudden and excessive. There is too little ttraactiveness in the heroine to account for a violent passion in such a man. The explanation is inadequate Why. should so much fondness be lavished upon this demure, keen-eyed little woman? Why should it be? we ask; and the reply is, It would not be so with us; and a feeling of contempt for the infatuation of this otherwise astute and daring man of the world is the result.

The characters, also, though drawn with mastery, are too strongly marked. Rochester is the type of one order of mind; St. John Rivers of another; and the features in each case are exaggerated to produce an effective contrast. Still, both are of the grand order of men. The broad-chested, grim-mouthed Rochester, sweeping past us on his black horse Mesrour, and followed by his Gytrash-like sleuth hound, is a modern apparition of Black Bothwell ... St. John is the warrior-priest, cool and inflexible as death. His integrity is austere, his con-scientiousness implacable. It is impossible to love him; nay even Rochester, in his devilish madness, is preferable to this inexorable priest. Yet the man is not tranquil; there is a passionate unrest at the bottom of his heart. A statue of snow, and fire burns underneath! But the fire will not thaw the ice. He will die ere the passion vanquish him ...

Shirley presents a notable contrast to Miss Brontë's other novels. In them there is a profound and frequently overmastering sense of the intense dreariness of existence to certain classes. The creative spirit of poetry and romance breaks at times through the dull and stagnant life; but as a rule it is different; and *Villette*, especially, becomes monotonous from the curb maintained upon the imagination. But *Shirley* is a Holiday of the Heart. It is glad, buoyant, sunshiny. The imagination is liberated, and revels in its liberty. It is the pleasant summer-time, and the worker is idling among the hills. The world of toil and suffering lies behind, but ever so far away ...

In *Villette* Miss Brontë returns to the realities of life; but with power more conscious and sustained. She is less absorbed and more compre-hensive. There is the same passionate force; but the horizon is wider ... *Villette* may be regarded as an elaborate psychological examination – the anatomy of a powerful but pained intellect – of exuberant emotions watchfully and vigilantly curbed. The character of this woman is peculiar, but drawn with a masterly hand. She *endures* much in a certain Pagan strength, not defiantly, but coldly and without submis-sion ... *She*, at least, will by all means look at the world as it is – a hard, dry, practical world, not wholly devoid of certain compensating elements – and she will not be cajoled into seeing it, or making others see it, under any other light. For herself, she will live honestly upon the earth, and invite or suffer no delusions; strong, composed, self-reliant, sedate in the sustaining sense of independence. But cold and reserved as she may appear, she is not without imagination – rich, even, and affluent as a poet's. This is in a measure, however, the root of her peculiar misery. The dull and cheerless routine of homely life is not in her case relieved and penetrated by the creative intellect, but on the contrary, acquires through its aid a subtle and sensitive energy to hurt, to afflict, and to annoy. Thus she is not always strong; her imagination sometimes becomes loaded and surcharged; but she is always passionately ashamed of weakness. And through all this torture she is very solitary: her heart is very empty; she bears her own burden. . . .

Miss Brontë always wrote earnestly, and in *Villette* she is peremptorily honest . . . She will therefore tolerate no hypocrisy, however decent or fastidious; and her subdued and direct insight goes at once to the root of the matter. She carries this perhaps too far – it may be she lacks a measure of charity and toleration, not for what is bad – for *that* there must be no toleration – but for what is humanly weak and insufficient. Graham Bretton, for instance, with his light hair and kind heart and pleasant sensitiveness, is ultimately treated with a certain implied contempt; and this solely because he happens to be what God made him, and not something deeper and more devout, the incarnation of another and more vivid kind of goodness, which it is not in his nature to be, and to which he makes no claim. It is the patience, the fortitude, the endurance, the strong love that has been consecrated by Death and the Grave, the spirit that has been tried in fire and mortal pain and temptation, – it is these alone she can utterly admire. We believe she is wrong. But as we recall the lone woman sitting by the desolate hearthstone, and remember all that she lost and suffered, we cannot blame very gravely the occasional harshness and impatience of her language when dealing with men who have been cast in a different mould.

Villette excels Miss Brontë's other fictions in the artistic skill with which the characters are – I use the word advisedly – *developed*. . . . Probably the most genuine power is manifested in the mode in which the interest is shifted from Graham Bretton to the ill-favoured little despot – Paul Emanuel. No essential change takes place in *their* characters, *they* remain the same, the colours in which they were originally painted were quite faithful, perfectly accurate – not by any means exaggerated for subsequent effect and contrast. It is only thaat deeper insight has been gained by *us* . . .

Leaf after leaf has been unfolded with a cold and impartial hand, until we have been let down into the innermost hearts of the men, and taught by the scrutiny a new sense of their relative value and worthiness. And Paul Emanuel is surely a very rich and genuine conception. *The Professor* will ever be associated in our memory with a certain soft and breezy laughter; for though the love he inspires in the heroine is very deep and even pathetic after its kind, yet the whole idea of the man is wrought and worked out in a spirit of joyous and mellow ridicule, that is full of affection, however, and perhaps at times closely akin to tears.

To ourselves, one of the most surprising gifts of the authoress of these volumes is the racy and inimitable English she writes. No other Englishwoman ever commanded such language – terse and compact, and yet fiercely eloquent. We have already had occasion to notice the absence of comparison or metaphor in her poetry; the same is true of her prose. The lava is at white heat; it pours down clear, silent, pitiless; there are no bright bubbles nor gleaming foam. A mind of this order – tempered, and which cuts like steel – uses none of the pretty dexterities of the imagination; for to use these infers a pause of satisfied reflection and conscious enjoyment which it seldom or never experiences. Its rigorous intellect seeks no trappings of pearl or gold. It is content to abide in its white veil of marble – naked and chaste, like 'Death' in the Vatican. Yet, the still severity is more effective than any paint could make it. The chisel has been held by a Greek, the marble hewed from Pentelicus.

Compare, side by side, these pictures of the Winter and Summer twilight.

[quotes from chapter 12, 'The ground was hard . . . sough of the most remote', and from chapter 23, 'A splendid midsummer sun . . . beneath the horizon']

And now, closing these volumes for the last time, a profound sense of regret comes upon us that a woman so powerfully and uniquely gifted should have been taken from us on the verge of her ripe maturity . . .

96. Charles Kingsley, letter

14 May 1857

Letter to Mrs Gaskell; from *Letters and Life*, ed. Mrs Kingsley (1877), ii, 24–5.

Let me renew our long-interrupted acquaintance by complimenting you on poor Miss Brontë's Life. You have had a delicate and a great work to do, and you have done it admirably. Be sure that the book will do good. It will shame literary people into some stronger belief that a simple, virtuous, practical home life is consistent with high imaginative genius; and it will shame, too, the prudery of a not over cleanly, though carefully white-washed age, into believing that purity is now (as in all ages till now) quite compatible with the knowledge of evil. I confess that the book has made me ashamed of myself. *Jane Eyre* I hardly looked into, very seldom reading a work of fiction – yours, indeed, and Thackeray's are the only ones I care to open.[1] *Shirley* disgusted me at the opening: and I gave up the writer and her books with the notion that she was a person who liked coarseness. How I misjudged her! and how thankful I am that I never put a word of my misconceptions into print, or recorded my misjudgments of one who is a whole heaven above me.

Well have you done your work, and given us the picture of a valiant woman made perfect by sufferings. I shall now read carefully and lovingly every word she has written, especially those poems, which ought not to have fallen dead as they did, and which seem to be (from a review in the current *Fraser*)[2] of remarkable strength and purity. I must add that Mrs Kingsley agrees fully with all I have said, and bids me tell you that she is more intensely interested in the book than in almost any which she has ever read.

---

[1] But see his review of *The Tenant of Wildfell Hall* (No. 78).
[2] See John Skelton's review of the *Life* (No. 95).

97. From an unsigned review of *The Professor*, *Athenaeum*

13 June 1857, 755–7

See Introduction, p. 38.

After nine years – the fitting Horatian interval – Currer Bell's rejected novel makes its posthumous appearance in print. The wondrous story of *Jane Eyre* has so much gratified, and the more wondrous, 'ower true,' and over-tragic life-drama of Charlotte Brontë so much amazed the world, that it feels disposed rather to err on the side of gentleness than rigour, and to question the justice of the criticism which refused, rather than the constructive power which was latent in the earlier tale. Accordingly friends, lovers, and biographer have moved for a new trial, and *The Professor* comes before the public with every advantage of typography, and with the best prospects of a hearing. Whether the counsel which prompted, or the love which consented, to publication was wise or considerate, is . . . fairly open to doubt. . . . The world has not gained greatly by *The Prelude*, and perhaps we ought to be resigned to the loss of a few sheets more of *The Opium-Eater*. That the work before us will be read and discussed by all who have read the *Life of Charlotte Brontë* is certain enough, but the interest excited will be rather curious than deep, and the impression left on the reader one of pain and incompleteness. It is a mere study for *Jane Eyre* or *Shirley*, – certainly displaying effects of the same force, the same characteristic keenness of perception, the same rough, bold, coarse truthfulness of expression, the same compressed style, offence of dialogue, preference for forbidden topics, and pre-Raphaelitish contempt for grace, – but with scarcely any relief or shadow, and with fewer descriptive or womanly touches. Unity or arrangement there is none. The sketches are carelessly left loose for the reader to connect or not, as he chooses, – a carelessness the result of a deliberate intention, as is clear enough from the Preface . . .

The incidents of the story are few; the principal parts are sustained

344

by an unnatural brother, a rough manufacturer, of the type of Mr Helstone, who interposes *ex machinâ* and rescues the hero, an obstinate but well-regulated character in difficulties. The hero, a younger son of a Yorkshire blue-dyer, is of patrician race by the mother's side, but though educated at Eton he declines to adopt the Church and the opinions of his titled uncles, and in preference offers himself as a clerk to his brother, a rich Yorkshire manufacturer, the husband of a childish-looking, *red-haired* lady, whom he terrifies by driving a restive quadruped, – 'only opening his lips to damn his horse.'

[outlines the rest of the story with extensive quotations]

Miss Brontë does not exhibit her characters in critical action, or under strong temptation. Low chicane, astuteness, sensuality, and tyranny, are keenly and observantly drawn; but throughout the novel the quietness is unnatural, the level of fact too uniform, the restraint and the theory of life too plain. The principles and the art of the writer, though true, excite no corresponding sympathy on the part of the reader, – few demands being made on his softer or gentler nature. There is no Helen Burns that we can watch or weep over, – no sprightly little Adele that we can sport with. Frances may possibly be the mother of Lucy Snow, and Mdlle. Reuter and M. Pelet the co-efficients of Madame Modeste and Paul Emanuel. Similarities of opinion respecting marriage may be traced, not as a crime, but an imbecility. Now and then there is a touch of grandiloquence that astonishes us. Words and events are utilized in a way that now, knowing the author's opportunities, appear to us **remark**able. On the whole, this tale bears to Currer Bell's later works the relation which a pre-Shakspearian story does to the drama, – it is curious to an artist or psychologist. On closing this posthumous chapter, and ending Charlotte Brontë's strange literary history, we are reminded of a saying of Jean Paul's[1] – 'God deals with poets as we do with nightingales, hanging a dark cloth round the cage until they sing the right tune.'

---

[1] Johann Paul Friedrich Richter 1763–1825), German romantic novelist.

98. W. C. Roscoe, from an unsigned review, *National Review*

June 1857, v, 127–64

William Caldwell Roscoe (1823–59), poet and essayist, was the grandson of the historian William Roscoe (1753–1831) and the friend of Walter Bagehot and R. H. Hutton; the latter were co-founders in 1855 of the *National Review* which they edited jointly until 1862, when Hutton resigned. Bagehot remained as editor until the periodical's demise in 1864.

Reprinted in W. C. Roscoe, *Poems and Essays* (1860), ii.

Friends and friendly biographers are apt to ask too much from 'the public,' and from the critic who expresses an individual atom of public judgment. There is such a thing as being unjust to the judges ... 'It is well,' Mrs Gaskell writes, 'that the thoughtless critics, who spoke of the sad and gloomy views of life presented by the Brontës in their tales, should know how such words were wrung out of them by the living recollection of the long agony they suffered.' Why thoughtless critics? They had penetration enough, it seems, to point out a leading feature in the books; and they must have been more than thoughtful to penetrate the secret domestic sorrows of the family and take them into account in characterizing their written productions. A living author is known to the world by his works only, or, if not so, it is with his works alone the public are concerned; and he has no cause of complaint if he is fairly judged by them without any allowance for the private conditions under which they were produced. On the other hand, he has the corresponding right to demand that personal considerations and private information shall not be dragged in as elements of literary judgment, and that his publicity as an artist shall give pretext for invading the seclusion of his private life ...

In writing the life of the late Mrs Nicholls, Mrs Gaskell ... had to depict an existence whose interest consisted in ... the spectacle of genius contending against circumstance, not on the wide stage of the world, but within the walls of one household ... The biographer who has to deal with such a life must choose between a mode of treatment which reduces his field to the limits of a memoir, and scarcely allows him to do justice to his task, or one which, on the other hand, is sure in its wider scope to do some injury to the rights and susceptibilities of others. Mrs Gaskell made her choice, and has un-flinchingly acted upon it. ... Frankly we will state our conviction, that she was mistaken; that the principles and the practice which in England make it indecorous to withdraw the veil from purely domestic affairs, – the joys, the griefs, the shames of the household, – have a true basis in fortitude and delicacy of feeling and are paramount to con-siderations of gratifying public curiosity, or even to that of securing a full appreciation for the private character of a distinguished artist. Don't let us deceive ourselves about the moral lesson in the present case; it is either so exceptional as to have no common application, or it is one which all who wish may gather for themselves within the range of their own family experience. And let us remember, too, that, without pressing real domestic events into the service, we have in our modern novels sufficient scope for supplying that pleasurable excite-ment of our better feelings, now so common a luxury, and which is in danger with many of us of replacing the effort to find them a field for their actual exercise.

After this protest, we are free to echo the universal opinion as to the skill with which a difficult work has been executed, and an absorbing interest given to the narrative; rather, we should say, to the felicity with which its native elements of interest have been marshalled and arrayed....

The close shadow of the Brontës' churchyard-home, the bitter winds, and the wild dark aspect of their moors, have left the mark of their influence upon the writings as well as upon the characters of the sisters. They want softness, variety, beauty; they are too often dark, hopeless, and discomfortable: on the other hand, they are vigorous and fresh, and bear welcome traces of Nature's close companionship with the minds from which they sprang. A personal impress is strongly marked on them. It is curious that, though the writers all had strong imaginations, not one of them had the power to get rid for a moment of her own individuality. It permeates with its subtle presence every page they write. They were not engaging persons; and they felt that they were not – felt it acutely, and made others unduly sensible of it. Nor did they care to see others in their more agreeable and engaging aspects. They had been brought into close contact with the darker shades of character, and they instinctively studied them and reproduced them; too often they used light to give a greater depth to shadow, rather than shadow to set off light. It is in Emily's works, as in her own nature, that the darkness lies deepest. None of them are at home in sunny weather; but Emily has drawn mid-winter and thunderous skies . . . Her temperament was a strange, even a distorted one. There must have been a fund of ferocity in her own nature strangely mingled with tenderness. 'Stronger than a man, simpler than a child, her . . . nature stood alone.' So says her sister. She could not tolerate the contact of other wills. Isolation became a necessary of her life; she could not endure her reserve to be infringed, and the demonstrations at least of her affection were reserved for the dumb creation . . . In her last illness, her sisters dared neither question nor assist her. As her body sank, her will seemed to get stronger. To the very gate of death she walked alone, not from necessity but from choice, rejecting all aid from medicine, refusing the sympathies that hung so tenderly around her. . . . A less degree of this sort of Stoicism and self-immolation is not uncommon in people of strong wills; but except in youth, before we have learnt the value of even the meanest of us to other hearts, it is not in general compatible with strong affections. . . . But Emily was young; and all the sisters seem to have been united by ties of deep and fervent, even passionate affection. Yet they all had that unhappy gift of feelings strong out of all proportion to their power of bringing them to the surface . . . Concentrated on few objects, love may become more strong; but the more it is concentrated, the closer it approaches to self-love. How mere a self-love it may become, how mere a passionate wilful surrender to native instincts, has no where received a more vivid and terrible artistic delineation than in Emily Brontë's tale of *Wuthering Heights*. In force of genius, in the power of conceiving and uttering intensity of passion, Emily surpassed her sister Charlotte. On the other hand, her range seems to have been still more confined. The atmosphere of the book obscures the elements of character and incident; it is like gazing on a storm which melts together and shrouds in rain and gloom all the distinctive features of the landscape. It is idle to deny that the book is revolting. That a wickedness, whose only claim to attention is its intensity, that the most frightful excesses of degrading vices, snarling hypocrisy, an almost idiotic imbecility of mind and body, combined with a cruel and utterly selfish nature, – that these things should not excite abhorrence is impossible; and they occupy so large a space in the book, they seem displayed so much for their own sake, that it is impossible the whole work should not obtain a share of the sentiment. We may admire, but not without horror, the stern, unflinching hand with which the author drives her keen plough through the worst recesses of the human heart, nothing surprised at what she finds there, nothing concerned at what she uproots; accepting every thing as the simple bent of nature, referring to no higher standard, and letting no sign escape her either of approval or condemnation ... The way in which the imagination of the author is imbued with the fierce uncontrolled tone of the work is shown remarkably in its overriding essential probabilities, as, for instance, in the way in which Isabella Linton's and the younger Catherine's temper and character become so immediately assimilated in coarseness and malice to those of Heathcliff's household. We dare not question Charlotte Brontë's judgment, when she says of her sisters that they were 'genuinely good and truly great'.... We cannot help shrinking from a mind which could conceive and describe, even as occurring in a dream, the rubbing backwards and forwards of a child's hand along the jagged glass in a broken window-pane till the blood flowed down upon the bed. 'Having formed these beings,' says Charlotte, 'she did not know what she had done' ...

Her sister goes on to prophesy that the matured fruits of her mind would have thrown into the shade this early and immature production. But we doubt it. We doubt, at least, whether she could ever have taken any very high place in dramatic literature. In *Wuthering Heights* there is an unmistakable tendency to subordinate differences of character to vividness of narration. Rather, we should say, perhaps it shows the absence of any power of intuitive insight into characters widely differing from one another and from the author. All the characters described in the book are within a very narrow range, and have a tendency to run into one another. Yet the whole story embodies a wonderful effort of imagination. It is not painted in detail from observation or reflection but caught up, as it were, into the highest heaven of imagination, and flung out from thence into the world, with scornful indifference to the restrictions of Art and the judgment of men. All is fused together as by fire; and the reader has neither power nor inclination to weigh probabilities or discuss defects. He shudders as he reads, and feels as one may imagine a modern Englishman would feel in gazing at the gladiatorial shows of ancient Rome; but the laceration of his feelings deadens him to the bearings of details. There is humour in Joseph, rude and harsh though it be; a quality not discernible in any of the other writings of the sisters (we do not except the curate scene); and once, though once only, Heathcliff shows in such a light that it is possible for pity to mingle with our detestation. It is when, after Catherine's death, he stands on his hearth-stone, his passion spent, and his spirit overwhelmed by the sense of his desolation.

[quotes chapter 17, '"Heathcliff did not glance my way ... The clouded windows of hell flashed a moment towards me; the fiend which usually looked out was so dimmed and drowned that I did not fear to hazard another sound of derision"']

'The clouded windows of hell flashed a moment towards me!' What a wealth of tragic utterance there is in the phrase! Entirely out of place, indeed, in the mouth by which it is uttered, as is the whole of this description; but in true keeping with the strain which underlies the whole wild harmony. Never, perhaps, has unbridled ferocity and unassuageable vindictiveness found so adequate a delineator as in this young girl. If her book have any moral, it serves, as we before observed, to show how fierce, how inhuman a passion, personal attachment to another may become, and how reckless of the welfare of its object; and this, too, not the love which sinks from the human level into the sensual appetite of the brutes, but the pure love of souls. For such is the passion of Heathcliff and Catherine. The life-like presentation of how such a love may be compatible with selfishness utterly unredeemed is, if not the conscious teaching of the author, yet the prominent lesson of her rude titanic story, 'rich with barbaric gems and crusted gold.' The only other evidence Emily Brontë has left of her remarkable genius, is to be found in her few short poems, for which Charlotte justly claimed an appreciation they have never obtained. They show a scarcely less forcible and a finer side of her nature than *Wuthering Heights*. They want the finish of an accomplished writer; but they have a true music of their own answering to the sense. It is rarely, indeed, that poetry written early in life stands so independent as does this of any trace of the influence of other minds. But here the writer has looked with her own eyes on nature and into her own heart (rarely, if ever, beyond these two), and with genuine simplicity and native vigour her poet's instinct gives a voice to what she has seen and experienced. The life in her imaginary world seems with her to have become positively more present and real than the outward daily world which surrounded her. To her uncompanioned spirit imagination was a comfort, almost a deity.

[quotes 'O, thy bright eyes must answer now . . .']

The following lines breathe a softer influence than most of the poetry. Wordsworth himself might have acknowledged them.

[quotes 'Often rebuked, yet always back returning . . .']

. . . 'Liberty,' says Charlotte, 'was the breath of Emily's nostrils;' and there are some verses, christened 'The Old Stoic,' which give expression to this deep-seated impatience of restraint which lay so near the heart of the young Stoic who wrote them.

[quotes 'Riches I hold in light esteem . . .']

There is something fine in her free undaunted spirit, her hidden tenderness, her passionate love of Nature and of home, her genius and her unconquerable fortitude. She died young, snatched away by rapid decline; and though we, who are strange to her, look on her with a sort of compelled and fearful admiration, there were passionate tears shed over her by those who associated with her in every-day life. In less than another six months the youngest sister, Anne, followed Emily to the grave . . . Anne was 'meek and retiring, while possessing more than ordinary talents; and her piety was genuine and unobtrusive.' Though gentle, she was not weak; she possessed her full share of that independence of external support which distinguished all the sisters, and her share too of their constitutional reserve. But she had an un-affected humility, and lived more in purposes entirely apart from herself than either of the others. Charlotte speaks of her life as having been passed under the tyranny of a too tender conscience, and of her religious feeling as partaking in a milder form of the sad hallucinations of Cowper. The former we can well understand; but neither her writings, nor the occasional glimpses of her life which we obtain, seem to warrant the idea that she suffered in any degree from the disease of religious melancholy. Indeed, her sister probably scarcely meant us to infer so much as this. *Agnes Grey* reflects so accurately all we hear of her, that we can scarcely be wrong in supposing it shadows forth her character as well as a part of her experiences. Without wishing to seem paradoxical, we cannot help thinking that Anne had more of the artist's faculties than either of her sisters. Her stories are much more homogeneous in their structure, her characters more consistent, and, though less original and striking, conducted with a nicer perception of dramatic propriety.[1] Grimsby, Hattersley, and Lord Lowborough –

[1] See Introduction, p. 40.

unfilled outlines as they are – are more of real men than Heathcliff, Rochester, or Dr John. The revolting scenes in *Wildfell Hall* were drawn, in despite of a natural reluctance for the task, from a sense of the duty of sparing no blackening touch in the picture of an odious vice; a mistaken duty we think it (for these gross pictures of excess cannot touch those whom alone they are adapted to benefit), but in the discharge of which the writer has displayed no common powers both of insight and delineation. The hero spoils the book. Anne meant him to be a gentleman; but she was ignorant of the manners and demeanour of a gentleman, and she has given us instead a truculent ill-bred young farmer, with strong feelings, an active mind, and a most offensively good opinion of himself. Lawrence, who is meant to be the not very strong, somewhat over-refined, reserved, fine gentleman, she is not able to draw at all. She had no materials to enable her to do so.

Charlotte Brontë, older than her two sisters, differed widely from them in character ... The absolute seclusion which was to Emily a necessary, and to Anne a protection, was too often felt by Charlotte as a prison, in which the ties of affection and the claims of duty, to which none ever yielded a more loyal and unconditional obedience, alone had power to bind her. Hers was an active, eager spirit, which thirsted for knowledge and experience ... Some of her letters indicate how much it cost her willingly to immure herself within the narrow sphere which Providence had assigned her ...

Absence of hope in her was not only a moral deficiency, but extended its influence over her intellect. She always looked at things as they were in the immediate present, without looking forward to the modifications they might undergo in the future. She never represents the growth of character, or the influence of circumstances and of the will in changing it. She accepts her own and that of others as something settled; and while displaying and advocating a rigid conformity to duty in action, she studies but little its reflex influence on the actor. Hence partly it is that she is too much disposed to accept all men's natures with a somewhat unusual tolerance. Emily, as we have before remarked, had the same tendency, though in a far greater degree; and some lines of hers express it so clearly that we are tempted to quote them, though we have already perhaps indulged ourselves sufficiently in this matter. But Emily Brontë's poetry is little known, and always worth reading.

[quotes 'Well, some may hate, and some may scorn' ...]

Strong as was her fancy, Miss Brontë's was an eminently practical mind ... Though her limited experience of the world may have betrayed her into some blunders, they were wonderfully few – a sound practical judgment distinguishes her: her letters to her publishers are perfectly business-like, clear, succinct, and direct to the purpose. She has the whip-hand of her genius, and compels it to go in harness and draw to a purpose. When the *Professor* was declined for want of 'startling incident' and 'thrilling excitement,' she sat down there and then to write a book which should be more to the public taste. Her object was to find not 'fit audience though few,' but a purchasing publisher and a reading public; and she went straight to her object. If she thus wrote worse than she might have done had she been more independent, the fault was not hers, but that of her necessities and the public taste ...

The union of strong imagination and strong love of living realities is the characteristic of her genius. It is she, however, who compels them together, and never permits the former faculty to work except upon a basis of close observation. Her method is the reverse of that of most writers, and does much to give to her works their great originality of style. Most writers draw upon imagination for their general conception both of character and incident, resting merely on a suggestion of fact, and work up their details from observation. Thackeray does so, Dickens does so; all great painters of manners necessarily do so. But Miss Brontë is no painter of manners, or of social conditions. Her creations inhabit an exceptional world of their own. She takes her characters and her main field of incident from the world of reality, and furnishes the filling-up from imagination. The phrase she and her sisters used for the creative workings of their young minds shows the bent of their genius. They called it 'making out.' They took favourite heroes and starting points of historical fact, and 'made out' sequels to them; and they pondered on them till the imagined part seemed as real, or more so, than the rest ... It is this power of 'making out' – the intense vividness with which she summoned up her creations before her own eyes – that gives their enthralling air of actual fact to her narrations. The events *were* so and so to her; she seemed to herself to be discovering rather than inventing. She could not fancy and build up at her leisure; she must wait till she could *see* how it really was. Her father was most anxious *Villette* should end happily; but how could it? Monsieur Paul Emanuel really *did* die at sea. There was no help for it; all she could do was to conceal his fate in ambiguous phrases ...

In her novels, it is not so much the whole story as the separate scenes and detached incidents that delight us; and it is not the characters themselves so much as the mode in which they display themselves under particular circumstances. She is perfectly master of the art of narration; her events are linked in so easy and continuous a succession, that the reader loses the sense of the exquisite art by which it is done; and the wonderful thing is, that there are no dull places. Long she is sometimes, but never dull. A certain sinewy vigour gives interest to every paragraph. Character is her favourite study; but, like most people who deliberately study character, she never thoroughly comprehends it. True perception of character seems to be something intuitive. It requires, at any rate, a nature of very extended though not necessarily deep sympathies, which finds something in itself answering to all hints, and ready to gather up all clues. Miss Brontë had nothing of this. She studies the manifestations, the workings of character; and it is these alone, for the most part, that she is enabled to reproduce. She does this with all her might. In *Shirley*, for instance, with intent and resolute eyes she sits gazing into the human heart. Darkness shades its penetralia; but her keen vision *shall* pierce the veil; she *will* compel its secrets to the light . . .

Miss Brontë never deals with mere abstractions; all her people have body, reality, definiteness. But they are too singular. The greatest poets have always been those who have done the greatest things with the old every-day materials . . . Something Jane Eyre, and Lewis Moore, and Madame Beck, have in common with us, no doubt; but no doubt also much of the charm of Currer Bell's works, and their great popularity, is due to this very thing – the minuteness and accuracy with which she has described unfamiliar scenes and characters; and to the thorough air of novelty which pervades both her subject-matter and her treatment. But this, though the most popular of attractions, is not the most lasting. New readers such works never lack; but few, if any, turn back to them as they do to Fielding, Scott, and Thackeray. It is wearisome to read them even twice over . . .

Mr Lewes, it would seem from one of her letters, warned her to distrust her imagination and rely on her observation. He told her, 'real experience is perennially interesting to all men.' This is true of experience in its narrowest sense, the personal experience of the recorder; it is much less true of that mixed observation which we usually include within the term. Wiser advice (if, indeed, advice avails any thing in these cases) would have been to rely more on her imagination, and to avoid raw mingling of fact and fancy. The truest and the

finest creation she ever made, the one which gives the most indisputable proof of the real greatness of her genius, – is the sensitive, deep-
hearted child Paulina;[1] we say the child, for the woman is much less
ably and less subtly drawn. To make experience and observation valuable as such, they must be given in their naked simplicity. To eke out
facts by the suggestions of imagination, or to conceal them by a varnish
of fancy, is a very deceptive and unsatisfactory process. And this is
what Currer Bell does with her characters . . .

They must be strange people who would not feel grievously injured
by being pointed out as the originals of that hard, contentious, selfish
set of people, the Yorke family. Miss Brontë represented in Rose and
Jessy two dear friends; they may be like, but they are not portraits,
they have over them exactly the dark, somewhat disproportioned and
forbidding aspect of a daguerreotype. Miss Brontë's drawing always
has this effect: she prided herself on not drawing flattering portraits of
human nature; but she was unaware how hard and dark her lines
were . . . Most of all, however, we confess we are moved for the three
curates. They seem so defenceless and so good-humoured about the
matter. Every one has a fling at them. The biographer tells us they
were 'so obtuse in perception.' They must be happy men if they don't
know how hard they have been hit; but even pachydermatous animals
have rights which should be respected. Can we be so sure, too, that
they did not feel it? perhaps they thought it the wiser course to laugh
it off; perhaps they exercised a Christian forgiveness. . . .

The *Professor*, now published, throws no new light on the characteristics of Miss Brontë's genius; no new ground is broken; indeed, the
greater part of it only retraces for us the Belgian experiences with
which we are already familiar. Here is the first draft of Madame Beck,
under the name of Mademoiselle Reuter; M. Pelet, the French master,
is a new and excellent sketch; but we have our old friend, the teacher
and intellectual subjugator of the female heart, in Mr William Crims-
worth, but mixed in his nature something of the sulky, secret-feeding
affections of Lucy Snowe; in Mr Hunsden, the educated and abnormal
Yorkshire manufacturer, a crude, ill-drawn, and exaggerated, as well
as badly-defined figure; and in Frances, the plain, piquant, strong-
minded, fascinating little girl. But Frances, though like, is unlike. She
gives a charm to the book; intellect is reconciled with a 'sweet, attractive kind of grace,' which Miss Brontë does not often indulge us by
delineating. Frances is a refined and softened Jane Eyre, and decidedly

[1] See Introduction, p. 39.

the most attractive female character that ever came from the pen of this author. She suffers the ordinary fate, however. Miss Brontë was a great upholder of the privileges of her sex, yet no writer in the world has ever so uniformly represented women at so great a disadvantage. They invariably fall victims to the man of strong intellect, and generally muscular frame, who lures them on with affected indifference and simulated harshness; by various ingenious trials assures himself they are worthy of him, and, when his own time has fully come, raises them with a bashaw-like air from their prostrate condition, presses them triumphantly to his heart, or seats them on his knee, as the case may be, and indulges in a condescending burst of passionate emotion. All these men are in their attachments utterly and undisguisedly selfish, and we must say we grudge them their easily won victories over the inexperienced placid little girls they lay siege to ... The *Professor* contains some very unsparing and outspoken expressions, especially in the sketches of two or three young ladies who occupied prominent places in the Brussels school described. Miss Brontë had had no opportunity of learning what in England is considered proper to be said, and naturally, from her foreign experience, adopted some touch of continental freedom of speech. While we are on this subject, we cannot pass without notice a passage in the Life in strange contrast with the general tone of universal admiration. A passage which few, we think, can have read without just indignation; and after penning which, we cannot help saying, we wonder the writer had the heart to accuse the *Quarterly* reviewer of injustice or pharisaism:[1]

'I do not deny for myself,' says Mrs Gaskell, with an air worthy of Mrs. Candour, 'the existence of coarseness here and there in her works, otherwise so entirely noble. I only ask those who read them to consider her life, which has been openly laid bare before them, and to say how it could be otherwise. She saw few men; and among these few were one or two with whom she had been acquainted since early girlhood, who had shown her much friendliness and kindness – through whose family she had received many pleasures – for whose intellect she had a great respect – but who talked before her, if not to her, with as little reticence as Rochester talked to Jane Eyre. Take this in connection with her poor brother's sad life, and the outspoken people among whom she lived; remember her strong feeling of the duty of representing life as it really is, not as it ought to be; and then do her justice for all that she was, and all that she would have been had God spared her, rather than censure her because circumstances forced her to touch pitch, as it were, and by it her hand was for a moment defiled. It was but skin-deep. Every change in her life was

[1] *Life*, chapter 26 (Haworth edition, 599–700.) See Introduction, p. 36.

purifying her; it hardly could raise her. Again I cry, "If she had but lived!"'

Charlotte Brontë's works are far from being 'otherwise so entirely noble;' they have defects in abundance; but there never were books more free from the stain here so quietly assumed, and so feelingly lamented as unavoidable. Rochester does *not* talk without reticence to Jane Eyre. The writer never *did* touch pitch: she might paint it; but it was in the safety of her own innocency, and we lose patience at being told, with all this array of exculpation, that she needed 'purifying.' Coarse materials, indeed, she too much deals with; and her own style has something rude and uncompromising in it, not always in accordance with customary ideas of what is becoming in a female writer; but it would be scarcely possible to name a writer who, in handling such difficult subject-matter, carried the reader so safely through by the unseen guardianship and unconsciously exercised influence of her stainless purity and unblemished rectitude. The conventional proprieties of speech and subject-matter she disregards, indeed; her delicacy lost some of its bloom abroad, and she may be said with justice to want refinement; but even that is the conventional refinement rather than the real one. It has been well said, and every reader perceives it, or ought to do so, that her plain speaking is itself the result of her purity. What she has that jars on us often in her writings is not so much these things as a certain harshness, a love of the naked fact too unsparing, and a tendency to believe that what is attractive scarcely can be true. In the school of ladylike refined writing, true in its own sphere, enlivening, softening, and elevating, which deals gently with weak mortality, and reversing the saying which dissuades us from breaking a butterfly on a wheel, punishes vice with a knitting-needle ... we have many proficients. High in the list stands Mrs Gaskell's own name. Her graceful fictions have power to beguile us, to cheer us, to instruct us; and if with too silver a voice she echoes the dread undertones of the mystery of sin and suffering and death, we remember that reality has more sides than one, that each side has its truth. ... But Miss Brontë had a different call: her feet were rougher shod to walk through both life and art; and if she does not lead us through the dark caverns of life, at least she does not attempt to measure their depths with a silken thread, or hang pale lights of fancy in their mouths. As she passes over the lesser evils of life, she describes them in their native ruggedness; through the depths she steals, in general, in the silence of fortitude; and only now and then some brief cry of personal anguish rings sharp and sudden through the darkness.

99. E. S. Dallas, from an unsigned review, *Blackwood's Magazine*

July 1857, lxxxii, 77–94

See John Blackwood's letter to George Lewes of 28 April 1857, *The George Eliot Letters* (1954), ii, 322–3:

I am greatly disposed to have a walk into the biographer of poor Charlotte Brontë, and a friend has proposed a paper to me. There is execrable taste in the book, and I detest this bookmaking out of the remains of the dead which must be so grating to the feelings of all whom the dead cared for.

Blackwood's 'friend' was the lively journalist and aesthetic theorist, Eneas Sweetland Dallas (1828–79), author of *Poetics* (1852), an abridgment of Richardson's *Clarissa* (1858) and *The Gay Science* (1866). His review opens with an account of the biographical facts concerning the Brontës' writing career; other omitted passages include for the most part additional biographical material and references to the narrative content of their books. See Introduction, pp. 39–40.

. . . The general verdict was, that the poems in this volume [*Poems . . .* (1846)] with the signature of Ellis Bell, are the most remarkable, and that verdict is not likely to be disputed. In all the contributions, the handwriting of the three sisters is very apparent; so that, in taking up any one of the poems, it is not difficult to discover the writer. Currer has the faculty of forgetting herself, and talking of things and persons exterior to herself, with a fine power of observation, and with a certain sense of pleasure in life. Acton writes rather in the Olney Hymn style, very contentedly, very beautifully, full of doubts of herself, but full of trust in her Redeemer. Ellis, on the other hand, is somewhat of a heathen, and writes in the utmost despair: she writes calmly, but with intensity; and from the intensity of her woe there issues a music of expression which Currer, with all her wonderful felicity of diction, never attained. Emily Brontë's character is certainly

358

enigmatical; but it seems to us that Mrs Gaskell has not done it justice, in attributing to selfishness what was due to the despair of her nature. Emily had powers greater than either of her sisters, and a heart not less warm than theirs. Charlotte, who adored her, and used to address her as 'mine dear love,' 'mine bonnie love,' attempted to give some idea of her noble nature in the character of Shirley. At the same time, Emily could never appear to the world as anything like Shirley; for she had that fearful defect which darkened her in the eyes of every stranger, and Mrs Gaskell was one of these strangers; – she was the victim of despair. With amazing powers, she had no confidence in her strength; with overflowing sympathies, she could not believe that anybody cared for aught she might say or do. Charlotte, in one of her poems entitled 'Frances,' seems to have had Emily in her eye.

[quotes the four stanzas beginning 'Unloved – I love . . .']

Emily herself at one time [in 'The Philosopher'] burst out with this feeling: –

> Oh for the time when I shall sleep
>   Without identity!
> And never care how rain may steep,
>   Or snow may cover me!
>
> No promised heaven these wild desires
>   Could all or half fulfil;
> No threaten'd hell with quenchless fires
>   Subdue this quenchless will!

And she probably described her own state when, in one of her finest poems ['Cold in the earth . . .'] she wrote, –

> Sweet love of youth, forgive if I forget thee,
>   While the world's tide is bearing me along;
> Other desires and other hopes beset me,
>   Hopes which obscure, but cannot do thee wrong!
>
> No later light has lighten'd up my heaven,
>   No second morn has ever shone for me;
> All my life's bliss from thy dear life was given,
>   All my life's bliss is in the grave with thee.

But when the days of golden dreams had perish'd,
And even Despair was powerless to destroy,
Then did I learn existence could be cherish'd,
Strengthen'd and fed without the aid of joy;

as she certainly described herself in the verses entitled a 'Day-Dream.'

On a sunny brae alone I lay
One summer afternoon;
It was the marriage time of May
With her young lover June.

The trees did wave their plumy crests,
The glad birds carol'd clear;
And I of all the wedding guests
Was only sullen there!

There was not one but wish'd to shun
My aspect, void of cheer;
The very grey rocks, looking on,
Asked, 'What do you do here?'

Similarly, also, one discovers a vain attempt at cheerfulness, and a miserable consolation from the sympathy of nature, in a poem ['There should be no despair for you . . .']

Now all this despair . . . is very unattractive, and quite unfits one for social life: it is indeed ruin; but it is not unamiable. Good Mrs Gaskell, who has a firm basis of self-esteem to go upon, and who probably was never troubled in her life with a doubt as to her own excellent qualities, has no idea of Emily Brontë's reserve proceeding from any other source than indifference and selfishness. Currer Bell was not a fool, and would never have loved her sister as she did, if that view of her character were the true one. How tenderly Emily Brontë could feel, how large and steadfast was her heart, these poems and her novel of *Wuthering Heights* amply testify. In this latter work, too, we find the developed expression of her despairing nature – a hopelessness which paralyses every power, and is intimately mingled with the most deadly fatalism. Although all the characters are more or less finely conceived, there is only one man of will and action in the book, and that is Heathcliff, who, almost without the slightest exercise of contrivance or power, has only to will, and his will is executed as by a fate. He is surrounded by people who might easily master him, or who, at all events, might get out of his reach, but there they remain motionless where he places them, and he has only to say 'Dilly, dilly, duckling,' and they come to be killed without an effort of resistance. Not that Heathcliff is a great man, with much discourse of reason; he too, like his victims, is actuated by a blind fate, is as helpless and hopeless as the other mortals who lie passive in his grasp. The whole gloomy tale is in its idea the nearest approach that has been made in our time to the pitiless fatality which is the dominant idea of Greek tragedy. And as if to illustrate the helpless despair which she so grandly conceived, poor Emily Brontë, very soon after writing her novel, died to the same dismal tune which inspired its pages. While she was yet dying, she refused all remedy; she was in the clutches of fate, and fate was fate. Throw physic to the dogs. If she was miserable, why not? – she was born to misery; if she was afflicted, why not? – she had only to endure. She refused to be comforted, she refused to be nursed; she bore up with indomitable patience to within two hours of her death; then she – this simple lass, in a lowly parsonage in the wilds of Yorkshire – laid her head upon her pillow and died like the heroine of a Grecian tragedy, who willingly approaches the altar when her life is required as a sacrifice to fate. 'Severed at last by time's all-severing wave,' we are reminded of her own beautiful lines ['Cold in the earth . . .'], which now there is no loved one left, save her father, to repeat over the place of her rest . . .

After many refusals, the novels of the two younger sisters were accepted on terms which rather impoverished the inexperienced authors. *The Professor*, however, was everywhere rejected; and now that . . . it has been thought proper to publish the tale, we are compelled to the conclusion that the award was substantially just. *The Professor* is a picture of school-life at Brussels; and although it is very remarkable as a literary curiosity, it is in itself the poorest of all Charlotte Brontë's productions . . . Afterwards, when she became more accustomed to the expression of impassioned thought, she rewrote the tale, and as by some volcanic agency interminable plains are elevated into mountains and sink into gloomy ravines, the story ceases to be flat, and becomes vigorous and lifelike as a land of hill and heather. The novel thus rewritten is known to the public under the name of *Villette*; and in the history of its origin, now revealed, we have some explanation of the fact that, if not the most powerful, it is the most finished of Currer Bell's performances. *The Professor*, too, while certainly deficient in dramatic interest, is, when read in connection with *Villette*, one of the most curious works that have ever been printed. It is strange to compare the two novels – alike, and yet so different; displaying in every page how conscientiously the writer laboured, as in the general design, which, in the later novel, is quite revolutionized, she proves how perfectly her art had been matured. In *Villette*, it will be remembered that the story is told by Lucy Snowe, and that the most important personage in the volume is the Professor, M. Paul Emanuel. In the earlier tale the Professor tells the story; he is himself rather commonplace, and the interest is centred in a sort of feminine Paul – a Mademoiselle Henri. In the first half of *Villette*, while she has only made up her mind to work out the idea of *The Professor*, the story is dull, and moves on but slowly. It is not till she seizes a new idea, and begins to work out the character of Paul in accordance with it, that she at length rises to the full height of her powers. In *The Professor*, however, as in *Villette*, and in *Jane Eyre*, she carries out her favourite idea of a heroine. In the general outline of character she is herself, in fact, her own heroine. She purposely made her heroines plain, if not ugly. Deeming the lovely houris of fiction to be a mistake, she said, I will take a woman as insignificant and as plain as myself, and I will make her more bewitching than the most romantic of the fine ladies. She endowed this ugly little woman with amazing self-control, made her very content, very gentle, very neat, and also very delicate. Full of strange fancies, morbid likings and dislikes, the heroine – the double of Miss Brontë – was the most matter-of-fact person in the world. . . . How was this humdrum little creature – this Frances Henri, this Lucy Snowe, this Jane Eyre, this Charlotte Brontë – raised into a heroine of romance? She was not only attractive, she was fascinating, because she had an eye which nothing could escape. Very retiring, very diligent, with that wondrous eye of hers she saw every motive, read every glance, understood every soul . . . Remarkable as a composition, by whomsoever written, *Jane Eyre*, as a woman's composition, is very remarkable. What first of all strikes one about it is the singular faculty for analysis . . . Men excel in analysis, women generally fail. Charlotte Brontë cannot help herself; she has a morbid tendency to anatomize every passion, every impulse, every expression. Hence what may per- haps be regarded as a defect of all Currer Bell's novels, she must find a motive for every little act, for the twirling of a thumb, and for every tol-de-rol that a man heedlessly sings: she has no idea of purposeless behaviour, uncontrollable impulses without meaning, and idle flapping of the sails of the Happy-go-lucky . . . But this very power of analysis which, in a general way may be regarded as something oppressive and intrusive, was one of the principal causes that contributed to the popularity of *Jane Eyre*. . . . It was a new sensation to see that class of feelings which regulates the relation of the sexes mercilessly and minutely laid bare upon the woman's side, and by the hand of a woman. How men are influenced has often been told; how women are influenced has very seldom been told, except in the most general terms, and simply because the novelists have principally been men, and of necessity know very, very little of the sex – far less than they think they do. And while in this direction Currer Bell very naturally outshone the masculine authors, she outvied them also in another direction, in which they might justly have hoped to excel her. Most novels merely enchant, and the writer's power is exhibited in an inability to lay down the tale until we have finished it. But the motto of Currer Bell is, Duty. Full of sentiment, often morbid, one might have expected to find her obedient to mere impulses; on the contrary, she has a marvellous power of self-control; she is moved by will rather than led by desire; she looks at life inexorably as the fulfilling of duty; and such is the force of the example which she sets, that even while the interest of the story is at its height, and we acknowledge to ourselves the magic of the tale, we are content to shut the volume, and turn to our appointed work. It is rather paradoxical praise to give to a novelist, but yet it is the highest, that, inspired by the stirring theme, we throw away sloth, we shut the book, we seize the pilgrim's staff, and forth-with ascend the Hill Difficulty. Never have novels been written that have in equal degree at once captivated the imagination, and, through the imagination, quickened the sense of duty – not duty distant or future, but present in all the mud and mire of our actual life.

100. From an unsigned review, *Christian Remembrancer*

July 1857, n.s., xcvii, 87–145

This lengthy article offers what is in effect an extensive moral commentary on the characters of the three Brontë sisters, and is of interest in view of the adverse comments on Charlotte's novels which appeared in this periodical during her lifetime (see Nos 16, 54). Those of the reviewer's moral judgments which have the closest bearing on the Brontës' writings are reproduced here.

We have spoken of the sensation caused by the present biography which would have had no common interest had its subject been hitherto unknown; but this is of course indefinitely enhanced by the startling juxtaposition in which it stands, to ordinary readers, with the preconceived conception of what the author of *Jane Eyre* must be. The genius and audacity of the story; the shrinking timidity of the writer, the decorous, uneventful simplicity of the life; the bold plunge into the whirl of passion in the novel; the rustic ignorance of the world the one presents; the deep knowledge of man's nature – original, rough, coarse man's nature – in those scenes and interests which remove them farthest from woman's sympathy and observation, found in her works – what every reader seeks to do, is to reconcile this seeming contradiction, and unravel the mystery how can so bashful a woman be so unbashful a writer? – and so on.

In the first place, the book proves that those who know least of the world do not always know its best part ... Charlotte Brontë's small glimpse of the world showed her but an indifferent part of it, and her home held a monster whom the strong ties of an inordinate family affection constrained her to love and care for and find excuses for. Whatever extenuation can be found for want of refinement – for grosser outrages on propriety than this expression indicates – the home and the neighbourhood of Charlotte Brontë certainly furnish; she wrote in ignorance of offending public opinion. She thought men habitually talked before women in the way she makes one of them talk; she thought men generally were like, in their principles, practice, and manners, the men she describes. As her eyes were opened her standard rises, till in her last portrait, the eccentric M. Paul, she gives us something really noble and high principled, though in as odd a shape as these fine qualities were ever embodied.

For practical purposes she lived in a less refined age than our own. Her early experience is drawn from a society a hundred years behind-hand in these matters. People talked very differently in the days of Richardson from what they do now. He was then regarded as a moralist. Men would justly hesitate to accord that praise if he wrote the same things in our day. She did not know this; and she had a Lovelace in the house with her, in the person of her brother Branwell. So that while she hated low vice for its own sake, and suffered miser-ably for its consequences, she was sadly and grievously familiar with it, and knew so much worse than she wrote, that she had no conception of offending the delicacy of her readers.

But this is not all; it must be confessed that her sympathies were more with human nature as she saw it than either with ideal perfection or with the same human nature disciplined and held in check by stern principle ... Her character was essentially unspiritual. No merely natural qualities have any merit in them; an abstract admiration of the ideal and perfect may leave the mere admirer no better than his neighbour; but it is not the less true that a want of this appreciation of an elevated form of goodness is an evil. And this void is felt alike in Charlotte Brontë's religion and imagination – it influences at once her life and works.

As far as it is shown to us in Mrs Gaskell's Memoir, her actuating religion was *natural* religion. Not that the doctrines of the Gospel were, as far as we see, ever *questioned* by her. Her external life showed a formal submission to them, which we would be the last to undervalue. She went constantly to church – there were family prayers, at which she punctually assisted. She was conscientious, often to the sacrifice of pleasure and convenience, in her attendance at the Sunday-school. No duty of the clergyman's daughter was omitted. She had an intimate acquaintance with the language of Scripture – its words were con-stantly on her lips, or rather her pen. But all that teaching which con-nects the Christian's life with the love of Christ, which shows us that we are one with Him, hidden with Him, bought with a price, and therefore no longer our own; that we are risen with Him, and must seek the things *above* – the second birth – the indwelling of the Spirit – mysteries – sacraments – all these heavenly things, as far as the Biography shows us (we are aware that there may not have been any diligent search for them, or quick apprehension of transient leanings towards the higher spiritual truths), are a dead letter. . . . Of the Deity as a fate to be feared, a Power to be propitiated, a Master to be obeyed, we recognize the influence everywhere in life and works; seldom surely as a Father and a Friend. And this feeble and low estimate of the Divine nature may explain her very defective notions of the evils of sin. She seems to view sin only on the side of its injury to man; not mainly as an offence against God . . . She is seriously grieved when her friend, Miss Martineau, published her infidel book;[1] such speculations depressed her, and made her unhappy. But there is no indignation – she thinks the feeling out of place, and censures it in others . . . She regards Miss Martineau as under persecution, because people are angry with her book. She has no jealousy for the honour of God . . . The natural affections are her true inspiration – they absorbed all the feeling of her nature . . . There are sufferings in their nature elevating; pain, poverty, bereavement, all may be turned to noblest uses, but not constant forced intercourse for years with shameless vice. . . . All the sisters, in some degree, suffered in moral tone from this familiarity with evil; 'like the dyers' hand' their own minds became tinged by the habitual soil. In the two younger, Emily and Anne, the result, to judge by their books, was frightful; all the wickedness of the world seems to be at their fingers' ends, and they have no perception that society at large has not been subject to the same contamination with themselves. Not that they manifest any *love* for vice, which is the reason most people write about it; the tone towards it is cold, moral, and misanthropical – but there it is unblushing and rampant, because as such they saw it in the only man (except their father) with whom they were brought into close contact – whose mind they could read . . . Branwell embitters their existence, destroys the health of body and mind of his sisters – they bear with him; no one thinks of placing him under salutary restraint and privation elsewhere. Finally the daughters die one by one, in consequence, as it really seems, of this system of blind acquiescence – one at least rejecting every attempt to avert the danger, clinging to the routine of existence to the last moment . . .

Emily Brontë is altogether an enigma . . . The intense love of life

[1] Harriet Martineau's and H. G. Atkinson's *Letters on the Laws of Man's Social Nature* (1851); see *Life*, chapter 23 (Haworth edition, 505–6; *LL*, iii, 208).

is as strange a feature as any. Why should she care for life, who would not endure intercourse with her fellow-creatures – who would receive no influence or impressions, even from her sisters? Her leanings and affinities were all of a weird character; the wild hold of her affections on the locality of her home, – the strange sympathy with the brute creation, so that one who knew her said, 'she never showed regard for any human creature, all her love was reserved for animals:' the knowledge of their nature, which gave a magic power over them, as we are to judge by her management of her bull-dog 'Keeper,' whom we regard as her familiar.[1] . . .

But strange as everything is about Emily Brontë, the strangest thing by far is her book, over which such passages as these throw a certain light. We cannot read many pages of *Wuthering Heights*, without being driven to construct a theory. Without such a refuge it would be impossible to proceed beyond the first chapter. But philosophers are never revolted or disgusted; what shocks plain incurious natures stimulates the analyser of causes and motives. And here her sympathy with *animals*, and utter want of sympathy with *human* nature, together with certain animal qualities in herself, as, for instance, a *dogged temper*, supply a solution to what would otherwise be an impenetrable mystery – how a quiet, reserved, as far as we are informed, steady and well-conducted young woman, a clergyman's daughter, living all her life in a remote parsonage, and seeing nobody, could have conceived such scenes, or couched her conceptions in such language. With this fresh scent, as it were, we can pursue the story to the end, not without amusement, for the language is vigorous, and the scenes energetic.

If the respectable bull-dog Keeper could have been endowed with the ambition and the power to describe graphically the passions of his race – if you could put a pen in his hand and tell him to delineate the springs and impulses which prompt the displays of dog nature, with the outer workings of which we are alone familiar – if he could tell us the secret causes of every yelp, bark, and snarl, and spring, and bite, which we know now only in their effects – he would write precisely such a book as *Wuthering Heights*; and as 'Life in the Kennel,' it would be a very striking and clever performance. Just such instinctive, soulless, savage creatures as compose a pack of hounds, form the *dramatis personae* of this unique story. A vicious dog, if he were endowed with human organs, would no doubt swear as well as growl, and shoot and stab as well as bite, if he understood the use of weapons.

[1] *Life* (Haworth edition, 275–6).

And because they are called men and women, and are invested with human attributes, these accomplishments are added in the story to their canine powers of offence and annoyance. But the disguise of humanity is, after all, but feebly assumed, and constantly disappears altogether; the whole company drop on all fours as the authoress warms with her subject. Her heroines *scratch*, and *tear*, and *bite*, and *slap*; their likings are merely instinctive, without a thought of reason or moral feeling; their mutual rivalries and triumphs, antipathies and hatreds, are brutal (we use the word in its merely literal sense) in the most extreme degree; that is, they are impossible in human nature, and natural to brutes. The men are even more furious and inhuman in their dog-nature. We see that it is *in* them all; the idea of change or reform is out of the question; they roll, and grapple, and struggle, and throttle, and clutch, and tear, and trample, not metaphorically, but with hands, and feet, and teeth. The thought of murder is habitual to them, the idea of conscience never interferes with their revenges. Their love is as vicious and cruel as their hate, they will *strike* the objects of their affection, and the spaniels do not resent it, and curse them in life and in death, and are savage in their grief. Their terrors and fears are animal shudderings; they say of themselves that they have no pity; the one solitary deed of kindness in the book is the cutting down a dog that is being hanged; they liken one another to dogs; they act 'the dog in the manger;' they turn tail. We meet with such phrases as 'his mouth watered to tear him with his teeth' – 'she ground her teeth into splinters' – not here and there, but in every chapter. Finally, their meals are dog-meals; if they begin with the thin disguise of tea and cake, they degenerate quickly into porridge and bones. They spill, and scatter, and 'slobber' and snarl over their food, and grudge if they be not satisfied.[1]

Our reader will think this a strong picture; let him read for himself if he will, and judge if we have not furnished the key to this phenomenon. Inasmuch as our interpretation throws the bad language into the background, the oaths and execrations, we have given only too favourable a report, and misjudged the animal creation, in representing the soul of a dog as possessing this turbid and sullen human nature, and using its gifts to his own purposes. Glancing over Emily's poems after the perusal of this monstrous performance, we the more regret that

[1] An amusing part-anticipation of Mark Schorer's analysis of Emily's use of language in 'Fiction and the Matrix of Analogy', *Kenyon Review* (1949; reprinted in *The World We Imagine* (1968)).

this phase of her nature should ever have found expression. Verse was her real utterance; here we find her 'clothed and in her right mind.' If she were our main subject, we would give our readers the opportunity of judging of what we cannot but think their unusual merit. Daring and questionable thoughts there are, but alleviated by tender human feeling, and set off by clear vivid imagery, in flowing harmonious numbers ...

Anne was not unnatural; the whole history of her illness is interesting, and impresses us most favourably. It is quite fitting that we should dwell on details like these, and find comfort in them, and contemplate them in juxtaposition with the eccentricities of *her* authorship, which would be very astounding indeed, if Emily's was not more so. Not that the *Tenant of Wildfell Hall* suggests the same ideas as her sister's; we are amongst men and women, such as they are – but such a set! Anne set it before her as a conscientious duty, to represent the progress from bad to worse of vice ... The book is not so clever as *Wuthering Heights*; there is not the same force or swing; but, instead, a deliberate, careful, step by step delineation of what only a very morbid conscience could think it to the interests of society to delineate. We are led by Mrs Gaskell ... to understand that this book does really represent Anne's experience of life, particularly of life seen in her brother Branwell's. And such a record of ruffianism surely no woman ever undertook to chronicle. The coarseness of manners and unfathomable vulgarity of tone, the brutality of the men and general offensiveness of the women, the atmosphere of low society that pervades every scene, make the story unique as a *moral* one. On this point it forms a marked distinction from Emily's, who sets no such task before her: but here there is a very serious and moral strain maintained throughout. All the villanies are recorded with the good intention of disgusting us with vice, and showing sin in its native deformity ... Not that anything will make us believe that any state of English society is represented by such unmixed repulsiveness. But it needs imagination, which Anne had not, to reproduce the world a writer lives in. A mere matter of fact transcript of certain errors and crimes and a certain false tone of morals, is sure to make things worse than they are, for all the redeeming points are forgotten, and the deformities stand out as they can hardly do in real life. But these sisters seem to have had an eye for defects. Great sins had a sort of fascination for them, not from the smallest desire to participate, but because activity and vigour in wrong doing offered an exciting contrast to their own existence. It cannot but be wished that they had sometimes seen a gentleman (we speak more especially of Emily and Anne), though how far they would have been accessible to his refining influence, or appreciated his refinement, we cannot guess. They never seem to have been sensible of a want in this respect. There are no elegant disguises in their novels; they speak of life exactly as they see it. The kitchen is the scene of half the events. Very comfortable its homely cheerfulness feels in *Shirley*; we do not at all object to it there; but somehow Anne's and Emily's kitchens are *low*, and tell a tale. It is no wonder to find afterwards that Charlotte felt the task of revising these tales ...

Though criticism was never more needed than in the case of Currer Bell, yet this is inevitably a sad book for critics. We do not blame ourselves for what has been said in our pages of the author of *Jane Eyre*.[1] We could not do otherwise than censure what was censurable. Where would books get their deserts, how could judgment be given, if private considerations had weight to restrain independent public opinion? Critics would then be no better than partial friends. But such revelations as this book gives us are a lesson to weigh words. We should never forget that the unknown author has a known side; that he is not an abstraction. And here we are taught that the private side of a character may be in strong contrast to its public manifestation; that it needs rare discernment to form a true estimate of a writer from his works; and that the boldest, most fearless style, may emanate from a nature which has its sensitive, shrinking, timid side. We believe that all the critics thought they had a tolerably tough nature to deal with, that there was no need to sugar the bitter draught in this instance; and when a woman assumed a masculine tone, wrote as well or better than any man amongst them, and showed herself afraid of nothing, that gallantry and patronizing tenderness which is commonly bestowed upon women was changed to gall. And now the administrators of the potion have to reflect on the private most feminine sorrows of this Amazon; of a patient life of monotonous duty; of the passionate hold the purest domestic affections had on her character; and which amongst them, if he could rewrite his criticism, would not now and then erase an epithet, spare a sarcasm, modify a sweeping condemnation? We own it wounds our tenderest feelings to know her sensitiveness to such

---

[1] Quotes in full Charlotte's letter to the editor of the *Christian Remembrancer*, 18 July 1853; the text differs considerably from the abridged version in *LL*, iv, 79, notably in including Charlotte's references to the effect upon other reviewers of the misrepresentation of her life and character.

attacks; and when she sheds tears over the *Times* critique – of all things in the world to weep over – our heart bleeds indeed.

101. From Caroline Fox's *Journals*

9 July 1857

From *Caroline Fox, Her Journals and Letters*, ed. Horace N. Pym (1883), 382.

We are reading the Life of Charlotte Brontë, a most striking book. Genius as she was, she is beautifully attentive to the smallest practical matters affecting the comfort of others. She is intensely true, and draws from actual life, cost what it may; and in that remote little world of hers – a village, as it seems of a hundred years back – facts came to light of a frightful unmitigated force; events accompanied them, burning with a lurid glow and setting their very hearts on fire. She is like her books, and her life explains much in them which needs explanation.

102. Émile Montégut, from an article, *Revue des deux mondes*

1 July 1857, tome 4, 139-84

Reprinted in *Écrivains modernes de l'Angleterre*, première série, 1885. See Introduction, p. 41 above.

Émile Montégut (1825–95), critic and essayist, had been associated since 1847 with the *Revue des deux mondes*. His books include *Libres Opinions: morales et historiques* (1858), *Essais sur la Littérature anglaise* (1883) and his series, *Écrivains modernes de l'Angleterre* (1885–92), which reprints various articles from the *Revue*. His naturally expansive style has been pruned for the sake of economy but the main lines of his argument are represented in these extracts.

The life of Charlotte Brontë is the very substance of her novels . . . In *Jane Eyre* she depicted her imaginative life; in *Villette*, her true moral life; in *Shirley*, coming out of herself a little . . . she depicted the corner of Yorkshire where she lived and what little she had seen of human society.

Each of her books has therefore a very marked character. In the first, *Jane Eyre*, the author – as I have said – put the whole of her imaginative life and nothing but her imaginative life . . . *Jane Eyre* has been reproached with being an immoral book and although no good reason for the accusation has ever been given, it is not entirely unfounded. The author has struck only one chord of the human heart, the most powerful it is true, and has set it vibrating alone, to the exclusion of all the rest . . . *Jane Eyre* is a passionate dream, a perfect castle in Spain. In this book . . . Charlotte Brontë, leaving reality and forgetting the vicissitudes of ordinary life, . . . imagines for us the life she might have had and . . . tells us how she would have liked to love and whom she could have loved . . . This is the romance; does the reality correspond to it? Charlotte Brontë . . . depicted reality in her novel *Villette* . . . Jane Eyre is the ideal and poetic Charlotte; Lucy Snowe is the prosaic, living Charlotte; they are sisters but there lies between them all the distance that separates reality from illusion ... Goethe, who knew that man does not live on reality alone ... gave to his memoirs the profound title, *Poetry and Truth* (*Dichtung und Wahrheit*). Charlotte's two novels could be considered as autobiography and could bear the same title: *Jane Eyre* would be entitled the *Poetic Life*; and *Villette*, the *True Life of Charlotte Brontë*. This time Charlotte makes no imaginative excursions. Lucy Snowe has not, and cannot have, a romance. She is plain, poor and abandoned. No hope for her of an Edward Rochester, or even a St John Rivers. But ... despised or not, she has a heart and will suffer, and – supreme cruelty of fate – she will suffer in silence ...

It is the nature of *Villette* to arouse quite the opposite feeling to that of *Jane Eyre*. In *Jane Eyre*, where imagination triumphs, the reader finally emerges, in spite of all, with an impression of happiness and joy. After reading *Villette*, one is as weary and defeated as the heroine ...

In *Shirley*, Miss Brontë ... wrote not a romance but a novel. And yet this novel still refers to her own life; in it she gathered all that she had seen of Yorkshire society, all that she knew of the lives of the people among whom she had spent her life ... A whole, singularly strange, little world is brought to life in this book: there are sketches of powerful natures, portraits in little of great characters, microscopic originals. It is as though one were looking at a series of genre paintings in the manner of Teniers or Van Ostade. ...

The characters in *Jane Eyre* can be painted full-length, with their full breadth and stature, since their natures are so powerful that there is no fear of exceeding them. ... Ordinary characters do not give the artist the same freedom. If the characters in *Shirley* are drawn half-size, it is because they are themselves small; they belong to the middle-classes. In this environment, their natural powers have not atrophied, they have shrunk and hardened; their characters all have something twisted, something crooked about them ... they display oddities rather than originality, callousness rather than real hardness, absurdities and faults rather than vices. ...

As *Shirley* is the most impersonal of Miss Brontë's novels, it is also the happiest.[1] It is still a very sad kind of happiness, it is true; reading it, we seem to be looking at one of those harsh moors that Emily loved so much, and that Shirley Keeldar (the very type of Emily) also loves, lit by a soft May sun. The feelings of these characters, rough, hard, prickly like the heather, also open out like the heather in the spring ...

[1] See also John Skelton, No. 95, p. 340.

The general tone of the book, therefore, is in complete contrast with that of the other two novels where, from the first page to the last, the mind is stretched to its limits to follow the violent passions expressed by the author. This very tension creates a certain monotony and slowness of impression that breaks the reader's attention and prevents the flight of the imagination ... *Shirley* is partly exempt from this fault; there is more air and light, there are more characters and so one's attention is better divided. Although inferior to the other two novels in thought and conception, *Shirley* perhaps surpasses them both in the richness, variety and beauty of the details ... We may note especially the portraits ... in the chapter entitled 'Old Maids'. The five or six pages in which the author recounts Caroline Helstone's visit to these two old maids and the reflections in which she summarizes the young woman's impressions may have been equalled in English literature but, in my opinion, they have not been surpassed. ... But, of the three books, undoubtedly the finest is that which belongs solely to the author's imagination – *Jane Eyre*. In spite of the immense success of this book, I venture to say that it is not esteemed at its true value. I attach little importance to certain glaringly artificial details ... The sentimental tales with which Cervantes and Le Sage sprinkle their masterpieces are not very excellent inventions either; there are in certain comedies of Molière ... dénouements which exceed in romantic improbability the worst improbabilities with which the author of *Jane Eyre* has been reproached. Moreover, these improbabilities are in my opinion much better motivated than has generally been acknowledged. Thus, the burning down of the house and Rochester's blindness have perfectly good cause. Again, it is said that melodramatic effects abound. This is true, but are these effects powerful, do they denote a vigorous and sound imagination? Imagine the mystery of the madwoman and her nocturnal visits as a dramatic tool in the hands of any ordinary writer; one side of *Jane Eyre* touches on the novels of Mrs Radcliffe ... In a letter to Lewes, who had reproached her with excessive use of melodramatic devices, Miss Brontë replied, quite rightly in our view, that imagination had its rights as well as experience. These methods are therefore legitimate: everything depends on how they are employed and one of the great aspects of Miss Brontë's talent is precisely this, that she had the art of employing them ...

When, in the episode of the red room, Jane Eyre as a child sees a ghost, we do not find her terror exaggerated and we do not for a moment doubt the reality of the apparition. The soul has risen to such

heights, has suffered so formidable a strain, that it needs, – so to speak –
to seek oblivion in swooning . . . In *Villette*, there is an admirable
chapter entitled 'The Long Vacation'. Harassed by the visions of fever
and the demons of solitude, Lucy Snowe . . . walks at random, urged
on by an involuntary impulse: she enters a church bathed in the shadows of twilight and sees a priest seated in a confessional; she goes up
to the confessional and kneels – she, a protestant and a determined
heretic . . . What surprises us is that she should have had the courage
to reply to the priest's first words: '*Mon père, je suis protestante*' . . .
After the varied emotions we have been through with her, it would be
no surprise to see her rush off and enter a Carmelite convent or seek
sympathy from the first passer-by. And it is not only in the representation of powerful and dramatic effects that Miss Brontë excels. All
intense emotions, violent or delicate, fall within her province . . .
Jane Eyre is full of these subtle and delicate impressions; but the author's
masterpiece in this line is the first fifty pages of *Villette* which describe
Paulina's childhood . . .

Miss Brontë is extremely eloquent and critics have almost made a
fault of this virtue. She has been blamed for the length of the conversations between Jane Eyre and Rochester. . . . I would not have
them a syllable shorter . . . The more one re-reads these singular conversations, the less one is surprised that *Jane Eyre* should so have shocked
English moral susceptibilities; they are as stifling as a hot summer day,
as intoxicating as the exhalations of nature; they possess the mind like
a contagion. They have another strangely original feature, which
distinguishes them from all the love-scenes I have read, and that is a
mixture of the irresistible eloquence of nature and the artificial charms
of a cunning and resourceful passion. Rochester, for all his passion, is
at the same time highly astute. Jane, reserved as she is, is singularly
provocative. These two lovers know all the passes in the dangerous
fencing match in which they are engaged. That Rochester should be a
past-master in the art of simulating anger or delivering a passionate
tirade at the required moment: this one has no difficulty in understanding. But Jane? She does, in truth, divine a great many things. This little
sorceress with the inquisitive eye, the alert mind, the ambitious heart,
knows how a word spoken in season and with just the right inflection
will calm the fury of the worst storm . . .

But the great merit of *Jane Eyre* . . . consists in the conception of the
three characters . . . Jane Eyre, Rochester and St John Rivers are . . .
drawn from *human nature at its grandest*; they belong to the most

interesting families of the broad and complex human race. . . . The most extraordinary of the three . . . is St John Rivers. If Edward Rochester belongs to the family of Mirabeau,[1] St John Rivers belongs to that of Calvin and Knox, hard and austere men, without tenderness, without love for creatures of flesh and blood. His are purely spiritual passions . . . *Jane Eyre* . . . is perhaps the finest novel of our time. In no other modern novel does one encounter three characters . . . which grip the imagination so powerfully as these. . . . The book will live and succeeding generations will no more notice its romantic improbabilities than we today notice the crudities of Fielding or the long sermons of Richardson. We remark on these defects and having done so place *Tom Jones* and *Clarissa* among the masterpieces of imagination.

I would like to say a word about the talent of Miss Brontë's sisters . . . These two remarkable people, whose works have not been esteemed at their true value, having been as it were buried under Charlotte's success, deserve more space than we can give them. However, a word is necessary to complete what we have to say of Miss Brontë's own talent. That of her sisters is absolutely of the same family. To read Anne's book, *Agnes Grey*, is a painful and harrowing experience. In it, she writes on the constant family theme, the sufferings of dependence, for Agnes Grey – like Jane Eyre – is a governess. It is fundamentally a realistic novel; none of the sharp angles of reality has been softened, no coarse or wounding detail has been omitted. One feels that the sensibility of the author is too highly strung and too exhausted for her to engage in even the shadow of a struggle. A dull half-light illumines these pages which are filled with accounts of small unhappinesses suffered without murmur, small happinesses accepted with a gentle gratitude with scarcely the strength to smile. Resignation is the soul of this little book.

Quite different in character is Emily Brontë's novel *Wuthering Heights*. From beginning to end, terror is dominant and we witness a succession of scenes presented in a light resembling that of a coal-fire, some of which achieve the intense horror of Hoffmann's *Majorat*.[2]

[1] See above, p. 185 n.
[2] Ernst Theodor Amadeus Hoffmann (1776–1822), German romantic writer and music critic, celebrated for his supernatural tales. His best known stories include 'Das Majorat' ('The Entail'), published in *Nachtstücke* (1817). The English translation by F. Gillies (1826) 'Rolandsitten or the Deed of Entail', is referred to at length by Scott, with substantial quotations, in his review of Hitzig's *Wife of Hoffmann* and Hoffmann's *Die Serapionsbrüder* and *Nanstück* (*Quarterly Review* (1827)). Many readers have seen some resemblance to 'Das Majorat' in *Wuthering Heights*, though there is no evidence that Emily had read Hoffmann either in English or the original. See Introduction, p. 32 and pp. 455–6 below.

Emily's dark imagination parades before us with perfect tranquillity and without a moment's anxiety characters and scenes which are all the more shocking in that the terror they inspire is principally of a moral order. They threaten you, not with apparitions and miraculous events, but with savage passions and criminal instincts. At first, one accosts them without fear: they have the appearance of stout country-people, a little rough and crude; but soon they fix on you their eyes, haggard as those of a madman or cruel as a tiger or mocking as those of a witch casting a spell she knows will take certain effect, and you are fascinated and disturbed. The poetic effect produced is all the greater in that the author never appears behind her characters. Emily tells her tale with soberness and brevity; the energetic firmness of the writer points to a soul familiar with terrible emotions and contemptuous of fear. Her imagination was fired by certain memories and certain local family chronicles, and she brooded on these memories with frantic passion until the moment when the swarm of criminal passions they contained was ready to hatch. I have spoken of Charlotte's talent for surprising the hidden perversity of the soul; but the perversities she describes are after all such as may be confessed since we all share them. Emily goes much further: she divines the secrets of the criminal passions, she looks with an avid eye on the play of guilty instincts. The material of the novel is strange and she has treated it without hypocrisy, without prudery, without false reticence. Her characters are criminal; she knows it, she declares it and seems to defy us not to love them. *Wuthering Heights* is the story of an irresistible and perverse passion. Catherine Earnshaw, the daughter of a rich country land-owner, has fallen in love with Heathcliff, a little gipsy her father found wandering in the streets of Manchester [sic], took in out of charity and raised with his own children. Catherine is a headstrong, energetic girl, full of wild and poetic instincts – a moorland flower armed with thorns. It would be wise not to breathe the scents of this flower from too close; they are dangerous. The law of mysterious attractions has been marvellously observed by Emily. One can very well understand how Catherine can prefer Heathcliff – a brutal, savage character with a strong bent towards crime, who would not stop at murder on occasion or shrink from vengeance – to the good, devoted, charming Edgar Linton. Alas! Edgar Linton has not enough spirit for Catherine and as a result she feels a certain pity for her husband; all that she loved in him was his wealth and his good looks. But Heathcliff! he and she are, so to speak, but a single person; together they form a hybrid monster, twin-sexed and twin-souled; he is the male soul of the monster, she the female. In him, Catherine recognizes her own energies no longer confined by the reserves imposed on her sex; in him, she sees in full bloom, like poetic, poisoned flowers, all her own secret perversities. The scene in which she confesses the secret of her love for Heathcliff is fine and terrible. 'He is *so much me*, she says, he is more myself than I am; he is the thunder and I am only the lightning.'[1] Another striking scene is the one in which Edgar Linton calls his servants to throw Heathcliff out of the house and Catherine calmly puts the keys in her pocket and looks at her husband with quiet contempt. Catherine does not want to be saved, the thought never even occurs to her, and her terrible passion runs its furious and irresistible course through the most shocking vicissitudes.

[1] A free paraphrase of Catherine's declaration to Nelly Dean in chapter 9. Montégut's subsequent account of the scene in chapter 11 is not completely accurate.

Footnote by the author (1885)
When these pages were written, *Wuthering Heights* had achieved only a very modest success, far inferior to its high merit. This injustice lasted, even in the author's own country, until – quite recently – an eminent poet took a strong, if belated, liking to the book and revealed to the English public its true character which is precisely such as we have outlined. We are not a little proud to have anticipated by so many years the opinion of so penetrating a judge as Mr. Algernon Swinburne. (See No. 112 and Introduction, p. 41)

103. Margaret Sweat, from an unsigned review, *North American Review*

October 1857, lxxxv, 293–329

Margaret Jane Sweat (born Portland, Maine, 1823), wife of the Democratic Congressman for Maine (serving 1863–5), contributed her first paper to the *North American Review* in 1856; the present review is assigned to her in the index volume to vols 1–125. She was the author of *Ethel's Love Life* (New York, 1859) and *Highways of Travel, or a Summer in Europe* (Boston, 1859). The omitted passages rehearse the biographical events recorded in the *Life*.

Few who read the Brontë novels when they first appeared could have suspected, in ever so faint a degree, the strangeness of the private history which lay concealed behind the friendly shelter of those oracular names. It is questionable whether the criticism which attacked them from some quarters so ferociously and so blindly did not, in the end, prove a benefit to them. It drew the more attention to the defects indisputably existing, in the works of the younger sisters especially, but with that attention has come a more impartial judgment and a higher award of praise; for the knowledge that the authors painted life as it lay around them in their daily path is sufficient refutation of the charge, that they revelled in coarseness for coarseness' sake, and drew pictures of vice in accordance with their own inherent depravity. The materials were not selected by them, but thrust upon them by circumstances clamorous for utterance. The narrowness of their general world-knowledge could hardly be suspected by themselves. They probably did not regard their sphere as an exceptional one, but supposed that in their circle they saw, in little, what the world was in large, and when their imaginations pictured fairer scenes and softer natures and gentler emotions, then they fancied that they were straying into realms of impossibility. And looking at these novels in the strong daylight cast upon them by our study of the hearts and brains in which they had their birth ... they come to us as the very outpouring of pent-up passion, the cry of fettered hearts, the panting of hungry intellects, restrained by the iron despotism of adverse and unconquerable circumstance ...

The public judgment still remains somewhat undecided as to the tendency of *Jane Eyre*, viewed simply in its moral aspect, and this is, perhaps, so long as the majority is on the side of a favorable judgment, no small testimonial to the general truthfulness and power of the story ...

The book has been too universally read and too fully criticized to need more than a passing notice from us in regard to its literary merit. But there are several points wherein our present knowledge of the author decidedly modifies, and others in which it totally changes, opinions passed upon it in the absence of such knowledge. Not long after the publication of the work, the world outside concluded that it was in great measure autobiographic; but this, so far from uniting the different opinions, only placed the battle upon a new ground, and the writer became as fruitful a topic for discussion as the work itself, while the point where truth blended with fiction was decided at the pleasure of the critic. We now know it to have been autobiographic chiefly in that sense in which true genius throws its very self into its work, pours its lifeblood through its creation, making it throb with vitality, and then, by right of kingship, calls its conquered territory by its own name. The first part of *Jane Eyre*, the child-life of the heroine, deserves a more special notice than it is apt to receive; for the more rapid and tumultuous play of passion that succeeds obliterates the impression made by it. It is, however, artistic in the highest degree, and, viewed as a prelude to the main plot, is almost unequalled in its preparatory movement ... There are no waste lines or uncertain etchings, and the fidelity with which the first conception of character is clung to is quite marvellous. The childhood of Jane, with its embryo qualities, its nascent strength, its nervous imaginings, and its strong antagonisms, develops in steady preparation for the fervid passion-life of the woman ... It was a kind of literary clairvoyance which enabled Currer Bell to see that the time was ripe for such utterances. Novel-readers now-a-days are not satisfied with pictures of external and social life, however brilliantly colored they may be, or however various in style. The demand – to speak in mercantile parlance – is for a better article. We ask for deeper insight into character, for the features of the mind and heart rather than of the face and figure ... The author plays the part of anatomist, and dissects heart, brain, and nerve, to lay them before the reader for examination and analysis. Perhaps Thackeray may be regarded as the most skilful in this dissection, though he enjoys the work more as if he were pulling an enemy to pieces with malice aforethought, than as a surgeon regarding the result only in a scientific light. Currer Bell is more genial than Thackeray, and never loses her faith in the heroic element of humanity. She delights and interests us in persons ... who have warm human hearts and active minds, and the battle of whose life is no ignoble struggle, though it may be a silent and single-handed one. It is this single-handed conflict, indeed, that she delights in, and depicts with greatest power ...

The characters in *Jane Eyre* are stronger than most of the surrounding circumstances, to which, with consummate skill, they are made to seem to yield. It is in the accumulation of circumstances tending in one direction, and the indomitable will of the heroine which breaks this linked chain when the crisis comes, that we find the moral of the tale ... Natures like hers present extremes and approach paradox; strength and vigor of action in a crisis are balanced by impressionableness and superior receptivity for the magnetic force in others, producing a sort of fascinated submission to a certain point, at which the tremendous revulsive power is awakened. In Rochester a study of another kind is placed before us, as successfully managed, though less admirable in itself ... The predominant feeling is, that the nature is bent out of its true course by adverse influences, not that it loves best of itself a distorted growth, and we keep hoping for calmer airs to allow it to rise erect once more. In St John, the third type of character, self-denial soars (paradoxical as it may seem) into an intense selfishness; and in laying aside all the humanizing and pleasurable influences within and around him, he immolates others at the shrine of self as remorselessly as Rochester's eager and impulsive selfishness would do. Jane in both instances enjoys the struggle with their iron wills; ultimate victory we are sure must be with her, and we watch the contest with faith in our chosen champion ...

The most prominent artistic defects in the work are, in our opinion, the too highly colored pictures of the physical distress endured by Jane after leaving Thornfield, and the somewhat hackneyed melodrama of the discovery of her cousins in the persons of her chance benefactors, and her subsequent acquisition of a fortune. The former removes our interest to a new range of antagonistic experiences without relieving the tension ... and the latter detracts from the generally unique management of the characters and the plot ...

The general tone of *Shirley* is somewhat unlike that of its predecessor; the characters are more numerous, the scenes more varied, the interest less concentrated. It lacks the impetuous impulse, the passionate glow, the lava-rush towards a single point, and gives us instead, more changing tableaux, more general friction, wider varieties of emotion. It retains the spiciness of seasoning however; the viands are still of racy flavor and delicate concoction, but we detect more common and familiar ingredients in them ... The characters in *Shirley* are nearly all of them drawn from life, and their behavior under the circumstances created for them by the author is in perfect keeping with the tendencies which her analysis of their characteristics enabled her to discover and set in motion ...

She sets it down against one of her characters in *Shirley*, that he 'was not a man given to close observation of nature, he could walk miles on the most varying April day, and never see the beautiful dallying of earth and heaven, never mark when a sunbeam kissed the hill-tops, making them smile clear in green light, or when a shower wept over them, hiding their crests with the low-hanging, dishevelled tresses of a cloud'; and we feel directly that Currer Bell neither likes, nor means that her readers shall like, that man. The heroine in *Shirley* was intended as an impersonation of Emily Brontë, as her sister fancied she would have shown herself under more genial circumstances than those which surrounded her in reality. We detect the touch of a loving finger in the arrangement of the drapery around this peculiar figure ... Caroline Helstone represents a much-loved friend of Charlotte, and is evidently a favorite with the author, though a stronger contrast than that between such a disposition and her own Jane Eyre-ish nature cannot well be imagined. She gives us in the two Moores men nearly as selfish as Rochester and St John, and endowed with the power which selfish men almost always possess when they are shrewd and energetic ... It is undeniable that Currer Bell's heroes love themselves very much even in loving their mistresses. Having acknowledged this, or any other element of character in her creations, she never avoids for them any legitimate consequence of its existence, never shrinks from any situation into which it brings them, from fear of jarring upon the prepossessions of the reader. Inexorable as Nemesis, she forces upon them the mortifications and the disasters which are their due ...

In 1852 *Villette*, Currer Bell's last work, was published. In this novel the scene of action is removed from England to the Continent, it being ... a transcript of her own residence in Belgium. In some respects

Villette is her most remarkable work. It possesses a more classic elegance of outline and a more delicate finish of detail than either *Jane Eyre* or *Shirley*. In its analysis of character it is absolutely clairvoyant. The heart of Lucy Snowe, – that name so rightly chosen, – a volcano white with drifts without, glowing with molten heat within, – is laid bare before us, and we may watch every flicker of the flame, every surging of the fiery billows. No anatomist could more clearly describe the physical vitality, than she has sketched this weird and wild, yet hushed and still nature. She plays in the romance a part similar to that of Charlotte Brontë herself in the world, – that of a silent, unsuspected analyzer of others . . . In eloquence of language, also, *Villette* bears the palm . . . Certain passages in *Villette* rise to a height of sublimity or reach a depth of pathos which moves the very soul.

There are, however, certain defects in *Villette* which Miss Brontë herself acknowledged . . . She writes to her publisher: 'I must pronounce you right again, in your complaint of the transfer of interest, in the third volume, from one set of characters to another. It is not pleasant, and it will probably be found as unwelcome to the reader, as it was, in a sense, compulsory upon the writer.'[1] The childhood of Paulina, also, promises more than it performs . . . The queer little girl impresses us as 'quite a character,' and we are disappointed when she degenerates into a mere pretty woman. The giddy, shrewd-witted Ginevra is decidedly more entertaining; her whimsicalities amuse and her absurdities provoke us as they did Lucy, while she manages to keep the same place in our liking. Paul Emanuel . . . is strangely effective in the pages of *Villette*, and our admiration for him grows with the progressive development of the story, till our affections twine about him whether we will or no . . .

From these three works we must make up our estimate of Currer Bell's genius; for *The Professor*, written first, but not published till the halo of an assured reputation surrounded the name of its author, hardly influences our judgment either way. Its faults, which are many, were redeemed in her subsequent works; its crudeness, which is great, gave place to exquisite finish both of plot and of character; and its choice of material, which reminds us of her sisters rather than of herself as we now know her, was replaced by more genial and more natural specimens of humanity. Its best portions are developed in *Villette* with more power and richer charm, and, so far as Currer Bell is con-

[1] Letter to George Smith, 6 December 1852 (*Life*, chapter 25; Haworth edition, 587; *LL*, iv, 22).

cerned, the publication of *The Professor* might still have been omitted;
but viewed by itself, and compared with most of the romances issuing
from the prolific and not over-fastidious press of the day, we confess
some surprise that the occasional flashes of talent in its details, and the
unquestionable strength of its conception, should not have won the
attention of some one of the publishers to whose inspection it was
submitted. One inference we may certainly draw from its perusal now;
if *The Professor* was destined to be followed by such works as *Jane Eyre*,
Shirley, and *Villette*, we might fairly have expected a rich harvest from
the minds that in their first efforts could originate *Wuthering Heights*
and *The Tenant of Wildfell Hall*. Had the two sisters been spared, 'the
Brontë novels' might have become a long and illustrious list of noble
fictions . . .

We have room for but a brief notice of Emily and Anne and their
works, but the public is familiar with their history . . . The best criticism of . . . *Wuthering Heights*, is by Charlotte, and that is an explanation rather than a criticism; for it is only in the author that the key to
such an extraordinary story can be found. She described human nature
as it appeared to her distorted fancy, and it bore the same resemblance
to healthful humanity, that a faithful description of an eclipse of the
sun, as seen through smoked glass, would bear to the usual appearance
of that luminary.

[quotes from Charlotte's preface, 'What her mind gathered of the real
. . . complainant of affectation']

The power of the creations is as great as it is grotesque, and there is,
after all, a fearful fascination in turning over the pages of *Wuthering
Heights*. It calls for no harsh judgment as a moral utterance; for its
monstrosity removes it from the range of moralities altogether, and
can no more be reduced to any practical application than the fancies
which perplex a brain in a paroxysm of nightmare.

Anne, the younger and more gentle sister, was of a different mould;
yet some passages of her *Tenant of Wildfell Hall* would lead us to
suppose that she was gentle chiefly through contrast with her Spartan
sister, and that the savage elements about her found an occasional echo
from within. *Agnes Grey*, which appeared with *Wuthering Heights*,
made little impression; her reputation rests upon her second and last
work, *The Tenant of Wildfell Hall*. For a criticism of this, we turn
again to Charlotte; for though different in scope and style from
Wuthering Heights, it is nearly as inexplicable at a first glance . . .

It must be owned that she did not 'varnish' the horrors which she painted, and which her first readers did not suspect of causing the artist so much suffering. We can now trace the quiverings of a sister's heart through the hateful details of a vicious manhood; and if the book fail somewhat in its attempt to become a warning, it may at least claim the merit of a well-meant effort.

The history of the Brontë family is a tragedy throughout ... With the death of Charlotte ends the sad history, and we have now only the memory of what they were. The world will not soon forget them, and would gladly offer them a more kindly tribute than it could conscientiously have given while ignorant of so much which now reveals the virtues, the struggles, and the sufferings of the sisters in that desolate Haworth parsonage. We once more thank Mrs Gaskell for her labor of love, so gracefully executed, and echo to the letter the indignant language with which she condemns the too hastily uttered comments of ignorant criticism.[1]

[1] Chapter 16 (Haworth edition, 549–50); see also Introduction, p. 29.

Part III

Judgments and opinions, 1858-99

104. Queen Victoria on *Jane Eyre*

1858 and 1880

The first extract is from the unpublished portion of Queen Victoria's diary, copied out by Princess Beatrice; reproduced *BST* (1968) 68, xiii (no. 3), 296, the information being 'kindly provided by Sir Owen Morshead, K.C.M.G., D.S.O., M.C., by the gracious permission of H.M. the Queen'. The second extract is from the entry dated 23 November 1880 in *The Letters and Journals of Queen Victoria*, III, ed. G. E. Buckle and A. C. Benson, 259.

1858:

March 7. Began reading *Jane Eyre* to my dear Albert, having finished *Northanger Abbey*, one of Miss Austen's admirable novels.

March 21. Read to Albert out of that melancholy, interesting book, *Jane Eyre*.

May 13. We dined alone and talked and read, going on reading till past 11 in that intensely interesting novel *Jane Eyre*.

May 19. We dined alone with Mama and read afterwards in *Jane Eyre*, in which we are so deeply interested.

May 21. We remained up reading in *Jane Eyre* till ½ p. 11 – quite creepy from the awful account of what happened the night before the marriage, which was interrupted in the church.

August 2. We read in *Jane Eyre*, which proved so interesting that we went on till quite late. It was the part in which comes the moment of her finding Rochester again, blind, and with the loss of a hand!

August 4. (On board the Victoria & Albert). At near 10 we went below and nearly finished reading that most interesting book *Jane Eyre*. A peaceful, happy evening.

1880:

Finished *Jane Eyre*, which is really a wonderful book, very peculiar in parts, but so powerfully and admirably written, such a fine tone in

it, such fine religious feeling, and such beautiful writings. The description of the mysterious maniac's nightly appearances awfully thrilling.
Mr Rochester's character a very remarkable one, and Jane Eyre's
herself a beautiful one. The end is very touching, when Jane Eyre
returns to him and finds him blind, with one hand gone from injuries
during the fire in his house, which was caused by his mad wife.

105. Margaret Oliphant on 'sensational' novels, *Blackwood's Magazine*

September 1867, cii, 257–80

From an unsigned review by Margaret Oliphant who continues
to lament the tendencies which she had noticed in 1855. See No.
90.

There can be no doubt that a singular change has passed upon our light
literature. It is not that its power has failed or its popularity diminished
– much the reverse; it is because a new impulse has been given and a
new current set in the flood of contemporary story-telling. We will
not ask whence or from whom the influence is derived. It has been
brought into being by society, and it naturally reacts upon society.
The change perhaps began at the time when Jane Eyre made what
advanced critics call her 'protest' against the conventionalities in which
the world clothes itself. We have had many 'protests' since that time,
but it is to be doubted how far they have been to our advantage. . . .
The English mind is still so far *borné* that we do not discuss the seventh
commandment with all that effusion and fulness of detail which is
common on the other side of the Channel, though even in that respect
progress is daily being made; but there are points in which we altogether outdo our French neighbours. To a French girl fresh from her
convent the novels of her own language are rigorously tabooed;

whereas we are all aware that they are the favourite reading of her contemporary in this country, and are not unfrequently even the production . . . of young women, moved either by the wild foolhardiness of inexperience, or by ignorance of everything that is natural and becoming to their condition. It is painful to inquire where it is that all those stories of bigamy and seduction, those *soidisant* revelations of things that lie below the surface of life, come from . . . They have taken, as it would seem, permanent possession of all the lower strata of light literature. Above there still remains, it is true, a purer atmosphere . . . but all our minor novelists, almost without exception, are of the school called sensational. Writers who have no genius and little talent, make up for it by displaying their acquaintance with the accessories and surroundings of vice, with the means of seduction, and with what they set forth as the secret tendencies of the heart – tendencies which, according to this interpretation, all point one way. When the curate's daughter in *Shirley* burst forth into passionate lamentation over her own position and the absence of any man whom she could marry, it was a new sensation to the world in general. That men and women should marry we had all of us acknowledged as one of the laws of humanity; but up to the present generation most young women had been brought up in the belief that their own feelings on this subject should be religiously kept to themselves. No doubt this was a conventionalism; and if a girl in a secluded parsonage is very much in earnest about a husband, there is no effectual reason we know of why she should not lift up her 'protest' against circumstances. But things have gone very much further since the days of *Shirley*. We have grown accustomed to the reproduction, not only of wails over female loneliness and the impossibility of finding anybody to marry, but to the narrative of many thrills of feeling much more practical and conclusive. What is held up to us as the story of the feminine soul as it really exists underneath its conventional coverings, is a very fleshly and unlovely record. Women driven wild with love for the man who leads them on to desperation before he accords that word of encouragement which carries them into the seventh heaven; women who marry their grooms in fits of sensual passion; women who pray their lovers to carry them off from husbands and homes they hate; women, at the very least of it, who give and receive burning kisses and frantic embraces, and live in a voluptuous dream, either waiting for or brooding over the inevitable lover, – such are the heroines who have been imported into modern fiction.

106. 'The life and writings of Emily Brontë', *Galaxy*

February 1873, 226–38

From an unsigned article which begins by relating the story of Emily's life. Other omitted passages include extracts illustrating her 'power of concentration' (Cathy's account of her dream and her feelings for Heathcliff (chapter 9), their last meeting (chapter 15)) and her descriptive gifts (Cathy Linton and Linton Heathcliff on their notions of heaven (chapter 24)). There are also reflections on Heine, whose treatment of hopeless passion is felt to resemble Emily's in intensity. See Introduction, p. 45.

It is more than twenty years since the first edition of Emily Brontë's works appeared, and still her poems, whose vigorous simplicity, passion, and concentration are unsurpassed – we had almost said unequalled – by any poems written by a woman in this century, are a sealed book to the American public; and even in England she is known principally, as in America she is known only, through the medium of *Wuthering Heights*. This is unfortunate, because, though every page of that work bears the stamp of true genius, its sombre and lurid colouring, and the gloomy and repellent qualities of its leading characters have procured for it so decided a prejudice that it has been only once or twice candidly criticized and fairly judged ... Indeed, its faults are too prominent to admit of either glozing or concealment. No amount of sophistry would persuade any one that Heathcliff was a noble nature, warped by adverse circumstances; or that the elder Catherine was anything but fierce, faithless, and foolish; or that such a swift succession of acts of coarse cruelty was probable or even possible in any Yorkshire manor-house, however isolated; or, finally, that an upper servant could ever have adorned a narrative with passages so eloquent and so elegant as those with which Nelly Dean not unfrequently adorns hers. But if *Wuthering Heights* admits in some respects neither of defence nor encomium, still less does it deserve the wholesale condemnation and unqualified abuse which have been heaped upon it. Though a brutal, it is not a sensual book; though coarse, it is not vulgar; though bad, it is not indecent. The passion of Heathcliff for Catherine, though it is 'a passion such as might boil and glow in the essence of some evil genius,' is still a passion of soul for soul; and full of savage ferocity as the whole story is, it contains some exquisite pictures of childlike simplicity and innocence ... and there are bits of moorland, and dimly lighted and quaint interiors, and here and there a grand outline of distant hills, and grander stretch of sky, which are drawn by a master hand ...

Emily shared Charlotte's rare power of making the unreal vividly real to the reader ... The grim old manor-house, with its belt of stunted firs, 'all blown aslant' by the fierce winds; the wide, gray moor stretching away into the distance on every side; the sombre interior and sombre inmates of the 'Heights' – how vividly real they are made to us! How strangely familiar is the aspect of the desolate chamber where Lockwood lies down to sleep, with the moaning wind for a lullaby and the frozen fir bough drawing its icy fingers ceaselessly along the lattice. How marvellously is the picture of his nightmare given, blending as it does so naturally with the black, stormy night, the wild wind, and the dreary old house; and how admirably is the deathless passion of Heathcliff for Catherine introduced, in all its weird power, as 'believing himself to be alone,' he wrenches open the lattice and stretches out hands of wild yearning to the pitiless night, with that cry of anguish: 'Cathy! of my heart's darling! Hear me this once, Catherine, at last!' The keynote of his life's tragedy is struck in that vain appeal; and the deep night, the driving snow, the moaning wind form a fitting accompaniment to its passion and its pain ... In the absorbing intensity of this passion, which sees nothing beyond or beside itself, which disdains all consolation other than the supreme joy of consummated union, which limits all hope and all desire, all existence, and all futurity, within the narrow bound of a single being, we are reminded of some of those brief but marvellous poems in which Heine ... has compressed the tragedy of a human life and love ... a love godless, hopeless, and desperate ...

Heathcliff's history – or rather the history of his love, for that love is himself, and apart from it he has no being – is full of poems of this kind. Those few lines – 'Disturbed her? No! She has disturbed me, night and day, through eighteen years – incessantly – remorselessly – till yesternight; and yesternight I was tranquil. *I dreamt I was sleeping*

by that sleeper, with my heart stopped and my cheek frozen against hers'
[chapter 29] – are in themselves a dramatic poem, containing the history
of a love as tragic and profound as any which Heine sung. Emily
Brontë stands alone among female poets, and, Robert Browning
excepted, alone among the English poets of the present century, in this
peculiar power, the power of concentrating into a small space a profound psychological study, and a complete history of human life and
love, and of expressing it with rare simplicity and strength of diction ...

From *Wuthering Heights* we turn ... to the thin volume of poems,
which is all that remains of the published writings of Ellis Bell ... here
her imagination finds its wings ... which in a few years would have
borne her aloft to the zenith of fame and the full blaze of public approbation. Genius illuminates every page of this little volume, though
some of the poems are crude and imperfect; and in others we feel that
great ideas have found inadequate expression, and that the authoress
when she wrote them had not yet got her wonderful powers sufficiently in hand to be able to manipulate them with ease and grace.
Again, several are unequal, being in some passages magnificent, and
in others weak and halting. But, taken altogether, many of these
poems are beautiful, powerful, and original, so entirely free from the
trace of the influence of any other mind upon the mind of the author –
the rarest praise that can be awarded to a poet or poetess in these days –
that a pang shoots through us as we reflect that we can have nothing
more from Emily Brontë's pen. And it provokes a sad smile, too, when
we recall the fact that she was so little conscious of the rare beauties
contained in this small volume, that it took 'days to persuade her that
such poems merited publication.' The first poem we shall quote was
written when she was a child of fifteen, and is not merely beautiful, but
remarkably vigorous and terse.

[quotes 'A little while, a little while ...', published 1850]

In the few short stanzas which follow, and which are among the
finest of her purely metaphysical poems, she has been marvellously
successful in reproducing in words the strange ecstasy of the creative
power ...

[quotes 'Aye, there it is ...', published 1850, ll. 9–24]

It is curiously indicative of the habit of her mind to give personality
to that power of imagination which was her 'solacer of human cares,'

that, though every line of this poem throbs with the personal passion of a lover, it is addressed to imagination only. As we read the first lines we hear the wild wind whistling without, and bending the groaning trees; we, too, look out over the snowy track and expect to see a mortal wooer, ardent and eager, coming to his love. But the power to which she addressed these lines was to her a lover, and endowed with more than a lover's power to soothe and enrapture.

[quotes 'Silent is the House . . .' ll. 1–12, published 1850 with the title 'The Visionary']

In all her writings a deep-seated despair of any happier fate is painfully evident; and nowhere is it more evident than in her address to those phantoms of the imagination which were her only comforters. . . . Imagination, indeed, was to her no mere abstraction, but a real, living, presence, a divine, immortal lover, who took her to his arms when the long day's toils were over, and bore her to that world of phantasy which is fairer than the fairest spot of earth. In one of the finest poems . . . which she ever wrote on this favourite theme, she admits that she 'trusts not to this phantom bliss,' but she adds immediately afterward:

> Yet still at evening's quiet hour,
> With never-failing thankfulness,
> I welcome thee, benignant power,
> Sure solacer of human cares,
> And sweeter hope, when hope despairs ['To

Imagination', ll. 32–6] . . .

'Death' ['Death, that struck when I was most confiding . . .'] is a fine instance of her rare power of treating old and time-worn subjects in a fresh and original manner, and of applying figures drawn from natural objects to the illustration of abstract ideas . . . In this poem we have something altogether new. Grander poems, doubtless, have been and will be written; Emily Brontë herself wrote grander poems, but perhaps not one more distinctly original, and therefore more characteristic of her bold, simple, and untrammelled mind [quotes the poem in full] . . .

'The Captive, a Fragment,' which seems to have been originally intended to form, perhaps originally did form, part of a much longer poem, contains four of the finest and most original stanzas she ever wrote.[1] She has been wonderfully ... successful in reproducing in words that strange ecstasy of mind which seems an earnest of the final change, and which almost transcends the power of language. We do not know of any four stanzas anywhere which express this mysterious rapture as do these. . . .

Another of these poems, which we cannot refrain from quoting entire, is 'Remembrance' ['Cold in the earth . . .'] . . .

The language, that is to say, the art of this poem, is absolutely perfect. Each word is in its right place, and each word expresses all that it is intended to express. The passion and the pain which throb in every line are real for all time ... Rarely has there been a more marked union of strength and true sentiment than in these lines, or a more marked absence of the usual soft sentimentality which tinges and too often emasculates poems of this kind.

---

[1] I.e. 'The Prisoner, A Fragment', the title given by Charlotte Brontë to the stanzas, (ll. 13–44, 65–92) from 'Julian M. to A. G. Rochelle', included in her 1850 selection of Emily's poems. The 'four stanzas' must be ll. 69–84, beginning, 'He comes with westering winds . . .'

107. T. W. Reid on the Brontës

1877

From *Charlotte Bronte, A Monograph* (1877); expanded from articles for *Macmillan's Magazine* (1876), by Sir Thomas Wemyss Reid (1842–1905), journalist, novelist and biographer (*Life of W. E. Forster* (1888), *Life of Monckton Milnes, Lord Houghton* (1890)). He wrote to Ellen Nussey on 11 May 1876:

I should esteem it a very great pleasure and privilege to be able to give the world a 'life' of Charlotte Brontë which should be free of some of the defects in Mrs Gaskell's admirably written story. My idea has been. . . to write . . . a sketch of her life and character which shall be faithful as a portrait, and not necessarily a mere repetition of Mrs Gaskell's book. To do that, I should weave as many of her letters as possible into the narrative, so that C.B. might . . . tell her own story to the world (*LL*, iv, 261–2),

and on 26 May 1876:

I have put aside a certain number of letters (about 100) from which I proposed to make extracts . . . I have arranged that the first article shall appear in *Macmillan* in August. The sketch is to occupy three numbers of the magazine – August, Sept. and Oct. and then I shall enlarge the monograph so as to make 250 pages which Macmillan will publish (*LL*, iv, 262).

He promised Ellen Nussey one third of his royalties in return for the use of her Brontë letters. His principal departures from Mrs Gaskell lie in his attentiveness to Emily's work, his comments on the *Poems* and his discussion of Branwell Brontë's part in influencing the Brontë novels (see also No. 111, p. 436). The extracts given below are taken from chapters 7 and 13, the latter comprising his principal attempt at a critical assessment of the Brontë novels, in particular those of Emily and Anne; his comments on Charlotte throughout are celebratory rather than analytical.

Poems (1846)

So it came to pass that in 1846, unknown to their nearest friends, they presented to the world – at their own cost and risk, poor souls! – that thin volume of poetry 'by Currer, Ellis, and Acton Bell,' now almost forgotten, the merits of which few readers have recognized and few critics proclaimed.

Strong, calm, sincere, most of these poems are; not the spasmodic or frothy outpourings of Byron-stricken girls; not even mere echoes, however skilful, of the grand music of the masters. When we dip into the pages of the book, we see that these women write because they feel. They write because they have something to say; they write not for the world, but for themselves, each sister wrapping her own secret within her own soul. Strangely enough, it is not Charlotte who carries off the palm in these poems. Verse seems to have been too narrow for the limits of her genius ... Here and there, it is true, we come upon lines which flash upon us with the brilliant light of genius; but, upon the whole, we need not wonder that Currer Bell achieved no reputation as a poet. Nor is Anne to be counted among great singers ... One or two of her little poems are now included in popular collections of hymns used in Yorkshire churches; but, as a rule, her compositions lack the vigorous life which belongs to those of her sisters. It is Emily who takes the first place in this volume. Some of her poems have a lyrical beauty which haunts the mind ever after it has become acquainted with them; others have a passionate emphasis, a depth of meaning, an intensity and gravity which are startling when we know who the singer is, and which furnish a key to many passages in *Wuthering Heights* which the world shudders at and hastily passes by. Such lines as these ought to make the name of Emily Brontë far more familiar than it is to the students of our modern English literature.

[quotes 'Death that struck when I was most confiding ...']

The Brontë novels: *Wuthering Heights*

The Brontë novels continued to sell largely for some time after Charlotte's death. The publication of Mrs Gaskell's *Life* added not a little to the sale, and both at home and abroad the fame of the three sisters was greatly increased. But in recent years the disposition has been almost to ignore these books; and though fresh editions have recently been issued they have had no circulation worthy of being compared with that which they maintained between 1850 and 1860. Yet ... they continue from time to time to attract the attention of literary critics both in this and other countries, the works of 'Currer

Bell' naturally holding the foremost place in the critiques upon the writings of the sisters.

Wuthering Heights, the solitary prose work of Emily Brontë, is now practically unread. Even those who admire the genius of the family, those who have the highest opinion of the qualities displayed in *Jane Eyre* or *Villette*, turn away with something like a shudder from 'that dreadful book,' as one who knew the Brontës intimately always calls it.[1] But I venture to invite the attention of my readers to this story, as being in its way as marvellous a *tour de force* as *Jane Eyre* itself. It is true that as a novel it is repulsive and almost ghastly. As one reads chapter after chapter of the horrible chronicles of Heathcliff's crimes, the only literary work that can be recalled for comparison with it is the gory tragedy of *Titus Andronicus*. From the first page to the last there is hardly a redeeming passage in the book. The atmosphere is lurid and storm-laden throughout, only lighted up occasionally by the blaze of passion and madness. The hero himself is the most unmitigated villain in fiction; and there is hardly a personage in the story who is not in some shape or another the victim of mental or moral deformities. Nobody can pretend that such a story as this ever ought to have been written; nobody can read it without feeling that its author must herself have had a morbid mind if not a diseased mind. Much, however, may be said in defence of Emily Brontë's conduct in writing *Wuthering Heights*. She was in her twenty-eighth year when it was written, and the reader has seen something of the circumstances of her life, and the motives which led her to take up her pen. The life had been, so far as the outer world could judge, singularly barren and unproductive. Its one eventful episode was the short visit to Brussels. But Brussels had made no such impression upon Emily as it made upon Charlotte. She went back to Haworth quite unchanged; her love for the moors stronger than ever; her self-reserve only strengthened by the assaults to which it had been exposed during her residence among strangers; her whole nature still crying out for the solitary life of home, and the sustenance which she drew from the congenial society of the animals she loved and the servants she understood. When, partly in the forlorn hope of making money by the use of her pen, but still more to give some relief to her pent-up feelings, she began to write *Wuthering Heights*, she knew nothing of the world . . . Love, except the love for nature and for her own nearest relatives, was a passion absolutely

---

[1] Presumably Ellen Nussey. For Swinburne's comments on Reid's analysis see headnote to No. 112.

unknown to her – as any one who cares to study the pictures of it in *Wuthering Heights* may easily perceive. Of harsh and brutal, or deliberate crime, she had no personal knowledge. She had before her, it is true, a sad instance of the results of vicious self-indulgence, and from that she drew materials for some portions of her story. But so far as the great movements of human nature were concerned – of those movements which are not to be mastered by book learning, but which must come as the tardy fruits of personal experience – she was in absolute ignorance. Little as Charlotte herself knew at this time of the world, and of men and women, she was an accomplished mistress of the secrets of life, in comparison with Emily . . .

Wuthering Heights, then, is the work of one who, in everything but years, was a mere child, and its great and glaring faults are to be forgiven as one forgives the mistakes of childhood. But how vast was the intellectual greatness displayed in this juvenile work! The author seizes the reader at the first moment at which they meet, holds him thrilled, entranced, terrified perhaps, in a grasp which never relaxes, and leaves him at last, after a perusal of the story, shaken and exhausted as by some great effort of the mind. Surely nowhere in modern English fiction can more striking proof be found of the possession of 'the creative gift' in an extraordinary degree than is to be obtained in *Wuthering Heights*. From what unfathomed recesses of her intellect did this shy, nervous, untrained girl produce such characters as those which hold the foremost place in her story? Mrs Dean, the faithful domestic, we can understand; for her model was at Emily's elbow in the kitchen at Haworth. Joseph, the quaint High Calvinist, whose fidelity to his creed is unredeemed by a single touch of fellow-feeling with the human creatures around him, was drawn from life; and vigorous and powerful though his portrait is, one can understand it also. But Heathcliff, and the two Catherines, and Hareton Earnshaw – none of these ever came within the ken of Emily Brontë. No persons approaching them in originality or force of character were to be found in her circle of friends. Here and there some psychologist, learned in the secrets of morbid human nature, may have conceived the existence of such persons – evolved them from an inner consciousness which had been enlightened by years of studious labour. But no such slow and painful process guided the pen of Emily Brontë in painting these weird and wonderful portraits. They come forth with all the vigour and freshness, the living reality and impressiveness, which can belong only to the spontaneous creations of genius. They are no copies, indeed, but living originals, owing their lives to her own travail and suffering.

Regarded in this light they must, I think, be counted among the greatest curiosities of literature. Their very repulsiveness adds to their force. I have said that Heathcliff is the greatest villain in fiction. The reader of the story is disposed to echo the agonized cry of his wife when she asks: 'Is Mr Heathcliff a man? If so, is he mad? And if not, is he a devil?' It is not pleasant to see such a character obtruded upon us in a novel; but ... it is far more difficult to paint a consummate villain of the Heathcliff type than to draw any of the more ordinary types of humanity. The concentration of power required in performing the task is enormous ... Light and shade there must be, or the portrait becomes a mere daub of blackness; and the man whom the author has desired to create stands forth as a monster, unrecognizable as a creature belonging to the same race as ourselves. But unless these lighter shades are introduced with a tact and a self-command which belong rather to genius than to art, there must, as I have said, be complete failure. Now, Emily Brontë has not failed in her portrait of Heathcliff ... We can compare him to nobody else among the creatures of fiction. We cannot even trace his literary pedigree. He is a distinct being, not less original than he is hateful. But this circumstance does not alter the fact that we accept him at once as a real being, not a merely grotesque monster. He stands as much alone as Frankenstein's creature did; but we recognize within him that subtle combination of elements which gives him kinship with the human race. Here, then, Emily Brontë has succeeded; and girl as she was when she wrote, she has succeeded where some of the most practised writers have failed entirely. Compare *Wuthering Heights*, for example, with the fantastic horrors of Lord Lytton's *Strange Story* [1862], and you feel at once how much more powerful and masterly is the touch of the woman. Lord Lytton's villain, though he has been drawn with so much care and skill, is often absurd and at last entirely wearisome. Emily Brontë's is consistent, terrible, fascinating, from beginning to end. Then, again, the writer never tries to frighten her reader with a bogey. She never hints at the possibility of supernatural agencies being at work behind the scene. Even when she is showing us that Heathcliff is for ever haunted by the dead Catherine, she makes it clear by the words she puts into his own mouth that his belief on the subject is nothing more than the delusion of a disordered brain, worried by a guilty conscience.

[quotes from chapter 29, 'I knew no living thing ... to be always disappointed']

Here is a picture of a man who is really haunted. No supernatural agency is invoked; no strain is put upon the reader's credulity. We are asked to believe in the suspension of no law of nature. In one word, we can all understand how a wicked man, whose brain has, as it were, been made drunk with the fumes of his own wickedness, can be persecuted throughout his whole life by terrors of this kind; and just because we are able to conceive and understand it, this haunting of Heathcliff by the ghost of his dead mistress is infinitely more terrible than if it had been accompanied either by the paraphernalia of rococo horrors which Mrs Radcliffe habitually invoked, or by those refined and subtle supernatural phenomena which Lord Lytton employs in his famous ghost story.

This strict honesty . . . is shown all through the novel. The workmanship is good from beginning to end, though the art is crude and clumsy. She never allows a date to escape her memory, nor are there any of those broken threads which usually abound in the works of inexperienced writers. All is neatly, clearly, carefully finished off. Every date fits into its place, and so does every incident. The reader is never allowed to wander into a blind alley. Though at the outset he finds himself in a bewildering maze, far too complicated in construction to comply with the canons of literary art, he has only to go straight on, and in the end he will find everything made plain. Emily permits no fact however minute to drop from her grasp . . . Thus there is no scamped work in the story; nor any sacrifice of details in order to obtain those broad effects in which the tale abounds . . .

Even these fragments, culled from the pages of *Wuthering Heights*, are sufficient to show how little the story has in common with the ordinary novel. Differing widely in every respect from *Jane Eyre*, dealing with characters and circumstances which belong to the romance rather than the reality of life, it is yet stamped by the same originality, the same daring, the same thoughtfulness, and the same intense individuality. It is a marvel to all who know anything of the secrets of literary work, that Haworth Parsonage should have produced *Jane Eyre*; but how is the marvel increased, when we know that at the same time it produced, from the brain of another inmate, the wonderful story of *Wuthering Heights*. Brimful of faults as it may be, that book is alone sufficient to prove that a rare and splendid genius was lost to the world when Emily Brontë died.

It is with a feeling of curious disappointment that one rises from the perusal of the writings of Anne Brontë. She wrote two novels, *Agnes*

Grey and *The Tenant of Wildfell Hall*, neither of which will really repay perusal. In the first she sought to set forth some of the experiences which had befallen her in that patient placid life which she led as a governess. They were not ordinary experiences, the reader should know. I have resolutely avoided, in writing this sketch of Charlotte Brontë and her sisters, all unnecessary reference to the tragedy of Branwell Brontë's life. But it is a strange sad feature of that story, that the pious and gentle youngest sister was compelled to be a closer and more constant witness of his sins and his sufferings than either Charlotte or Emily. She was living under the same roof with him when he went astray and was thrust out in deep disgrace. I have said already that the effect of his career upon her own was as strong and deep as Mrs Gaskell represents it to have been. Branwell's fall formed the dark turning-point in Anne Brontë's life. So it was not unnatural that it should colour her literary labours. Accordingly, whilst *Agnes Grey* gives us some of the scenes of her governess life, dressed up in the fashion of the ordinary romances of thirty years ago, *The Tenant of Wildfell Hall* presents us with a dreary and repulsive picture of Branwell Brontë's condition after his fall.

108. Swinburne, a note on Charlotte Brontë

1877

From *Charlotte Brontë. A Note*, which was stimulated by Reid's monograph (No. 107). See Introduction (pp. 43–4) and also Edmund Gosse (to whom Swinburne read part of his essay in June 1877):

. . . a 'note' which extended to a volume . . . intended to undermine the reputation of George Eliot, . . . by insistence on the superior claims of Charlotte Brontë . . . [He] deserves great credit for having set the pendulum swinging back in favour of the Brontës. Nor was his praise of Charlotte, though expressed in dithyrambic language, excessive. It sweeps away *The Professor* and pronounces *Shirley* essentially a failure, while basing the triumphant claim of Charlotte Brontë to eternal fame on *Jane Eyre* and *Villette*. Swinburne took the opportunity to celebrate the genius of Emily, and criticism has in the main accepted a view which he was the earliest to state with vigour . . . There are offences against taste; he seriously grieved a number of his own friends by calling George Eliot 'an Amazon thrown sprawling over the crupper of her spavined and spurgalled Pegasus' (*Algernon Charles Swinburne* (1917), 235–6).

Swinburne's dithyrambic 'note' has needed severe pruning; omitted passages include various digressions, among them discussions of George Eliot and other contemporary women writers. For his letter to Reid of September 1877 on Emily Brontë see headnote to No. 112.

The priceless contribution to our knowledge of one of the greatest among women, for which the thanks of all students who have at heart the honour of English literature are due to Mr Wemyss Reid, had on its first appearance the singular good fortune to evoke from a weekly paper . . . one of the most profound and memorable remarks ever put forth even in the columns of the contemporary *Spectator*. On the 11th of November 1876, there appeared in that quarter a written assurance that its literary critic did actually 'agree with this biographer' in thinking that the works of Charlotte Brontë 'will one day again be regarded as evidences of exceptional intellectual power.' The present writer for once feels himself emboldened to express ... his own agreement with this critic in the opinion that they not impossibly may; he will even venture to avow his humble conviction that they may ... be expected ... to be read with delight and wonder, and re-read with reverence and admiration ... when even *Daniel Deronda* has gone the way of all waxwork, when even Miss Broughton no longer cometh up as a flower,[1] and even Mrs Oliphant is at length cut down like the grass. It is under the rash and reckless impulse of this unfashionable belief that I would offer a superfluous word or two of remark on the twin-born genius of the less mortal sisters who left with us for ever the legacies of *Jane Eyre* and *Wuthering Heights*.

The one sovereign quality common alike to the spirit and the work of these two great women, whose names make up with Mrs Browning's the perfect trinity for England of highest female fame, is one which even the prodigal Genius or God who presided at her birth could not or would not accord to the passionate and lyric-minded poetess. It is possibly the very rarest of all powers or faculties of imagination applied to actual life and individual character ... But in Charlotte and Emily Brontë this innate personal quality was manifested, as far as my knowledge or power of comparison extends, at a quite incomparable degree of excellence; of perfection, I would have written, but for the fear of giving too Irish a turn to the parting phrase of my sentence. It is a quality as hard to define as impossible to mistake ... But its absence or its presence is or should be anywhere and always recognizable at a glance ...

Perhaps we may reasonably attempt some indication of the difference which divides pure genius from mere intellect as by a great gulf fixed; the quality of the latter, we may say, is constructive, the property of the former is creative. Adam Bede, for instance, or even Tito Melema, is an example of construction – and the latter is one of the finest in literature; Edward Rochester and Paul Emanuel are creations. And the inevitable test or touchstone of this indefinable difference is the immediate and enduring impression set at once and engraved for ever on the simplest or the subtlest mind of the most

---

[1] *Cometh up as a Flower* (1867), one of the numerous novels published by Rhoda Broughton (1840–1920).

careless or the most careful student. In every work of pure genius we
feel while it is yet before us . . . the sense of something inevitable, some
quality incorporate and innate, which determines that it shall be thus
and not otherwise . . . Perhaps we may reasonably divide all imaginative work into three classes; the lowest, which leaves us in a complacent
mood of acquiescence with the graceful or natural inventions and
fancies of an honest and ingenious workman . . ., the second, of high
enough quality to engage our judgment in its service, and make direct
demands on our grave attention for deliberate assent or dissent; the
third, which in the exercise of its highest faculties at their best . . .
compels us without question to positive acceptance and belief. Of the
first class it would be superfluous to cite instances from among writers
of our own day, not undeserving of serious respect and of genuine
gratitude for much honest work done and honest pleasure conferred
on us. Of the second order our literature has no more apt and brilliant
examples than George Eliot and George Meredith. Of the third, if
in such a matter as this I may trust my own instinct – that last resource
and ultimate reason of all critics in every case and on every question –
there is no clearer and more positive instance in the whole world of
letters than that supplied by the genius of Charlotte Brontë.

I do not mean that such an instance is to be found in the treatment of
each figure in each of her great three books . . . [But] I must take leave
to reiterate my conviction that no living English or female writer can
rationally be held her equal in what I cannot but regard as the highest
and the rarest quality which supplies the hardest and the surest proof
of a great and absolute genius for the painting and the handling of
human characters in mutual relation and reaction. Even the glorious
mistress of all forms and powers of imaginative prose, who has lately
left France afresh in mourning – even George Sand herself had not this
gift in like measure with those great twin sisters in genius who were
born to the stern and strong-hearted old Rector of Haworth.

The gift of which I would speak is that of a power to make us feel
in every nerve, at every step forward which our imagination is compelled to take under the guidance of another's, that thus and not
otherwise . . . it was and it must have been with the human figures
set before us in their action and their suffering; that thus and not otherwise they absolutely must and would have felt and thought and spoken
under the proposed conditions . . . In almost all other great works of
its kind, in almost all the sovereign masterpieces even of Fielding, of
Thackeray, of the royal and imperial master, Sir Walter Scott him-

self ... we do not find this one great good quality so innate, so im-
manent as in hers ... When Catherine Earnshaw says to Nelly Dean,
'I *am* Heathcliff!' and when Jane Eyre answers Edward Rochester's
question, whether she feels in him the absolute sense of fitness and
correspondence to herself which he feels to himself in her, with the
words which close and crown the history of their twin-born spirits –
'To the finest fibre of my nature, sir' – we feel to the finest fibre of our
own that these are no mere words. On this ground at least it might
for once be not unpardonable to borrow ... and say, as was said on
another score of Emily Brontë ... by Sydney Dobell, in an admirable
paper [No. 80] ... that either sister in this single point 'has done no
less' than Shakespeare ...

If I turn again for contrast or comparison with their works to the
work of George Eliot, it will be attributed by no one above the spiritual
rank and type of Pope's representative dunces to irreverence or ingratitude for the large and liberal beneficence of her genius at its best. But
she alone among our living writers is generally admitted or assumed
as the rightful occupant, or at least as the legitimate claimant, of that
foremost place in the front rank of artists in this kind ... In knowledge,
in culture, perhaps in capacity for knowledge and for culture, Charlotte Brontë was no more comparable to George Eliot than George
Eliot is comparable to Charlotte Brontë in purity of passion, in depth
and ardour of feeling, in spiritual force and fervour of forthright
inspiration. It would be rather a rough and sweeping than a loose, or
inaccurate division which should define the one as a type of genius
distinguished from intellect, the other of intellect as opposed to genius.
But it would, as I venture to think, be little or nothing more or less
than accurate to recognize in George Eliot a type of intelligence vivified
and coloured by a vein of genius, in Charlotte Brontë a type of genius
directed and moulded by the touch of intelligence. No better test of
this distinction could be desired than a comparison of their respective
shortcomings or failures ...

That Charlotte Brontë, a woman of the first order of genius, could
go very wrong indeed, there are whole scenes and entire characters
in her work which afford more than ample proof. But George Eliot,
a woman of the first order of intellect, has once and again shown how
much further and more steadily and more hopelessly and more
irretrievably and more intolerably wrong it is possible for mere
intellect to go than it ever can be possible for mere genius. Having no
taste for the dissection of dolls, I shall leave Daniel Deronda in his

natural place above the ragshop door; and having no ear for the melodies of a Jew's harp, I shall leave the Spanish Gipsy to perform on that
instrument to such audience as she may collect. It would be unjust and
impertinent to dwell much on Charlotte Brontë's brief and modest
attempts in verse; but it would be unmanly and unkindly to touch at
all on George Eliot's ...

And first we will examine ... what may be the very gravest flaws
or shortcomings perceptible in the work of Charlotte Brontë ...
Whatever in *Jane Eyre* is other than good is also less than important.
The accident which brings a famished wanderer to the door of unknown kinsfolk might be a damning flaw in a novel of mere incident;
but incident is not the keystone and commonplace is not the touchstone
of this. The vulgar insolence and brutish malignity of the well-born
guests at Thornfield Hall are grotesque and incredible in speakers of
their imputed station; these are the natural properties of that class of
persons which then supplied, as it yet supplies, the writers of such
articles as one of memorable infamy and imbecility on *Jane Eyre* to the
artistic and literary department of the *Quarterly Review*. So gross and
grievous a blunder would entail no less than ruin on a mere novel of
manners; but accuracy in the distinction and reproduction of social
characteristics is not the test of capacity for such work as this. That
test is only to be found in the grasp and manipulation of manly and
womanly character. And, to my mind, the figure of Edward Rochester
in this book remains, and seems like to remain, one of the only two
male figures of wholly truthful workmanship and vitally heroic mould
ever carved and coloured by a woman's hand. The other it is superfluous to mention; all possible readers will have uttered before I can
transcribe the name of Paul Emanuel ...

And now we must regretfully and respectfully consider of what
quality and what kind may be the faults which deform the best and
ripest work of Charlotte Brontë's chosen rival. Few or none, I should
suppose, of her most passionate and intelligent admirers would refuse
to accept *The Mill on the Floss* as on the whole at once the highest and
the purest and the fullest example of her magnificent and matchless
powers. ... The two first volumes have all the intensity and all the
perfection of George Sand's best work, tempered by all the simple
purity and interfused with all the stainless pathos of Mrs Gaskell's ...
But what shall any one say of the upshot? If we are really to take it on
trust ... that a woman of Maggie Tulliver's kind can be moved to
any sense but that of bitter disgust and sickening disdain by a thing – I

will not write, a man – of Stephen Guest's[1]; our only remark, as our only comfort, must be that now at least the last word of realism has surely been spoken, the last abyss of cynicism has surely been sounded and laid bare.

No outrage of this kind on womanly loyalty and manly instinct was among the possible errors of Charlotte Brontë's heroic soul . . .

Another not insignificant point of difference, though less notable than this, we find in the broad sharp contrast offered by the singular perfection of George Eliot's earliest imaginative work with its gracious union of ease and strength . . . to the doubtful, heavy-gaited, floundering tread of Charlotte Brontë's immature and tentative genius, at its first start on the road to so triumphal a goal as lay ahead of it. No reader of average capacity could so far have failed to appreciate the delicate and subtle strength of hand put forth in the *Scenes of Clerical Life* as to feel any wonder mingling with his sense of admiration when the same fine and potent hand had gathered its latter laurels in a wider field of work; but even the wise and cordial judgment which had discerned the note of power and sincerity perceptible in the crude coarse outlines of *The Professor* may well have been startled and shaken out of all judicial balance and critical reserve at sight of the sudden sunrise which followed so fast on that diffident uncertain dawn. . . . There is yet a third point of contrast . . . No man or woman . . . has ever written of children with such . . . fidelity of affection as the spiritual mother of Tottie, of Eppie, and of Lillo . . . There is a certain charm of attraction as well as compassion wrought upon us by the tragic childhood of Jane Eyre; and no study can exceed for exquisite veracity and pathos the subtle and faultless portrait of the child Paulina in the opening chapters of *Villette*; but the attraction of these is not wholly or mainly the charm of infancy . . . it comes rather from the latent suggestion or refraction of the woman yet to be, struck sharply back or dimly shaded out from the deep glass held up to us of a passionate and visionary childhood. We begin at once to consider how the children in Charlotte Brontë's books will grow up; it is too evident that they are not there for their own childish sake – a fatal and infallible note of inferiority from the baby-worshipper's point of view . . . the dread and repulsion felt by a forsaken wife and tortured mother for the very beauty and dainty sweetness of her only new-born child, as recalling the cruel sleek charm of the human tiger who had begotten it, that we are wellnigh moved to think one of the most powerfully and

[1] Anticipates F. R. Leavis's strictures in *The Great Tradition* (1948) 40–1.

exquisitely written chapters in *Shirley* ... could hardly have been written at all by a woman, or for that matter by a man, of however kindly and noble a nature, in whom the instinct or nerve or organ of love for children was even of average natural strength and sensibility.[1]

But saving for her 'plentiful lack' of inborn baby-worship I cannot think of any great good quality most proper to the most noble among women which was not eminent in the genius as in the nature of Charlotte Brontë. Take for example neither of her great two masterpieces, but the most unequal and least fortunate of her three great books. Weakest on that very side where the others are strongest, *Shirley* is doubtless a notable example of failure in the central and crucial point of masculine character. Robert Moore is rather dubious than damnable as a study from the male; but for his brother the most fervent of special pleaders can hardly find much to say on that score. No quainter example of a woman of genius in breeches – and very badly fashioned and badly fitting breeches too – was ever exhibited by George Sand's very self ... Assuredly Louis Moore would never have passed muster with the very stolidest of all Swiss as the one unmistakable young man in a masquerading party of questionably mingled sexes ... Miss Brontë has written nothing finer, nothing of more vivid and exquisite eloquence, than the best passages of his diary. No other woman that I know of, not George Sand herself, could have written a prose sentence of such exalted and perfect poetry as this:– 'The moon reigns glorious, glad of the gale; as glad as if she gave herself to its fierce caress with love.'[2] Nothing can beat that ... It paints wind like David Cox, and light like Turner. To find anything like it in verse we must go to the highest springs of all; to Pindar or to Shelley or to Hugo. And these, in the famous phrase of Brummell's valet – these are her failures.

But what shall be said of her successes?

Supreme as is the spiritual triumph of Cervantes in the person of his perfect knight over all insult and mockery of brutal chance and ruffianly realities ... it is hardly a completer example of imaginative and moral mastery than the triumph of Charlotte Brontë in the quaint person of her grim little Professor over his own eccentric infirmities of habit and temper ... a triumph so ... delicately displayed in the swift steady gradations of change and development ... through which

[1] Cf. G. H. Lewes's objections, p. 167 above.
[2] Chapter 29; the passage appears in the opening paragraphs, before the record of Louis Moore's diary.

the figure of M. Paul seems to pass as under summer lights and shadows, till it gradually opens upon us in human fullness of self-unconscious charm and almost sacred beauty – yet always with the sense of some latent infusion, some tender native admixture of a quality at once loveable and laughable ... The figure of the young missionary St John Rivers is by no means to be rated as one of her great unsurpassable successes in spiritual portraiture ... but the imperishable passion and perfection of the words describing the moorland scene of which his eyes at parting take their long last look must have drawn the tears to many another man's that his own were not soft enough to shed.

This instinct (if I may so call it) for the tragic use of landscape was wellnigh even more potent and conspicuous in Emily than in Charlotte ... All the heart of the league-long billows of rolling and breathing and brightening heather is blown with the breath of it on our faces as we read; all the wind and all the sound and all the fragrance and freedom and gloom and glory of the high north moorland ... There is nothing known to me in any book of quite equal or similar effect ... Take for instance that marvellous note of landscape ... which serves as overture to the last fierce rapturous passage of raging love and mad recrimination between Heathcliff and the dying Catherine; the mention of the church-bell that in winter could just be heard ringing right across the naked little glen, but in summer the sound was lost, muffled by the murmur of blowing foliage and branches full of birds. The one thing I know or can remember as in some sort comparable in its effect to this passage is of course that notice of the temple-haunting martlet and its loved mansionry which serves as prelude to the entrance of Lady Macbeth from under the buttresses where its pendant bed and procreant cradle bore witness to the delicate air in which incarnate murder also was now to breed and haunt. Even more wonderful perhaps in serene perfection of subdued and sovereign power is the last brief paragraph of that stormy and fiery tale. There was a dark unconscious instinct as of primitive nature-worship in the passionate great genius of Emily Brontë, which found no corresponding quality in her sister's. It is into the lips of her representative Shirley Keeldar that Charlotte puts the fervent 'pagan' hymn of visionary praise to her mother nature – Hertha, Demeter, 'la déesse des dieux,' which follows on her fearless indignant repudiation of Milton and his Eve.[1] Nor had Charlotte's less old-world and Titanic soul any touch of the self-dependent solitary contempt for all outward objects of faith

[1] *Shirley*, chapter 18.

and hope, for all aspiration after a changed heart or a contrite spirit or a converted mind, which speaks in the plain-song note of Emily's clear stern verse with such grandeur of anti-christian fortitude and self-controlling self-reliance[1] . . . No other poet's imagination could have conceived that agony of the girl who dreams she is in heaven, and weeps so bitterly for the loss of earth that the angels cast her out in anger, and she finds herself fallen on the moss and heather of the mid moor-head, and wakes herself with sobbing for joy . . . it was assuredly with no less justice of insight and accuracy of judgment than humility of self-knowledge and fidelity of love that Charlotte in her day of solitary fame assigned to her dead sister the crown of poetic honour which she as rightfully disclaimed for herself . . . But the pure note of absolutely right expression for things inexpressible in full by prose at its highest point of adequacy . . . If here is not the pure distinctive note of song as opposed to speech – the 'lyrical cry,' as Mr Arnold calls it – I know not where to seek it in English verse since Shelley. Another such unmistakable note is struck in the verses headed 'Remembrance'.

[quotes 'Silent is the house . . .', ll. 69–74, 85–8 (i.e. the stanzas beginning 'He comes with westering winds . . .')

Here too is the same profound perception of an abiding power in the old dumb divinities of Earth and Time – gods only not yet found strong enough to divide long love from death;

> Severed at last by Time's all-severing wave.[2]

The praise of Emily Brontë can be no alien or discursive episode in the briefest and most cursory notice, the least adequate or exhaustive panegyric of her sister; and far less would it have seemed less than indispensable to that most faithful and devoted spirit of indomitable love which kept such constant watch over her memory; and fought so good a fight for her fame.

---

[1] Swinburne is thinking of the lines that also moved Matthew Arnold (No. 89).
[2] 'Cold in the earth . . .', l. 4.

109. Leslie Stephen on Charlotte Brontë, *Cornhill Magazine*

December 1877, 723–9

Reprinted in *Hours in a Library*, third series, 1879.
Designed as a reply to Swinburne (No. 108, and see Introduction, p. 44 above). Leslie Stephen was editor during 1871–82 of the *Cornhill Magazine* for which he wrote his *Hours in a Library* (first series 1874; second series 1876).

Mr. Swinburne, in his recent essay upon Miss Brontë, has, as usual bestowed the most enthusiastic and generous praise with a lavish hand, and bestowed it upon worthy objects. And, as usual, he seems to be a little too much impressed with the necessary connection between illuminating in honour of a hero and breaking the windows or burning the effigies of the hero's rivals. I do not wish to examine the justice of his assaults, and still less to limp on halting and prosaic feet after his eloquent discourse. I propose only to follow an inquiry suggested by a part of his argument. After all, though criticism cannot boast of being a science, it ought to aim at something like a scientific basis, or at least to proceed in a scientific spirit. The critic, therefore, before abandoning himself to the oratorical impulse, should endeavour to classify the phenomena with which he is dealing as calmly as if he were ticketing a fossil in a museum. The most glowing eulogy, the most bitter denunciation, have their proper place; but they belong to the art of persuasion, and form no part of scientific method. Our literary, like our religious, creed should rest upon a purely rational ground, and be exposed to logical tests. Our faith in an author must, in the first instance, be the product of instinctive sympathy, instead of deliberate reason. It may be propagated by the contagion of enthusiasm, and preached with all the fervour of proselytism. But when we are seeking to justify our emotions, we must endeavour to get for the time into the position of an independent spectator, applying with rigid impartiality such methods as are best calculated to free us from the influence of personal bias.

Undoubtedly it is a very difficult task to be alternately witness and judge; to feel strongly, and yet to analyze coolly; to love every feature in a familiar face, and yet to decide calmly upon its intrinsic ugliness or beauty ... It is especially difficult in the case of writers like Miss Brontë, and of critics who were in the most enthusiastic age when her fame was in its early freshness. It is almost impossible not to have overpowering prejudices in regard to a character so intense, original, and full of special idiosyncracy. If you did not love her you must hate her: or ... feel strongly a hopeless uncongeniality of temperament. The power of exciting such feelings is, indeed, some testimony to an author's intrinsic force ... Charlotte Brontë, and perhaps her sister Emily in an even higher degree, must have a certain interest for all intelligent observers of character. But only a minority will thoroughly and unreservedly enjoy the writings which embody so peculiar an essence. Some scenery – rich pasturage and abounding rivers and forest-clad hills – appeals more or less to everybody. It is only a few who really love the lonely cairn on a wind-swept moor ...

The comparative eclipse, then – if eclipse there be – of Charlotte Brontë's fame, does not imply want of power, but want of comprehensiveness. There is a certain *Primâ facie* presumption against a writer who appeals only to a few, though it may be amply rebutted by showing that the few are also fit. The two problems must go together; why is the charm so powerful, and why is it so limited? ...

Mr Swinburne takes Miss Brontë to illustrate the distinction between 'genius' and 'intellect.' Genius, he says, as the most potent faculty, can most safely dispense with its ally. If genius be taken to mean the poetic as distinguished from the scientific type of mind – that which sees intuitively, prefers synthesis to analysis, and embodies ideas in concrete symbols instead of proceeding by rule and measure, and constructing diagrams in preference to drawing pictures – the truth is undeniable and important. The reasoner gives us mechanism and constructs automata where the seer creates living and feeling begins ...

Miss Brontë, as her warmest admirers would grant, was not and did not in the least affect to be a philosophical thinker. And because a great writer, to whom she had been gratuitously compared, is strong just where she is weak, her friends have an injudicious desire to make out that the matter is of no importance, and that her comparative poverty of thought is no injury to her work. There is no difficulty in following them so far as to admit that her work is none the worse for containing no theological or philosophical disquisitions, or for showing no familiarity with the technicalities of modern science and meta-physics. But the admission by no means follows that her work does not suffer very materially by the comparative narrowness of the circle of ideas in which her mind habitually revolved. . . . There is no province of inquiry – historical, scientific, or philosophical – from which the artist may not derive useful material; the sole question is whether it has been properly assimilated and transformed by the action of the poetic imagination. By attempting to define how far Miss Brontë's powers were in fact thus bounded, we shall approximately decide her place in the great hierarchy of imaginative authors. That it was a very high one, I take to be undeniable. Putting aside living writers, the only female novelist whom one can put distinctly above her is George Sand; for Miss Austen, whom most critics place upon a still higher level, differs so widely in every way that 'comparison' is absurd. It is almost silly to draw a parallel between writers when every great quality in one is 'conspicuous by its absence' in the other.

The most obvious of all remarks about Miss Brontë is the close connection between her life and her writings. In no books is the author more completely incarnated. She is the heroine of her two most powerful novels; for Lucy Snowe is avowedly her own likeness, and Lucy Snowe differs only by accidents from Jane Eyre; whilst her sister is the heroine of the third novel. All the minor characters, with scarcely an exception, are simply portraits, and the more successful in proportion to their fidelity. The scenery and even the incidents are, for the most part, equally direct transcripts from reality. And, as this is almost too palpable a peculiarity to be expressly mentioned, it seems to be an identical proposition that the study of her life is the study of her novels. More or less true of all imaginative writers, this must be pre-eminently true of Miss Brontë. Her experience, we might say, has been scarcely transformed in passing through her mind . . . *Shirley* contains a continuous series of photographs of Haworth and its neighbourhood; as *Villette* does of Brussels: and if *Jane Eyre* is not so literal, except in the opening account of the school-life, much of it is almost as strictly autobiographical . . .

The sisters . . . differed widely, though with a strong resemblance. The iron had not entered so deeply into Charlotte's nature. Emily's naturally subjective mode of thought – to use the unpleasant technical phrase – found its most appropriate utterance in lyrical poetry. She represents, that is, the mood of pure passion, and is rather encumbered than otherwise by the necessity of using the more indirect method of concrete symbols. She feels, rather than observes; whereas Charlotte feels in observing. Charlotte had not that strange self-concentration which made the external world unreal to her sister. Her powers of observation, though restricted by circumstances and narrowed by limitations of her intellect, showed amazing penetration within her proper province. The greatest of all her triumphs in this direction is the character of Paul Emanuel, which has tasked Mr Swinburne's powers of expressing admiration, and which one feels to be, in its way, inimitable. A more charming hero was never drawn, or one whose reality is more vivid and unmistakable . . .

Mr Swinburne compares this masterpiece of Miss Brontë's art with the famous heroes of fiction, Don Quixote, Uncle Toby, and Colonel Newcombe . . . Sterne, in describing Uncle Toby, gave a concrete symbol for one of the most important currents of thought of the time, which took religious, moral, and political, as well as artistic, shapes. In many ways the sentiment has lost much of its interest for us; but though an utterance of an imperfect doctrine, we may infer that Uncle Toby's soul will transmigrate into new shapes, and perhaps develop into higher forms.

When we measure M. Paul Emanuel by this test, we feel instinctively that there is something wanting. The most obvious contrast is that M. Emanuel is no humourist himself, nor even a product of humour. The imperfections, the lovable absurdities, of Uncle Toby are imbedded in the structure of his character. His whims and oddities always leave us in the appropriate mood of blended smiles and tears. Many people, especially 'earnest' young ladies, will prefer M. Paul Emanuel, who, like his creator, is always in deadly earnest. At bottom he is always (like all ladies' heroes) a true woman, simple, pure, heroic and loving – a real Joan of Arc, as Mr Thackeray said of his creator, in the beard and blouse of a French professor. He attaches extravagant importance to trifles, indeed, for his irascible and impetuous temperament is always converting him into an Æolus of the duck-pond. So far there is, we may admit, a kind of pseudo-humorous element in his composition; but the humour, such as it is, lies entirely on the surface. He is perfectly sane and sensible, though a trifle choleric. Give him a larger sphere of action, and his impetuosity will be imposing instead of absurd. It is the mere accident of situation which gives, even for a moment, a ludicrous tinge to his proceedings.

Uncle Toby, on the contrary, would be even more of a humourist as a general on the battle-field than in his mimic sieges on the bowling-green. The humour is in his very marrow, not in his surroundings; and the reason is that Sterne feels what every genuine humourist feels, and what, indeed, it is his main function to express – a strong sense of the irony of fate, of the queer mixture of good and bad, of the heroic and the ludicrous, of this world of ours, and of what we may call the perversity of things in general. Whether such a treatment is altogether right and healthy is another question; and most certainly Sterne's view of life is in many respects not only unworthy, but positively base. But it remains true that the deep humourist is finding a voice for one of the most pervading and profound of the sentiments raised in a philosophical observer who is struck by the discords of the universe. Sensitiveness to such discords is one of the marks of a truly reflective intellect, though a humourist suggests one mode of escape from the pain which they cause, whilst a philosophic and religious mind may find another and perhaps a more profound solution.

Now M. Paul Emanuel, admirable and amiable as he is, never carries us into the higher regions of thought. We are told, even ostentatiously, of the narrow prejudices which he shares, though they do not make him harsh and uncharitable. The prejudices were obvious in this case to the creator, because her own happened to be of a different kind. The 'Tory and clergyman's daughter' was rather puzzled by finding that a bigoted Papist with a Jesuit education might still be a good man, and points out conscientiously the defects which she ascribes to his early training. But the mere fact of the narrowness, the want of familiarity with a wider sphere of thought, the acceptance of a narrow code of belief and morality, does not strike her as in itself having either a comic or a melancholy side. M. Paul has the wrong set of prejudices, but is not as wrong as prejudiced; and therefore we feel that a Sterne, or, say, a George Sand, whilst doing equal justice to M. Emanuel's excellent qualities, would have had a feeling (which in her was altogether wanting) of his limitation and his incongruity with the great system of the world. Seen from an intellectual point of view, placed in his due relation to the great currents of thought and feeling of the time, we should have been made to feel the pathetic and humorous aspects of M. Emanuel's character, and he might have been equally a living individual and yet a type of some more general idea. The philosopher might ask, for example, what is the exact value of unselfish heroism guided by narrow theories or employed on unworthy tasks; and the philosophic humourist or artist might embody the answer in a portrait of M. Emanuel considered from a cosmic or a cosmopolitan point of view. From the lower standpoint accessible to Miss Brontë he is still most attractive; but we see only his relations to the little scholastic circle, and have no such perception as the greatest writers would give us of his relations to the universe, or, as the next order would give, of his relations to the great world without.

Although the secret of Miss Brontë's power lies, to a great extent, in the singular force with which she can reproduce acute observations of character from without, her most esoteric teaching, the most accurate reflex from her familiar idiosyncracies, is of course to be found in the characters painted from within. We may infer her personality more or less accurately from the mode in which she contemplates her neighbours, but it is directly manifested in various avatars of her own spirit. Among the characters who are more or less mouthpieces of her peculiar sentiment we may reckon not only Lucy Snowe and Jane Eyre, but, to some extent, Shirley, and, even more decidedly, Rochester. When they speak we are really listening to her own voice, though it is more or less disguised in conformity to dramatic necessity. There are great differences between them; but they are such differences as would exist between members of the same family, or might be explained by change of health or internal circumstances. Jane Eyre has not had such bitter experience as Lucy Snowe; Shirley is generally Jane Eyre in high spirits, and freed from harassing anxiety; and Rochester is really a spirited sister of Shirley's, though he does his very best to be a man, and even an unusually masculine specimen of his sex.

Mr Rochester, indeed, has imposed upon a good many people; and he is probably responsible in part for some of the muscular heroes who have appeared since his time in the world of fiction. I must, however, admit that, in spite of some opposing authority, he does not appear to me to be a real character at all, except as a reflection of a certain side of his creator. He is in reality the personification of a true woman's longing (may one say it now?) for a strong master.[1] But the knowledge is wanting. He is a very bold but necessarily unsuccessful attempt at an impossibility. The parson's daughter did not really know anything about the class of which he is supposed to be a type, and he remains vague and inconsistent in spite of all his vigour. He is intended to be a person who has surfeited from the fruit of the tree of knowledge, and addresses the inexperienced governess from the height – or depth – of his worldly wisdom. And he really knows just as little of the world as she does. He has to impose upon her by giving an account of his

[1]The point is developed by Peter Bayne in 1881; see No. 110, p. 429 n.

adventures taken from the first novel at hand of the early Bulwer school, or a diluted recollection of Byron. There is not a trace of real cynicism – of the strong nature turned sour by experience – in his whole conversation. He is supposed to be specially simple and masculine, and yet he is as self-conscious as a young lady on her first appearance in society, and can do nothing but discourse about his feelings, and his looks, and his phrenological symptoms, to his admiring hearer. Set him beside any man's character of a man, and one feels at once that he has no real solidity or vitality in him. He has, of course, strong nerves and muscles, but those are articles which can be supplied in unlimited quantities with little expense to the imagination. Nor can one deny that his conduct to Miss Eyre is abominable. If he had proposed to her to ignore the existence of the mad Mrs Rochester, he would have acted like a rake, but not like a sneak. But the attempt to entrap Jane into a bigamous connection by concealing the wife's existence, is a piece of treachery for which it is hard to forgive him. When he challenges the lawyer and the clergyman to condemn him after putting themselves in his place, their answer is surely obvious. One may take a lenient view of a man who chooses by his own will to annul his marriage to a filthy lunatic; but he was a knave for trying to entrap a defenceless girl by a mock ceremony. He puts himself in a position in which the contemptible Mr Mason has a moral advantage.

This is by far the worst blot in Miss Brontë's work, and may partly explain, though it cannot justify, the harsh criticisms made at the time. It is easy now to win a cheap reputation for generosity by trampling upon the dead bodies of the luckless critics who blundered so hopelessly. The time for anger is past; and mere oblivion is the fittest doom for such offenders. Inexperience, and consequently inadequate appreciation of the demands of the situation, was Miss Brontë's chief fault in this matter, and most certainly not any want of true purity and moral elevation. But the fact that she, in whom an instinctive nobility of spirit is, perhaps, the most marked characteristic, should have given scandal to the respectable, is suggestive of another inference. What, in fact, is the true significance of this singular strain of thought and feeling, which puts on various and yet closely-allied forms in the three remarkable novels we have been considering? It displays itself at one moment in some vivid description, or – for 'description' seems too faint a word – some forcible presentation to our mind's eye of a fragment of moorland scenery; at another, it appears as an ardently sympathetic portrayal of some trait of character at once vigorous and tender;

then it utters itself in a passionate soliloquy, which establishes the fact that its author possessed the proverbial claim to knowledge of the heavenly powers; or again, it produces one of those singular little prose-poems – such as Shirley's description of Eve – which, with all their force, have just enough flavour of the 'devoirs' at M. Heger's establishment to suggest that they are the work of an inspired school-girl. To gather up into a single formula the meaning of such a character as Lucy Snowe, or, in other words, of Charlotte Brontë, is, of course, impossible. But at least such utterances always give the impression of a fiery soul imprisoned in too narrow and too frail a tenement. The fire is pure and intense. It is kindled in a nature intensely emotional, and yet aided by a heroic sense of duty. The imprisonment is not merely that of a feeble body in uncongenial regions, but that of a narrow circle of thought, and consequently of a mind which has never worked itself clear by reflection, or developed a harmonious and consistent view of life. There is a certain feverish disquiet which is marked by the peculiar mannerism of the style. At its best, we have admirable flashes of vivid expression, where the material of language is the incarnation of keen intuitive thought. At its worst, it is strangely contorted, crowded by rather awkward personifications, and degenerates towards a rather unpleasant Ossianesque. More severity of taste would increase the power by restraining the abuse. We feel an aspiration after more than can be accomplished, an unsatisfied yearning for potent excitement, which is sometimes more fretful than forcible.

The symptoms are significant of the pervading flaw in otherwise most effective workmanship. They imply what, in a scientific sense, would be an inconsistent theory, and, in an aesthetic sense, an in-harmonious representation of life. One great aim of the writing, explained in the preface to the second edition of *Jane Eyre*, is a protest against conventionality. But the protest is combined with a most un-flinching adherence to the proper conventions of society; and we are left in great doubt as to where the line ought to be drawn. Where does the unlawful pressure of society upon the individual begin, and what are the demands which it may rightfully make upon our respect? At one moment in *Jane Eyre* we seem to be drifting towards the solution that strong passion is the one really good thing in the world, and that all human conventions which oppose it should be disregarded. This was the tendency which shocked the respectable reviewers of the time. Of course they should have seen that the strongest sympathy of the author goes with the heroic self-conquest of the heroine under temptation. She triumphs at the cost of a determined self sacrifice, and undoubtedly we are meant to sympathize with the martyr. Yet it is also true that we are left with the sense of an unsolved discord. Sheer stoical regard for duty is represented as something repulsive, however imposing, in the figure of St John Rivers, and virtue is rewarded by the arbitrary removal of the obstacles which made it unpleasant. What would Jane Eyre have done, and what would our sympathies have been, had she found that Mrs Rochester had not been burnt in the fire at Thornfield? That is rather an awkward question. Duty is supreme, seems to be the moral of the story; but duty sometimes involves a strain almost too hard for mortal faculties.

If in the conflict between duty and passion the good so often borders upon the impracticable, the greatest blessing in the world should be a will powerful enough to be an inflexible law for itself under all pressure of circumstances. Even a will directed to evil purposes has a kind of royal prerogative, and we may rightly do it homage. That seems to be the seminal thought in *Wuthering Heights*, that strange book to which we can hardly find a parallel in our literature, unless in such works as the *Revenger's Tragedy*, and some other crude but startling productions of the Elizabethan dramatists. But Emily Brontë's feeble grasp of external facts makes her book a kind of baseless nightmare, which we read with wonder and with distressing curiosity, but with even more pain than pleasure or profit. Charlotte's mode of conceiving the problem is given most fully in *Villette*, the book of which one can hardly say, with a recent critic, that it represents her 'ripest wisdom,'[1] but which seems to give her best solution of the great problem of life. Wisdom, in fact, is not the word to apply to a state of mind which seems to be radically inconsistent and tentative. The spontaneous and intense affection of kindred and noble natures is the one really precious thing in life, it seems to say; and, so far, the thought is true, or a partial aspect of the truth; and the high feeling undeniable. But then, the author seems to add, such happiness is all but chimerical. It falls to the lot only of a few exceptional people, upon whom fortune or Providence has delighted to shower its gifts. To all others life is either a wretched grovelling business, an affair of making money and gratifying sensuality, or else it is a prolonged martyrdom. Yield to your feelings, and the chances are enormously great that you are trampled upon by the selfish, or that you come into collision with some of those con-

[1] See T. W. Reid on *Villette*, '. . . a great masterpiece, destined to hold its own among the ripest and finest fruits of English genius' (*Charlotte Brontë*, (1877) 127–8).

ventions which must be venerated, for they are the only barriers against moral degradation, and which yet somehow seem to make in favour of the cruel and the self-seeking. The only safe plan is that of the lady in the ballad, to 'lock your heart in a case of gold, and pin it with a silver pin.' Mortify your affections, scourge yourself with rods, and sit in sackcloth and ashes; stamp vigorously upon the cruel thorns that strew your pathway, and learn not to shrink, when they lacerate the most tender flesh. Be an ascetic, in brief, and yet without the true aim of the ascetic. For, unlike him, you must admit that these affections are precisely the best part of you, and that the offers of the Church, which proposes to wean you from the world and reward you by a loftier prize, are a delusion and a snare. They are the lessons of a designing priesthood, and imply a blasphemy against the most divine instincts of human nature.

This is the unhappy discord which runs through Miss Brontë's conceptions of life, and whilst it gives an indescribable pathos to many pages, leaves us with a sense of something morbid and unsatisfactory. She seems to be turning for relief alternately to different teachers, to the promptings of her own heart, to the precepts of those whom she has been taught to revere, and occasionally, though timidly and tentatively, to alien schools of thought. The attitude of mind is, indeed, best indicated by the story (a true story, like most of her incidents) of her visit to the confessional in Brussels. Had she been a Catholic, or a Positivist, or a rebel against all the creeds, she might have reached some consistency of doctrine, and therefore some harmony of design. As it is, she seems to be under a desire which makes her restless and unhappy, because her best impulses are continually warring against each other. She is between the opposite poles of duty and happiness, and cannot see how to reconcile their claims, or even – for perhaps no one can solve that or any other great problem exhaustively – how distinctly to state the question at issue. She pursues one path energetically, till she feels herself to be in danger, and then shrinks with a kind of instinctive dread, and resolves not only that life is a mystery, but that happiness must be sought by courting misery. Undoubtedly such a position speaks of a mind diseased, and a more powerful intellect would even under her conditions have worked out some more comprehensible and harmonious solution.

For us, however, it is allowable to interpret her complaints in our own fashion, whatever it may be. We may give our own answer to the dark problem, or at least indicate the path by which an answer must be reached. For a poor soul so grievously beset within and without by troubles in which we all have a share, we can but feel the strongest sympathy. We cannot sit at her feet as a great teacher, nor admit that her view of life is satisfactory, or even intelligible. But we feel for her as for a fellow-sufferer who has at least felt with extraordinary keenness the sorrows and disappointments which torture most cruelly the most noble virtues, and has clung throughout her troubles to beliefs which must in some form or other be the guiding lights of all worthy actions. She is not in the highest rank amongst those who have fought their way to a clearer atmosphere, and can help us to clearer conceptions; but she is among the first of those who have felt the necessity of consolation, and therefore stimulated to more successful efforts.

110. Peter Bayne on the Brontës

1881

From *Two Great Englishwomen: Mrs Browning and Charlotte Brontë* (1881). Contains copiously detailed discussions of Charlotte and Emily, extensively revised from his earlier study of 1857 (No. 93). Some representative extracts are given here, notably his new analysis of Emily Brontë's metaphysical beliefs (see No. 93 and Introduction, p. 45) and his attempt to assess the relative literary standing of the three sisters.

I have never changed the opinion, formed and expressed by me many years ago, that the poems of Emily Brontë excel those of her sisters. They are superior in occasional splendour and concentrated force of expression; in serene intensity; in penetration and power of thought. Take as a sample of her gift of expression the following poem.

[quotes 'Stars']

Lovely also, with a grave, high solemn loveliness, especially towards its close, is the poem entitled 'A Death Scene'.

['Oh day, he cannot die . . .']

But the most important of Emily Brontë's poems – the most original in thought, the most powerful in imagination, the most intensely sincere and impassioned in feeling – is one too vaguely called *The Philosopher*. It consists of an interchange of confidences between two sages, or two personified moods of the same sage, on the question of questions, – God or no God? The one sage believes; the other, to say the least, hesitates. The second sage has the last word, and this appears to show that the position he takes up is adopted by the author. Let us hear first the believing sage.

> I saw a Spirit, standing, man,
>> Where thou dost stand – an hour ago,
> And round his feet three rivers ran,
>> Of equal depth and equal flow –
> A golden stream – and one of blood –
>> And one of sapphire seemed to be;
> But when they joined their triple flood
>> It tumbled in an inky sea.
> The Spirit sent his dazzling gaze
>> Down through that ocean's gloomy night;
> Then, kindling all, with sudden blaze,
>> The glad deep sparkled wide and bright –
> White as the sun, far, far more fair
> Than its divided sources were!

Such is the statement of his experience, such the profession of his faith, by the believer in God. Observe the imaginative grandeur, combined with intellectual subtlety, of the similitude made use of. Every painter knows that the three primitive colours, red, yellow, blue – here represented by blood, gold, and sapphire – yield, when mingled, an 'inky', or, at least, brown-black tint. Yet out of those same colours, linked in celestial harmony, arises the pure white light. The seer, the proclaimer of faith in God, avers that, while he looked upon the colours mixing in the blackness of chaos – the blackness of matter – the blackness of an universal inky ocean unvisited by light – he saw a Spirit send from His eye an irradiating beam, which turned blackness

into beauty and night into day, kindling the universe with sudden
blaze of order, life, and joy. That Spirit was God.

To have devised and worked out a conception like this would have
satisfied almost any woman-poet that ever lived; but it is only the
prelude to what Emily Brontë has to say. She has uttered the challenge:
now for the reply. It is the philosophical sceptic, the representative of
earnest doubt, that speaks.

> And even for that Spirit, seer,
>   I've watched and sought my lifetime long;
> Sought Him in heaven, hell, earth, and air,
>   An endless search, and always wrong.
> Had I but seen His glorious eye
>   *Once* light the clouds that wilder me,
> I ne'er had raised this coward cry
>   To cease to think and cease to be;
> I ne'er had called oblivion blest,
>   Nor, stretching eager hands to death,
> Implored to change for senseless rest
>   This sentient soul, this living breath.
> Oh, let me die! – that power and will
>   Their cruel strife may close;
> And conquered good, and conquering ill,
>   Be lost in one repose!

To this Emily Brontë gives no answer. By all rules of interpretation,
the speaker must be held to stand for the poet. It seems, therefore, to be
Emily Brontë who, deliberately and intensely, but without the
remotest suggestion of irreverence, affirms that she has looked for the
Spirit announced by the seer who spoke first, and has not seen Him.
One glimpse, she says, would have been enough, but that one glimpse
she did not obtain; and in colossal sincerity, though with unspeakable
distress, she turns to the universe, which is for her a grave, and accepts
the eternal death that is her portion. Whether it is in the mere dramatic
sympathy of an artist that Emily Brontë puts words into the mouth
of the philosopher; or whether the words are her own, and reveal a
secret that might throw some light on her stern, reserved, ungenial
existence, and on the mood of mind in which *Wuthering Heights* was
composed; – I shall not undertake to decide.

I confess, however, that I look upon the second of these hypotheses
as in a high degree probable. The verses come, if ever verses came, from

the heart, and I cannot help thinking that the fire within them searched with its burnings the soul of Emily Brontë. Charlotte, I fancy, never fathomed the depths of her sister's mind. At all events, the girl who wrote these stanzas had uttered the last and deepest word that has been spoken, or can rationally be spoken, by modern doubt ...

Wuthering Heights is one of the most remarkable of all the Brontë books ... The secret of her life, if we may read that secret in the terrible poem which I attempted to analyze, is to be discerned between the lines of the novel. The purport of the poem is that Emily Brontë had searched the universe for God, and that God had never, by so much as one glimpse of His eye, revealed Himself to her. The burden of *Wuthering Heights* is the potency of evil – its potency to pervert good. Old Mr Earnshaw does a deed of kindness – relieves the helpless, shelters the homeless – and thus brings a fiend in human shape into his house. Emily Brontë, with a strange reserve of power in so young an artist, generally covers up her secret; but she is vividly conscious of her own meaning, and sometimes lets us have more than a hint of it. 'It's a cuckoo's, sir,' answers Nelly Dean, when Lockwood asks her what is Heathcliff's history. Now the ways of the cuckoo are deeply suggestive. The green-finch builds her nest in the hedge, and lays her eggs; the cuckoo comes and inserts her egg among the rest; and if you go and look six weeks afterwards, you find that the young cuckoo has utterly dispossessed the young finches, by way of thanks to their mother for giving it a warm place, while still unfledged, among her eggs ... This is one of those mysterious facts which are not usually mentioned by preachers when expatiating on the bounty and beneficence of nature, but which, at a time when nature-worship is fashionable, ought not to be overlooked. Heathcliff, the little castaway Lascar, or gipsy, whom Mr Earnshaw picked out of the gutter in Liverpool and brought home, was the human cuckoo of Wuthering Heights. In like manner, the hospitable deed of Mr and Mrs Linton, of Thrushcross Grange, in sheltering Catherine Earnshaw, leading, as it did, to an intimacy between the families of the Heights and of the Grange, brought sorrow and death to their offspring.

Strange and appalling thesis to be expounded by an English girl! In the *Iliad* it is of tyrannic rapacity on the one hand, and proud resentment and moody wrath on the other, that the curse is born whence spring unnumbered woes. In the great Greek tragedies it is sin always that is the fountain-head of sorrow ... In the tremendous tragedy of *Lear* ... it is from folly and lawless passion that the subsequent blighting of the earth and blackening of the heavens proceed. But in *Wuthering Heights* the root of pain and misery is goodness, and the world in which we move seems God-forsaken. And yet – this can, I think, be proved – the tale is told without violation of natural possibility. That is to say, we are always made aware of the means by which good is neutralized or perverted and the triumph of evil prepared. Herein is displayed the consummate skill of the author; while at the same time the main doctrine of the book, that there is no over-ruling Divine force to be counted on to 'make for' righteousness, or for those who work righteousness, is fearfully illustrated.

It is not indeed wholly without glimpses of joy and brightness ... There is much tenderness, as well as sense of the wild joy of the moors, in the loving inspection and enumeration of the feathers of moorland birds drawn from her pillow by Cathy Linton on her death-bed. Sometimes the darkness is dispersed, like mist by a sudden burst of sunlight, and the joy breaks out in a loud, ringing, lark-like song of gladness, as in that admirable passage where the younger Catherine gives an account of the dispute which she and her boy-lover had as to the best way of imagining happiness and heaven [chapter 24] ... It is not, however, too much to say that there is only enough brightness in *Wuthering Heights* to bring out the gloom of the book in its deepest murky glow ... *Wuthering Heights* ... is a work of great genius, but of genius reared within sight of graves, and amid the winds and mists of the moorland. The morbid and maddening affection with which Heathcliff and Catherine cling to each other was exactly such an affection, so intense, so unreasonable, so original, as that with which Emily Brontë clung to Haworth ... The book cannot be pronounced a good or a wholesome book. It exaggerates the evil that is in the world, for it does not show the light in due proportion to the darkness. If Haworth Parsonage, beside its graves, moaned around by the wind of the moors, were all the world, then might the gloom of *Wuthering Heights* be accepted for the atmosphere of the planet. But it is not so; and the best that can be said for the book is that it is the product of marvellous genius that never freely and genially expanded ... that seems to have watched, and wailed, and waited for God, and yet never *once* saw His eye light up the 'wildering clouds' above and around ... Against this, however, we must in fairness set the fact, that the execution of *Wuthering Heights* is singularly mature – the style such as practised and consummate writers use, the sentiment free of young-mannish bravura, and, still more, of a young-womanish syllabub. The author never seems for one moment to lose her self-possession and self-command. Had Shakespeare written *Lear* before he was thirty, and died, we should have had a right to believe that he took a pessimistic view of life . . .

It is, however, the sunny book – above all, it is the sunny novel – that the world most cordially takes to; and we may doubt whether Emily Brontë's name would ever have obtained a place in the chronicles of English literature, if the more buoyant and happy genius of her sister had not . . . drawn all eyes to the wonder that had appeared somewhere among the Yorkshire hills.

Mr Wemyss Reid seems to me to be correct in deciding that the main determining incident in Charlotte's life was not the death of her brother, but her own residence, at two successive periods in Brussels . . .

Of her experience in Brussels, Charlotte Brontë availed herself in the composition of two novels, her first and her last – *The Professor* and *Villette*. Critics have loudly praised *Villette*, and I do not recollect seeing anything in commendation of *The Professor*; but I own to finding it a stiffer business to read the later than the earlier book. *The Professor*, I make bold to say, has not received due appreciation. It is by no means a wonderful book, but it has signal merits. Nothing could be more sharp than the chiselling of the characters, which are neither uninteresting nor commonplace, and the story is full of life. Hunsden is unmistakably a first sketch of the Yorke of *Shirley*, and the school scenes, though not so carefully elaborated as those in *Villette*, are, to my thinking, more fresh, and, in general respects, about as good. Frances, of *The Professor*, is perhaps somewhat too commonplace for a heroine: but not even a critic has, to my knowledge, been found who could care for the Lucy Snowe of *Villette* . . . Charlotte Brontë, when writing of Miss Austen, seems to be quite aware that the novelist must have suitable materials if he is to succeed. She complains that, in *Pride and Prejudice*, we have 'a carefully-fenced, highly-cultivated garden, with neat borders and delicate flowers; but no glance of a bright, vivid physiognomy, no open country, no fresh air, no blue hill, no bonny beck.'[1] And what have we in *Villette*? The routine of what Mrs Gaskell calls a 'pension' – the schoolrooms and dwelling-rooms and fine gardens of an educational establishment in Brussels. It must be confessed that the interest of mankind in education, as a subject of entertainment, is limited . . . And then the charm at which Charlotte so felicitously hints – the charm of blue hill and bonny beck,

[1] See Introduction, p. 24.

of woods and moors, and craggy heathery dells – the charm whose fascination is so pervasively felt in *Jane Eyre* and *Shirley*, is absent in *Villette* . . .

But it was France that lighted the torch of Charlotte's genius. After being partly educated in England, and serving some time, with in-domitable energy, as a governess, she went to Brussels, and came under the influence of M. Heger. He saw the powers of her mind, encouraged her in composition, taught her to sharpen and burnish her French *devoirs*, and thus prepared her to make her *début* as an English author in one of the most nervous, terse, and brilliant styles in the whole range of English prose – a style with no fault except a certain uniformity, a too sustained alertness and trenchancy, – a style quite perfect as a music of battle and of march, but far less adapted than some styles, notably than the style of Thackeray, to express the sauntering moods, to suit the meditative hours, that will not fail to occur in our earthly pilgrimage. One cannot think without a smile of the immense part played by M. Heger and her Brussels residence in the history of Charlotte Brontë. Choleric yet good-hearted, highly intelligent yet not without moodiness and whimsicality, M. Heger displayed that 'force du caractère recouvrant une vibrante tendresse,' that combination of masculine strength with feminine tenderness, which M. Eugène Forçade, in his admirable critique on *Shirley*, declares to be irresistibly attractive to women, and which is the keynote of all Charlotte Brontë's characteristic heroes. In her first and last books – the *Professor* and *Villette* – the scene is principally laid in a Brussels school; and in *Shirley* she puts Flemish blood into the veins of the brothers Moore, and avails herself of the opportunity thus offered her of airing her French. In *Villette* there is more French than belongs legitimately to an English novel.

It is beautiful, however, to see how the genial, brave, and healthy nature of our Yorkshire girl takes what is good, and rejects all that is evil, in the influence of the Continent and of France . . .

I have spoken of Emily Brontë as a woman of, in some sense, more wonderful and original genius than that of her sister. Charlotte has not left anything evincing such subtle, far-brought, and magical power as the group of Heathcliff and Cathy, nor had her intellectual glance, in the last resort, the same penetrating finality as Emily's; and she herself agreed with all the best judges in awarding the palm of poetic superiority to Ellis Bell. Nevertheless, it is Charlotte that must be pronounced, on the whole, the chief of the sisters . . . Charlotte stands between Emily and Anne, the mean between two extremes. Emily was hard – too hard. In her books and in her life she lacked expansion and geniality. She was unhealthy, with deficient stamina, a circumstance quite compatible with spasmodic and contracted strength. She has left little, and that little imperfect; and yet it may be doubted whether, if she had lived, she would have done much more or much better; for there is hardly a trace of youngness in her work. Anne, though also a woman of unquestionable genius, fell short in force ... Charlotte had ten times the power of Anne, and her nature was more healthy and genial, her culture more comprehensive, than Emily's. On the whole, therefore, we must, I repeat, assign her the first place among the sisters.

111. A. Mary F. Robinson, 'The Origin of *Wuthering Heights*'

1883

From *Emily Brontë* (1883), the first full-length biography, written
with the help of information supplied by Ellen Nussey which
helped to correct the grim image of Emily in Mrs Gaskell's *Life*
(Introduction, p. 36); Ellen Nussey was dissatisfied with the result
though the book was well received (*LL*, iv, 281–3) and inspired
Swinburne's seminal essay (No. 112).

Agnes Mary Frances Robinson, later Darmesteter, later Duclaux
(1857–1944), was a hugely prolific writer and had already produced
two volumes of verse and several stories and critical studies (*LL*,
iv, 268). The extracts below are taken from chapters 12 ('Writing
Poetry') and 14 (*'Wuthering Heights:* its origin'; chapter 15 contains a detailed analysis of the story). The author's speculations
about the origins of *Wuthering Heights* succeed a recapitulation of
Emily's restricted range of experience at Haworth and a *resumé*
of Charlotte's views concerning the independent workings of
Emily's imagination (No. 81).

The Poems

These poems with their surplus of imagination, their instinctive music
and irregular rightness of form, their sweeping impressiveness, effects
of landscape, their scant allusions to dogma or perfidious man, are,
indeed, not at all like the poetry women generally write. The hand that
painted this single line,

> The dim moon struggling in the sky,

should have shaken hands with Coleridge. The voice might have sung
in concert with Blake that sang this single bit of a song:

> Hope was but a timid friend;
> She sat without the grated den,

Watching how my fate would tend,
　Even as selfish-hearted men.

She was cruel in her fear;
　Through the bars, one dreary day,
I looked out to see her there,
　And she turned her face away!

Had the poem ended here it would have been perfect, but it and many more of these lyrics have the uncertainty of close that usually marks early work. Often incoherent, too, the pictures of a dream rapidly succeeding each other without logical connection; yet scarcely marred by the incoherence, since the effect they seek to produce is not an emotion, not a conviction, but an impression of beauty, or horror, or ecstacy. The uncertain outlines are bathed in a vague golden air of imagination, and are shown to us with the magic touch of a Coleridge, a Leopardi – the touch which gives a mood, a scene, with scarce an obvious detail of either mood or scene.

[quotes 'The Philosopher'] . . .

Some semblance of coherence may, no doubt, be given to this poem by making the three first and the last stanzas to be spoken by the questioner, and the fourth by the philosopher. Even so, the subject has little charm. What we care for is the surprising energy with which the successive images are projected, the earnest ring of the verse, the imagination which invests all its changes. . . . The finest songs, the most peculiarly her own, are all of defiance and mourning, moods so natural to her that she seems to scarcely need the intervention of words in their confession. The wild, melancholy, and elevating music of which Charlotte wisely speaks is strong . . . in such verses as the following.

[quotes 'Death! that struck . . .']

A finer poem yet is 'Remembrance', written two years later, in the March of 1845 . . . It has vital passion in it; though it can scarcely be personal passion, since, 'fifteen wild Decembers' before 1845, Emily Brontë was a girl of twelve years old, companionless, save for still living sisters, Branwell, her aunt, and the vicarage servants. Here, as elsewhere . . . the creative instinct reveals itself in imagining emotions and not characters. The artist has supplied the passion of the lover.

Throughout the book one recognizes the capacity for producing something finer and quite different from what is here produced; one recognizes so much, but not the author of *Wuthering Heights*. Grand impressions of mood and landscape reveal a remarkably receptive artistic temperament; splendid and vigorous movement of lines shows that the artist is a poet. Then we are in a *cul-de-sac*. There is no hint of what kind of poet – too reserved to be consistently lyric, there is not sufficient evidence of the dramatic faculty to help us on to the true scent. All we can say is that we have before us a mind capable of very complete and real illusions, haunted by imagination, always fantastic, and often terrible; a temperament reserved, fearless and brooding; a character of great strength and ruggedness, extremely tenacious of impressions. We must call in Monsieur Taine and his *Milieu* to account for *Wuthering Heights*.

No human being is wholly free, none wholly independent, of surroundings. And Emily Brontë least of all could claim such immunity. We can with difficulty just imagine her a prosperous heiress, loving and loved, high-spirited and even hoydenish; but with her cavalier fantasy informed by a gracious splendour all her own, we can just imagine Emily Brontë as Shirley Keeldar, but scarcely Shirley Keeldar writing *Wuthering Heights*. Emily Brontë away from her moors, her loneliness, her poverty, her discipline, her companionship with genius, violence and degradation, would have taken another colour, as hydrangeas grow now red, now blue, according to the nature of the soil. It was not her lack of knowledge of the world that made the novel she wrote become *Wuthering Heights*, not her inexperience, but rather her experience, limited and perverse, indeed, and specialized by a most singular temperament, yet close and very real. Her imagination was as much inspired by the circumstances of her life, as was Anne's when she wrote the *Tenant of Wildfell Hall*, or Charlotte's in her masterpiece *Villette*; but, as in each case the imagination was of a different quality, experience, acting upon it, produced a distinct and dissimilar result; a result obtained no less by the contrariety than by the harmony of circumstance. For our surroundings affect us in two ways; subtly and permanently, tinging us through and through as wine tinges water,[1] or, by some violent neighbourhood of antipathetic force, sending us off at a tangent as far as possible from the antagonistic presence that so

---

[1] Echoing Catherine Earnshaw's 'dreams that have stayed with me ever after, and changed my ideas; they've gone through and through me like wine through water, and altered the colour of my mind' (chapter 9).

detestably environs us. The fact that Charlotte Brontë knew chiefly clergymen is largely responsible for *Shirley*, that satirical eulogy of the Church and apotheosis of Sunday-school teachers. But Emily, living in this same clerical evangelistic atmosphere, is revolted, forced to the other extreme; and, while sheltering her true opinions from herself under the all-embracing term 'Broad Church,'[1] we find in her writings no belief so strong as the belief in the present use and glory of life; no love so great as her love for earth – earth the mother and grave; no assertion of immortality, but a deep certainty of rest. There is no note so often struck in all her work, and struck with such variety of emphasis, as this: that good for goodness' sake is desirable, evil for evil's sake is detestable, and that for the just and the unjust alike there is rest in the grave.

This quiet clergyman's daughter, always hearing evil of Dissenters, has therefore from pure courage and revolted justice become a dissenter herself. A dissenter in more ways than one. Never was a nature more sensitive to the stupidities and narrowness of conventional opinion, a nature more likely to be found in the ranks of the opposition ... What, then, would this inexperienced Yorkshire parson's daughter reveal? The unlikeness of life to the authorized pictures of life; the force of evil, only conquerable by the slow-revolving process of nature which admits not the eternal duration of the perverse; the grim and fearful lessons of heredity; the sufficiency of the finite to the finite, of life to life, with no other reward than the conduct of life fulfils to him that lives; the all-penetrating kinship of living things, heather-sprig, singing lark, confident child, relentless tyrant; and, not least to her already in its shadow, the sure and universal peace of death.

A strange evangel from such a preacher; but a faith evermore emphasized and deeper rooted in Emily's mind by her incapacity to acquiesce in the stiff, pragmatic teaching, the narrow prejudice, of the Calvinists of Haworth ... Nevertheless, so dual-natured is the force of environment, this antagonistic faith ... did not send her out from it before she had assimilated some of its sternest tenets. From this doctrine of reward and punishment she learned that for every unchecked evil tendency there is a fearful expiation; though she placed it not indeed in the flames of hell, but in the perverted instincts of our own

---

[1] Perhaps inferred from conversations with Ellen Nussey. The single recorded comment by Emily Brontë on religious belief is preserved by Mary Taylor, 'I said that [the question of my religion[[was between God and me; – Emily ... exclaimed, "That's right". This was all I ever heard Emily say on religious subjects' (*LL*, i, 137).

children. Terrible theories of doomed incurable sin and predestined loss warned her that an evil stock will only beget contamination: the children of the mad must be liable to madness; the children of the depraved, bent towards depravity; the seed of the poison-plant springs up to blast and ruin, only to be overcome by uprooting and sterilization, or by the judicious grafting, the patient training of many years . . .

No use, she seems to be saying, in waiting for the children of evil parents to grow, of their own will and unassisted, straight and noble. The very quality of their will is as inherited as their eyes and hair. Heathcliff is no fiend or goblin; the untrained doomed child of some half-savage sailor's holiday, violent and treacherous. And how far shall we hold the sinner responsible for a nature which is itself the punishment of some forefather's crime. Even for such there must be rest. No possibility in the just and reverent mind of Emily Brontë that the God whom she believed to be the very fount and soul of life could condemn to everlasting fire the victims of morbid tendencies not chosen by themselves. No purgatory, and no everlasting flame, is needed to purify the sins of Heathcliff; his grave on the hillside will grow as green as any other spot of grass . . .

So much for the theories of life and evil that the clash of circumstance and character struck out from Emily Brontë. It happened, as we know, that she had occasion to test these theories; and but for that she could never have written *Wuthering Heights*. Not that the story, the conception, would have failed. After all there is nothing more appalling in the violent history of that upland farm than many a midland manor set thick in elms, many a wild country-house of Wales or Cornwall could unfold. Stories more socially painful than the mere brute violence of the Earnshaws; of madness and treachery, stories of girls entrapped unwillingly into a lunatic marriage that the estate might have an heir; legends of fearful violence, of outcast children, dishonoured wives, horrible and persistent evil. . . .[1] Emily, with all this eerie lore at her finger-ends, would have the less difficulty in combining and working the separate motives into a consistent whole, that she did not know the real people whose histories she knew by heart. No memory of individual manner, dominance or preference for an individual type, caught and disarranged her theories, her conception being the completer from

[1] Cf. Swinburne's letter to T. W. Reid of 24 September 1877, recording the impressions of his correspondent from Westmorland who admired *Wuthering Heights* and 'had known wilder instances of lawless and law-defying passion and tyranny, far more horrible than any cruelty of Heathcliff's in her own immediate neighbourhood' (*LL*, ii, 279–80).

her ignorance. This much her strong reason and her creative power enabled her to effect. But this is not all . . . Branwell, who sat to Anne sorrily enough for the portrait of Henry Huntingdon, served his sister, Emily, not indeed as a model, a thing to copy, but as a chart of proportions by which to measure, and to which to refer, for correct investiture, the inspired idea. Mr Wemyss Reid (whose great knowledge of the Brontë history and still greater kindness in admitting me to his advantages as much as might be, I cannot sufficiently acknowledge) – this capable critic perceives a *bona fide* resemblance between the character of Heathcliff and the character of Branwell Brontë as he appeared to his sister Emily. So much, bearing in mind the verse concerning the leveret,[1] I own I cannot see. Branwell seems to me more nearly akin to Heathcliff's miserable son than to Heathcliff. But that, in depicting Heathcliff's outrageous thwarted love for Catharine, Emily did draw upon her experience of her brother's suffering, this extract from an unpublished lecture of Mr Reid's will sufficiently reveal . . .

Has it not been said over and over again by critics of every kind that *Wuthering Heights* reads like the dream of an opium-eater? And here we find that during the whole time of the writing of the book an habitual and avowed opium-eater was at Emily's elbow. . .[2] Whole pages of the story are filled with the ravings and ragings of the villain against the man whose life stands between him and the woman he loves. Similar ravings are to be found in all the letters of Branwell Brontë written as this period of his career; and we may be sure that similar ravings were always on his lips as, moody and more than half mad, he wandered about the rooms of the parsonage at Haworth . . . In one of his own letters there are these words in reference to the object of his passion: 'My own life without her will be hell. What can the so-called love of her wretched sickly husband be to her compared with mine?' Now, turn to *Wuthering Heights* and you will read these words: 'Two words would comprehend my future – death and hell; existence after losing her would be hell. Yet I was a fool to fancy for a moment that she valued Edgar Linton's attachment more than mine. If he loved with all the powers of his puny being, he couldn't love in eighty years as much as I could in a day.' [chapter 14]

So much share in *Wuthering Heights* Branwell certainly had. He was a page of the book in which his sister studied . . .

To the three favouring circumstances of Emily's masterpiece, which we have already mentioned – the neighbourhood of her home, the

---

[1] See, 'Well, some may hate and some may scorn . . .', stanzas 4–5.
[2] Branwell's addiction to opium is discussed in Margaret Lane's *The Brontë Story* (1953), 101–2.

character of her disposition, the quality of her experience – a fourth must be added, inferior in degree, and yet not absolutely unimportant. This is her acquaintance with German literature, and especially with Hoffmann's tales ...[1]

Of the materialistic influence of Italy, of atheist Shelley, Byron with his audacity and realism, sensuous Keats, she would have little experience in her remote parsonage. And, had she known them, they would probably have made no impression on a nature only susceptible to kindred influences. Thackeray, her sister's hero, might have never lived for all the trace of him we find in Emily's writings; never is there any single allusion in her work to the most eventful period of her life, that sight of the lusher fields and taller elms of middle England; that glimpse of hurrying vast London; that night on the river, the sun slipping behind the masts, doubly large through the mist and smoke in which the houses, bridges, ships are all spectral and dim. No hint of this, nor of the sea, nor of Belgium, with its quaint foreign life; nor yet of that French style and method so carefully impressed upon her by Monsieur Heger, and which so decidedly moulded her elder sister's art. But in the midst of her business at Haworth we catch a glimpse of her reading her German book at night, as she sits on the hearthrug with her arm round Keeper's neck ... to her the study of German was not – like French and music – the mere necessary acquirement of a governess, but an influence that entered her mind and helped to shape the fashion of her thoughts.

So much preface is necessary to explain, not the genius of Emily Brontë, but the conditions of that genius.

[1] See above, p. 376, n.

112. Swinburne on Emily Brontë, *Athenaeum*

16 June 1883, 762–3

Reprinted in *Miscellanies*, 1895.

Designed as a review of Mary Robinson's *Emily Brontë* (No. 111) and the most influential critical essay about Emily Brontë to appear since the 1850s. For Swinburne's emphasis on the 'poetic' qualities of *Wuthering Heights*, see further Introduction, pp. 17, 44–5 and for his early enthusiasm for both Charlotte and Emily see his letter to T. W. Reid of 24 September 1877 (written after his own 'Note' [No. 108] and part quoted above, p. 435, n.),

From the first hour when as a schoolboy I read *Jane Eyre* and *Wuthering Heights* I have always retained the first intense desire I felt then to know all that I might or ought to know about the two women who wrote them. The only reference . . . in your book [*Charlotte Brontë* (1877): see No. 107] which seemed to indicate a different point of view from my own was the passage in which you seem to depreciate the tone, if not . . . the merit, of *Wuthering Heights*. . . . Seeing that Emily Brontë was a tragic poet . . . I cannot think that anything in her book is at all excessive or unjustifiable, – And, with all its horror, it is so beautiful, but I must not go off into fresh rhapsodies about 'that dreadful book' [*LL*, ii, 279–80; see above p. 399, n.].

To the England of our own time, it has often enough been remarked, the novel is what the drama was to the England of Shakespeare's. The same general interest produces the same incessant demand for the same inexhaustible supply of imaginative produce, in a shape more suited to the genius of a later day and the conditions of a changed society. Assuming this simple explanation to be sufficient for the obvious fact that in the modern world of English letters the novel is everywhere and the drama is nowhere, we may remark one radical point of difference between the taste of playgoers in the age of Shakespeare and the taste of novel-readers in our own. Tragedy was then at least as popular as either romantic or realistic comedy; whereas nothing would seem to be more unpopular with the run of modern readers than the threatening shadow of tragedy projected across the whole length of a story, inevitable and unmistakable from the lurid harshness of its dawn to the fiery softness of its sunset. The objection to a novel in which the tragic element has an air of incongruity and caprice – in which a tragic surprise is, as it were, sprung upon the reader, with a jarring shock such as might be given by the actual news of some unforeseen and grievous accident – this objection seems to me thoroughly reasonable, grounded on a true critical sense of fitness and unfitness; but the distaste for high and pure tragedy, where the close is in perfect and simple harmony with the opening, seems not less thoroughly pitiable and irrational.

A recent work of singular and admirable power, in which the freshness of humour is as real and vital as the fervour of passion, was at once on its appearance compared with Emily Brontë's now famous story. And certainly not without good cause; for in point of local colour *Mehalah*[1] is, as far as I know, the one other book which can bear and may challenge the comparison. Its pages, for one thing, reflect the sterile glitter and desolate fascination of the salt marshes, their minute splendours and barren beauties and multitudinous monotony of measureless expanse, with the same instinctive and unlaborious accuracy which brings all the moorland before us in a breath when we open any chapter of *Wuthering Heights*. And the humour is even better; and the passion is not less genuine. But the accumulated horrors of the close, however possible in fact, are wanting in the one quality which justifies and ennobles all admissible horror in fiction: they hardly seem inevitable; they lack the impression of logical and moral certitude. All the realism in the world will not suffice to convey this impression; and a work of art which wants it wants the one final and irreplaceable requisite of inner harmony. Now in *Wuthering Heights* this one thing needful is as perfectly and triumphantly attained as in *King Lear* or *The Duchess of Malfi*, in *The Bride of Lammermoor* or *Notre-Dame de Paris*. From the first we breathe the fresh dark air of tragic passion and presage; and to the last the changing wind and flying sunlight are in keeping with the stormy promise of the dawn. There is no monotony, there is no repetition, but there is no discord. This is the first and last necessity, the foundation of all labour and the crown of all success, for a poem worthy of the name; and this it is that distinguishes the hand of Emily from the hand of Charlotte Brontë. All the works of the elder sister are rich in poetic spirit, poetic feeling, and poetic detail; but the younger sister's work is essentially and definitely a poem in the

[1] *Mahalah, a story of the Salt Marshes* (1880), by Sabine Baring-Gould.

fullest and most positive sense of the term. It was therefore all the more proper that the honour of raising a biographical and critical monument to the author of *Wuthering Heights* should have been reserved for a poetess of the next generation to her own. And those who had already in their mind's eye the clearest and most definite conception of Emily Brontë will be the readiest to acknowledge their obligation and express their gratitude to Miss Robinson for the additional light which she has been enabled to throw upon a great and singular character. It is true that when all has been said the main features of that character stand out before us unchanged. The sweet and noble genius of Mrs Gaskell did not enable her to see far into so strange and sublime a problem; but, after all, the main difference between the biographer of Emily and the biographer of Charlotte is that Miss Robinson has been interested and attracted where Mrs Gaskell was scared and perplexed. On one point, however, the new light afforded us is of the very utmost value and interest. We all knew how great was Emily Brontë's tenderness for the lower animals; we find, with surprise as well as admiration, that the range of this charity was so vast as to include even her own miserable brother. Of that lamentable and contemptible caitiff – contemptible not so much for his commonplace debauchery as for his abject selfishness, his lying pretension, and his nerveless cowardice – there is far too much in this memoir . . . but this error is almost atoned for by the revelation that of all the three sisters in that silent home 'it was the silent Emily who had ever a cheering word for Branwell; it was Emily who still remembered that he was her brother, without that remembrance freezing her heart to numbness.'

I cannot however but think that Miss Robinson makes a little too much of the influence exercised on Emily Brontë's work by the bitter, narrow, and ignoble misery of the life which she had watched burn down into such pitiful ruins. . . . The impression of this miserable experience is visible only in Anne Brontë's second work, *The Tenant of Wildfell Hall*; which deserves perhaps a little more notice and recognition than it has ever received. . . . On the other hand, the intelligent reader of *Wuthering Heights* cannot fail to recognize that what he is reading is a tragedy simply because it is the work of a writer whose genius is essentially tragic. Those who believe that Heathcliff was called into existence by the accident that his creator had witnessed the agonies of a violent weakling in love and in disgrace might believe that Shakespeare wrote *King Lear* because he had witnessed the bad effects of parental indulgence, and that Æschylus wrote the *Eumenides* because he had witnessed the uncomfortable results of matricide. The book is what it is because the author was what she was; this is the main and central fact to be remembered. Circumstances have modified the details; they have not implanted the conception.

It is a fine and accurate instinct that has inevitably led Miss Robinson to cite in chosen illustration of the book's quality at its highest those two incomparable pictures of dreamland and delirium[1] which no poet that ever lived has ever surpassed or equalled for passionate and lifelike beauty of imaginative truth. But it is even somewhat less than exact to say that the latter scene 'is given with a masterly pathos that Webster need not have made more strong, nor Fletcher more lovely and appealing.' Fletcher could not have made it as lovely and appealing as it is; he would have made it exquisitely pretty and effectively theatrical; but the depth, the force, the sincerity, recalling here so vividly the 'several forms of distraction' through which Webster's Cornelia passes after the murder of her son by his brother, excel everything else of the kind in imaginative art; not excepting, if truth may be spoken on such a subject, the madness of Ophelia or even of Madge Wildfire ... these two crowning passages could never have been written by any one to whom the motherhood of earth was less than the brotherhood of man – to whom the anguish, the intolerable and mortal yearning, of insatiate and insuppressible homesickness, was less than the bitterest of all other sufferings endurable or conceivable in youth. But in Emily Brontë this passion was twin-born with the passion for truth and rectitude. The stale and futile epithet of Titaness has in this instance a deeper meaning than appears; her goddess mother was in both senses the same who gave birth to the divine martyr of Æschylean legend: Earth under one aspect and one name, but under the other Righteousness. And therefore was the first and last word uttered out of the depth of her nature a cry for that one thing needful without which all virtue is as worthless as all pleasure is vile, all hope as shameful as all faith is abject – a cry for liberty.

And therefore too, perhaps we may say, it is that any seeming confusion or incoherence in her work is merely external and accidental, not inward and spiritual. Belief in the personal or positive immortality of the individual and indivisible spirit was not apparently, in her case, swallowed up or nullified or made nebulous by any doctrine or dream of simple reabsorption into some indefinite infinity of eternal life. So

[1] See Mary Robinson's *Emily Brontë* (1883) 190; the passage prefaces her extract from *Wuthering Heights*, chapter 12, depicting the onset of Catherine's delirium.

at least it seems to me that her last ardent confession of dauntless and triumphant faith should properly be read, however capable certain phrases in it may seem of the vaguer and more impersonalinterpreta- tion ... As an author she has not perhaps even yet received her full due or taken her final place. Again and again has the same obvious objection been taken to that awkwardness of construction or presenta- tion which no reader of *Wuthering Heights* can undertake to deny. But, to judge by the vigour with which this objection is urged, it might be supposed that the rules of narrative observed by all great novelists were of an almost legal or logical strictness and exactitude with regard to probability of detail. Now most assuredly the indirect method of relation through which the story of Heathcliff is conveyed, however unlikely or clumsy it may seem from the realistic point of view,[1] does not make this narrative more liable to the charge of actual impossibility than others of the kind. Defoe still remains the one writer of narrative in the first person who has always kept the stringent law of possibilities before the eye of his invention. Even the admirable ingenuity and the singular painstaking which distinguish the method of Mr Wilkie Collins can only give external and transient plausibility to the record of long conversations overheard or shared in by the narrator only a few hours before the supposed date of the report drawn up from memory. The very greatest masters in their kind, Walter Scott and Charles Dickens, are of all narrators the most superbly regardless of this objection. From *Rob Roy* and *Redgauntlet*, from *David Copper- field* and *Bleak House*, we might select at almost any stage of the auto- biographic record some instance of detail in which the violation of plausibility, probability, or even possibility, is at least as daring and as glaring as any to be found in the narrative of Nelly Dean. Even when that narrative is removed, so to speak, yet one degree further back – even when we are supposed to be reading a minute detail of incident and dialogue transcribed by the hand of the lay figure Mr Lockwood from Nelly Dean's report of the account conveyed to her years ago by Heathcliff's fugitive wife or gadding servant, each invested for the nonce with the peculiar force and distinctive style of the author – even then we are not asked to put such an overwhelming strain on our faculty of imaginative belief as is exacted by the great writer who invites us to accept the report drawn up by Mr Pendennis of everything that takes place – down even to the minutest points of dialogue, accent, and gesture – in the household of the Newcomes or the

[1] See Introduction, pp. 31, 46.

Firmins during the absence no less than in the presence of their friend the reporter. Yet all this we glady and gratefully admit, without demur or cavil, to be thoroughly authentic and credible, because the whole matter of the report, however we get at it, is found when we do get at it to be vivid and lifelike as an actual experience of living fact. Here, if ever anywhere, the attainment of the end justifies the employment of the means. If we are to enjoy imaginative work at all, we must 'assume the virtue' of imagination, even if we have it not; we must, as children say, 'pretend' or make believe a little as a very condition of the game.

A graver and perhaps a somewhat more plausible charge is brought against the author of *Wuthering Heights* by those who find here and there in her book the savage note or the sickly symptom of a morbid ferocity. Twice or thrice especially the details of deliberate or passionate brutality in Heathcliff's treatment of his victims make the reader feel for a moment as though he were reading a police report or even a novel by some French 'naturalist' of the latest and brutallest order.[1] But the pervading atmosphere of the book is so high and healthy that the effect even of those 'vivid and fearful scenes' which impaired the rest of Charlotte Brontë is almost at once neutralized – we may hardly say softened, but sweetened, dispersed, and transfigured – by the general impression of noble purity and passionate straight-forwardness, which removes it at once and for ever from any such ugly possibility of association or comparison. The whole work is not more incomparable in the effect of its atmosphere or landscape than in the peculiar note of its wild and bitter pathos; but most of all is it unique in the special and distinctive character of its passion. The love which devours life itself, which devastates the present and desolates the future with unquenchable and raging fire, has nothing less pure in it than flame or sunlight. And this passionate and ardent chastity is utterly and unmistakably spontaneous and unconscious. Not till the story is ended, not till the effect of it has been thoroughly absorbed and diges-ted, does the reader even perceive the simple and natural absence of any grosser element, any hint or suggestion of a baser alloy in the ingredients of its human emotion than in the splendour of lightning or the roll of a gathered wave. Then, as on issuing sometimes from the tumult of charging waters, he finds with something of wonder how absolutely pure and sweet was the element of living storm with which

[1] Objections to the seamy subject matter encouraged by Naturalist doctrines were al-ready being voiced in France at this time, esp. in F. Brunetière's *Le Roman Naturaliste* (1883).

his own nature has been for a while made one; not a grain in it of soiling sand, not a waif of clogging weed. As was the author's life, so is her book in all things: troubled and taintless, with little of rest in it, and nothing of reproach. It may be true that not many will ever take it to their hearts; it is certain that those who do like it will like nothing very much better in the whole world of poetry or prose.

113. Anthony Trollope on Charlotte Brontë

1883

From *An Autobiography* (1883), chapter 13, 'On English Novelists of the Present Day'. Trollope places Charlotte Brontë fourth in order after Thackeray, George Eliot and Dickens.

Charlotte Brontë was surely a marvellous woman. If it could be right to judge the work of a novelist from one small portion of one novel, and to say of an author that he is to be accounted as strong as he shows himself to be in his strongest morsel of work, I should be inclined to put Miss Brontë very high indeed. I know no interest more thrilling than that which she has been able to throw into the characters of Rochester and the governess, in the second volume of *Jane Eyre*. She lived with those characters, and felt with every fibre of her heart, the longings of the one and the sufferings of the other. And therefore, though the end of the book is weak, and the beginning not very good, I venture to predict that *Jane Eyre* will be read among English novels when many whose names are now better known shall have been forgotten. *Jane Eyre*, and *Esmond*, and *Adam Bede* will be in the hands of our grandchildren, when *Pickwick*, and *Pelham* and *Harry Lorreque* are forgotten; because the men and women depicted are human in their aspirations, human in their sympathies, and human in their actions

In *Villette*, too, and in *Shirley*, there is to be found human life a natural and as real, though in circumstances not so full of interest as those told in *Jane Eyre*. The character of Paul in the former of the two is a wonderful study. She must herself have been in love with some Paul when she wrote the book, and have been determined to prove to herself that she was capable of loving one whose exterior circumstances were mean and in every way unprepossessing.

114. Walter Pater on Emily Brontë

1889

From the discussion of the terms 'classical' and 'romantic' in the 'Postscript' to *Appreciations* (1889).

As the term, *classical*, has been used in a too absolute, and therefore in a misleading sense, so the term, *romantic*, has been used much too vaguely, in various accidental senses. The sense in which Scott is called a romantic writer is chiefly this; that, in opposition to the literary tradition of the last century, he loved strange adventure, and sought it in the Middle Age. Much later, in a Yorkshire village, the spirit of romanticism bore a more really characteristic fruit in the work of a young girl, Emily Brontë, the romance of *Wuthering Heights*; the figures of Hareton Earnshaw, of Catherine Linton, and of Heathcliff – tearing open Catherine's grave, removing one side of her coffin, that he may really lie beside her in death – figures so passionate, yet woven on a background of delicately beautiful, moorland scenery, being typical examples of that spirit. In Germany, again, that spirit is shown less in Tieck, its professional representative, than in Meinhold, the author of Sidonia the Sorceress and the Amber-Witch.[1]

[1] John Ludwig Tieck (1773–1853), prolific German poet, novelist and critic: for Mrs Humphry Ward's reference to him see p. 455. Wilhelm Meinhold (1797–1851). German theologian and writer: his *Maria Schweidler die Bernsteinhexe* ('The Amber Witch') was translated into English 1844 by E. A. Friedlander and 1885 by Lady Duff Gordon; his *Sidonia von Bork, die Klosterhexe* (*Sidonia the Sorceress*) was translated into English 1847 by Mrs W. R. Wilde. See D. G. Rossetti, p. 300 above.

115. Angus Mackay on Emily Brontë, *Westminster Review*

August 1898, c, 217–18

Angus M. Mackay published *The Brontës, Fact and Fiction* (1897, expanded from his essay of 1895 in the *Westminster Review*) as a point-by-point rebuttal of William Wright's wildly improbable account in *The Brontës in Ireland* (1893; see Introduction, p. 42 n. 96) of Patrick Brontë's Irish relatives, whose colourful lives were supposed to have dictated the subject matter of the Brontë novels. Mackay's emphasis in 1898 on the dramatic power and the mingling of naturalistic and non-naturalistic elements in *Wuthering Heights* is in keeping with Swinburne's reading in 1883 (No. 112) and with the readings of various readers in the 1850s (Introduction, p. 33).

Emily Brontë's rank as a poet is to be measured, not by her verse, but by her single romance. The quantity as well [as] the quality of work must needs be taken into account in estimating the genius of a writer, and it may seem that a beginner's first volume forms a slender foundation for a claim to high rank. But if we look only to the *quality* of the imagination displayed in *Wuthering Heights* – its power, its intensity, its absolute originality – it is scarcely too much to say of Emily that she might have been Shakespeare's youngest sister. To the many, of course, this will seem merely fantastic; but the few who have really learnt to appreciate *Wuthering Heights* will see no exaggeration in the title. Putting aside the clumsiness of the framework – the only mark of the prentice-hand in the whole book – what is there comparable to this romance except the greater tragedies of Shakespeare? The single peasant in the story, Joseph, is of the kin of Shakespeare's clowns, and yet is quite distinct from them. Heathcliff is one of the most vivid creations in all literature, he fascinates the imagination, and in some scenes almost paralyses us with horror, and yet that subtle human touch is added which wrings from us pity and almost respect. H reminds us of Shylock and Iago – not, indeed, by any likeness to their characters, but by the sense of wonder he awakens in us at the power that could create such a being. Catherine Earnshaw, again, and Catherine Linton – are not these by their piquancy and winsomeness almost worthy of a place in Shakespeare's gallery of fair women? The whole story has something of the pathos of *King Lear* and much of the tragic force of *Macbeth*, and yet both characters and story are, perhaps, as absolutely original as any that can be named in English literature. It is not, of course, meant that Emily Brontë achieved anything comparable to Shakespeare's greatest work: Shakespeare lived to become a great artist, while Emily only once tried her prentice-hand. Shakespeare knew the world in all its phases, while Emily passed her life in the seclusion of a remote village: but the material out of which the two wrought their work, the protoplasm of their creations, so to speak, was the same. Suppose Shakespeare had died, as Emily did, after completing his first work – *Love's Labours Lost* – would he have lived in men's memories at all? Or suppose the great dramatist's career to have closed at the same age as Emily's – twenty-nine: he would then have written a group of five complete plays, many of them comparatively immature, and none of them of the first rank as showing the real supremacy of his genius. Thus considered, the claim that Emily Brontë's creative power had something of the nature of Shakespeare's will not appear extravagant to those who can justly estimate what she has accomplished in *Wuthering Heights*.

It would be profitless, perhaps, to speculate on the work which this powerful imagination might have achieved had time been granted; let us rather be grateful for the imperishable work with which she has enriched our literature, and cherish the careless preludes which show how great a poet was lost to the world when Emily Brontë died.

116. Mary Ward on Charlotte, Emily and Anne Brontë

1899–1900

Mary Augusta Ward, better known as Mrs Humphry Ward (1851–1920), was the wife of T. H. Ward and niece of Matthew Arnold. She was a prolific novelist – her best known novels include *Robert Elsmere* (1885) and *Helbeck of Bannisdale* (1898) – and in 1898 was asked by George Smith to write the prefaces for the Haworth edition of the Brontës' work (see Introduction, pp. 46–7). These comprehensive and sensible introductions are perhaps not as widely known now as they should be; the extracts given here illustrate the writer's assessment of the relative imaginative strengths of the three sisters and her insight into Charlotte and Emily's affinities with various aspects of English and European romanticism.

The true subject of *Jane Eyre* is the courage with which a friendless and loving girl confronts her own passion, and, in the interest of some strange social instinct which she knows as 'duty,' which she cannot explain and can only obey, tramples her love underfoot, and goes out miserable into the world. Beside this wrestle of the human will, everything else is trivial or vulgar. The various expedients – legacies, uncles, fires, and coincidences – by which Jane Eyre is ultimately brought to happiness, cheapen and degrade the book without convincing the reader. In fact – to return to our *advocatus diaboli* – *Jane Eyre* is on the one side a rather poor novel of incident, planned on the conventional pattern, and full of clumsy execution; on another side it is a picture of passion and of ideas, for which in truth the writer had no sufficient equipment; she moves imprisoned, to quote Mr Leslie Stephen, in 'a narrow circle of thoughts; if you press it, the psychology of the book is really childish; Rochester is absurd, Jane Eyre, in spite of the stir that she makes, only half-realized and half-conscious.'

So far the objector; yet, in spite of it all, *Jane Eyre* persists, and

Charlotte Brontë is with the immortals. What is it that a critic of this type forgets [?] . . .

Simply, one might say, Charlotte Brontë herself. Literature, says Joubert, has been called the expression of society; and so no doubt it is, looked at as a whole. In the single writer, however, it appears rather as the expression of studies, or temper, or personality. And this last is the best. There are books so fine that literature in them is but the expression of those that write them. In other words, there are books where the writer seems to be everything, the material employed, the environment, almost nothing. The main secret of the charm that clings to Charlotte Brontë's books is, and will always be, the contact which they give us with her own fresh, indomitable, surprising personality – surprising, above all. In spite of its conventionalities of scheme, *Jane Eyre* has, in detail, in conversation, in the painting of character, that perpetual magic of the unexpected which overrides a thousand faults, and keeps the mood of the reader happy and alert . . . The general plan may be commonplace, the ideas even of no great profundity; but the book is original. How often in the early scenes of childhood or school-life does one instinctively expect the conventional solution, the conventional softening, the conventional prettiness or quaintness . . . And it never comes. Hammer-like, the blows of a passionate realism descend. Jane Eyre, the little helpless child, is never comforted; Mrs Reid, the cruel aunt, is never sorry for her cruelties; Bessie, the kind nurse, is not *very* kind . . . she only just makes the story credible, the reader's assent possible. So, at Lowood, Helen Burns is not a suffering angel; there is nothing consciously pretty or touching in the wonderful picture of her: reality, with its discords, its infinite novelties, lends word and magic to the passion of Charlotte's memory of her dead sister, all is varied, living, poignant, full of the inexhaustible savour of truth, and warm with the fire of the heart . . .

Personality then – strong, free, passionate personality – is the sole but the sufficient spell of these books. Can we analyze some of its elements? – so far, at least, as their literary expression is concerned?

In the first place, has it ever been sufficiently recognized that Charlotte Brontë is first and foremost *an Irishwoman*, that her genius is at bottom a Celtic genius? The main characteristics indeed of the Celt are all hers – disinterestedness, melancholy, wildness, a wayward force and passion, for ever wooed by sounds and sights to which other natures are insensible – by murmurs from the earth, by colours in the sky, by tones and accents of the soul, that speak to the Celtic sense as to no other . . . Idealism, understood as a life-long discontent; passion, conceived as an inner thirst and longing that wears and kills more often than it makes happy; a love of home and kindred entwined with the very roots of life, so that home-sickness may easily exhaust and threaten life; an art directed rather to expression than to form – ragged often and broken, but always poignant, always suggestive, touched with reverie and emotion; who does not recognize in these qualities, these essentially Celtic qualities, the qualities of the Brontës? . . .

Then, as to the Celtic pride, the Celtic shyness, the Celtic endurance, – Charlotte Brontë was rich in them all. . . .

And all three qualities – pride, shrinking, endurance – are writ large in her books. With passion added, they *are* Jane Eyre and Lucy Snowe. They supply the atmosphere, the peculiar note, of all the stories. A contempt for mean and easy living, for common gains, and common luxuries, breathes in them, and makes them harsh and bracing as the air of her own moors.

And one other Celtic quality there is in Charlotte Brontë and her books, which is responsible perhaps for half their defects. It is a quality of exuberance, of extravagance, of what her contemporaries called 'bad taste.' Charles Kingsley threw *Shirley* aside because the opening seemed to him vulgar [see No. 96]. Miss Martineau expressed much the same judgment on *Villette* [see No. 41]. And there can be no doubt that there was in Miss Brontë a curious vein of recklessness, roughness, one might also say – *hoydenism* – that exists side by side with an exquisite delicacy and a true dignity, and is none the less Irish and Celtic for that. It disappears, so far as one can see, with the publication of *Shirley*; but, up till then, it has to be reckoned with. . . . There is one sentence in the first chapter of *Shirley*, which may serve both as an illustration of this defect, and as a landmark pointing to certain radical differences of feeling that separate 1900 from 1850. It occurs in the course of an address to the reader, warning him to expect neither sentiment, poetry, nor passion from the book before him. 'Calm your expectations; reduce them to a lowly standard . . . It is not positively affirmed that you shall not have a taste of the exciting, perhaps towards the middle and close of the meal, but it is resolved that the first dish set upon the table shall be one that a Catholic – *aye, even an Anglo-Catholic – might eat on Good Friday on Passion Week: it shall be cold lentils and vinegar without oil; it shall be unleavened bread with bitter herbs, and no roast lamb.*'

These lines that I have thrown into italics were written in 1850, five years after Newman's secession, in the midst no doubt of a swelling tide of Liberal reaction, destined, however, as we all know now, to interfere very little with the spread and power of those deep under-currents setting from the Oxford Movement. The hasty arrogance, the failure in feeling and right instinct, which the passage shows, mark the chief limitation and weakness in the artist who wrote it. It is a weakness of taste, a limitation, as Mr Leslie Stephen would perhaps insist, of thought and idea. Taken together with the country-house scenes in *Jane Eyre*, with some of the curate scenes in *Shirley*, with various passages of raw didactic and rather shrill preaching, this utter-ance, and some others like it, suggest a lack of social intelligence, of a wide outlook, of that sense, above all, for measure and urbanity which belongs to other and more perfect art – like George Sand's – or to a more exquisitely tempered instinct – like that of Burns . . .

The Irish and Celtic element in Charlotte Brontë, however, is not all . . . Crossing, controlling the wild impetuous temper of the Irish-woman is an influence from another world, an influence of habit and long association, breathed from Yorkshire, and the hard, frugal, persistent North. One has but to climb her Haworth hills to feel it flowing around one . . .

Amid this rude full-blooded keen-brained, world grew up the four wonderful children who had survived their fragile mother and their two elder sisters. From the beginning they showed the Celtic qualities – the Celtic vision that re-makes the world, throws it into groups and pictures, seen with a magical edge and sharpness . . . Yet all the time there are secret bonds between these four small creatures – the children of an Irish father and a Cornish mother – and the stern practical Yorkshire world about them. For they come not from the typical and Catholic Ireland, but from the Ireland of the North, on which com-merce and Protestantism have set their grasp, the Ireland which has half yielded itself to England. In the girls, at any rate, the Bible and Puritanism have mingled with their Celtic blood. Economy, self-discipline, constancy, self-repression, order, – these things come easily to them, so far as the outer conduct of life is concerned. They take their revenge in dreams, – in the whims and passions of the imagina-tion. But they cook and clean and sew . . . They are docile, hard-working, hard-living. They are poor, saving, industrious, keenly alive to the value of money and of work, like the world about them.

And it is this mixture of Celtic dreaming with English realism and self-control which gives value and originality to all they do – to Emily's *Wuthering Heights*, to Charlotte's four stories. . . . There were no children's books in Haworth Parsonage. The children there were nourished upon the food of their elders: the Bible, Shakspeare, Addison, Johnson, Sheridan, Cowper, for the past; Scott, Byron, Southey, Wordsworth, Coleridge, *Blackwood's Magazine, Fraser's Magazine,* and Leigh Hunt for the moderns; on a constant supply of newspapers, Whig and Tory – Charlotte once said to a friend that she had taken an interest in politics since she was five years old – on current biographies, such as Lockhart's *Life of Burns,* Moore's Lives of Byron and Sheridan, Southey's *Nelson,* Wolfe's *Remains*; and on miscellaneous readings of old Methodist magazines containing visions and miraculous conversions, Mrs Rowe's *Letters from the Dead to the Living,* the *British Essayists,* collected from the *Rambler,* the *Mirror,* and elsewhere, and stories from the *Lady's Magazine.* They breathed, therefore, as far as books were concerned, a bracing and stimulating air from the beginning . . .

Thus strongly were the foundations laid, deep in the rich main soil of English life and letters . . . Later on, both in Charlotte and in Emily, certain foreign influences come in. Just as Emily certainly owed something to Hofmann's Tales,[1] so Charlotte probably owed much – more, I am inclined to believe, than has yet been recognized – to the books of French Romanticism. . . . In 1840, before the visit to Brussels, Charlotte writes that she has received 'another bale of French books from [Gomersal] . . . containing upwards of forty volumes. They are like the rest, clever, wicked, sophistical, and immoral. The best of it is, that they give one a thorough idea of France and Paris.'[2] By 1840 Victor Hugo had written *Marion Delorme, Hernani, Le Roi s'amuse, Ruy blas,* six volumes of poems, *Notre Dame de Paris,* and much else. Alfred de Musset, who was thirty in 1840, had done all his work of any importance, and sunk into premature exhaustion; *Premières Poésies, Rolla, Confession d'un Enfant du Siècle, Espoir en Dieu* – were they in the packet that reached Charlotte in 1840? George Sand, making her first great success with *Indiana* in 1832, had produced *Valentine, Lélia, Jacques, Léone Leoni, André, Mauprat,* and some others. Balzac, herald of another age and another world, had been ten years at work on the *Comédie Humaine.* We know, however, from a letter of Charlotte's in 1848, that she never read a novel of Balzac's till after the publication of *Jane Eyre.*[3]

[1] See above, p. 376 n. 2.
[2] *LL,* i, 215.
[3] See above, p. 173 n.

But she did read George Sand, as the same letter informs us, and the influence of that great romantic artist in whom restless imagination went hand in hand with a fine and chosen realism, was probably of some true importance in the development of Charlotte Brontë's genius ... It has not yet, I think, been pointed out that there is in *Jacques* – a novel written in 1834 – a very curious anticipation of the cry of Rochester to Jane. The passage occurs in a letter from Sylvia, the sisterly friend, to Jacques, about to become the husband of Fernande ...

The ... romantic suggestion of these sentences may very possibly have mingled with, perhaps given birth to, some later fancy or experience, of which she spoke to Mrs Gaskell, and so found shape ultimately in the thrilling scene of *Jane Eyre*. Of direct imitation of George Sand there is nowhere any trace; but in certain parts of *Shirley*, in the 'Marriage of Genius and Humanity'[1] for instance, the stimulating influence of certain famous passages in *Lélia* suggests itself readily; and throughout *Villette* there is constantly something in her mode of approaching her subject, even in the turn of the sentences, especially in the use of participles, which is French rather than English. All the books testify to her pride in her French culture. She had won it at great cost; it had opened fresh worlds to her, and she makes free use of it in numerous scenes of *Shirley* and *Villette*, and in the whole portraiture of the Moores.

The differences, of course, between her and the author of *Jacques* are great and fundamental. Charlotte Brontë's main *stuff* is English, Protestant, law-respecting, conventional even. No judgment was ever more foolish than that which detected a social rebel in the writer of *Jane Eyre*. She thought the French books, as we have seen, 'clever, wicked, sophistical, and immoral.' But she read them; and for all her revolt from them, they quickened and fertilized her genius. More than this. The influence which she absorbed from them has given her a special place in our literature of imagination. She stands between Jane Austen, the gentle and witty successor of Miss Burney and Richardson, and George Eliot, upon whom played influences of quite another kind – German, critical, scientific – representing the world which succeeded the world of *Hernani*. Midway appears the work of Charlotte Brontë, linked in various significant ways with the French romantic movement, which began with *Atala* in 1801, and had run its course abroad before 1847, the year of *Jane Eyre*. One may almost say of it, indeed,

[1] *Shirley*, chapter 27.

453

that it belongs more to the European than to the special English tradition. For all its strongly marked national and provincial elements, it was very early understood and praised in France; and it was of a French critic, and a French critic only, that Charlotte Brontë said with gratitude, in the case of *Shirley*, 'he follows Currer Bell through every winding, discerns every point, discriminates every shade, proves himself master of the subject, and lord of the aim.'[1]

Wuthering Heights

When we are under the spell of the Brontë stories we admire and we protest with almost equal warmth ... And if this is the case with Charlotte Brontë, it is still more so with Emily. Emily's genius was the greater of the two, yet of a similar quality and fibre. It provokes even more vivid reactions of feeling in the reader; and yet, in those who have felt her spell, she wins an ultimate sympathy and compels an ultimate admiration so strong that no one wishes to examine the stages of his own conquest. ...

Nevertheless, criticism has still a real work to do with this strange novel and these few passionate poems of Emily Brontë's. In the first place, the novel has not even yet taken the place which rightly belongs to it. In Mr Saintsbury's belief, for instance, Emily Brontë's work, though he grants its originality, has been 'extravagantly praised', and is 'too small in bulk and too limited in character to be put really high.'[2] ... And even for Mr Leslie Stephen's generous and catholic taste, Emily Brontë in *Wuthering Heights* 'feels rather than observes'; so that 'her feeble grasp upon external facts makes her book a kind of baseless nightmare, which we read with wonder and with distressing curiosity, but with even more pain than pleasure or profit.' Matthew Arnold, indeed, in the well-known lines

> whose soul
> Knew no fellow for might,
> Passion, vehemence, grief,
> Daring, since Byron died –

– has paid the natural tribute of one true poet to another. But it may be doubted whether in writing it he thought of *Wuthering Heights*, and not rather of those four or five poems of the first order which Emily Brontë has added to our literature. While for an earlier genera-

---

[1] Eugene Forçade: see No. 33.
[2] G. Saintsbury, 'Three mid-century novelists', *Corrected Impressions* (1895).

tion of critics, *Wuthering Heights* was, as a rule, matter for denunciation rather than praise; and it was again a poet – Sydney Dobell in the *Palladium* – who, almost alone, had the courage to understand . . .[1]

Indeed, Charlotte Brontë herself, in the touching and eloquent preface which she wrote for a new edition of *Wuthering Heights* in 1850, adopts a tone towards her sister's work which contains more than a shade of apology. . . .[2] But for us fifty years later . . . *Wuthering Heights* lives as great imagination, of which we must take the consequences, the bad with the good; and will continue to live, whether it pleases us personally or no. Moreover, the book has much more than a mere local or personal significance. It belongs to a particular European moment, and like Charlotte's work, though not in the same way, it holds a typical and representative place in the English literature of the century . . . During their eager, enthusiastic youth the Brontë sisters . . . were readers of Christopher North, Hogg, De Quincey, and Maginn in *Blackwood*, of Carlyle's early essays and translations in *Fraser*, of Scott and Lockhart, no less than of Wordsworth, Southey, and Coleridge. Charlotte asked Southey and Coleridge for an opinion on her poems; Branwell did the same with Hartley Coleridge; and no careful reader of Emily Brontë's verse can fail to see in it the fiery and decisive influence of S. T. C.[3] . . .

There can be no question that they were 'romantic' influences, and . . . among them were many kindling sparks from that 'unextinguished hearth' of German poetry and fiction which played so large a part in English imagination during the first half of the century . . . In 1830, Carlyle . . . reports triumphantly 'a rapidly growing favour for German literature' . . . During the time that he was writing and translating for the *Edinburgh*, the *Foreign Review* and *Fraser* – in *Blackwood* also, through the years which Charlotte and Emily Brontë . . . were delighting in it, one may find a constant series of translations from the German, of articles on German memoirs and German poets . . . *Blackwood* published [in 1839] a translation of Tieck's *Pietro d'Abano*,[4] a wild robber-and-magician story, of the type which spread the love

---

[1] No. 80.

[2] No. 81.

[3] A view shared by Mary Robinson (p. 431 above).

[4] On Tieck see above, p. 445 n. His *Pietro von Abano oder Pietrus Apone, Zaubergeschichte* was published 1824, translated into English 1831, 1839. The latter version appeared in *Blackwood's* August 1839, xlvi, 228–55. The unlikelihood of a direct influence on *Wuthering Heights* is discussed by Emily Brontë's modern French critic, Jacques Blondel, in his full-length study (see Bibliography).

of monster and vampire, witch and werewolf, through a Europe tired for the moment of eighteenth-century commonsense; and, more important still, a long section, excellently rendered, from Goethe's *Dichtung and Wahrheit*.[1] In that year Emily Brontë was alone with her father and aunt at Haworth . . . *Blackwood* came as usual, and one may surely imagine the long, thin girl bending in the firelight over these pages from Goethe, receiving the impress of their lucidity, their charm, their sentiment and 'natural magic' . . .[2] In 1842 she and Charlotte journeyed to Brussels . . . While Charlotte . . . was carried into that profounder appreciation of the French Romantic spirit and method which shows itself thenceforward in all her books, Emily . . . learnt German diligently, and it has always been assumed, I hardly know on what first authority, that she read a good deal of German fiction, and especially Hoffmann's tales, at Brussels. Certainly we hear of her in the following year, when she was once more at Haworth, and Charlotte was still at Brussels, as doing her household work 'with a German book open beside her' . . .

It is important to realize that of the three books written simultaneously by the three sisters, Emily's alone shows genius already matured and master of its tools . . . The common, hasty, didactic note that Charlotte often strikes is never heard in *Wuthering Heights*. The artist remains hidden and self-contained; the work, however morbid and violent may be the scenes and creatures it presents, has always that distinction which belongs to high talent working solely for its own joy and satisfaction, with no thought of a spectator, or any aim but that of an ideal and imaginative whole. She has that highest power – which was typically Shakespeare's power, and which in our day is typically the power of such an artist as Turgueniev – the power which gives life, intensest life, to the creatures of imagination, and, in doing so, endows them with an independence behind which the maker is forgotten . . .

Yet, at the same time, *Wuthering Heights* is a book of the later Romantic movement, betraying the influences of German Romantic imagination, as Charlotte's work betrays the influences of Victor Hugo and George Sand. The Romantic tendency to invent and delight in monsters, the *exaltation du moi*, which has been said to be the secret

---

[1] Goethe's *Dichtung und Wahrheit* (*Poetry and Truth*) was completed 1831; an English version of the first two books appeared in *Blackwood's*, October–November 1839, xlvi, 475–93, 597–613.

[2] Matthew Arnold's phrase in his essay, 'Mauric de Gérin,' *Essays in Criticism* (1865).

of the whole Romantic revolt against classical models and restraints; the love of violence in speech and action, the preference for the hideous in character and the abnormal in situation – of all these there are abundant examples in *Wuthering Heights*. The dream of Mr Lockwood in Catherine's box bed, when in the terror of nightmare he pulled the wrist of the little wailing ghost outside on to the broken glass of the window, 'and rubbed it to and fro till the blood ran down and soaked the bed-clothes' – one of the most gruesome fancies of literature! – Heathcliffs' long and fiendish revenge on Hindley Earnshaw; the ghastly quarrel between Linton and Heathcliff in Catherine's presence after Heathcliff's return; Catherine's three days' fast, and her delirium when she 'tore the pillow with her teeth'; Heathcliff dashing his head against the trees of her garden, leaving his blood upon their bark, and 'howling, not like a man, but like a savage beast being goaded to death with knives and spears'; the fight between Heathcliff and Earnshaw after Heathcliff's marriage to Isabella; the kidnapping of the younger Catherine, and the horror rather suggested than described of Heathcliff's brutality towards his sickly son: – all these things would not have been written precisely as they were written but for the 'Germanism' of the thirties and forties, but for the translations of *Blackwood* and *Fraser*, and but for those German tales, whether of Hoffmann or others, which there is evidence that Emily Brontë read both at Brussels and after her return.

As to the 'exaltation of the Self,' its claims, sensibilities and passions, in defiance of all social law and duty, there is no more vivid expression of it throughout Romantic literature than is contained in the conversation between the elder Catherine and Nelly Dean before Catherine marries Edgar Linton. And the violent, clashing egotisms of Heathcliff and Catherine in the last scene of passion before Catherine's death, are as it were an epitome of a whole *genre* in literature, and a whole phase of European feeling.

Nevertheless, horror and extravagance are not really the characteristic mark and quality of *Wuthering Heights*. If they were, it would have no more claim upon us than a hundred other forgotten books – Lady Caroline Lamb's *Glenarvon* [1816] amongst them – which represent the dregs and refuse of a great literary movement. As in the case of Charlotte Brontë, the peculiar force of Emily's work lies in the fact that it represents the grafting of a European tradition upon a mind already richly stored with English and local reality, possessing at command a style at once strong and simple, capable both of homeliness and magnificence. The form of Romantic imagination which influenced Emily was not the same as that which influenced Charlotte; whether from a secret stubbornness and desire of difference, or no, there is not a mention of the French language, or of French books, in Emily's work, while Charlotte's abounds in a kind of display of French affinities, and French scholarship. The dithyrambs of *Shirley* and *Villette*, the 'Vision of Eve' of *Shirley*, and the description of Rachel in *Villette*, would have been impossible to Emily; they come to a great extent from the reading of Victor Hugo and George Sand. But in both sisters there is a similar *fonds* of stern and simple realism; a similar faculty of observation at once shrewd, and passionate; and it is by these that they produce their ultimate literary effect. The difference between them is almost wholly in Emily's favour. The uneven, amateurish manner of so many pages in *Jane Eyre* and *Shirley*; the lack of literary reticence which is responsible for Charlotte's frequent intrusion of her own personality, and for her occasional temptations to scream and preach, which are not wholly resisted even in her masterpiece, *Villette*; the ugly, tawdry sentences which disfigure some of her noblest passages, and make quotation from her so difficult: – you will find none of these things in *Wuthering Heights*. Emily is never flurried, never self-conscious; she is master of herself at the most rushing moments of feeling or narrative; her style is simple, sensuous, adequate and varied from first to last; she has fewer purple patches than Charlotte, but at its best, her insight no less than her power of phrase, is of a diviner and more exquisite quality . . .

Wuthering Heights, then, is the product of romantic imagination, working probably under influences from German literature, and marvellously fused with local knowledge and a realistic power which, within its own range, has seldom been surpassed . . .

Anne Brontë

Anne Brontë serves a twofold purpose in the study of what the Brontës wrote and were. In the first place, her gentle and delicate presence, her sad, short story, her hard life and early death, enter deeply into the poetry and tragedy that have always been entwined with the memory of the Brontës, as women and as writers; in the second, the books and poems that she wrote serve as matter of comparison by which to test the greatness of her two sisters. She is the measure of their genius – like them, yet not with them.

There can be no question that Branwell's opium madness, his bouts of drunkenness at the Black Bull, his violence at home, his free and coarse talk, and his perpetual boast of guilty secrets, influenced the imagination of his wholly pure and inexperienced sisters. Much of *Wuthering Heights* and all of *Wildfell Hall*, show Branwell's mark, and there are many passages in Charlotte's books also where those who know the history of the parsonage can hear the voice of those sharp moral repulsions, those dismal moral questionings, to which Branwell's misconduct and ruin gave rise. Their brother's fate was an element in the genius of Emily and Charlotte which they were strong enough to assimilate . . .

But Anne was not strong enough, her gift was not vigorous enough, to enable her thus to transmute experience and grief. The probability is that when she left Thorpe Green in 1845 she was already suffering from that religious melancholy of which Charlotte discovered such piteous evidence among her papers after death. It did not much affect the writing of *Agnes Grey*, which was completed in 1846, and reflected the minor pains and discomforts of her teaching experience, but it combined with the spectacle of Branwell's increasing moral and physical decay to produce that bitter mandate of conscience under which she wrote *The Tenant of Wildfell Hall* . . .

And there was and is a considerable narrative ability, a sheer moral energy in *Wildfell Hall*, which would not be enough, indeed, to keep it alive if it were not the work of a Brontë, but still betray its kinship and source . . . But the book's truth, so far as it is true, is scarcely the truth of imagination; it is rather the truth of a tract or a report . . . The same material might have been used by Emily or Charlotte; Emily, as we know, did make use of it in *Wuthering Heights*; but only after it had passed through that ineffable transformation, that mysterious, incommunicable heightening which makes and gives rank in literature . . .

The same world of difference appears between her poems and those of her playfellow and comrade, Emily. If ever our descendants should establish the schools for writers which are even now threatened or attempted, they will hardly know perhaps any better than we what genius is, nor how it can be produced. But if they try to teach by example, then Anne and Emily Brontë are ready to their hand. Take the verses written by Emily at Roehead ['Still, as I mused the naked room . . .']. Just before those lines there are two or three verses which it is worth while to compare with a poem of Anne's called 'Home'. Emily was sixteen at the time of writing; Anne about twenty-one or twenty-two. Both sisters take for their motive the exile's longing thought of home. Emily's lines are full of faults, but they have the indefinable quality – here, no doubt, only in the bud, only as a matter of promise – which Anne's are entirely without.

[quotes Emily's 'A little while, a little while . . .' and Anne's 'How brightly glistening in the sun . . .']

And so we are brought back to the point from which we started. It is not as the writer of *Wildfell Hall*, but as the sister of Charlotte and Emily Brontë, that Anne Brontë escapes oblivion.

Bibliography

It will be understood from my comments on modern criticism of the Brontës (Introduction, pp. 47–50) that this list is necessarily highly selective. Other studies are referred to elsewhere in this book.

ALLOTT, MIRIAM (ed.), *Wuthering Heights: Casebook* (1970); *Jane Eyre* and *Villette: Casebook* (1973). Represents early critical reviews and modern opinions from 1900 to the 1960s.

BENTLEY, PHYLLIS, *The Brontës and their World* (1969). An attractive collection of pictures illustrating Yorkshire scenes familiar to the Brontës from their childhood and youth (contains a biographical survey).

BLONDEL, JACQUES, *Emily Brontë: expérience spirituelle et création poétique* (Paris, 1955). The fullest biographical and critical account to appear, with a substantial bibliography.

CECIL, DAVID, 'Charlotte Brontë' and 'Emily Brontë and *Wuthering Heights*', *Early Victorian Novelists* (1934). The most influential of the Brontës, modern critics in establishing Emily Brontë's reputation and promoting twentieth-century debate about the meaning of her novel. His views on the relative standing of the sisters have much in common with those of Mrs Humphry Ward.

CHRISTIAN, MILDRED, 'The Brontës', in *Victorian Fiction: A Guide to Research*, ed. Lionel Stevenson (1964). A comprehensive survey of Brontë criticism.

COLBY, R. A., '*Villette* and the life of the mind', *PMLA* (1960). Analyses Charlotte's novels in order to show her as a writer in whom 'the romantic imagination finally reconciles itself to real life'.

CRAIK, WENDY, *The Brontë Novels* (1968). Reflects some recent tendencies in Brontë criticism in dealing with the sisters as a group, avoiding biographical detail and seeking to establish Charlotte's artistic equality with Emily; Anne's work is also given serious critical attention. A closely argued essay in revaluation.

CROMPTON, D. W., 'The new criticism: a caveat', *Essays in Criticism*

(July 1960). Includes a brief commentary on *Jane Eyre* indicating the inappropriateness of seeking in Charlotte's work the structural complexity found in *Wuthering Heights*.

EWBANK, INGA-STINA, *Their Proper Sphere: a study of the Brontë sisters as Early Victorian female novelists* (1966). One of two or three studies appearing in the later 1960s which revive the practice of studying the three sisters as a family group, the emphasis in this case being laid on their relationship with other early nineteenth-century women writers.

FRASER, JOHN, 'The name of action: Nelly Dean and *Wuthering Heights*', *Nineteenth-Century Fiction* (19) (1965). Dismisses contemporary 'sentimental disengagement' which encourages an uncritical acceptance of the wickedness in Catherine and Heathcliff and the depreciation of Nelly Dean as 'an agent of repression'.

GERIN, WINIFRED, *Anne Brontë* (1959); *Charlotte Brontë* (1967); *Emily Brontë* (1971). The most ambitious modern biographical studies and as such indispensable, in spite of occasionally uneven documentation and reliance on conjecture (for example in accounts of Charlotte's and Emily's attitudes to Branwell).

HALE, W. T., *Anne Brontë: Her Life and Writings* (1929). Brief but sensible monograph.

HANSON, L. and E. M., *The Four Brontës* (1949; revised 1967). Still one of the most useful general surveys (the account of Emily's attitude to Branwell after his dismissal from Thorp Green in 1845 is necessarily conjectural).

HARRISON, ADA and STANFORD, DEREK, *Anne Brontë: Her Life and Work* (1959). Contains biographical material and critical discussions of her poems and novels.

HATFIELD, C. W. (ed.), *The Complete Poems of Emily Jane Brontë* (1941). The standard edition.

HEILMAN, R. B., 'Charlotte Brontë's "new" Gothic', in *From Jane Austen to Joseph Conrad*, ed. R. C. Rathburn and M. Steinmann (1958); 'Charlotte Brontë, reason and the moon', *Nineteenth-Century Fiction* (1960). The essays signal the renewed attention given to Charlotte Brontë in the late 1950s. In the first essay, the author explores the interplay of reason and intuition throughout her work, and in the second concentrates on her use of moon imagery in *Jane Eyre*.

HEWISH, JOHN, *Emily Brontë: a critical and biographical survey* (1969). An economical *résumé* of salient facts concerning Emily Brontë's life and critical reception since 1847·

LEAVIS, Q. D., 'A fresh approach to *Wuthering Heights*', in *Lectures in America* by F. R. and Q. D. Leavis (1969). Emphasizes the book's 'human centrality' and provides interesting background material in the four Appendices.

MARTIN, R. B., *Accents of Persuasion* (1966). Abjures biographical material and concentrates on critical analysis of each in turn of Charlotte Brontë's novels, stressing 'the self-reliant Protestant ethic' that dominated her life.

RATCHFORD, F. E., *The Brontës' Web of Childhood* (1941). Seminal study of the Brontë children's creative fantasies, including Emily's and Anne's world of Gondal (Emily's chronicles were reconstructed by the same author in *Gondal's Queen*, 1955).

SHERRY, NORMAN, *The Brontë sisters: Charlotte and Emily* (1969). Succinct introductory primer.

TILLOTSON, KATHLEEN, *The Novels of the Eighteen-Forties* (1954). Contains valuable background material and discusses *Jane Eyre* in the context both of prevailing attitudes to prose fiction and of Charlotte's personal development as a novelist.

Index

This index is divided into three sections: I. The Brontës: writings; II. The Brontës: characteristics; III. General.

I. THE BRONTËS: WRITINGS

II. THE BRONTËS: CHARACTERISTICS

III. GENERAL